A BOOK OF

Middle Eastern

FOOD

TO PAUL, SIMON, NADIA, AND ANNA

Acknowledgments

I gratefully extend my thanks to the many people of the Middle East who so generously contributed recipes, advice, and their culinary experience, and whose enthusiasm and strong conviction of the value of their culinary tradition were the origin of this book.

I wish to thank my parents: my father, whose enjoyment of life and appreciation of Middle Eastern food urged me to perpetuate the tradition, and my mother, who advised and guided me throughout.

I wish to thank my husband, my brothers, Ellis and Zaki Douek, their wives, and my friend Suzy Benghiat (the last particularly for her love of food and cooking), for their constant sympathetic support, encouragement, and valuable advice, many friends for their interest and gracious sampling of my food, and my children, who allowed me to write the book.

Of those who contributed recipes, I am particularly indebted to Mrs. Iris Galante, Mrs. Lily Galante, my aunt Régine Douek, Mrs. R. Afif, Mrs. Irene Harari, Mrs. I. Laski, and Mrs. S. Gaon.

I would like to express my warmest appreciation of the overwhelming generosity I encountered at the various Arab and North African Embassies, and the Islamic Centre, and for the recipes, help, and advice given to me by members of the embassy staffs and their wives, some of whom extended the hospitality of their homes.

I am equally indebted to the Israeli Embassy for their generous advice, and to the Israeli Government Tourist Office for supplying me with recipes.

I wish to extend my deepest gratitude to Miss Belinda Bather, whose rich experience was the major source of the Turkish recipes, and to Mrs. V. Afsharian, who contributed many Persian dishes.

I wish to record my gratitude to Professor A. J. Arberry, with whose kind permission I have been able to include many recipes from al-Baghdadi's medieval manual and various culinary poems which he translated, and to M. Maxime Rodinson, from whose valuable studies in Arab culinary history and translation of the *Wusla il al Habib* I have drawn much information.

I also wish to acknowledge my debt to certain Arab, Turkish, and Persian cookbooks which I have studied.*

Finally, I wish to thank my editor, Helena Radecka, for her constant invaluable guidance from the early stages of my project, and for her enthusiasm and understanding throughout. Without her the book would not have been as it is, and perhaps not at all.

---

* A bibliography of cookbooks of the Middle East is given on page 451.

Contents

‡ *Whenever this symbol appears,*
  check the List of Sources on pages 452–3,
  if necessary.

INTRODUCTION

My compilation of recipes is the joint creation of numerous Middle Easterners who, like me, are in exile, either forced and permanent, or voluntary and temporary. It is the fruit of nostalgic longing for, and delighted savoring of, a food that was the constant joy of life in a world so different from the Western one. The Arab sayings "He who has a certain habit will have no peace from it" and "The dancer dies and does not forget the shaking of his shoulders" apply to us.

The collection began fifteen years ago with a recipe for *ful medames*. I was a schoolgirl in Paris then. Every Sunday I was invited together with my brothers and a cousin to eat *ful medames* with some relatives. This meal became a ritual. Considered in Egypt to be a poor man's dish, in Paris the little brown beans became invested with all the glories and warmth of Cairo, our hometown, and the embodiment of all that for which we were homesick.

Our hosts lived in a one-room apartment, and were both working, so it was possible for them to prepare the dish only with tinned *ful*. Ceremoniously, we sprinkled the beans with olive oil, squeezed a little lemon over them, seasoned them with salt and pepper, and placed a hot hard-boiled egg in their midst. Delicious ecstasy! Silently, we ate the beans, whole and firm at first; then we squashed them with our forks and combined their floury texture and slightly dull, earthy taste with the acid tang of lemon, mellowed by the olive oil; finally, we crumbled the egg, matching its earthiness with that of the beans, its pale warm yellow with their dull brown.

Since that time, I and many relatives (Sephardic Jews), acquaintances and friends, exiled from our Middle Eastern homelands, have settled in various countries. We have kept in close touch by letter and occasional visits. Some of us have tried to re-create certain aspects of the way of life to which we were accustomed after centuries of integrated life in the Ottoman and Arab worlds, in particular the food, which meant so much in the Middle East and has come to mean even more in exile.

It has been, for me, a matter of great delight to acquire an extra recipe from some relative passing through London, a well-known ex-restaurateur from Alexandria, or somebody's aunt in Buenos

Aires—another treasure to pass on to the Middle Eastern community in Paris, Geneva, or Milan.

Friday night dinners at my parents' and gatherings of friends at my own home have been opportunities to rejoice in our food and to summon the ghosts of the past.

Each dish has filled our house in turn with the smells of the *Muski*, the Cairo market, of the *corniche* in Alexandria, of Groppi's and the famous Hati Restaurant. Each dish has brought back memories of great and small occasions, of festivals, of the emotions of those times, and of the sayings invariably said. They have conjured up memories of street vendors, bakeries and pastry shops, and of the brilliant colors and sounds of the markets. Pickles and cheeses have re-created for us the atmosphere of the grocery shop around the corner, down to which a constant flow of baskets would be lowered from the windows above, descending with coins, and going up again with food. It is these smells, emotions, habits, and traditions, attached to and inseparable from our dishes, a small part of our distinctive culture, that I have tried to convey with the food.

At first, on leaving Egypt, I imagined our food to be uniquely Egyptian. In Europe, I discovered that the Turks claimed most of our dishes, and that the Syrians, Lebanese, and Persians claimed the rest, leaving us with only a few specialties, our "national dishes." Nearly all our food was common to other Middle Eastern countries, so to write about "our food" was to write about Middle Eastern food generally. I have not been able to disentangle what is an Egyptian culinary tradition from a Turkish, Persian, or Syrian one, and I have had to include various countries which I did not intend to at first, but which were necessary to make a complete and comprehensible picture of what was originally my "family's food." The countries which imposed themselves were, in a broad sense, the countries of the Middle East.

The Middle East is a broad and fluid term which today means different things to different people. Its more recent history and events, tragic, intricate, and tumultuous, have made it, for all those who have any mild involvement with it, loaded with explosive emotion. I cannot attempt in this book of food to make any sort of political or geographical definition, since even the latter is tragically complex and unsettled.

The region embraces many different countries, races, and religions.

The people call themselves "Orientals," a term more often used in the West when referring to the Far East. The area is one of geographical, climatic, human, and social contrasts. It has been the birthplace of our present civilization, and the battleground of most of the creeds, philosophies, and religions which form the basis of those now occupying the minds of much of the world today.

. Some parts of the Middle East are racially pure, such as those inhabited by Bedouin Arabs. Others, such as the Mediterranean coast, inhabited by people loosely termed "Levantines," are extremely mixed in racial origin, nationality, and religion, embodying the numerous human changes brought about by various empires, invasions, foreign settlers, and traders. A name invented by my community for these people is "Bazramites."

With a few exceptions, the Arabic language is spoken throughout the region in its numerous and varied dialects. The religion is that of Islam, but each country until recently sheltered a large number of small communities of Christians and Jews, and various small sects and factions of these.

Here is my choice of countries included in this book: Syria, the Lebanon, Egypt, Iran, Turkey, Greece, Iraq, Saudi Arabia, the Yemen, the Sudan, Algeria, Tunisia, Morocco, and Israel. All are inextricably linked culinarywise.

Although the Balkan countries have adopted culinary traditions from their former Ottoman rulers, I have not included them, since they are now far removed from the Middle East, and they have not notably fed many dishes back to the common pool. I have dealt with Greece inasmuch as its tradition is almost identical with the Turkish one, and probably inspired it at the time of the Ottoman Empire. I have included the North African countries of Tunisia, Algeria, and Morocco, which until recently were the French Maghreb, but today have shown their allegiance to, and become part of, the Arab World. I have done so, too, because I have recognized in their food a strong and mysterious similarity with medieval Persian and Arab dishes, and because of the recent adoption of their more popular national dishes by other Middle Eastern countries.

I have treated the food of the individual countries arbitrarily, giving preference and most careful scrutiny to all aspects of food belonging to my own personal background, but, I hope, doing justice to the food of other countries objectively. Iran, Lebanon, Syria, Turkey, and

Morocco I found ready to pour out an abundant variety of splendid recipes, while other countries, possessing a poorer and more limited range, had only a few dishes to offer.

The early sources of my collection of recipes have been my family and my own community from Egypt; people who were either born in Egypt or had lived, themselves and their forefathers, for centuries in various countries of the Middle East, and had come to settle in Egypt. Their culture and traditions ran parallel to, and were part of, wider national traditions.

To explore the food of the different countries was made easy for me by the fact that we were particularly spoiled in the very cosmopolitan atmosphere of Egypt, which contained communities of other Middle Eastern nationals. My own family has a Syrian and a Turkish branch, and many of my relatives have married into families coming from Lebanon, North Africa, and Iran. This enabled us to savor the best of many worlds.

I was extremely lucky in having the help of Turks, Syrians, Persians, Lebanese, Saudi Arabians, Armenians, Israelis, and North Africans, whom I met in London and with whom I spent long, rich, and interesting hours, taking in their experience, sampling the dishes they prepared for me before trying them myself. All those who contributed recipes have a feeling for, and deep understanding of, food.

Most of these people explained in the minutest detail the washing and the handling of ingredients, the feel, the smell, and the color of the food—but usually omitted quantities, weights, and cooking times. I learned that to some "leave it a minute" meant an hour, that "five spoonfuls" was in order to make a round figure or because five was for them a lucky number, and that a pinch could be anything from an eighth of a teaspoon to a heaping tablespoon.

Remarking how delicious the dishes they described were, they related the circumstances in which they used to prepare them. It gave them, I think, as much pleasure to describe the recipes as it gave me to record them. Through them I have gathered humble peasant food, flamboyant Mediterranean dishes, the elaborate dishes developed during the times of the great empires as well as the everyday dishes of the middle classes throughout the Middle East.

I have tried to be faithful to the old traditions of cooking, but I have also introduced dishes in which the European influence of the present century can be felt. These I have classed as modern dishes or modern variations. Among them are several newly developed prize-winning Israeli recipes.

I have tried to trace the origins of dishes and to understand their variations, to detect the influences brought about by conquering nations, mass emigrations, and religious prohibitions, and I have discovered that, to a certain extent, I can only guess at these.

I was thrilled to find at the British Museum library and at the School of Oriental Languages translations of two medieval cooking manuals, one by Professor A. J. Arberry, and the other by M. Maxime Rodinson (into French). I could not resist including recipes from both those books. I have quoted them with the kind permission of the authors, as they are so clearly and beautifully described. Out of well over two hundred recipes, I have chosen a few, some because they were so familiar that it was interesting to compare them with the modern variations they inspired, others simply because they appealed to me, and I would like to be permitted to return them to the culinary repertoire of the Middle East. Since exact measures are not given, I have indicated the quantities that I would personally choose through my own experience of cooking.

With this collection of dishes I wish to offer what to me is a treasure, the detailed and simple explanation of the way in which the women of the Middle East (and, of course, the professional male cooks) have prepared their food for centuries, some even since Pharaonic times. I would like to pass on the experience which has been transferred from mother and mother-in-law to daughter and daughter-in-law, with the keen encouragement of their husbands, fathers, and brothers.

Middle Eastern cooking, though sometimes elaborate, is easy. Some of the dishes, such as stuffed vine leaves, may take some time to prepare; but if you consider cooking to be a pleasurable and creative activity, you are adding to the enjoyment of serving and eating the dish the peace and pleasure derived from rolling up the leaves. Women in the West like to knit while watching television, or while sitting with their children. Could rolling vine leaves and stuffing tomatoes not be yet another such soothing activity?

The preparation of most of these dishes is short and simple. Some require lengthy cooking, but these often need very little work and hardly any attention. They can usually be cooked a day in advance and become richer in this way. Sometimes the cooking time can be greatly reduced by the use of modern labor-saving devices such as electric blenders or pressure cookers.

Middle Eastern food is economical, lamb and minced meat being the favorite meats. The recipes can give inspiration for subtle and exciting ways of cooking familiar and cheaper cuts of meat. Alcohol, which usually brings up the cost of cosmopolitan *haute cuisine*, is absent (except for a few modern dishes), owing to its prohibition by Muslim dietary law.

The vegetables, used because of their abundance in the Middle East, are available almost everywhere today, either imported or home grown.

Spices can be found in most supermarkets as well as in Greek and Indian shops. Some ingredients, such as vine leaves, pine nuts, and *fila* pastry, not generally available in ordinary shops, can usually be found in all Greek shops or where there are Greek or Cypriot communities, and in some delicatessens.

I have included with my recipes a few tales, poems, and descriptions of ceremonies, rituals and myths, customs and manners, all relating to food. I believe that they will make the dishes more interesting and familiar by placing them in their natural and traditional setting, and add to the pleasure of eating them.

I have allowed myself to include riddles, proverbs, and sayings, in the hope that through them a little of the wit and spirit of the peoples of the Middle East may be discovered. Although I have used instances of my own experience, and songs and proverbs of particular regions, these are not foreign to other parts of the Middle East, but common and general.

In particular, I have included stories of Goha, the folk hero of the Middle East, sometimes called Goha Ibn Insh'Allah al Masri in Egypt, and known in various countries as Joha, Abbu Nawwas, and Nasr-ed-Dine Hodja. He is, in turn, an itinerant *imam* (priest), a peasant, a *qadi* (judge), husband, donkeyman, and court buffoon.

Since the Arabic names of the dishes vary a little from one country to another, I have chosen to use those by which they are most familiarly known in Egypt, except in cases of particularly national specialties.

Origins and Influences

Having collected a rich and rather extraordinary assortment of recipes from a great number of people, many of whom did not know the origins of their favorite dishes, and had picked them up at some point in their wanderings—from a place they had visited, from a relative, or from someone they had met—I tried to give them a national identity.

I then set about trying to learn more of their history. This search became fascinating, although it was soon clear that, to a certain extent, it would be impossible to determine their true sources. The same recipes seemed to turn up in several countries. One could not be certain as to when exactly they had come or from where, and who had introduced them to whom, especially in the absence of early culinary literature. Culinary manuals have been found dating from the twelfth and thirteenth centuries. Earlier ones are mentioned in various works, but have unfortunately been lost to us. It was a thrill to discover a dish mentioned in some historical or literary work, in a poem or in a proverb, and to conjure up the circumstances of its arrival in a particular place, to guess which battle and which conquering general had brought it, and to wonder why one country had adopted it while another had rejected it.

The history of this food is that of the Middle East. Dishes carry the triumphs and glories, the defeats, the loves and sorrows of the past. We owe some to an event, or to one man: the Caliph who commissioned it, the poet who sang it, or the *imam* who "fainted on receiving it."

The early origins of Middle Eastern food can be found in Bedouin dishes and the peasant dishes of each of the countries involved. In the case of Egypt, one can go back as far as Pharaonic times to find the same dishes, still eaten today by the Egyptians: roast goose, *melokhia* soup, *bamia*, and *batarekh*. In his *Dictionary of the Bible*, J. Hastings writes that the "Hebrews in the wilderness looked back wistfully on the cucumbers, melons, leeks, onions and garlic of Egypt; all of these were subsequently cultivated by them in Palestine." He also lists other foods mentioned in the Bible, such as varieties of beans and lentils, chickpeas, bitter herbs (still eaten today in the Passover ritual), olives, figs, grapes and raisins, dates, almonds, and nuts.

These were prepared in a manner similar to that of the Egyptians, probably remembered by the Jews from their time in Egypt. One specialty the Hebrews adopted was a fish, split open, salted and dried in the sun. It was very useful to take on long journeys, and it is still considered a great delicacy all over the Middle East.

Little is known about what the other ancient inhabitants of the Middle East ate—the Syrians, Lydians, Phrygians, Cappadocians, Armenians, Assyrians, Babylonians, Cilicians, and Mesopotamians. One can assume that these prosperous and highly civilized states must have had highly developed and luxurious culinary traditions, undoubtedly influenced by Greek and Roman customs, which fused together at different times during their history of invasions and conquests, whereas the inhabitants of the arid desert areas of Arabia and the Sahara could only have produced the spartan food still popular with the Bedouins today.

The Persian Empire of c. 500 B.C. was the earliest empire to envelop the whole region. Macedonian Greeks followed to radiate their culture, culinary and other. As the Romans and Parthians fought for dominance, the states they governed assimilated their traditions —and their recipes. And while these empires were won and lost, the character and style of Middle Eastern food was unknowingly being born.

It is in the Persia of the Sassanid period (third to seventh century) that it blossomed. The reign of King Khusrow I inaugurated the most brilliant period of the Sassanid era, and with it the decline of Byzantine power. Alexander the Great and his successors had made part of Persia, as well as parts of India, Hellenic strongholds. The debris of Hellenic civilization remained for many centuries, mingling and fusing with the Persian and Indian civilizations, philosophies, myths, and cultures, cross-fertilizing and leading to multiple variations. Similarities in food in these countries today, particularly between India and Persia, bear witness to these early influences.

In the reign of Khusrow II (early seventh century), Byzantium was finally defeated, and the Persian generals conquered Antioch, Damascus, Jerusalem, and Alexandria. The triumphs of this great king were matched by his growing cruelty, vanity, and greed. Enormous sums were spent on his pleasures and those of his court. Persian tales and legends describe his fantastic banquets, lavishly laid, dazzling with luxury and extravagance. In his book *L'Iran sous les Sassanides,* Arthur Christensen describes some of the dishes popular at the time, and the court's favorite recipes. It is then that some of the dishes so familiar today made their first appearance. A "dish for the King" consisted of hot and cold meats, rice jelly, stuffed vine leaves, marinated chicken, and a sweet date purée. A "Khorassanian dish" was composed of meat grilled on the spit and meat fried in butter with a sauce. A "Greek dish" was made with eggs, honey, milk, butter, rice, and sugar—a sort of rice pudding. A "Dehkan dish" consisted of slices of salted mutton with pomegranate juice, served with eggs.

Young kid was popular; so was beef cooked with spinach and vinegar. All kinds of game and poultry were eaten; in particular, hens fed on *chènevis* (hempseed) were hunted and "frightened" before they were killed, and then grilled on the spit. The lower part of the chicken's back was considered the tastiest. Today it is still a delicacy, sometimes called "the mother-in-law's morsel." Meat was marinated in yogurt and flavored with spices. Many different kinds of almond pastry were prepared, jams were made with quinces, dates stuffed with almonds and walnuts. All this is still done today. Our dishes were savored by Khusrow and his favorite wife, Shirin.

The decline of the Sassanids had started by the end of Khusrow's reign, but even after this grandiose empire had crumbled, its music and its food survived. Arab dishes today betray their origins by their Persian names.

The death of the Prophet Muhammad in A.D. 632 was followed by victorious wars waged by Muslim Arabs against Byzantines and Persians. The conquest and conversion to Islam of vast territories led to the establishment of an enormous Islamic empire stretching across North Africa, Spain, and Sicily. Its capital was first Damascus, and then Baghdad (now the capital of Iraq), ruled initially by the family of Muhammad, the Umayyads, followed by the Abbassids.

The Arabs themselves, unsophisticated and primitive, possessed a very limited culinary tradition based on Bedouin and peasant food. The Bedouin tradition included milk, sheep, and dates—the food of the desert and oasis. After a century of high moral standards, strict living, and restraint, the Abbassid Arabs, dazzled by the aristocratic brilliance of the Persians they had conquered, adopted their traditions of chivalry and good living, thus perpetuating the glories of the Persian past, as well as that of their Greek and Roman predecessors. This became a period of Persian ascendancy and cosmopolitan culture. Baghdad, the Abbassid capital, was built on Persian soil. It was then (from the end of the eighth to the tenth century) that cooking reached the height of magnificence. A creative culinary genius flourished at the banquets of the Caliphs of Baghdad, which became proverbial for their variety and lavishness. Manuals on the noble art of cooking are known to have been written at that time, but unfortunately none have survived. Songs were sung about food, poems were written and legends born of the great feasts which featured in the Arabian Nights. Mas'ūdī, a writer of the period, relates in his *Meadows of Gold* that one day the Caliph Mustakfi said: "It is my desire that we should assemble on such and such a day, and converse together about the different varieties of food, and the poetry that has been composed on the subject." Those present agreed. On the day prescribed, Mustakfi joined the party, and bade every man produce what he had prepared. Each member of the circle spoke up in turn, addressing the Commander of the Faithful. One recited verses by Ibn al Mu'tazz, the tragic prince who ruled for one day only and was put to death in 908, in which bowls of *kämakh* are described. Another recited a work by the poet-astrologer and culinary expert Husain al Kushajun, describing a table of delicacies, of roast kid, partridges, chickens, *tardina, sanbūsaj, nad, buran,* and sweet lozenges. Another then stood up and recited a poem of Ibn al-Rumi, describing *wast*. Another quoted Ibrāhīm of Mosul on the marvel of *sanbūsaj*.* Yet others glorified *harisa, madira, judhaba,* and *qada'if*. Each time, Mustakfi ordered that everything that had been mentioned in the poem should be served. They ate to the sound of music and sweet maidens' voices. Never had the narrator seen the Caliph so happy since the day of his accession. To all present, revelers, singers, and musicians, he gave money and gifts. Sadly, the narrator adds, this Caliph was one day to be seized by Ahmad ibn Buwaith the Buwayhid, who had his eyes "put out."

During the decline and dissolution of Abbassid power, in times of rebellion and strife, the incredible and inexhaustible wealth of the area still survived. Art, trade, philosophy, and gastronomy flourished. Maxime Rodinson, in his "Recherches sur les Documents relatifs à la Cuisine" in the *Revue des Etudes Islamiques*

* See pages 89–90.

(1949), has made a valuable study of the social climate of this period —which ended in the thirteenth century—and of the society for which dishes were created and thus glamorized. A ruling class had emerged whose members led a life of luxury and who devised a code of *savoir-vivre*. Manuals on how to be a connoisseur appeared. In *Meadows of Gold* Mas'ūdī advised people to read his other work *Ahbar Az-Zaman*, unfortunately lost, in which he says, "One can be instructed in detail on the variety of wines, on desserts, on the manner of arranging them in baskets or on plates, either piled up in pyramids, or otherwise, a culinary summary the knowledge of which is essential and which cannot be ignored by a well-bred man. One can also read about the new fashions in the way of dishes, the art of combining aromas and spices for the seasoning; subjects of conversation, as well as the way to wash one's hands in the presence of one's host." *

This literary gastronomical overabundance had been bitterly criticized as early as the eighth century by the heretic scientist Salih b. Abd al-Quddus, who wrote: "We live among animals who roam in quest of pastures, but who do not wish to understand. If one writes about fish and vegetables, one is invested in their eyes with superior merit, but if one writes of truly scientific subjects, it is for them painful and boring."

Two manuscripts of recipes have been found dating from the period of the collapse of Abbassid rule. One, the *Kitab al Wusla il al Habib*, probably written in the thirteenth century by a person of high

* From the French translation by Barbier de Meynard.

rank accustomed to the life of the court, received a detailed description in Maxime Rodinson's study. M. Rodinson believes that the writer(s)—there may be three—was from Syria. My father originally came from Syria, and I was thrilled to trace the origin of several of my own family's recipes. The other manual was written in Baghdad in the year 1226, a few years before the sack of the town by the Mongols. The dishes described are in the Persian tradition and bear Persian names. The author was a serious man and an enthusiast by the name of Muhammad ibn Hasan ibn Muhammad ibn al-Karim al-Katib al-Baghdadi. Professor A. J. Arberry has translated the manuscript of recipes, which was discovered by the Iraqi scholar Dr. Daoud Celebi in 1934. These were published in *Islamic Culture* in 1939.

Al-Baghdadi wrote, as was required at the time, "in the name of God the Merciful, the Compassionate." He divided pleasure into six classes: food, drink, clothes, sex, scent, and sound. Of these, he said, the noblest and most consequential was food. He subscribed to the doctrine of the preexcellence of the pleasure of eating above all other pleasures, and for that reason he composed the book. Al-Baghdadi chose to include from among the recipes popular at the time only those which he personally liked, and discarded what he describes as "strange and unfamiliar dishes, in the composition of which unwholesome and unsatisfying ingredients are used."

The dishes described in both these cookbooks belonged to the court cuisine. Vegetables such as *bamia* (okra) and numerous varieties of beans were left out, since they grew abundantly and were too common to be considered important. Ingredients that came from afar, such as expensive spices from China, India, and East Africa, were used.

It is this *haute cuisine*, or rather various *hautes cuisines* (from Baghdad, Damascus, and other centers), which was introduced by the conquerors who conducted the Muhammadan armies to the four corners of the earth. The Muslim invasion of the Middle East, North Africa, and parts of Asia, Sicily, Spain, and Portugal introduced Arab dishes to all these countries, the peasant food brought by the soldiers, the court cuisine by their generals. It was probably then, too, that the *couscous* of the Maghreb was introduced to the Arab world, and that the Turkish burghul (cracked wheat) was adopted in most countries. All the best dishes were put into the common culinary pool, and trade between the countries of the Arab Empire made it possible for ingredients grown in one country to become available in others.

The next great culinary period was that of the Ottoman Empire. Yet another new cuisine emerged, partly based on, and similar to, the Arab one, and partly adopted from the new countries conquered by the Turkish Ottoman warriors. A great number of dishes common to the Balkan countries bear Turkish names. The Greeks claim that this cuisine originated in their country, and although no description or record of dishes appears in ancient Greek literature or history, the fact that theirs was such a highly sophisticated civilization would support this claim. However, the Turkish contribution is undeniable regarding dishes such as shish kebab, which is believed to have evolved when the Ottoman invading armies had to camp outdoors in tents, awaiting a new assault. And whatever the source, it is to Selim the Cruel and Suleiman the Magnificent that we owe our stuffed vegetables and *mousakas*, and our glorious pastries such as *baklava* and *konafa*.

The sixteenth-century Turkish poet Revānī, in his *Isret Nāme*, deals with festive themes, and writes of the glorious banquets of the time: cultured revelers seated in a circle around crystal cups and flagons, each excelling in some art or other, debating a point of literature or philosophy, while a few musicians play the plaintive melodies of the East, a singer tells of tragic loves, and a fair young cupbearer goes her rounds. He also describes the various delicacies which figure at these banquets: sausages lying as if they were serpents keeping guard over a treasure, roast fowl dancing with delight to see the wine, grains of rice like pearls, saffron dishes like yellow-haired beauties, *börek* which might flout the sun, *chorek* shaped like the moon, jelly on which the almond fixeth her eyes, *qada'if* like a silver-bodied loveling.

In more recent history, from the early part of this century after the collapse of the Ottoman Empire, the Middle East became cosmopolitan, crowded with people from all parts of the world, in particular Greeks, French, Italians, and British. This was the Middle East of Lawrence Durrell, the Alexandria where Greek and Italian were spoken on the *corniche*, the Lebanon where most people spoke French. In this cosmopolitan and Europeanized climate, the food in general tended to become lighter, and cooking fats more digestible.

Dishes appeared in which the tastes of the East and the West had fused. Today, the renowned restaurants of the Middle East offer a double menu: traditional and cosmopolitan. Looking through a recent Egyptian cookbook published in Arabic, I found it abounding in recipes such as *roly-poly bel costarda* (a type of Swiss roll with custard) and *macaroni al Italiani*. The Grand Hotel of Khartoum used to offer (and probably still does) only one menu, devised in the time of Gordon, which was (or is) very reminiscent of British Rail fare. However, clients would be served local food on request.

Social Aspects

The activities of cooking and eating reflect many subtly intricate facets of the Middle Eastern character and way of life. They are intensely social activities, while the dishes hold within them centuries of local culture, art, and tradition.

Hospitality is a stringent duty all over the Middle East. "If people are standing at the door of your house, don't shut it before them," and "Give the guest food to eat even though you yourself are starving," are only two of a large number of sayings which serve to remind people of this duty.

Sayings of Muhammad in the Quran, folk proverbs, religious, mystical, and superstitious beliefs set up rules of social *savoir-vivre* to the minutest detail—sweetly tyrannical, immutable, and indisputable rules of civility and manners—to dictate the social behavior of people toward each other, and sometimes submerge and entangle them in social obligations.

The ultimate aim of civility and good manners is to please: to please one's guest or to please one's host. To this end one uses the rules strictly laid down by tradition: of welcome, generosity, affability, cheerfulness, and consideration for others.

People entertain warmly and joyously. To persuade a friend to stay for lunch is a triumph and a precious honor. To entertain many together is to honor them all mutually.

It is equally an honor to be a guest. Besides the customary obligations of cordiality and welcome, there is the need for the warmth of personal contact and cheerful company, the desire to congregate in groups, and the wish to please. It is common when preparing food to allow for an extra helping in case an unexpected guest should arrive. Many of the old recipes for soups and stews carry a note at the end saying that one can add water if a guest should arrive. When a meal is over there should always be a good portion of food left, otherwise one might think that someone has not been fully satisfied and could have eaten more.

The host should set before his guest all the food he has in the house, and apologize for its meagerness, uttering excuses such as: "This is all the grocer had," or "I was just on my way down to the confectioner's," or "For the past two weeks I have been preparing for my niece's wedding and have not had time to make anything else."

If a guest comes unexpectedly, the host must never ask why he has come, but receive him with a smiling face and a look of intense pleasure. After a ceremony of greetings, he should remark on the pleasure of seeing him and the honor of such a visit. The guest should never say right away why he has come, if there is a reason, but first inquire about the family, friends, and affairs of his host. The latter must treat his guests as though he were their servant; to quarrel with them would be a disgrace. He must never argue with them about politics or religion, but should always acquiesce. He must never ask his guests if they would like food or drink, but provide these automatically, insisting that they have them and ignoring repeated refusals.

"The first duty of a host is cheerfulness" is a maxim strictly abided by. A host must amuse and entertain, provide light gossip, jokes, and, occasionally, riddles and a little satire. He may also offer a tour of the house and an inspection of new acquisitions.

A guest, in turn, must also play his role correctly. He should "guard his voice, shorten his sight, and beautify (praise) the food." That is, although he must commend everything, exclaim in admiration, and congratulate, he should not look about too much, nor inspect too closely. The Quran advises him to talk nicely and politely: "Sow wheat, do not sow thorns; all the people will like you and love you." "Don't enter other people's houses, except with permission and good manners." "Beautify your tongue and you will obtain what you desire."

A guest must at first refuse the food offered to him, but eventually give in on being urgently pressed. In particular, he must never refuse dishes which have already been sampled by others of the company, as this would put them in an uncomfortable position. If he comes invited, he must bring a present, and if this happens to be a box of confectionery, the host must open it immediately and offer him some.

The Quran advises that "It is not right for a man to stay so long as to incommodate his host." When a guest leaves, he must bless his host and he is under an obligation to speak well of him to others.

However, this beautifully laid-out pattern has its pitfalls. The wrong sort of admiration might be mistaken for envy, and give rise to a fear of the "evil eye," of which it is said that "half of humanity dies." Folklore provides phrases to avoid this. The words "five on your eye" are equivalent to the Western "touch wood." Blessings uttered toward various saints and the invocation of the name of God also act as a protection from evil. The person who is the object of admiration may protect himself by denouncing the reality of his good fortune and protesting that he has also been the victim of various misfortunes. However, a remark of admiration directed toward a personal possession may oblige the owner to offer it instantly and pressingly.

Cooks always cook to suit the taste of those who will eat the food. They need and expect approval. Often, dishes for the evening are lengthily discussed in the morning. Husbands express their wishes as to what they would like for dinner and, while they are eating, often remark on the success of the dish. However, a few husbands of my acquaintance believe that they must criticize something in a meal or complain that the dish requires a little more of one thing or another, thereby preventing their wives from becoming complacent.

Cooks are constantly coaxed and encouraged to surpass themselves and to perfect family favorites. Cooking ability is rated highly among female accomplishments. One Arab saying goes: "A woman first holds her husband with a pretty face, then by his tummy, and lastly with the help of a *sheb-sheb* (a wooden slipper)."

Cooking is often done in company. Mothers and daughters, sisters, cousins, and friends love to talk about what they will serve their family for lunch or dinner, and they sit together or help each other to prepare delicacies which require time and skill. At all special occasions, such as family gatherings and national or religious holidays, the hostess can count on the help of many eager and generous relatives and friends, who come to help prepare the food, sometimes two or three days ahead. If they are unable to be present at the preparations, they will often send a plateful of their own particular specialty instead.

People always turn to food to mark important events. Weddings, circumcisions, religious festivals, new arrivals, in fact, most occasions, call for a particular dish or delicacy, or even a whole range of specialties. If these are lacking when it is customary to include them, it is a cause for offense and gossip. Criticism and disapproval are feared most by those who wish to impress and do the right or customary thing. This accounts for the fact that parties, though often extraordinarily lavish and varied, are also repetitive within each community. No table could be without stuffed vine leaves, *kahk*, *ma'amoul*, or *baklava* and the usual range of delicacies. How fearful one is of the critical gaze of a guest searching for some specialty which is missing from the table!

It is said that there is a language of flowers. In the Middle East there exists a language of food. A code of etiquette for serving and presenting particular dishes expresses subtle social distinctions. Which piece, of what, and in what order gives away the status of the person who is being served. There are rules of procedure according to social and family status and age. A dignitary or the head of the family is served the best helping first. A guest who comes seldom or who comes from afar is served before one who is a regular and familiar visitor to the house. A bride-to-be is served ceremoniously at the house of her husband-to-be. But when she is married, her status drops considerably at the table (as it does everywhere else), to rise again when she is expecting a baby. Then, she is often pampered and allowed to indulge in extravagant yearnings. If she then gives birth to a son, her status remains high.

A person of "low extraction" who insists on sitting next to one of high birth or importance might be asked: "What brought the sardine to the red mullet?" A proverb advises men to pay respect to status, and to give to each according to his station: "Divide the meat and look at the faces." And a saying describes this regard: "When a wealthy man comes to a feast, the host tells some poor man to get up and give his place to the newcomer."

In some parts of the Middle East where folklore is rich in beliefs about the evil eye, *djinns,* and omens, some foods are believed to have magical powers.

Garlic is believed by some to ward off the evil eye and is sometimes hung at the front door of a house to protect its inhabitants. For its disinfectant qualities it is hung on a string around children's necks during epidemics. In some parts, people do not eat brains for fear of becoming as stupid as the animal; in others, they eat it to fortify their own brains and become more intelligent. Some do not eat the hearts of birds in case they might acquire their timidity.

Certain beliefs are uncommon and localized, and few people will have even heard of them. Others are widespread in all the countries and communities. One of these is that eating yellow things will result in laughter and happiness; another, that eating honey and sweet things will sweeten life and protect one from sadness and evil. Predictably, things colored black, such as very black eggplant, are considered by some to be unlucky, while green foods encourage the repetition of happy and prosperous events.

In the past, some foods were believed to have aphrodisiac qualities. Cheikh Umar ibn Muhammed al Nefzawi, in his now famous sixteenth-century work, *The Perfumed Garden,* recommends various foods as a cure for impotence or as powerful sexual stimulants. For the former, he recommends eating "a stimulant pastry containing honey, ginger, pyrether, syrup of vinegar, hellebore, garlic, cinnamon, nutmeg, cardamoms, sparrow's tongues, Chinese cinnamon, long pepper, and other spices"; also "nutmeg and incense mixed with honey." Of foods which "all learned men" acknowledge to have a positive effect in stimulating amorous desires are: an asparagus omelet, a fried onion omelet, camel's milk mixed with honey, eggs boiled with myrrh, coarse cinnamon and pepper, eggs fried in butter, then immersed in honey and eaten with a little bread, and simply plain chickpeas. He assures his readers that "the efficacy of all these remedies is well known, and I have tested them." Even today, a certain belief in the aphrodisiac powers of some foods still exists.

· · ·

Cooking in the Middle East is deeply traditional and nonintellectual —an inherited art. It is not precise and sophisticated like Chinese cooking, nor is it experimental and progressive like American cooking today. Its virtues are loyalty and respect for custom and tradition, reflected in the unwavering attachment to the dishes of the past. Many have been cooked for centuries, from the time they were evolved, basically unchanged.

Yet each cook feels that within the boundaries of tradition she can improvise. She can pit her artfulness and wits, her sensuous feeling for the food, its texture and aroma, to create a unique and exquisite dish with the imprint of her own individual taste.

Of the people who have given me recipes, most added remarks such as: "Personally, I like to add a little mint," implying that this was their own innovation; or "I always put double the usual amount of ground almonds," meaning that they are extravagant; or "I use dry bread crumbs instead of soaked bread," to show their ingenuity; or, with a touch of guilt, "I use stock cubes instead of making a chicken stock because it is easier, but I find it very acceptable." Somebody even devised a way of stuffing zucchini without actually doing so, by curling them around a compact ball of meat and rice filling and securing them tightly with a toothpick.

Nevertheless, if I suggested to those same people a totally new taste or a totally new form or method for a dish, they were mildly outraged or laughed incredulously at the folly of such a suggestion.

A certain malleability and a capacity to absorb new cultures while still remaining true to themselves have enabled the people of the Middle East to adopt dishes brought back by the Moors from Spain, those introduced by the Crusaders, Greek dishes, North African dishes such as *couscous*, and, more recently, French, Italian, and even English dishes, and then to adapt them to suit local tastes.

Of the dishes created by the local way of life and general character are the large variety of *mezze*, served before a meal, or to accompany drinks at any time of the day. These reflect the passion that the Middle Eastern peoples have for leisure and the importance they attach to their peace of mind, the luxury of tranquil enjoyment which they call *keif*. It is for them a delight to sit at home on their balconies, in their courtyards, or at the café, slowly sipping drinks and savoring *mezze*.

The numerous stuffed *mahshi*, *börek*, *sanbusak*, and pastries, all requiring artful handiwork, denote a local pride in craftsmanship and skill. The traditional decoration of dishes down to the humblest sauce or soup with a dusting of red paprika or brown cumin and a sprinkling of chopped parsley is the result of a love of beauty and ornamentation, the same that has produced the luscious Islamic decorative arts. The sensuous blue and green patterns of the ceramics are echoed in the green chopped pistachios and pale chopped blanched almonds adorning cream puddings. The crisscross wooden patterns of the balconies behind which the women used to hide haunt the lozenge shapes of *basbousa* and *baklava*. The colors of confectioneries, syrups, and pickles are those of the brilliant dresses which appear at *mûlids* (festivals).

The Traditional Table

Before proceeding to the table, guests are entertained in a different room, where they often sit on sofas at floor level. A maid comes around with a large copper basin and flask, pouring out water (sometimes lightly perfumed with rose or orange blossom) for the guests to wash their hands. A towel is passed around at the same time.

Dining tables are low and round—large metal trays resting on a type of stool, or on short, carved, folding wooden legs, sometimes inlaid with mother-of-pearl and tortoise shell. The trays themselves are of copper, brass, or silver, beaten and engraved, sometimes inlaid

with silver or other metals. Thin threads of the metal are beaten into crevices with a little hammer, making traditional Oriental decorative patterns and writing: words of blessing, charms against the evil eye, and words in praise of Allah. Usually several tables are placed in the room, and the diners sit around them on cushions.

Several bowls containing a variety of dishes are placed on each table for guests to enjoy the pleasure of deciding which dish to start with, and with which delicacy to follow.

Before the meal is started, the word *Bismillah* (In the name of God!) is uttered by all.

In eating, a strict code of etiquette is observed. It is related that the Imam Hassan (son of Ali) listed twelve rules of etiquette to be observed.

"The first four are *necessary*, namely: to know that God is the Provider; to be satisfied with what he has provided; to say 'In the name of God!' when beginning to eat and to say 'To God be thanks!' when you finish. The next four are *customary*, and it is well to observe them, though they are not required: to wash the hands before eating; to sit at the left of the table; to eat with three fingers; and to lick the fingers after eating. The last four are rules of particular politeness: to eat out of the dish that is immediately in front of you and out of your own side of the dish; to take small pieces; to chew the food well; and not to gaze at the others at the table with you. These twelve rules form the traditional basis for the table manners of the majority of the people."

Besides these rules, there are other, subtler points of *savoir-vivre*. It is tolerated to eat with five fingers when eating food of a not too solid consistency, such as *couscous*.

It is considered sociable and polite to detach choice morsels such as chicken hearts or livers, or fish roes, and to offer these to a neighbor.

If one feels satiated, one should nevertheless continue to nibble at a dish from which others are still eating, since if one person stops eating, everyone else may feel compelled to stop too, and the dish will be removed from the table.

One must lick one's fingers at the end of a meal only. To do so before would be a sign that one had finished.

One must always talk about pleasant and joyful things and never introduce a sad or bitter note into the conversation. One must be cheerful and entertaining, and remark on the perfection of dishes, saying, "Your fingers are green!" if the hostess has prepared them or helped in their preparation; and "May your table always be generous to all!"—a phrase entertaining the hope that one will be asked to eat there again soon.

Sometimes, in parts where women have not yet become emancipated, men only are invited. Islam looks upon women with suspicion. According to Muslim tradition, the Prophet Muhammad said: "I have not left any calamity more hurtful to man than woman." In some parts, women are believed to have more power to cast the evil eye, so they are served first, before their look of longing can have a harmful effect on the food.

If two people have eaten together, they are compelled to treat each other well, as the food contains a conditional curse. This is alluded to in the sayings: "God and the food will repay him for it" and "Cursed, son of a cursed one, is he who eats food and deceives him who shared it with him." Host and guest in particular are tied in a relationship governed by this conditional curse.

When the meal is finished, guests leave the table to go through the hand-washing ceremony again and to partake of coffee or tea.

Similar rules to these are added to Western manners in homes where Western habits of eating have been adopted, and certain actions and words reveal this attachment to ancient tradition. At buffet dinner parties in our house, for example, the guests stood far away from the table and had to be urged and pressed to eat. Although the mechanics of the table, the knife and fork, and the table napkin had been adopted, the old, Middle Eastern manners and rules of *bienséance* remained.

To those of the Middle East who might misunderstand my motives and feel offended, as I believe some will, by my description of "table manners," I would like to say that the manner of eating with the fingers is most delicate and at least as refined as any belonging to the culture of the West, and I have only respect for the elegance of these rules of *savoir-vivre*.

Muslim Dietary Laws

A note on Muslim dietary laws is relevant in a book of food which has been influenced by them.

The religion of Islam is the most important part of Middle Eastern culture and the main foundation of the customs and traditions of the region. The code of religion is derived mainly from the Quran, which serves the faithful as a model and rule of life in every particular.

The Quran consists of a collection of the revelations or commands which the Prophet Muhammad received through the Angel Gabriel as messages from God, and which he delivered to those about him, on divine direction. As Muhammad received the messages in moments of divine inspiration he recited them to those of his Companions, or followers, who were with him, and who wrote them down on any object available, such as a stone or a piece of cloth.

These fragments were copied and preserved after the Prophet's death, to be compiled and collected later by a certain Zayd b. Thabit. The *Suras*, or chapters, were not arranged in chronological order and are out of their original context. Without the certainty of the occasion and period at which they were revealed, it is possible to interpret them in different ways. To appreciate them, one should be aware of the social environment of the time, and of the influence of the customs and superstitions of previous centuries.

Muhammad mentioned food many times throughout the Quran, and insisted particularly on its beneficial character as a gift from God. He repeated injunctions about kinds of food permitted and not permitted.

"So eat of what God has given you, lawful or good, and give thanks for God's favor if Him it is you serve."

"Say I find not in that which is revealed to me aught forbidden for an eater to eat thereof, except that it be what dies of itself, or blood poured forth, or flesh of swine—for that surely is unclean—or what is a transgression other than (the name of) God having been invoked on it. But whoever is driven by necessity, not desiring nor exceeding the limit, then surely thy Lord is Forgiving, Merciful."

In actual fact, the following are forbidden: 1. animals dead before they are slaughtered, or those killed for reasons other than that of food; 2. blood; 3. pig's flesh; 4. animals slaughtered as an offering to a pagan deity or in the name of the deity; 5. alcoholic or fermented liquids, and all inebriating liquors, although they were favored at first. They are forbidden in cooking, too.

An animal that is killed for the food of man must be slaughtered in a particular manner: the person who is about to do it must say: "In the name of God, God is most great!" and then cut its throat.

These dietary laws are observed in varying degrees of laxity throughout the Muslim world. It is very uncommon for people to eat pork. Some Muslims drink wine, liqueurs, and other types of alcohol, and some use them in their food. This is quite common practice today in Turkey, but generally, cooking with wine and alcohol is more an individual and personal preference, rather than a national or traditional characteristic.

General Features of Middle Eastern Food

I have noted below a few features which make up the general patterns or rhythms of Middle Eastern cooking. This may help to form an understanding of the character of the cuisine.

Cooking fats used in most countries in the past were rather heavy. In particular, *alya*, the rendered fat from a sheep's or lamb's tail, was extremely popular. Many of the medieval recipes I have included start with "melt tail" or "fry in tail." They refer to *alya*. Today, however, although this fat is still used for cooking in a few districts, it has generally been replaced by a clarified butter called *samna*, ordinary butter, margarine, and oil.

Samna is butter (usually made from buffalo's milk) which has been melted over boiling water and clarified by straining it through thin dampened muslin. The impurities which cause butter to burn and darken are eliminated, as well as much of the water content. It is rich and strong with a distinctive taste, and a little of it will give the same result as a much larger quantity of butter. It also keeps well. A type of *samna* sold in jars in Indian shops is called *ghee*. Although *samna* is much used and favored all over the Middle East, it, too, is sometimes replaced by butter or margarine.

Oil, usually corn or nut oil, is generally used by Jews for all their cooking, while Copts prefer sesame oil. All countries use olive oil for dishes which are to be eaten cold. For most deep frying, corn or nut oil is used, but for deep frying fish, olive oil is preferred.

In the medieval recipes, I have suggested using butter or oil (instead of "tail") for frying meat, and nut or corn oil for sesame oil.

As a general rule, people like to fry or sauté their meat and vegetables before adding water to make stews and soups. These acquire a rather darker color and a somewhat richer flavor, while the meat, sealed by the preliminary frying, retains its juices. The Moroccans of Fez are an exception; their pale, delicate lamb stews are distinguished from those of the inhabitants of other Moroccan towns. They do not fry the ingredients, but boil them from the start in water with a little oil, relying on the stocks which result, and the variety and quality of the other ingredients, to give color, texture, and body to their dishes. To them it is a crime against refinement to fry meats or vegetables destined for a stew.

A large variety of spices is used. The region, which in early times served as a spice route between the Far East and Europe, and between Central Africa and Europe, succumbed to their charms.

Practically every main Middle Eastern town has its *attarine*, or spice street, containing very small shops (some as small as a cupboard) which sell spices. Passing through it, one is in turn soothed and excited, and one feels compelled to acquire almost every spice to be had. Vendors fill little cones made out of tightly rolled pieces of paper, and offer them as though they were magic potions.

Each country seems to have a favorite combination of spices or herbs. In the medieval recipes, the same spices and flavorings— cumin, coriander, cinnamon, ginger, and mastic—are used again and again (sometimes in a "spice bag").

A favorite Lebanese spice mixture is made up of one part of hot pepper (cayenne), two parts of sweet pepper (paprika), and two parts of cinnamon. Another Arab favorite, called *taklia*, is ground coriander fried with crushed garlic, the smell of which trickles out through the door of every home in Egypt, be it hovel or palace, and lingers in the little alleyways. Yet another is a mixture of cinnamon, nutmeg, cloves, and ginger, named the "four spices," which is sometimes replaced by the one spice called allspice or Jamaican pepper, whose taste rather resembles that of the four together. A combination of coriander and cumin is also very popular.

Moroccans use an enormous range of spices, often all at once, but only in extremely small quantities, so that even when they are using three different types of pepper of varying strengths, the general flavor of the dish is still gentle and mild. A rather extraordinary spice mixture called *Harissa* or *Ras el Hanout* (see page 149) is used for winter dishes and is said to "warm up" and render virile.

Fresh coriander is an herb often used by Arabs in their salads and stews. Dill is popular in Turkey and Iran, while mint is a great favorite everywhere. A type of parsley rather like chervil in appearance is much used, as well as *rigani*, oregano, and marjoram. Sesame seed, aniseed, caraway seed, and fennel flavor breads and savories.

Saffron, the pistil of a certain variety of crocus, is highly prized. In certain parts, such as Morocco and Persia, it is used extensively in all types of dishes for its faint, delicate aroma, and for the magnificent yellow color it gives the food. It is used either in its natural pistil form, crushed with salt or sugar, or as a powder.

In a legal treatise from twelfth-century Spain by Ibn Abdun, translated into French by E. Lévi-Provençal in *Seville Musulmanne*, it is requested that *"le safran ne doit pas être vendu sous forme de pâte découpée en pastilles, car il est fort falsifié et mauvais."* Various imitations and "false" saffrons which are infinitely cheaper and which may be used for color only still exist today. They come in varying shades, ranging from yellow to red, and can be found in Indian shops. I would personally omit saffron from many of the recipes where it is optional, an omission justified, I feel, by its very high cost, and by the fact that the dishes are equally good without it.

Another coloring spice which is much favored for its taste and for its acid yellow shade is turmeric, used in powdered form. Sometimes called "Oriental saffron," it is often substituted for the latter. I particularly like it with chicken, veal, potatoes, and chickpeas.

In many countries, roasted spice, seed, and nut mixtures are sold ready-prepared from jars in groceries, or in paper cones in the streets. In Egypt these mixtures are called *dukkah* (see page 51). Dried crushed mint seasoned with salt and pepper is sold to accompany rings of bread covered with sesame seeds, called *semit* (see page 369). Such mixtures are also featured in the medieval *Wusla il al Habib* and in al-Baghdadi's manual.

People generally roast their spice seeds themselves and grate or crush them as they need them so as to retain the maximum of their aroma, since freshly ground spices are more flavorful than ground spices which have been stored in jars for a long time. However, those who enjoy visits to the spice street prefer to buy small amounts of ground spices at a time, and more frequently.

I would like to suggest that when trying a dish for the first time you add only very small quantities of spices or herbs to begin with, then increase them after tasting, if you find the flavor agreeable.

·   ·   ·

The utensils and the type of heat available have to a large extent determined the style of cooking. Ovens have only recently been introduced in most homes. In the past, cooking was generally done over a type of portable oil stove called a *fatayel*. It was a long, slow procedure, and pans were sometimes left to simmer overnight. This habit has remained to the present day, although the necessity may have passed, and it is more usual for food to be prepared over heat than for it to be baked or roasted in an oven.

It was customary in the past, and to a lesser degree it still is even today, to send certain dishes to be cooked in the ovens of the local bakery. This was a feature of the way of life. People hurried about in the streets with huge trays or casseroles, sometimes balancing them on their heads. Life at the ovens bustled with activity and humor. I am told of great-aunts who sealed their pans with a paste made of flour and water, ostensibly in order to cook the dish under pressure, but also to ensure that no one introduced an unwholesome, impure, or prohibited ingredient out of spite. Many people specified precisely in what position they wanted their pans placed in the enormous ovens. Others, perfectionists, sat by the ovens on wicker stools throughout the cooking time, watching their food and giving directions for the pans to be moved this way and that, in order to vary the degree of the heat. Today, dishes which would in the past have gone to the district oven (such as a roast leg of lamb surrounded by vegetables) are cooked in domestic ovens, but slowly, as before.

Another factor which helped to perpetuate the tradition of slow, lengthy cooking, as well as that of the more elaborate dishes which require time and craftsmanship, is the social custom which has kept women in the home until very recently.

Nuts have been used since ancient times in a variety of dishes and in unexpected ways. One of the regional characteristics which denotes the nationality of the cook is the selective use of nuts. Where an Egyptian or Syrian would use ground almonds or pine nuts to thicken a sauce such as *tarator* (page 166) or almond sauce (page 355), a Turk would use ground walnuts. Persians also use ground almonds, for example in their *faisinjan* sauce (page 193) for chicken or duck, in the same way as they are used for the Circassian chicken (page 185). In Persia, pomegranate or sour cherry sauce is added to the walnut sauce, while in Turkey it is sprinkled with the favorite garnish of red paprika melted in oil.

In most countries, it is customary to place a bowl of fresh yogurt on the table, to be eaten with such varied foods as *eggah*, pilavs, stuffed vegetables, salads, and kebabs. It is sometimes flavored with salt, mint, and crushed garlic. In Turkey, yogurt is used extensively as a bed for meat or vegetables, or to be poured over salads, eggs, vegetables, rice, almost anything in fact. It is also used as a cooking liquid, particularly in the Lebanon, Turkey, and Persia.

Persians favor dishes delicately balanced in flavor between sweet and sour, cooked with vinegar, lemon, and sugar, and the sour juice of pomegranates. They share with Moroccans a predilection and a skill for combining the textures and flavors of meats and fruits. They also habitually thicken their stews and sauces with lentils or yellow split peas.

Measurements have been translated for this edition into common American usage.

I have indicated precise quantities and measures in the recipes, and have given a few variations to allow for the natural fluidity and variability of the dishes. I would like to stress, however, that many more variations exist, according to region and even to individual families. Another cook might use slightly different ingredients (or the same in varying proportions) for a dish similar to one I have given, equally successfully. On a different day, in different moods, I might prepare the same dish in a different manner from what I have recorded.

Three tomatoes can sometimes be used instead of one, and onions and garlic may be used abundantly or omitted entirely without spoiling a dish. Parsley may be used when fresh coriander or chervil is not available, turmeric may occasionally be substituted for saffron, and cinnamon and allspice may often be interchanged. Soups may be made thick or thin, and salads more or less lemony, according to taste.

I would like to suggest that after the initial "trying out" of a new recipe, the reader should trust his taste and allow himself greater freedom in its preparation.

All the recipes are designed to serve six people unless otherwise stated, but they may be thought rather on the generous side since I, too, suffer from the Oriental urge to prepare more than is actually required for my guests.

HORS D'ŒUVRES

Mezze

Mezze are one of the most delightful features of Middle Eastern food —indeed they are almost a way of life. Form the cafés by the Nile to mountain resorts in the Lebanon and palatial villas in Morocco and Persia, savoring *mezze* with an *ouzo*, a beer, a syrup, or a coffee can be a delight approaching ecstasy, part sensual, part mystical. The pleasure of savoring the little pieces of food is accompanied by feelings of peace and serenity, and sometimes by deep meditation.

Mezze are ideally suited to the Western way of life. A small assortment can be served with drinks at parties, and a wider choice provides an exciting buffet dinner.

There are many different kinds of *mezze*, simple and elaborate.

Nuts of all types; salted and soaked chickpeas; olives; cucumbers cut into long thin slices and sprinkled with salt half an hour before serving; quartered tomatoes; pieces of cheese cut into small cubes or long sticks, sometimes grilled or fried—these provide *mezze* which require little or no work.

Salads are popular as *mezze*. So is every type of pickle. Sauces or dips made with *tahini* (sesame paste), chickpeas, and eggplant are greatly favored. They are eaten with little pieces of Arab bread.

Myriads of "miniature foods," sometimes exact but diminished replicas of main dishes of meat, chicken, and fish, can be served. Favorites are grilled or fried chicken livers, fried cubes of lamb's or calf's liver served hot or cold, small minced meat, chicken, or fish balls, and savory little pastries such as *börek* (page 92) and pies.

Stuffed vine leaves are popular in all their forms. So are *ta'amia* or *falafel* in Egypt (page 47), and an assortment of fresh herbs in Persia (page 32).

In this chapter, I shall give the dishes which are more commonly thought of as hors d'œuvre dishes, although some of them are also served as salads or as accompaniments to main dishes. Other *mezze* will be found in the chapters on salads, savories, and pickles. Recipes for meat, chicken, and fish balls and other dishes in the meat, poultry, and fish chapters can also be reduced in size and served as an appetizer or first course. *Hamine* eggs, for instance (page 136), or boiled or deep-fried eggs sprinkled with cumin, make good *mezze*. They will be found in the chapter on egg dishes.

When preparing an assortment of appetizers, arrange them so that you make the most of the color and texture of each, by its contrast or affinity to its neighbor. Place the small, sharply defined shapes of fish sticks or *ta'amia*, for instance, next to smooth, pale sauces and dips. Set shiny black olives next to faintly beige *tahini* cream, and light green cucumber fingers beside a gently tinted eggplant purée. If necessary, decorate the *mezze* with chopped parsley, tomato and onion slices, radishes, gherkins, lemon wedges, paprika, olives, almonds, or chickpeas.

Limit your selection of *mezze* with strict self-discipline if you are serving them before a large meal, or appetites may easily be spoiled.

In the recipes which follow, quantities given are quite large, designed for six people who will be offered only one, or perhaps two, dishes. Reduce the quantity by half if you wish, as is customary, to serve a large variety.

A Bowl of Fresh Herbs

In Persia fresh herbs are served as *mezze*, and a bowl containing a varied assortment of these is placed on the table at most meals.

An ancient custom is for women to eat the herbs with bread and cheese at the end of a meal. According to an old belief, this will help them to keep their husbands away from a rival. Job's-tears and mandrake in particular should turn him against a "co-wife." *

A Persian friend of mine grows a large variety of Persian herbs in her London garden, where they thrive throughout the English summer.

Wash a few sprigs of fresh parsley, mint, chives, cress, dill, coriander, tarragon, scallions—in fact any fresh herbs you like which are available—and arrange them in a bowl.

Persian saying: "Even the worm inside a stone eats herbs."

* Donaldson, *The Wild Rue.*

An Egg Hors d'Œuvre / A Sephardic Dish

3 large eggs, hard-boiled
1 large potato, boiled

2½ tablespoons goose or chicken fat, or softened butter
Salt and black pepper

Shell and chop the eggs. Mash the potato before it cools. Cream the fat with salt and pepper to taste, and mix it lightly with the egg and potato. Serve lukewarm or cold.

Wara Einab / Dolma or Stuffed Vine Leaves

Popular in every country throughout the Middle East, stuffed vine leaves are a very intriguing and delightful delicacy. There are numerous variations. As a general rule, ground meat is used in the making of hot *dolma*, and cold *dolma* are made without meat. Nevertheless, leftover vine leaves stuffed with meat are sometimes eaten cold, and invariably they turn out to be delicious.

The leaves can be bought preserved in brine in Greek and Oriental stores, and they are also sold in cans in many delicatessens.

Hot Stuffed Vine Leaves

40–50 preserved, drained vine leaves (a 1-lb. jar)
¾ cup long-grain rice
½ lb. beef or lamb, ground
1 tomato, skinned and chopped
1 small onion, finely chopped
4 tablespoons finely chopped parsley

4 tablespoons finely chopped celery leaves [optional]
Salt and black pepper
2½ tablespoons tomato paste [optional]
2 tomatoes, sliced [optional]
2 cloves garlic, halved or slivered
Juice of 1 lemon, or more

If using vine leaves preserved in brine, put them in a large bowl and pour boiling water over them. Make sure that the water penetrates well between the layers, and let the leaves soak for 20 minutes. Drain. Soak in fresh cold water, then drain again, and repeat the process once more. This will remove excess salt.

If using fresh vine leaves, soften them by plunging them, a few at a time, in boiling water for a few minutes until they become limp.

Soak and wash the rice in boiling water, and then rinse it under the cold tap. Drain it well. In a large bowl, mix the rice with the meat, chopped tomato, onion, parsley, celery, salt and pepper. And 2 tablespoons or more tomato paste for a particularly Greek flavor.

Place one leaf on a plate vein side up. Place 1 heaping teaspoon of the filling in the center of the leaf near the stem edge. Fold the stem end up over the filling, then fold both sides toward the middle and roll up like a small cigar. Squeeze lightly in the palm of your hand. This process will become very easy after you have rolled a few.

Fill the rest of the leaves in the same way. Continue until all the filling is used up.

Line the bottom of a large saucepan with a layer of tomato slices or leftover vine leaves to prevent the stuffed leaves from sticking to the pan and burning. Pack the stuffed leaves in tight layers on top, pushing small pieces of garlic here and there between them. Sprinkle with lemon juice and add about ½ cup water. Some cooks mix a little saffron with the water to give a pale yellow color to the cooked filling, but in my opinion this is unnecessary since it does not seem to improve the taste and the leaves themselves give a beautiful pale lemon color to the rice anyway.

Put a small plate over the rolled leaves to prevent them from coming undone, and cover with a lid. Cook the leaves over very gentle heat for at least 2 hours, or until tender, adding water gradually as it becomes absorbed. The cooking time can be reduced to 20 minutes if a pressure cooker is used, but the taste is improved by the long simmering.

Turn out onto a serving dish and serve hot.

A Lebanese cook may add 4 or more cloves of crushed garlic (in addition to the slivered ones) and a tablespoon of crushed dried mint with a little water about 20 minutes before the end of cooking time. Others, including Persians, Lebanese, and Greeks, like to add about ½ teaspoon ground cinnamon to the filling.

Cold Stuffed Vine Leaves

This is an exquisite dish in which the delicate aromas of the spices blend with the taste of the vine leaves against a background of acid lemon and sweet garlic.

40–50 preserved, drained vine leaves (a 1-lb. jar)	¼ level teaspoon ground cinnamon
¾ cup long-grain rice	¼ level teaspoon ground allspice
2–3 tomatoes, skinned and chopped	Salt and black pepper
1 large onion, finely chopped, or 5 tablespoons finely chopped scallions	2 tomatoes, sliced [optional]
	3–4 cloves garlic [optional]
	½ cup olive oil
2½ tablespoons finely chopped parsley	¼ teaspoon powdered saffron [optional]
2½ tablespoons dried crushed mint	1 teaspoon sugar
	Juice of 1 lemon, or more

Prepare the leaves as described in the previous recipe. Soak and stir the rice in boiling water, and then rinse it under the cold tap. Drain it thoroughly. In a bowl, mix the rice with the tomatoes, onion or scallions, parsley, mint, cinnamon, allspice, and salt and pepper to taste.

Stuff the leaves with this mixture and roll them up as described in the previous recipe. Pack them tightly in a large pan lined with tomato slices or leftover, torn, or imperfect vine leaves, occasionally slipping a whole clove of garlic in between them if you like.

Mix the olive oil with ½ cup water and the saffron, if used. Add the sugar and lemon juice, and pour the mixture over the stuffed leaves. Put a small plate on top of the leaves to prevent their un-winding, cover the pan, and simmer very gently for at least 2 hours, until the rolls are thoroughly cooked; add water occasionally, a cup at a time, as the liquid in the pan becomes absorbed. Cool in the pan before turning out. Serve cold.

Persians like to add about 2 tablespoons chopped dill and ¾ cup seedless raisins or currants to the filling. Another variation which adds a new element to the texture uses *hummus* or chickpeas. Soak about ½ cup in water overnight. Then crush them in a mortar and add them to the filling. In this case use ⅓ cup less rice. Pine nuts (⅓ cup) can also be added, and make a delicious variation.

Eggplant Purée

This way of preparing eggplants, sometimes called "poor man's caviar," is a favorite all over the Middle East.

3 eggplants	1–2 cloves garlic, crushed
4 tablespoons olive oil	Juice of 1 lemon, or more
3 tablespoons chopped parsley	Salt and black pepper

The best way of preparing this purée is to grill the eggplants over charcoal, which gives them a distinctive flavor. However, it will probably be more convenient to grill them under a broiler or place them over a gas flame; either way is very successful. Sear them until the skins are black and start to blister, and the flesh soft and juicy. Rub the skins off under the cold tap, taking care to remove any charred particles. Gently squeeze out as much of the juice as possible, since it is very bitter.

Put the eggplants in a bowl and mash them with a fork, or pound them to a smooth paste in a mortar. An electric blender will give excellent results. Add the oil gradually, beating all the time. Then add the remaining ingredients, mixing vigorously to blend them into the purée. Taste and add more lemon juice, garlic, or seasonings as you wish.

Serve as an appetizer or salad.

Eggplant Purée with Yogurt

A *similar recipe to this one, called* buran, *is to be found in al-Baghdadi's thirteenth-century cooking manual. Fried meatballs are added to the purée, and the dish is seasoned with ground cumin and cinnamon.*

3 eggplants
4 tablespoons olive oil
1¼ cups yogurt
Juice of 1 lemon

1–2 cloves garlic, crushed
Salt
2 tablespoons finely chopped parsley
[optional]

Cook and peel the eggplants as described in the previous recipe, and squeeze them to remove the bitter juices.

Mash them with a fork in a bowl or pound to a smooth paste in a mortar. Add the olive oil gradually, beating constantly. Then add the yogurt and mix vigorously until it is thoroughly blended with the eggplant purée. Mix in the remaining ingredients (except parsley), spoon into a serving bowl, and garnish with chopped parsley if desired. Serve cold.

Fried Eggplant with Yogurt

3 eggplants
Salt
Oil

2 cloves garlic, crushed
1¼ cups yogurt
Dried crushed mint, to garnish

Cut the eggplants into ½-inch-thick slices. Sprinkle them with salt and leave them in a colander for about ½ hour to allow the bitter juices to drain away. Rinse them with cold water and wipe dry.

Fry the eggplant slices in hot oil for a few minutes on each side until lightly browned. Add the crushed garlic and fry for a minute or two longer until golden and aromatic. Remove the eggplant slices and garlic, and drain on absorbent paper. Allow to cool.

Season the yogurt with salt. (Some people prefer to add the crushed garlic raw to the yogurt instead of frying it with the eggplant.) Arrange and spread alternate layers of yogurt and fried eggplant slices in a dish. Start with a layer of yogurt, and top the dish with yogurt too. Garnish with dried crushed mint and serve as an appetizer or salad.

Gebna Beida / White Cheese

2½ quarts milk   5 tablespoons liquid essence of
1 tablespoon salt, or more   rennet *

Use at least 2½ quarts of milk, as the amount of cheese produced even from this quantity is really quite small.

Pour the milk into a saucepan and heat gently. Add the salt and rennet, and continue to heat the milk slowly until you can just bear to keep your finger in it without feeling any sting. Do not cover the pan, as condensed steam would spoil the process, and do not allow the milk to become too hot, as this will cause failure. Boiling would ruin it.

Turn off the heat and cover the pan with a cloth. The milk will separate into curds and whey. Leave undisturbed for at least 6 hours or overnight.

Pour the mixture into a colander or large sieve lined with damp cheesecloth, and let it drain overnight. The following day, turn out the piece of cheese formed into a small round wicker or plastic basket with little holes in it. This will allow it to dry out further and will give it the shape and texture of the basket. Leave the cheese for another whole day. Then turn the beautiful, porcelain-white cheese out onto a plate and serve as an appetizer, cutting it up into little cubes. It is also delicious sliced and fried with eggs when it is a few days old and rather dry.

The same cheese, made with little or no salt, is excellent eaten with jam.

Fried or Grilled Cheese

Greek cheeses such as Halumi, Kephalotyri, and Kasseri, which are hard and salty, or the popular Kashkaval,‡ are delicious when cut into cubes, grilled or fried, and served with a squeeze of lemon juice.

Grill the cheese over charcoal or under the broiler, turning it over once, until it starts to melt. Alternatively, fry the cheese in very hot

---

* Rennet contains rennin from the stomach of the calf. It coagulates the milk proteins, and activates the curd. Its use for making cheese is forbidden by Jewish dietary law.

oil or butter, rolling the pieces in flour first if you like. Serve very hot, sprinkled with lemon juice.

This idea can be adapted to other cheeses, such as Gruyère or hard Cheddar.

Fried cheese used to be served in cafés in Cairo in two-handled frying pans straight from the fire, to be eaten with bread and a squeeze of lemon.

Sidqi Effendi, in his Turkish cooking manual written in the nineteenth century, gives this recipe for grilling cheese. "Put a portion of cheese in silver paper. Wrap it up and put it over a fire. When the paper starts to glow the cheese is ready to eat and deliciously creamy. . . . This is good food which enhances sex for married men."

Fried Liver Pieces, Hot or Cold

4–6 slices calf's or lamb's liver
  [about ¾ lb.]
2½ tablespoons olive oil
2½ tablespoons vinegar
Salt and black pepper
Oil
Juice of ½ lemon

2 tablespoons finely chopped
  parsley [optional]
1 small mild (Spanish or Bermuda)
  onion, thinly sliced [optional]
A good pinch of ground cumin
  [optional]

Calf's liver is tastier than lamb's, but of course very much more expensive. Wash the liver, cut it into small, neat pieces, and remove any sinews or membranes. Mix the olive oil, vinegar, and seasonings, to make a marinade. Marinate the liver for an hour, or longer if possible.

Drain the liver pieces well. Fry them in hot oil, turning the pieces once, for only a minute or two so that they are well done on the outside but still very juicy inside. (Liver dries very quickly and is not good overcooked.) Cook a little longer if serving cold. The liver pieces can equally well be broiled gently. In this case, they should be eaten hot.

Serve sprinkled with lemon juice; if you like, garnish the liver pieces with chopped parsley and very thin slices of mild onion. They are also good lightly dusted with cumin.

Onions with Vinegar

It is said that the Prophet Muhammad did not like the smell of onions although he liked to eat them, and he therefore asked people not to attend the mosque smelling of onion or garlic. Even today, people are sometimes turned away from holy places for this reason. But, although according to numerous sayings and proverbs, onions have a low rating in Arab folklore, they are very much appreciated and often eaten raw, quartered or sliced.

A Persian way of serving onions.

2 large mild onions (Spanish or Bermuda)	3 tablespoons wine vinegar
	1 tablespoon dried crushed mint
Salt	

Slice the onions into half-moon shapes. Sprinkle with a little salt, add the vinegar and mint. Toss the onions in this seasoning, and leave them to stand for at least 1 hour before serving. They will become soft, lose much of their pungency, and absorb the other flavors.

They can then be served as an appetizer, or be placed in little bowls on the table to accompany a main dish.

Arab saying: "He fasted for a year, then he broke his fast on an onion." (Implying that it was not worth fasting.)

Brain Salad

Brains are considered a great delicacy by many people in the Middle East. A Syrian student I met in London admitted to cooking and eating three a day in his bed-sitting room, such was his passion for them.

In some parts of the Middle East, it is believed that they feed one's own brain and render one more intelligent. In other places, it is thought that eating brains reduces one's intelligence to that of the animal, and people who hold such beliefs cannot be persuaded to touch them.

2 calf's brains or 4 lamb's brains	6 tablespoons olive oil
Salt	Black pepper
Vinegar	3 tablespoons finely chopped
½ large mild onion or 4–6 scallions,	parsley
finely chopped	½ teaspoon ground cumin
Juice of ½–1 lemon, or more	[optional]

Brains should be cooked when they are very fresh, preferably on the day they are bought. Soak them for 1 hour in cold water with salt and 1 tablespoon vinegar. Carefully remove the thin outer membranes, and wash under cold running water. Simmer gently for 10 minutes in salted water to which you have added a teaspoon of vinegar.

In the meantime, marinate the chopped onions in lemon juice. Drain the brains and let them dry. Slice them. They should be firm enough to keep their shape. Arrange the slices in a single layer in a shallow serving dish.

Stir the olive oil into the onion-and-lemon mixture, season to taste with salt and pepper, and sprinkle over the brains. Garnish the dish with chopped parsley and, if you like, dust it with a little cumin (although this is uncommon).

Serve as an appetizer or salad.

Fried Brains

2 calf's brains or 4 lamb's brains	Fine dry bread crumbs
3 teaspoons vinegar	Oil for deep frying
Salt	2½ tablespoons finely chopped
White or black pepper	parsley
Flour	Juice of ½ lemon [optional]
1 egg yolk, beaten	

Soak the brains for 1 hour in water acidulated with 2 teaspoons of the vinegar. Remove the thin membranes in which they are encased and wash the brains under cold running water. Drop the brains into boiling salted water acidulated with the remaining teaspoon of vinegar, and simmer for about 3 minutes. Remove and drain thoroughly. Cut into smallish pieces. Roll the pieces first in seasoned flour, then in beaten egg yolk seasoned with a little salt and pepper, and lastly in bread crumbs. Fry in deep, hot oil for a few minutes until golden brown, and drain on absorbent paper.

Serve hot or cold, garnished with chopped parsley and, if you like, sprinkled with lemon juice.

CREAM SALADS

Tahini Cream Salad

Tahini *in its various forms is a great Middle Eastern favorite. It is served as an appetizer with Arab bread (page 364), and invariably appears as an accompaniment to most cold, and some hot, main dishes.*

Tahini itself is a paste made from sesame meal, and can be found canned in all Greek stores and a few delicatessens.‡

1–3 cloves garlic, to taste	½ teaspoon ground cumin [optional]
Salt	
½ cup lemon juice or the juice of 2½ lemons, or more	6 tablespoons finely chopped parsley, or 2 only to garnish
½ cup tahini	Sliced hard-boiled egg, to garnish [optional]

Crush the garlic with salt. Mix it with a little of the lemon juice in a large bowl. Add the *tahini* and mix well. Then add the remaining lemon juice and enough cold water to achieve a thick smooth cream, beating vigorously. Season with salt and cumin, if liked; taste and add more lemon juice, garlic, or salt until the flavor is fairly strong and tart. Add a few drops more water if too thick.

Tahini cream prepared in this way is most often served as it is, sprinkled with a little chopped parsley; but sometimes it is mixed with the larger amount of parsley given above. As with all *tahini*-based salads and creams, the flavorings are combined to taste, and the cream must be tasted several times while adjusting the seasonings in order to achieve a good balance.

This mixture can be made very quickly and easily in an electric mixer or blender. In fact, the result will be smoother and creamier than mixing by hand.

Serve the *tahini* cream in a bowl and provide Arab or other bread to dip in it. Slices of hard-boiled egg are sometimes used as a garnish.

An alternative seasoning is white wine vinegar. A few teaspoons of it can be used to replace a little of the lemon juice; or vinegar can be substituted for all the lemon juice. A little mustard is also added by some people.

Tahini Cream Salad with Almonds

An exquisite and very delicate variation on the *tahini* theme.

Prepare a *tahini* cream salad with ½ cup *tahini* as described above, but omit the parsley and perhaps use only 1 clove of garlic. Add ½ teaspoon sugar and 6 tablespoons ground almonds. Stir well and blend the sugar and almonds into the mixture, adding a few tablespoons more water if necessary to achieve a creamy texture. Use an electric mixer or blender if available.

Decorate with 5 whole blanched almonds arranged in a daisy on top. Serve with bread, or as an accompaniment to cold chicken and fish dishes.

Tahini Cream Salad with Yogurt

This version has a very definite flavor of its own and is rather creamier than most. My mother discovered it in the Sudan, and has made it ever since.

2–3 cloves garlic	½ cup yogurt
Salt	Juice of 2½ lemons, or more
½ cup *tahini*	Finely chopped parsley, to garnish

As in the first *tahini* cream salad recipe, crush the garlic with a little salt and mix it with the *tahini*. Add the yogurt and lemon juice gradually, beating vigorously to make a smooth, thick cream. Taste and add more salt, lemon juice, or garlic if necessary. (Here, again, an electric mixer or blender can be very useful.)

Serve in a bowl, garnished with finely chopped parsley, and provide Arab or other bread to dip into it.

Serve as an appetizer, or to accompany grilled or fried meat dishes and salads.

Teradot / Tahini with Walnuts

This is a Turkish variation of the tarator *sauce on page 166, and is a specialty of Jehan in Southern Turkey.*

¼ lb. (1 cup) shelled walnuts
2 cloves garlic
Salt

4–5 tablespoons *tahini*
Juice of 2 lemons
5 tablespoons chopped parsley

Pound the walnuts and garlic in a mortar with a little salt until the walnuts are almost, but not quite, ground to a paste. Add the *tahini* and lemon juice gradually, stirring well. Then mix in the chopped parsley.

An electric blender can be used. In this case, add the lemon juice and *tahini* at the same time as the walnuts and garlic, to allow them enough time to blend together without overblending the walnuts, which might then lose their slightly rough texture. A few tablespoons of water are also necessary to achieve the right texture in a blender.

Serve with fried mussels, baked fish, or as an accompaniment to various salads and plainly cooked vegetables, such as steamed string beans or cauliflower.

Hummus / Chickpeas

These hard, round, corn-colored peas, earthy in flavor and aesthetically attractive, lend themselves, as do most ingredients in the hands of Middle Eastern cooks, to an infinite variety of dishes. Mashed and smoothly puréed, they make an excellent base for a *tahini* cream or a meat soup. Whole, they combine deliciously with chicken, meat, and calf's feet. Mixed with rice and vermicelli or in a stew destined for *couscous* (page 279), they provide excitement in texture and flavor.

In the past, chickpeas had to be soaked for hours in cold water with bicarbonate of soda, and then required prolonged cooking. In addition, it was often necessary to remove their tough outer skins, a long and tedious operation, especially when a large quantity was required. The chickpeas sold today are of a superior quality. It is necessary only to soak them in plain cold water overnight—the bicarbonate of soda, no longer necessary, used to leave a peculiar taste —and they are usually tender after ¾ to 1 hour's cooking in boiling, salted water. However, this cooking time, although generally short, does vary according to the quality of the chickpeas, their place of origin, and their age.

It is virtually impossible to spoil chickpeas through overcooking, as it in no way changes their shape or spoils their flavor.

Hummus bi Tahini / Chickpeas with Tahini

This tahini *salad is the most widely known and appreciated of all outside the Middle East; its aroma blends so well with that of its constant companions, shish kebab and* ta'amia, *in Oriental restaurants. Its particular quality is a rich, earthy one.*

It makes an excellent appetizer served as a dip with bread, fish, eggplant—practically anything—and can also be used as a salad with a main dish.

¾–1 cup chickpeas, soaked
  overnight
Juice of 2–3 lemons, or to taste
2–3 cloves garlic
Salt
½ cup *tahini*

GARNISH
1 tablespoon olive oil
1 teaspoon paprika
1 tablespoon finely chopped parsley

Boil the soaked chickpeas in fresh water for about 1 hour, or until they are soft. The cooking time will depend on their age and quality. Drain the chickpeas and put aside a few whole ones to garnish the dish. Press the rest through a sieve or pound them in a mortar; or better still, use an electric mixer or blender to reduce them to a purée. In this case, you will have to pour the lemon juice and a little water into the bowl or container first to provide enough liquid for the blending to be successful. Add the remaining ingredients and blend to a creamy paste, adding more water if necessary.

If you are blending by hand, crush the garlic cloves with salt, add them to the crushed chickpeas, and pound them together until well mixed. Add the *tahini* gradually, followed by the lemon juice, and mix vigorously. If the paste seems too thick, beat in a little water to thin it to the consistency of a creamy mayonnaise. Keep tasting and adjusting the seasoning, adding more lemon juice, garlic, or salt if necessary.

This is one of the dishes which, for centuries, have been traditionally decorated in the same manner. Pour the cream into a serving dish and dribble a little red paprika mixed with olive oil over the surface. Sprinkle with chopped parsley and arrange a decorative pattern of whole chickpeas on top.

Serve as a dip with Arab bread, or *pitta*.

An alternative, rather stronger cream is made by using a generous pinch of cayenne pepper instead of paprika. Some of it is mixed into the cream, the rest is sprinkled over the top together with a little ground cumin, in a star design of alternating red and brown.

Baba Ghanoush / Eggplants with Tahini

This rich cream is a combination of two strong flavors: the smoky one of eggplants prepared as below, and the strong taste of tahini *sharpened by lemon and garlic. It is exciting and vulgarly seductive. The ingredients are added almost entirely to taste, the harmony of flavors depending largely on the size and flavor of the eggplants used.*

The quantities below give a fairly large amount, enough to be served as a dip at a party.

3 large eggplants
2–4 cloves garlic, or to taste
Salt
½ cup tahini or less,
    depending on the size of the
    eggplants

Juice of 3 lemons, or more to taste
½ teaspoon ground cumin
    [optional]
2 tablespoons finely chopped parsley
A few black olives or 1 tomato,
    thinly sliced, to garnish

Cook the eggplants over charcoal or under a gas or electric broiler as described in the recipe for eggplant purée (page 36), until the skin blackens and blisters. Peel and wash the eggplants, and squeeze out as much of the bitter juice as possible.

Crush the garlic cloves with salt. Mash the eggplants with a potato masher or fork, then add the crushed garlic and a little more salt, and pound to a smooth, creamy purée. Alternatively, use an electric blender to make the purée.

Add the *tahini* and lemon juice alternately, beating well or blending for a few seconds between each addition. Taste and add more salt, lemon juice, garlic, or *tahini* if you think it necessary, and if you like, a little cumin.

Pour the cream into a bowl or a few smaller serving dishes. Garnish with finely chopped parsley and black olives, or with a few tomato slices. Serve as an appetizer with Arab or other bread, as a salad, or as a party dip.

Tahini bil Fessih / Tahini with Salt Fish

Fessih is a fish which has been salted and left buried in the hot sand to "mature." It has a soft, salty texture. A popular way of eating it is to cut it into small pieces and mix it with *tahini* salad and sliced onions.

A modern variation which can be made in the West substitutes anchovy fillets or pickled herrings for the *fessih*.

Prepare a plain *tahini* cream salad as described on page 42, omitting the parsley. Mix it with a medium-sized can of anchovy fillets, drained and roughly chopped, or with 2 sliced pickled herrings and a medium-sized Spanish or Bermuda onion, thinly sliced. Sprinkle the top with chopped parsley and serve with Arab bread or *pitta*.

Ta'amia or Falafel

This is one of Egypt's national dishes, a specialty of which rich and poor alike never tire. It is welcome at all times, for breakfast, lunch, or supper.

The Christian Copts, who are said to be pure representatives of the ancient Egyptians, claim this dish as their own, along with melokhia *soup (page 111). Their claim is quite probably justified, since these dishes, whose origins cannot be traced, are nevertheless believed to be extremely old. During Coptic religious festivals, and particularly during Lent, when they are not allowed to eat meat for many weeks, every Coptic family produces platefuls of* ta'amia *daily; it consumes large quantities itself and distributes the rest to non-Coptic friends.*

Ta'amia are patties or rissoles made from a dried, white fava or broad bean (ful nabed),‡ *splendidly spiced and flavored, and deep-fried in oil. They are delicious, and I have never known anyone who has not liked them instantly.*

The best ta'amia *I have eaten were in Alexandria, with my aunt and uncle. Every year they rented an apartment there, the balcony of which was directly above a café which specialized in* ta'amia. *My relatives were both rather large, which was not surprising, since we always seemed to come upon them eating; and I could never visualize them eloping, gazelle-like, in their youth, which was the romantic legend related to us.*

On each visit, we would sit with them for hours on their balcony overlooking the sea. Time and again, a basket would be lowered on a rope to the café below and pulled up again with a haul of fresh ta'amia, *sometimes nestling in the pouch of warm, newly baked Arab bread. We would devour them avidly with pieces of the bread dipped in* tahini *salad, and then wait anxiously for the basket to be filled up again.*

1 lb. dried white fava beans [ful nabed]	1 bunch parsley, finely chopped
2 red or Spanish onions, very finely chopped or grated, or 1 bunch scallions, finely chopped	1–2 teaspoons ground cumin
	1–2 teaspoons ground coriander
	½ teaspoon baking powder
2 large cloves garlic, crushed	Salt and cayenne pepper
	Oil for deep frying

The dried white beans can be found in all Greek stores and in many delicatessens. Buy them already skinned if possible.

Soak the beans in cold water for 24 hours. Remove the skins if this has not been done. Drain, and mince or pound them. Mix this with the onions, garlic, parsley, cumin, coriander, baking powder, and salt and cayenne pepper to taste. Pound the ingredients together to a smooth paste. This will take a long time and much effort, so if a

grinder is available, put the mixture through the fine blade twice before pounding it. Let the paste rest for ½ hour at least.

Take walnut-sized lumps and make flat, round shapes 1½ inches in diameter. Let them rest for 15 minutes longer, then fry them in deep hot oil until they are a dark, rich golden brown.

Serve hot, accompanied by a tomato and cucumber salad and *tahini* cream salad (page 42). *Ta'amia* are delicious served as an appetizer, or as a main dish for a luncheon party, accompanied by a variety of salads and bread.

I have recently been told that the baking powder is sometimes replaced by ½ oz. (1 cake) fresh yeast, or ¼ oz. (1 package) dried yeast dissolved in a few tablespoons of lukewarm water. A dry *falafel* "ready mix" is now available in all Greek and Oriental Shops.‡ Add water as directed on the package, allow the paste to rest for a while, then shape and fry in deep fat as above. This "ready mix" is not nearly as good as the real thing, but you can use it for making appetizers if you are short of time. To improve the flavor, add a little finely chopped parsley, finely chopped scallion, crushed garlic, and other seasonings to taste. Israelis have practically adopted *ta'amia* as a national dish. They are sold, ready to eat, in the streets and cafés all over Israel, and are prepared in the same way as the Egyptian ones, but chickpeas are substituted for the beans, and I am told that yeast is often used instead of baking powder.

Artichoke Hearts Stewed in Oil

2 lemons

6 artichokes or a 14-oz. can
  artichoke hearts

5 tablespoons olive oil

2 cloves garlic

Salt and white pepper

Have ready a bowl of water to which you have added the juice of ½ lemon. Cut off the stems and the hard outer leaves of the artichokes, and slice off the remaining leaves to within ½ inch of the hearts. Scoop out the chokes. Rub each prepared artichoke with the squeezed lemon half and put it into the bowl of acidulated water. This will prevent the artichokes from discoloring.

Bring 2 cups water to a boil with the juice of the remaining 1½ lemons, olive oil, the 2 whole garlic cloves, and salt and pepper to taste. Throw in the artichoke hearts and simmer them, uncovered, for about 20 minutes, or until tender. Cool.

Serve cold, whole if small, halved or quartered if large, in their own liquid, which will have reduced considerably during the cooking.

If canned artichokes are used, drain them well and let them simmer, covered, for about 15 minutes only in the lemon juice and olive oil, flavored with garlic, salt, and pepper. No water is necessary.

Koftit Ferakh / Fried Ground Chicken Balls

Here is one variety of ground chicken balls which is easily prepared from leftovers and which, rolled into shapes the size of small marbles, makes a marvelous appetizer.

2 cooked chicken quarters, preferably breasts	Pinch of turmeric [optional]
	Salt and black pepper
2 large slices white bread	Flour
Milk	Oil for deep frying
1 large egg	Juice of ½ lemon [optional]

Skin and bone the chicken, and remove any sinews and hard membranes. Grind the flesh, or chop it very finely if a meat grinder is not available. Remove the crusts from the bread. Soak the slices in a little milk and squeeze dry. In a bowl mix the chicken, bread, egg, and seasonings. Knead well and shape into marble-sized balls. Roll them in flour and fry in deep hot oil until cooked and a dark golden color.

Serve the balls hot or cold, with a few drops of lemon juice squeezed over them, if you like.

Dukkah

This is another dearly loved and old Egyptian specialty. It is a loose mixture of nuts and spices in a dry, crushed but not powdered form, usually eaten with bread dipped in olive oil. In Egypt it is served at breakfast time, as an appetizer, or as a snack in the evening. It is a very personal and individual mixture which varies from one family to another. Here are two mixtures, the first my mother's, the second from a book published in 1860.

4 cups sesame seed	Salt and pepper to taste—try 1
2 cups coriander seed	teaspoon salt and ½ teaspoon
¼ lb. (1 cup) hazelnuts	black pepper
1 cup ground cumin	

Roast or broil the ingredients separately. Pound them together until they are finely crushed but not pulverized. The crushing can be done in a meat grinder or an electric blender. In the last case run it for a very short time only, as otherwise the oil from the too finely ground seeds and nuts will form a paste with the pulverized ingredients. *Dukkah* should always be a crushed dry mixture, and definitely not a paste.

The quantities above make a good deal of *dukkah*, but it can be stored indefinitely in covered jars.

"A meal is often made by those who cannot afford luxuries of bread and a mixture called 'dukkah,' which is commonly composed of salt and pepper with za'atar or wild marjoram or mint or cumin-seed, and with one or more, or all, of the following ingredients—namely, coriander seed, cinnamon, sesame, and hummus (or chickpeas). Each mouthful of bread is dipped in this mixture." *

Try mixing the ingredients to taste and improvise the proportions. Roast or grill the ingredients separately before pounding them. If you use chickpeas, buy those sold precooked, salted, and dried, available in most Greek shops. They are tiny, white, and very round.

Another very humble preparation, a mixture of dried crushed mint, salt, and pepper, is sold in the streets in little paper cornets as dukkah to sprinkle over bread.

Eggplant Slices Stuffed with Cream Cheese

2 long, large eggplants	3–4 eggs
Salt	4 tablespoons finely chopped
Oil	parsley
½ lb. cream cheese, Greek Halumi cheese, or mozzarella	Fine dry bread crumbs

An elegant Turkish delicacy. Slice the eggplants lengthwise, and cut each slice in three to make smallish rectangles. Sprinkle the slices with salt and leave them for about ½ hour in a colander to allow the bitter juices to drain away. This will also prevent their absorbing too much oil. Rinse off the salt with cold water and pat the slices dry. Fry them lightly in oil until soft and colored. Remove from the pan and drain on absorbent paper.

Mash the cream cheese with a fork, or grate the Halumi or mozzarella if used. Add 2 eggs, beaten, and the parsley, and mix well. Spread a little of this mixture on a slice of eggplant and top with another one to make a sandwich. Continue with the remaining slices and cheese mixture. The cheese and egg mixture will hold the slices together firmly.

Beat the remaining egg or eggs. Dip the eggplant "sandwiches" in

* Lane, Manners and Customs of the Modern Egyptians.

beaten egg and coat them with bread crumbs. Fry in deep hot oil for 2 or 3 minutes until golden. Drain on absorbent paper and serve hot.

Batarekh / French Boutargue

Known and favored as a great delicacy since the time of the Pharaohs, and still considered so by Egyptians today, *batarekh* is the salted, dried roe of the gray mullet. It is a deep, orangy, sienna-brown color, rich and strongly flavored.

In Egypt, we used to buy *batarekh* already dried and ready to eat. I was thrilled to eat a perfect one last year in Paris. It had been made by Mrs. R. Telio, who now lives in Montreal and who had sent it, properly waxed and sealed, to her brother in Paris. Here is her recipe.

Gray mullet roes are sold in Canada from barrels, where they are kept frozen. They are held together by a thin skin and look like rather long sausages. You may like to experiment with fresh cod's roes instead.

Choose roes with skins which are intact, free from tears or holes. This is important to the success of the recipe. Roll the roes in kitchen salt and arrange them on a thick layer of absorbent paper. They will begin to lose their moisture. Keep changing the papers as they become saturated. Turn the roes over when you change the papers, and sprinkle with more salt. The secret of success lies in changing the papers frequently until they remain quite dry. This will take a few days.

At this stage, put the roes on a tray in front of an open window, or hang them on a string in a very airy place such as an airing cupboard, to dry out still more. This part of the process will take about 8 days, longer for fresh cod's roes. The process can be speeded up by placing the roes occasionally in a turned-off warm oven, but care must be taken not to overdry them, or they will be crumbly. When the roes are hard and rather dry, they are ready to eat.

Slice the *batarekh* very thinly and serve it with bread, either buttered bread or dipped in olive oil. If you like, squeeze a little lemon juice over it. The taste is an acquired one which can become a passion.

The dried *batarekh* can be preserved for months in a refrigerator. Each one must be individually wrapped in a plastic bag and sealed. If you wish to preserve them in a home freezer, it will be necessary to expose them to the air for a little while to dry out again before they can be eaten.

Mrs. Telio, who usually travels with presents of *batarekh* to distribute to friends, covers them with wax to preserve them hermetically sealed on long journeys. Dipping them in melted wax also prevents overdrying.

I have dried *smoked* cod's roes by putting them occasionally in a turned-off warm oven and by hanging them in a very airy, dry place for a few days. The results were excellent, and were achieved with very little effort. So I can highly recommend this as a substitute for *batarekh*.

Taramasalata

This "cream salad," well known in the West, is a Greek and Turkish specialty. Tarama is the dried, salted, and pressed roe of the gray mullet, but you can use smoked cod's roe instead. I myself prefer to use potted (skinned) roes because they have a smoother texture. If using the whole roes sold in fish shops, choose a soft quality.

3 thick slices white bread
Milk
3 oz. *tarama* or smoked cod's roe,
    potted or otherwise
1–2 cloves garlic, crushed, or 2
    tablespoons grated onion, or
    both

Juice of 1–2 lemons
5 tablespoons olive oil
Black olives, to garnish [optional]

Remove the crusts from the bread and soak the slices in a little milk. If using smoked cod's roes, remove their natural skins and pound them vigorously in a mortar to eliminate their gritty texture. Add the soaked bread, squeezed dry, the garlic and/or onion, and continue pounding until smooth. Gradually add lemon juice and olive oil, tasting until you get the flavor you like; more or less lemon, garlic, or onion may be added to taste. Then work the mixture into a creamy, pale pink paste by vigorous beating.

Alternatively, put all the ingredients in an electric mixer, and beat at a fairly high speed. Add a few tablespoons of water or milk if required.

Taramasalata is sometimes garnished with black olives, and usually served with thin toast.

Numerous variations on *taramasalata* exist. Some people like to add a boiled, mashed potato or an egg yolk to bind the paste.

Here is an excellent recipe which gives a rather firmer cream with the texture of a stiff mayonnaise.

3 oz. smoked cod's roe, potted or otherwise

2 slices slightly dry, crustless white bread, soaked in water and squeezed dry

1 clove garlic, crushed

Generous pinch of cayenne pepper

Juice of 1–2 lemons

About ¾ cup corn or nut oil [not olive oil]

Skin the roes and pound in a mortar or, preferably, beat in an electric mixer or blender. Mix in the other ingredients as in the previous recipe. Add the lemon juice and corn or nut oil gradually, as for a mayonnaise, mixing in first a little of one and then the other. Mix or beat vigorously all the time until you achieve a rich, smooth cream. Blend in 1 tablespoon hot water to finish the paste.

Midye Tavasi / Turkish Fried Mussels

BATTER
½ oz. (1 cake) fresh yeast or ¼ oz. (1 package) dried yeast
Pinch of sugar
1 cup all-purpose flour
2½ tablespoons melted butter
Pinch of salt
2 eggs, separated

30 large mussels
½ cup white wine [optional]
Salt
Flour
Oil for deep frying

Make the batter. Dissolve the yeast in ½ cup lukewarm water to which you have added a pinch of sugar. Leave in a warm place for about 10 minutes, or until it begins to froth. Sift the flour into a large mixing bowl. Add the melted butter, salt, and egg yolks, and mix well. Gradually add the yeast mixture, beating constantly with a wooden spoon. The batter should be fairly liquid. Leave it in a warm place to rise for about 1 hour. Just before using, fold in the stiffly beaten egg whites.

Meanwhile, wash the mussels thoroughly in a bowl under the tap. Throw away broken or open shells, and scrape away beards, seaweed, and barnacles with a sharp knife. Then scrub the shells one by one under running water, changing the water in the bowl frequently until there is no trace of sand or grit left.

Put the mussels in a large saucepan with ½ cup water or white wine (which greatly enhances the flavor). Season lightly with salt, cover the pan, and boil vigorously until the shells open. This takes 5 to 7 minutes. Remove the mussels from their shells and put them on a clean cloth to dry.

When the batter is ready, roll the mussels quickly in flour, dip them in the batter, and drop 3 or 4 at a time into the hot oil—preferably olive oil, although any other oil will do. Fry for about 1 minute, until crisp and brown.

Serve immediately with *teradot* (page 44) or with *tarator* sauce (page 167).

Blehat Samak / Miniature Fish Sticks

Prepare the recipe for fish sticks on page 162, but roll the mixture into smaller, marble-sized balls or tiny fingers and fry them in oil until golden brown. They will cook more quickly, being smaller. Serve hot or cold.

These little snacks can also be simmered in fish stock or the tomato sauce given with the main recipe, and serve cold.

Cold Mussels Plaki

48 large mussels	2–3 cloves garlic
Salt	1 tablespoon superfine sugar
2 medium onions, chopped	3 tomatoes, skinned and chopped
⅓ cup olive oil	4 tablespoons chopped parsley
1 medium carrot, diced	2½ tablespoons tomato paste
1 large potato, diced	Black pepper
1 medium celeriac, diced	

Wash and scrape the mussels as described in the recipe above. Open them by boiling them vigorously in a covered saucepan with about 1 cup water and a little salt for 5 to 7 minutes. Remove the mussels from their shells, and keep the cooking liquor.

Fry the onions in olive oil until soft and golden. Add the diced carrot and continue to fry gently for another 2 minutes. Then add the potato, celeriac, garlic cloves, sugar, tomatoes, parsley, and tomato paste. Season with salt and pepper to taste, and moisten with the reserved mussel liquor. Stir gently and simmer over very low heat until all the vegetables are well cooked and the sauce is rich and reduced, adding a little more water if necessary. Be careful not to let the vegetables stick to the pan or burn. Finally, add the mussels and simmer for 5 minutes. Remove from the heat and allow to cool.

Serve cold as an hors d'œuvre or as a main luncheon dish.

Carmel Avocado Purée

A modern Israeli hors d'œuvre, made possible in the Middle East for the first time by the recent introduction of avocados.

3 ripe avocados
Juice of 1 lemon, or to taste
1–2 cloves garlic, crushed with salt
Salt
½ large mild onion, grated
White pepper
4–5 tablespoons olive oil
4 tablespoons finely chopped parsley

Cut open the avocados and remove pits. Scoop out the flesh and mash it with a silver fork. Stir in the remaining ingredients and beat to a smooth, creamy paste. Taste, and adjust the seasoning. If an electric blender can be used, it will give you a beautifully smooth purée in a very short time.

This cream is very rich. Serve it heaped on small crackers or thin toast.

AVOCADO PURÉE WITH TUNA

Mash the flesh of 2 ripe avocados to a purée with a silver fork. Drain a 7-oz. can of tuna and combine the flaked fish with the avocado purée. Stir in a little mayonnaise, season, and serve on small crackers or thin toast.

AVOCADO PURÉE WITH CREAM CHEESE

Mash and combine the flesh of 2 ripe avocados with half its weight of cream cheese. Season and serve as above.

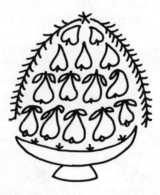

SALADS

Salatat

Simple and unpretentious, rich and exotic, salads are present at practically every type of Middle Eastern meal. Almost anything can be made into a salad: fresh, raw vegetables, cooked vegetables, legumes, cracked wheat (burghul), bread, cheese, and meat, including brains and tongue (see also the preceding chapter). Chopped red Italian, Bermuda, or Spanish onions, crushed garlic, and chopped parsley are favorite ingredients.

Great care is taken with the presentation, and color plays an important part, as well as taste and texture.

As a general rule, boiled vegetables are usually dressed with olive oil and lemon, while raw vegetables can be dressed with olive oil and lemon or vinegar. The oil is used lavishly. Prepared commercially or by peasants, it ranges accordingly from a pure, pale golden color to a coarser, brownish shade. People love it and sometimes drink it neat by the glass when they feel anemic or tired. In the past, it was believed that olive oil would cure every illness except the one by which a person was destined to die. "It is related that Adam was suffering with pain and complained to God; Gabriel descended from heaven with an olive tree and presented it to Adam, and told him to plant it, to pick the fruit, to extract the oil and use it whenever he had pain, assuring him that it would be a cure for all ills. . . ." *

Besides its many other properties, olive oil is widely believed to have a powerful aphrodisiac effect. According to a recent report in a Greek newspaper, a man who had been accused of seducing a young woman cleared himself in court by swearing, and providing witnesses to testify, that he had eaten an extra large salad dressed particularly lavishly with olive oil.

If pure olive oil proves too expensive, other salad oils will make an adequate substitute.

As a general rule, the ingredients of a salad should be as fresh as possible. Raw vegetables and lettuce must be unbruised, well washed, cold, crisp, and dry. Cooked vegetables must *not* be overcooked, but rather firm. Legumes must be cooked carefully until they are tender but not too soft if they are to be kept whole, longer if they are to be

* Donaldson, *The Wild Rue.*

puréed. These, as well as cooked vegetables, absorb their dressing better if dressed while still hot. They are seasoned with a lemon and olive oil dressing in varying proportions, as the cook pleases.

Salad Dressings

Middle Eastern dressings for salads are a mixture of olive oil and lemon juice or vinegar (preferably wine vinegar), used in much the same proportions as in the French vinaigrette sauce. Crushed garlic is usually added with the salt and pepper. Sometimes, too, lemon dressings are sharper than in the West; more lemon is used in proportion to the oil. Occasionally, the Middle Eastern cook uses as much lemon as oil, or more, for instance in dressing dried vegetable salads.

Unless otherwise stated, the dressing for the salads which follow is made in the proportions below with the proviso that more oil and lemon juice or vinegar can always be added if you feel that the salad requires it:

1 tablespoon lemon juice or vinegar   1–2 cloves garlic, crushed [optional]
3 tablespoons olive oil   Salt and black pepper

Common additional flavorings are chopped parsley, fresh or dried mint, dill, fresh coriander, scallions (usually mixed into the salad, but sometimes added with the dressing).

Na'na Mukhalal

A medieval recipe from al-Baghdadi for a vinegar dressing.

"Take fresh large-leafed mint, and strip the leaf from the stalk. Wash and dry in the shade: sprinkle with aromatic herbs. If desired, add celery leaves and quarters of peeled garlic. Put into a glass bottle and cover with good vinegar, colored with a little saffron. Leave until the mint has absorbed the sourness of the vinegar so that the latter has lost its sharpness: then serve."

Tomato Salad

1½ lbs. firm tomatoes, sliced
1 red Italian or large mild onion, or
    a few scallions, chopped
2 tablespoons finely chopped parsley

½ teaspoon ground cumin
    [optional]
Salad dressing [page 60]

It is not necessary to skin the tomatoes. Scallions will do beautifully instead of an onion when they are in season.

Mix the tomatoes, onions, parsley, and cumin, if used, in a bowl. Mix the dressing, pour it over the vegetables, and toss well. Or arrange the tomatoes in overlapping rows on a serving dish. Pour the mixed dressing over them, and sprinkle with the onions, chopped parsley, and cumin.

Sweet Pepper Salad

3 sweet green peppers
Salad dressing [page 60]

1 tablespoon finely chopped parsley

Cut the peppers in half and taste a small piece from each one in case it is too strong. Remove the seeds and broil the peppers under a low flame until their skins blister and darken, and their flesh becomes soft. Skin them, and cut them into long strips. Crisp and sharp when raw, they become mellow and sweet when broiled.

Put the peppers in a serving bowl. Mix the dressing ingredients together, using either salad oil or olive oil. Stir in parsley, pour over the peppers, and mix well.

Israeli Mixed Salad

The many cultures which have been fused into modern Israel, each contributing its own culinary influence, have resulted in a tentative national cuisine. In this, a wide range of salads has emerged. The fruit of foreign inspiration, experimental intuition, and local ingredients, they have not escaped the influence of the Orient.

The ingredients are often chopped or cut into small pieces in the traditional Arab fashion. Often, too, tahini cream salad is used as a dressing instead of mayonnaise.

Here is one combination. I leave it to your own imagination to devise others.

2 tomatoes	1–2 avocados, peeled and pitted
2 small cucumbers	2 firm potatoes, boiled
6 olives, pitted if you like	1 large mild onion
1 large raw carrot, peeled	1 sweet pepper
1 raw beet, peeled	2 hard-boiled eggs

Chop all the ingredients or cut them into very small dice. Mix them together in a bowl and dress with *Tahini* Cream Salad (page 42), sour cream, or a vinaigrette sauce.

Salatit Khodar Meshakel / Mixed Fresh Vegetable Salad

This popular Arab salad is different from conventional Western salads in that all the ingredients are finely chopped and absorb the dressing and each others' flavors better. Do not prepare it too long before serving, as the ingredients will wilt. Dress it just before putting it on the table. Ingredients can vary according to taste.

1 small romaine or cos lettuce or ½ large one
2 small cucumbers or 1 longer one
3 tomatoes
1–2 red Italian onions if available, or 1 large mild onion, or 1 small bunch scallions
6 radishes, thinly sliced [optional]
4–5 tablespoons finely chopped parsley
1 tablespoon finely chopped fresh dill or chervil [optional]
2 tablespoons finely chopped fresh mint or 1 teaspoon dried crushed mint [optional]

DRESSING
3 tablespoons olive oil
1 tablespoon lemon juice or wine vinegar
1 clove garlic, crushed with salt [optional]
Salt and black pepper

Wash the lettuce, if necessary. Peel the onion or scallions. Shred the lettuce; cut the cucumbers (peeled or unpeeled, as you wish) into small dice. Dice the tomatoes (remove the seeds and juice first), and chop the onions finely, using a sharp knife, or an Italian *mezzaluna* chopper if you have one. Put the prepared vegetables in a salad bowl and mix lightly with the radishes and herbs.

Mix the dressing ingredients thoroughly, sprinkle over the salad, and toss well.

Cabbage Salad

1 small firm cabbage or ½ large one
Salt

DRESSING
3 tablespoons olive oil
1 tablespoon lemon juice or wine
    vinegar
1–2 cloves garlic, crushed [optional]
Black pepper
½ teaspoon sugar [optional]

Either red or white cabbage can be used. Cut off the tough outer leaves, the central core and hard stems, and slice it. Either take a few leaves at a time and shred them, or cut thin slices across the whole cabbage, starting at the top, then cut through the slices again vertically. Sprinkle the thinly shredded cabbage lightly with salt, working it in well with your hands. Leave it for at least ½ hour in a colander with a weight on top. It will lose much of its water and become soft and pliable.

Squeeze the cabbage out tightly in your hands and put in a salad bowl. Pour over the dressing, mixed separately. Add salt with care, taking into account the saltiness of the cabbage. Mix salad and dressing together thoroughly.

Cacik / Cucumber and Yogurt Salad

A Turkish salad, extremely popular throughout the Middle East.

1 large cucumber or 2 small ones,
    peeled and diced
Salt
2–3 cloves garlic
2 cups yogurt

White pepper
1 tablespoon dried crushed mint or
    3 tablespoons finely chopped
    fresh mint, or to taste
Additional dried mint, to garnish

Sprinkle the diced cucumber with salt, and leave in a colander to drain for ½ hour. Crush the garlic with a little salt; use more than 3 cloves if you like. Mix a few tablespoons of the yogurt with the garlic, then add the mixture to the rest of the yogurt and mix well. Add more salt and pepper to taste. Finally add the mint, whose aroma and flavor make the salad deliciously refreshing. Drain the cucumbers and mix with the yogurt dressing.

Pour into a serving dish and decorate with more mint.

Salata Meshwiya

This salad is very popular all over North Africa, particularly in Tunisia. It is not unlike the French salade niçoise, *so its origin might just as well be Nice as Tunis.*

2 firm tomatoes
2 sweet peppers
1 mild onion or 6–7 scallions
1 hot dried chili pepper [optional]
A 3½-oz. can tuna fish
2 hard-boiled eggs, sliced
1 tablespoon capers
2½ tablespoons finely chopped
    parsley

DRESSING
1 tablespoon lemon juice
3 tablespoons olive oil
Salt and black pepper

If you wish to skin the tomatoes, plunge them in boiling water for a minute or two first. Halve the sweet peppers and broil them skin side up until they are soft and mellow. Skin and seed them. Chop the onions and the chili pepper finely. Slice off one end of the tomatoes, scoop out the seeds, squeeze gently to release the juice, and slice them. Cut the sweet peppers into narrow ribbons.

Put all the vegetables in a large serving dish. Add the tuna fish, drained and crumbled, the sliced hard-boiled eggs, and the capers. Mix the dressing ingredients together, pour them over the salad, and mix well. Serve sprinkled with finely chopped parsley.

Cream Cheese and Celery Salad

½ lb. cream cheese
Juice of 1 lemon
2½ tablespoons olive oil

½ cup yogurt
Salt and white pepper
1 head celery, finely chopped

With a fork, work the cream cheese with the lemon juice and olive oil until smooth. Add the yogurt and salt and pepper to taste. Stir well. Lightly stir in the chopped celery and serve.

Michoteta / Cream Cheese and Cucumber Salad

This delightful Egyptian salad is usually made with salty Greek cream cheese, either Teleme or feta. For an authentic salad, these can be found in most Greek stores,‡ but good-quality cottage or curd cheese makes a good substitute.

½ lb. soft cheese
Juice of 1 lemon
2½ tablespoons olive oil

1 red Italian or large mild onion,
  finely chopped
½ large cucumber, peeled and diced
Salt and black pepper

Crumble the cheese with a tablespoon of water, using a fork, and work in the lemon juice and olive oil. Mix in the onion and cucumber, and season to taste with salt and pepper.

This salad is wonderful as an appetizer or as an accompaniment to the dish of brown beans called *ful medames* (page 268).

Toureto / Israeli Cucumber and Bread Salad

5–6 slices dry white bread, crusts removed
1 large cucumber, peeled and chopped
2 cloves garlic, crushed

5 tablespoons olive oil
Juice of ½ lemon, or more
Salt and white pepper
1 level teaspoon paprika mixed with 1½ tablespoons olive oil

Soak the bread in water and squeeze it dry. Mix it with the other ingredients and rub through a sieve or purée in an electric blender. If necessary, sieve the purée twice to make a smooth, soft cream. Chill.

Serve garnished with a dribble of olive oil mixed with paprika.

Hamud Shami

Although shami *means Syrian, this is an Egyptian salad, characterized by its definite taste of lemon and garlic. It is more like a chicken jelly than a salad.*

2½ cups chicken stock
1½ tablespoons oil
2 large cloves garlic, crushed

5 tablespoons ground rice ‡
Juice of 1 lemon, or a little more
½ teaspoon turmeric

Prepare a well-flavored chicken stock.

Heat the oil in a saucepan and fry the crushed garlic until it turns golden and aromatic. Pour in a ladleful of the stock. Dissolve the ground rice in a little cold water and mix it with the garlic-flavored stock. With the saucepan still over gentle heat, add the rest of the chicken stock gradually, stirring all the time. Continue cooking and stirring until the mixture becomes very thick. Add the lemon juice and turmeric, and bring the mixture gently to the boil, stirring vigorously. Pour into a serving dish.

Allow to cool fully, and chill if you wish. The mixture will become a delicate yellow jelly. It looks beautifully translucent in a transparent bowl.

This unusual salad is delicious served with cold chicken and plain hot rice. It is often served as an appetizer, with bread or vine leaves to dip into it.

Orange Salads

MOROCCAN ORANGE SALAD

Peel 3 large oranges, taking care to remove all the bitter white pith. Slice very thinly. Arrange on a plate. Sprinkle with orange blossom water and dust lightly with ground cinnamon.

ORANGE AND RADISH SALAD

In this Moroccan salad, a bunch of radishes is thinly sliced, and one or two oranges are peeled, sliced, and divided into small pieces. The whole is seasoned lightly with salt and a little lemon juice.

ORANGE AND AVOCADO SALAD

A modern Israeli salad. Two oranges are peeled, cut into slices and then into medium-sized pieces. They are then mixed with the flesh of a firm, not too ripe avocado, also cut into pieces. The whole is seasoned to taste with lemon juice, olive oil, salt, white pepper, and a pinch of sugar.

COOKED FRESH VEGETABLE SALADS

Mixed Salad of Boiled Vegetables

Any vegetables available can go into this salad, but those listed below are the ones most commonly used.

2 potatoes
1 beet
2 zucchini
¼ lb. string beans
½ small cauliflower
Salt
Salad dressing [page 60]

Peel the potatoes, scrub the beet and zucchini, string and rinse the string beans, and wash the cauliflower. Boil the vegetables separately in salted water until just tender, or, preferably, steam them.

Drain. Cube the potatoes and the peeled beet, slice the zucchini into rounds and the string beans lengthwise, and separate the cauliflower into flowerets.

Arrange the vegetables in separate little groups on a large serving dish and sprinkle with well-mixed dressing.

Spinach Salad with Yogurt

Spinach has a remarkable affinity with yogurt, and it is delicious prepared in this particular manner.

1 lb. fresh spinach or ½ lb. frozen   1 clove garlic, crushed
   leaf spinach   Salt and black pepper
½ cup yogurt

Wash the spinach carefully, snipping off any hard stems. Drain. Chop the leaves and stew them in their own juice in a large covered saucepan until tender, about 15 minutes. If using frozen spinach, defrost it in a colander and simmer until cooked. Allow to cool.

Beat the yogurt and garlic together, and add the mixture to the pan. Mix well and season to taste with salt and pepper.

Beet Salad

Beets are commonly served boiled and sliced, dressed with olive oil, lemon, salt, and pepper, and sprinkled with chopped parsley. A more unusual way is to dress them with yogurt, olive or corn oil, lemon juice, and salt.

2 tablespoons lemon juice   ½ lb. boiled beets, diced
2 tablespoons olive or corn oil   Slices of boiled beets and
1 cup yogurt   1 tablespoon finely chopped
Salt   parsley, to garnish

Mix the lemon juice with the oil. Add the yogurt, add salt to taste, and beat well. Fold in the diced beets and mix thoroughly. Pour into a serving dish and decorate the top with slices of beets and chopped parsley.

Fresh Fava Bean Salad

1 lb. fresh or frozen fava beans
Salt
3 tablespoons finely chopped
    parsley, or fresh coriander
    leaves if available

DRESSING
4 tablespoons olive or salad oil
2 tablespoons lemon juice
1–2 cloves garlic, crushed [optional]
Salt and black pepper

Boil the beans in lightly salted water until tender. Frozen beans will do when fresh ones are out of season, but they must be thoroughly defrosted. Drain and cool.

Prepare the dressing separately, and pour it over the beans in a serving dish. Add the chopped parsley or coriander, and mix well.

STRING BEAN SALAD

Wash 1 lb. fresh young string beans, remove stems, and string them if necessary. Cut lengthwise or crosswise. Boil the beans in lightly salted water until tender. Frozen beans will do very well and they need only a few minutes' cooking.

Drain the beans and cool them. Put them in a serving bowl and dress them with the dressing given for fresh fava bean salad above, using only 1 clove garlic. Sprinkle with 2 tablespoons finely chopped parsley; mix lightly and serve.

ZUCCHINI SALAD

This salad is better made with small zucchini, but if they are not available, larger ones will do. Boil 1 lb. zucchini, whole or sliced, in a little salted water until tender (they will only take a few minutes); or steam them over boiling water. If using large ones, cut into ½-inch cubes. Cook in the same way and drain well.

If the zucchini have been cooked whole, cut them into ½-inch slices. Prepare the dressing for fresh fava bean salad above. Pour it over the zucchini. Sprinkle with 1 or 2 tablespoons finely chopped parsley, toss lightly and serve.

LEEK SALAD

Use 1 lb. leeks. Split the green parts lengthwise and wash the leeks carefully, fanning them out in the water to remove all traces of soil between the leaves. Discard the tough outer leaves; trim the tops and roots. Cut the leeks into 1- or 2-inch lengths and boil them in lightly salted water until only just tender (about 15 to 20 minutes). Drain and cool.

Prepare the dressing for fresh fava bean salad above, and pour it over the leeks in a serving dish. Add 1 tablespoon finely chopped parsley and mix well.

A variation is to simmer the leeks very gently in the juice of ½ lemon, 4 tablespoons oil, and their own juice, seasoned with salt, black pepper, and about ¾ teaspoon sugar. Cover and simmer until very soft, about 20 minutes.

Allow to cool in their liquid and serve cold, garnished with chopped parsley.

Turkish Tarator Sauce

This is similar to the Syrian and Lebanese tarator (page 166), but uses ground walnuts or hazelnuts instead of pine nuts and almonds. It is usually served separately, in a bowl, with the plainer boiled vegetable salads such as string bean or zucchini salad; so I have included it in this chapter.

2 thin slices bread, crusts removed	4 tablespoons wine vinegar
¼ lb. (1 cup) walnuts or hazelnuts, ground	1–2 cloves garlic, crushed
½ cup olive oil	Salt and black pepper

Dip the bread in water and squeeze dry. Crumble it, and add it to the ground nuts. Gradually add the olive oil, beating constantly. Stir in the vinegar and garlic, and season to taste with salt and pepper. The sauce should be very smooth and creamy. For an even smoother texture, blend the mixture in an electric blender.

Salade Rachèle

This salad was the specialty of a cook called Rachèle who helped to prepare many of the parties for our community in Cairo. In Egypt we used English pickles to make it. It is extremely simple, and always a great favorite because of its strong taste of pickles.

I have given amounts for rather a large quantity, enough for a party, or as a stock supply to be prepared and stored for future occasions. This salad is unusual because it keeps for many weeks in a covered jar if the surface is covered with a thin layer of oil.

2 lbs. eggplant
Salt
Oil

1 lb. tomatoes, skinned and sliced
1 medium jar mustard pickle

Slice the eggplants, sprinkle them with salt, and leave them in a colander for at least ½ hour to allow the bitter juices to drain away. Pat the slices dry and fry them in oil until soft and golden brown on both sides.

In a large pan, arrange layers of eggplant and tomato slices, sprinkling each layer with a little salt. Stew very gently, covered, for ½ hour, preferably without adding any water. Remove the pan from the heat and allow to cool.

Chop the pickles into small pieces and mix them lightly with the eggplant and tomato slices.

This salad is often served as an hors d'œuvre.

Mushrooms in Olive Oil / A Greek Dish

½ lb. small button mushrooms
4 tablespoons olive oil
1½ tablespoons water
Salt and black pepper
Juice of ½–1 lemon

½ teaspoon dried thyme [optional]
1–2 cloves garlic, crushed
5 tablespoons finely chopped
    parsley

Wash and dry the mushrooms, or wipe them clean with a damp cloth. Cut them in half if they are a little large. Pour the oil and water into a deep frying pan. Stir in all the remaining ingredients except the mushrooms and bring to the boil. Finally, add the mushrooms and simmer gently for about 10 minutes, or until the mushrooms are tender, turning them over occasionally. Pour into a serving dish and allow to cool.

Taste and adjust the seasoning before serving, as its intensity changes with the drop in temperature. Serve cold.

The mushrooms are not stewed by some; instead they are left to marinate in the refrigerator in the same dressing as above (but without the water) for 24 hours.

DRIED VEGETABLE SALADS

Dried vegetables make rich, nourishing salads to accompany lighter main dishes. Their earthy texture is given excitement by a really sharp, lemony dressing flavored with crushed garlic, sometimes with a little ground cumin or coriander, and always with finely chopped parsley or fresh coriander.

The vegetables are soaked overnight if necessary, then drained and brought to a boil in a fresh portion of unsalted water. They are simmered until tender but not completely soft, and salted just before the end of their cooking time. Finally, they are drained and dressed, preferably while still hot, mixed with herbs, and allowed to cool.

These dried vegetable salads are also sometimes served puréed. In this case, they are simmered rather longer, drained well, seasoned, and mashed with a fork; or they are made into a paste in an electric blender, using a little of the cooking liquor if necessary. They are then cooled and served garnished with chopped parsley, sprinklings of oil and paprika, and black olives.

The proportion of oil and lemon juice used in the seasoning is different from that of the vinaigrette type of dressing for fresh salads. Tastes vary, but usually more lemon is used, sometimes as much as, or more than, oil.

Lentil Salad

½ lb. (1 cup) lentils, soaked overnight if necessary (check package directions)
Salt
3 tablespoons finely chopped parsley

DRESSING
7–8 tablespoons olive or salad oil
Juice of 1½–2 lemons, or more
1–2 cloves garlic, crushed [optional]
Black pepper
½ teaspoon ground coriander or cumin [optional]

Use the large, dark brown lentils for this salad. Drain them after soaking, and boil them in a half-covered pan in fresh water until barely tender. This will take ¾ to 1½ hours. A pressure cooker will reduce the cooking time to between 10 and 20 minutes, but care must be taken not to overcook the lentils. Add salt only toward the end of cooking time. Drain well.

Mix the dressing ingredients and pour over the lentils while still quite hot. Stir in parsley, and arrange in a serving dish.

One variation is to soften a finely chopped onion in about 7 tablespoons oil, add the lentils, the juice of 1 lemon, a crushed clove of garlic, and about 2½ cups of water (but no salt). The mixture is simmered until tender (about ¾ to 1 hour), water being added from time to time if necessary. Salt and black pepper are added near the end of the cooking time, together with 2 tablespoons chopped parsley and, if desired, a little ground cumin or coriander. The whole mixture is then cooked for just a few minutes more. The lentils can also be cooked as in the variation above, but for longer, until they are very soft. They are spiced in the same way, and are then mashed to a paste and served as a purée.

Tabbouleh / Burghul (Cracked Wheat) Salad

Rich, earthy, and beautifully seasoned, this is a wonderful party dish. Burghul gives the tabbouleh *its earthy quality. This is harmoniously balanced by the light, refreshing aromas of parsley and mint, and the acid tang of lemon.*

As with most dishes, the preparation is highly individual. Quanties of ingredients vary with every family, but parsley is always used abundantly. This is a great Lebanese favorite.

½ lb. (2 cups) fine burghul

4 tablespoons finely chopped scallions and/or 1 large onion, finely chopped

Salt and black pepper

About ¾ cup finely chopped parsley

4 tablespoons finely chopped fresh mint or 2½ tablespoons dried crushed mint

5 tablespoons olive oil, or more

5 tablespoons lemon juice

Cooked vine leaves, raw lettuce or tender cabbage leaves

Soak the burghul in water for about ½ hour before preparing the salad. It will expand enormously. Drain and squeeze out as much moisture as possible with your hands. Spread out to dry further on a cloth.

Mix the burghul with the chopped onions, squeezing with your hands to crush the onions so that their juices penetrate the burghul. Season to taste with salt and pepper. Add the parsley, mint, olive oil and lemon juice, and mix well. Taste to see if more salt, pepper or lemon are required. The salad should be distinctly lemony.

Tabbouleh is traditionally served in individual plates lined with boiled vine leaves, or raw lettuce or cabbage leaves. People scoop the salad up with more leaves, served in a separate bowl beside it.

A more dramatic way of serving *tabbouleh is* to pile it in a pyramid on a large platter, and to decorate it with black olives, scarlet tomatoes, pale green cucumber slices, or dark green ribbons of sweet pepper, and sprigs of parsley.

A little finely chopped cucumber and tomato may be added to the salad, but it is absolutely necessary to salt and drain the cucumber for ½ hour first. Otherwise the water from these vegetables can unbalance the delicate seasoning, without which the burghul would be quite uninteresting.

Ful Nabed / Purée of Dried White Fava Beans

Choose the white fava beans to be found in all Greek shops and some delicatessens, usually skinned.

2 onions, finely chopped
7 tablespoons olive oil
½ lb. dried white fava beans,
   soaked for 24 hours
Juice of 1 lemon
1 level teaspoon superfine sugar
Salt

DRESSING
2½ tablespoons olive oil
Juice of ½ lemon
3 tablespoons finely chopped fresh
   dill or parsley
1 teaspoon paprika or a pinch of
   cayenne pepper [optional]

Fry the onions gently in oil in a large saucepan until they are only just soft and a very pale golden color. Add about 2½ cups water and bring to the boil. Drain the beans of their soaking water, add them to the saucepan, and cook over low heat without any salt until they practically disintegrate. Add more water during the cooking time if necessary. This will take from 1 to 1½ hours, according to the quality of the beans.

When the beans are ready, there should be hardly any liquid left. Mash them to a paste. Season with the lemon juice, sugar, and salt. For a very creamy consistency put the mixture through a sieve or in an electric blender.

Pour the purée into a serving bowl. When cold, decorate with a dribble of olive oil, lemon juice, and chopped dill or parsley. Red paprika may be added to this mixture for color, or cayenne pepper for strength.

Fattoush / Bread Salad

This is a very much loved Syrian peasant salad in which pieces of soaked toasted bread provide an unusual texture.

It is preferable to sprinkle the cucumber with salt and allow it to drain in a colander for ½ hour before preparing the rest of the salad. If the cucumber drains into the toasted bread, it will unbalance the seasoning and make the salad rather dull.

½ flat Arab bread or 4 thin slices white bread, toasted and broken into small pieces
Juice of 1–2 lemons, or to taste
1 large cucumber or 2 small ones, chopped
3–4 firm tomatoes, chopped
1 medium-sized mild onion or a bunch of scallions, chopped
2½ tablespoons finely chopped parsley
2½ tablespoons finely chopped fresh mint or 1 tablespoon dried crushed mint
4 tablespoons chopped fresh coriander [optional]
2 cloves garlic, crushed [optional]
8–10 tablespoons olive oil
Salt and black pepper

The ingredients and proportions of this salad vary with every family. Romaine or cos lettuce can be used instead of cucumber, and sometimes chopped sweet peppers are added.

Put the broken pieces of toast in a bowl. Moisten and soften with a little cold water or lemon juice. Mix with the remaining ingredients. Taste and adjust seasoning.

Purée of Dried White Beans

½ lb. dried white beans (navy, pea, or Great Northern), soaked overnight
5 tablespoons olive oil
Juice of 1 lemon, or more
Salt and black pepper
4 black olives [optional]

Boil the beans until very soft. The time required will, as usual, depend on their quality and age. A pressure cooker can reduce it considerably.

Drain the beans thoroughly. Save a few whole beans for garnish, and mash, pound, or blend the rest to a smooth paste in an electric blender. Add the olive oil and lemon juice, salt, and pepper, beating with a wooden spoon to blend them into the purée. Thin with a little water if necessary.

Serve in a bowl, decorated with the whole beans and, if you like, a few black olives.

Piaz

A Turkish white bean salad.

¼ lb. dried white beans (navy, pea, or Great Northern), soaked overnight
5 tablespoons olive oil
Juice of ½ lemon, or more
Salt and black pepper
2 hard-boiled eggs
4 black olives
1 tomato, thinly sliced

Boil the beans until very tender and soft, bearing in mind their age and quality in assessing the cooking time. Take care not to overcook them if using a pressure cooker. They must be firm.

Drain the beans well. While still hot, add the olive oil, lemon juice, salt, and pepper. Mix in the eggs cut into eighths, the black olives, pitted and halved, and thinly sliced tomato, taking care not to crumble or crush them, or the beans.

Nougada / Almond Salad

½ lb. (1 cup) ground almonds
Pinch of superfine sugar
Salt and white pepper
1 clove garlic, crushed
Juice of 1½–2 lemons
About ½ cup olive or corn oil [I prefer corn]
3–4 tablespoons finely chopped parsley
Slivered or flaked almonds, to garnish

Put the ground almonds in a bowl. Add sugar and a very little salt and white pepper. Add garlic. Stir in the lemon juice and oil alternately, a little at a time, beating well with a fork. Pour into a serving bowl. Sprinkle the top with more oil and the parsley, and garnish with slivered or flaked almonds.

An excellent salad to serve with cold fish, cold chicken, or *kibbeh* (pages 226 ff.).

YOGURT

Laban

In every Middle Eastern household, the making of yogurt is a regular activity, a creative ritual which gives a satisfaction similar to that of planting a seed and watching it grow and flourish. With a little experience one learns the rhythm of preparation and the exact warmth required to turn milk into yogurt. The actual preparation of yogurt is in fact extremely easy, but the right conditions are necessary for success. If these are fulfilled, the "magic" cannot fail.

Yogurt is an essential part of the Middle Eastern diet. In al-Baghdadi's medieval manual it was referred to as "Persian milk." In Iran it is known as *mâst*, in Turkey as *yoğurt*. Syrians and Lebanese call it *laban*, Egyptians *laban zabadi*, Armenians refer to it as *madzoon*.

In parts of the Middle East, as in the Balkans, yogurt is believed by some people to have medicinal and therapeutic qualities—longevity and a strong constitution are sometimes attributed to the daily consumption of yogurt.

More recently, the Western world, too, has discovered the wholesome and diet-regulating qualities of yogurt. But it is still unfortunately restricted to a minor role as a dessert, too often sweetened or synthetically flavored. Yogurt has yet to be allowed the freedom and versatility it enjoys throughout the Middle East, where it is, in turn, a hot or cold soup, a salad, a marinade for meat, or the basic liquid element in a meat and vegetable dish. The West has also still to discover the vast number of dishes which are refreshed, soothed, and glorified when accompanied by yogurt, and the splendid drink called *ayran* or *abdug* (see page 444), made with yogurt and water.

To Make Yogurt

If yogurt is to be adopted as an important element in cookery, it is well worth learning to make it at home. All sorts of equipment have been recommended as being needed: cake pans lined with padding, feather cushions, thermometers, different-sized bottles, jars, cork tops, to name a few. Commercial firms sell rather expensive sets of equipment, but you can do perfectly well without them. All that is necessary, or at least for me, is a large earthenware or glass bowl, a plate to cover it entirely, and a small woolen blanket—I use two old shawls.

The proportions are a tablespoon of starter or activator (culture of the bacteria *bulgaris*) or fresh, live yogurt (I use ordinary, commercial *plain* yogurt) to each 2½ cups of milk. If you increase the quantity of milk, increase that of the starter accordingly, but do not use too much of the latter, or the new batch of yogurt will be excessively sour.

Bring the milk to a boil in a large pan. When the froth rises, lower the heat and let the milk barely simmer for about 2 minutes. Turn off the heat, and allow the milk to cool to the point where you can just dip your finger in (about 106°–109°F.) and leave it there while you count to ten. If the milk is much cooler or hotter than this, the yogurt is likely to fail.

Remove any skin that has formed on the surface of the milk.

Beat the activator or plain yogurt in a large glass or earthenware bowl until it is quite liquid. Add a few tablespoons of the hot milk, one at a time, beating vigorously. Then add the rest of the milk slowly, beating constantly until thoroughly mixed.

Cover the bowl with a large plate or with a sheet of plastic secured tightly with an elastic band. Wrap the whole bowl in a woolen blanket or shawl and leave it undisturbed in a warm place such as an airing cupboard, *free of drafts*, for at least 8 hours or overnight. It should then be ready, thick like a creamy custard. Do not leave the bowl in the warmth too long, or the yogurt will become too sour.

As soon as the yogurt is ready, you can cool it in the refrigerator. The yogurt will keep for a week, but it is preferable to make a new batch every 4 days, using some of the previous one as an activator. This will ensure a constant supply of sweet, fresh-tasting yogurt.

To "Stabilize" Yogurt

Many Middle Eastern dishes call for yogurt as a cooking liquid or sauce which needs to be cooked (boiled or simmered) rather than just heated. Salted goat's milk, which was used in these recipes in olden times, can be cooked without curdling, which explains why medieval recipes do not give any indication of ways of preventing yogurt from curdling. Lengthy cooking, however, causes yogurt made with cow's milk to curdle, and stabilizers such as cornstarch or egg white are required to prevent this.

5 cups yogurt	1 egg white, lightly beaten, or 1
¾ teaspoon salt	tablespoon cornstarch mixed
	with a little cold water or milk

Beat yogurt in a large saucepan until liquid. Add the egg white, or the cornstarch mixed to a light paste with water or milk, and a little salt. Stir well with a wooden spoon. Bring to a boil slowly, stirring constantly *in one direction only*, then reduce the heat to as low as possible and let the yogurt barely simmer, uncovered, for about 10 minutes, or until it has acquired a thick, rich consistency. Don't cover the pan: dripping steam could ruin it.

After simmering, the yogurt can be mixed and cooked with other ingredients such as meat or vegetables with no danger of curdling.

If carefully handled, this process can also be carried out successfully after the yogurt has been mixed with other ingredients.

Labna / Cream Cheese

This is a delightful cream cheese. It is made by salting the yogurt, adding from ½ to 1 teaspoon salt per pint of yogurt, according to taste. The yogurt should be poured into a strainer or colander lined with damp cheesecloth. Allow it to drain overnight, or tie the corners of the cloth together and suspend the bundle over a bowl or the sink. The whey will drain away, leaving a very light, soft, creamy white curd cheese. Shape this cheese into little balls. Sprinkle them with olive oil and a little paprika, or roll them in it.

This great Arab favorite is often served at breakfast.

SAVORY PASTRIES

In his *Kanju'l Ishtiha* (Treasure of the Appetite) the fifteenth-century Persian poet of food, Abu Ishaq of Shiraz, wrote: "We came into the kitchen for this purpose, that we might show the fried meat to the pastry."

The Middle East has "shown to the pastry" not only meat, but also chicken, brains, cheese, eggs, spinach, eggplants, and all the nuts they have had available.

Savory pastries are one of the most interesting features of Oriental food: *sanbusak, börek, pasteles, bstilla, fila, brik, spanakopitta, lahma bi ajeen*—a vast family of glorious little pastries, half-moon shapes, triangles, fingers, small pots, little parcels of all types, as well as medium-sized pies and enormous ones. Various doughs are used, each country and community favoring a particular type; and to make it more confusing, different names are given to the same pastries by different countries and communities, while sometimes the same name can apply to two very different pastries.

Pie pastry, flaky pastry, a paper-thin pastry called *fila* (somewhat thinner than strudel pastry), and bread dough can all be used. Fillings for small pies can be any combination of cheese and egg, spinach and cheese, brains and parsley, ground meat and nuts, and fried eggplant. Large pies are filled with chicken, pigeon, and meat stews thickened with eggs, as well as the fillings used for the smaller ones.

For the smaller pastries, some regions favor a certain shape to which the people are touchingly attached, and from which they would never allow themselves to deviate. They require a certain amount of skill, but it is easily acquired; it is a skill well worth possessing, since the results are particularly delicious and never cease to provoke general admiration. It is indeed a pleasure to master the art of molding perfect, dainty little pots, to make elegant, festoon-type edges, and to fold tidy little envelopes.

These savory pastries make excellent appetizers and first courses, served hot or cold; they also make splendid buffet and party dishes, particularly in their smaller versions. Mountains of crisp, golden savories are a familiar sight at parties. The larger pies such as the Moroccan *bstilla* (page 102) and the Tunisian *tagine malsouka* (page

104) make a magnificent main dish and are practically a meal in themselves.

Quantities given for the smaller pastries are usually for making 30 or more pastries, and are appropriate for parties or buffet meals.

Raghîf Alsinîyyeh

An extraordinary pie or pastry is described by Abd al-Latif al-Baghdadi,* the versatile Arab scholar, scientist, historian, philosopher, and traveler, in an account of conditions and events in Egypt in the early part of the thirteenth-century, the *Kitab al-ifadah wa'l-l'tibar*.

"One of the most singular foods made in Egypt is that called *raghîf alsinîyyeh*. This is how it is made: they take 30 *rotles* (Baghdad weight) of wheat flour. They knead it with 5½ *rotles* of sesame oil in the same way as they make the bread called *khoschcnan*. They divide the whole into two parts, spreading one of the two parts in a round shape of a *raghîf* [cakc] in a coppcr plate made for this purpose of about 4 spans in diameter, and which has strong handles. After that they arrange on the dough three roasted lambs stuffed with chopped meats fried in sesame oil, crushed pistachios, various hot and aromatic spices like pepper, ginger, cloves, lentisk, coriander, caraway, cardamom, nuts and others. They sprinkle rose water, in which they have infused musk, over all. After that they put on the lambs and in the spaces left, a score of fowls, as many pullets, and fifty small birds, some roasted and stuffed with eggs, others stuffed with meat, others fried in the juice of sour grapes or lemon or some other similar liquor. They put above them pastry, and little boxes filled, some with the meat, some with sugar and sweetmeats. If one would add one lamb more, cut into morsels, it would not be out of place, and one could also add fried cheese.

"When the whole is arranged in the form of a dome they again sprinkle rose water in which musk has been infused, or wood of aloes. They cover it again with the other part of the dough, to which they begin to give the shape of a broad cake. They are careful to join the

* *Not* the al-Baghdadi from whom I have quoted extensively in this book.

two cakes of dough, as one makes pastry, so that no vapour escapes. After that they put the whole near the top of the oven until the pastry is solid and begins a degree of cooking. Then they lower the dish in the oven little by little, holding it by the handles, and leave it until the crust is well cooked and takes on a rose red colour. When it is at this point it is taken out and wiped with a sponge, and again sprinkled with rose and musk water, and then brought out to be eaten.

"This dish is fit to be put before kings and wealthy persons when they go hunting far from home or take part in pleasures in far off places; for in this one dish is found a great variety. It is easy to transport, difficult to break, pleasing to the sight, satisfying to the taste, and keeps hot a very long time." *

Savory Fillings

Certain fillings are common to many savory pastries. Here are a few.
    For a dough made with 1 lb. (3½ cups) flour:

CHEESE FILLING I

1 lb. cheese, grated   White pepper
2 eggs, beaten

Use Greek Halumi, Gruyère, Cheddar, Wensleydale, Edam, Gouda, or a mixture of any of these with a little Parmesan; try also Italian mozzarella. Mix the grated cheese with beaten eggs and season to taste with pepper.

CHEESE FILLING II

1 lb. crumbly white feta   4–5 tablespoons finely chopped
    cheese or about equal   fresh parsley, dill, mint, or
    quantities of feta and cottage   chives
    cheese   White pepper

Crumble the cheese with a fork. Do not use a cream cheese because it melts. Mix in chopped herbs and season to taste with white pepper,

* Zand and Videan, *The Eastern Key.*

but do not add salt unless the cheese requires it. (Feta is very salty, for instance.) Work the ingredients into a paste.

MEAT FILLING I—This is called a *tatbila*.

1 medium or large onion, finely
    chopped
2½ tablespoons oil or butter
1 lb. lean lamb or beef, ground
2½ tablespoons pine nuts

Salt and black pepper
1 teaspoon ground cinnamon or
½ teaspoon ground allspice
    [optional]

Gently fry the onion in the oil or butter (I prefer to use oil) until soft and a pale golden color. Add the meat and fry lightly until it changes color. Stir in the pine nuts and fry for 2 minutes longer. The pine nuts can also be fried separately and added at the end. Season to taste with salt and pepper and, if liked, cinnamon or allspice (these flavorings are particularly excellent). Some even add a little sugar. Moisten with about 6 tablespoons water. The meat will otherwise be too dry for a filling. Cook for a few minutes more until the water is absorbed and the meat tender.

MEAT FILLING II

Prepare the filling as above but omit the pine nuts. When cooked, mix with the calf's brains, cleaned, washed, and boiled in acidulated water, then drained and mashed with a fork (see following recipe).

    This serves to hold the minced meat together and gives the filling a creamy consistency.

BRAIN FILLING

1 lb. calf's or lamb's brains
Vinegar
Salt
2–3 tablespoons finely chopped
    parsley

White pepper
1 hard-boiled egg, chopped
    [optional]

Soak the brains in water with a tablespoon of vinegar for 1 hour. Drain and wash under cold running water, removing the thin outer membranes. Drop into boiling salted water acidulated with 1 tablespoon vinegar and simmer for about 10 minutes. Drain. Mash with a fork, adding parsley and a generous amount of salt and pepper, and mix well.

A rather good addition is to stir in a chopped hard-boiled egg.

SPINACH FILLING I

1 lb. fresh spinach or ½ lb. frozen chopped or leaf spinach
1 tablespoon butter
¼ lb. Gruyère, Gouda, or Wensleydale cheese, grated

1 egg
Black pepper
¼ teaspoon grated nutmeg [optional]

Trim stems of fresh spinach; wash carefully and chop the leaves finely. Put in a pan with a tablespoon of butter. Cover and let it cook in its own juice over very low heat, stirring occasionally, until tender. If using frozen spinach, defrost it and make sure water drains away entirely. Cook with the butter.

Stir in the grated cheese, the lightly beaten egg, and black pepper to taste. Do not add salt unless necessary. Take into account the saltiness of the cheese melting into the spinach. Add a little nutmeg if you like, and mix well.

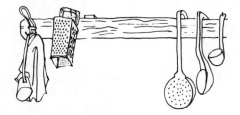

SPINACH FILLING II

1 lb. fresh spinach or ½ lb. frozen chopped or leaf spinach
1 onion, finely chopped
Oil

2½ tablespoons pine nuts or chopped walnuts
1–2 tablespoons raisins
Salt and black pepper

Trim stems of fresh spinach. Wash, drain, and chop finely. If using frozen spinach, defrost it and make sure that the water drains away entirely.

Fry the onion gently in 2 tablespoons oil until soft. Add the spinach and stew it in its own juice until tender. Lightly fry the pine nuts or chopped walnuts separately in oil for 2 minutes. Drain, and add to the spinach with the raisins. Season to taste with salt and pepper, and mix well.

SPINACH FILLING III

1 lb. fresh spinach or ½ lb. frozen chopped or leaf spinach	Salt and black pepper
1 tablespoon butter	½ lb. calf's brains

Trim stems of fresh spinach. Wash, drain, and chop finely. If using frozen spinach, defrost it and make sure that the water drains away entirely. Simmer the spinach in its own juice with a little butter until soft. Season to taste with salt and pepper.

Clean, wash, and simmer the brains in acidulated water as described in the recipe for brain filling on page 86. Mash with a fork and mix with the spinach. They will act as a rather creamy binder.

KHANDRAJO (EGGPLANT) FILLING—This is a Sephardic Jewish filling similar to the French *ratatouille*.

1 lb. unpeeled eggplants, cut into small cubes	1 large onion, finely chopped
Salt	3 tomatoes, skinned and chopped
Oil	Black pepper

Sprinkle cubed eggplant with salt and leave in a colander for about ½ hour to allow the bitter juices to drain away. Squeeze lightly, rinse well, and drain.

Heat 2 tablespoons oil in a saucepan and fry the chopped onion to a dark golden color. Add the eggplant and fry lightly until tender and a little colored. Add the tomatoes and season generously with pepper. Add salt only if required, taking into account the eggplant, which is salty already. Simmer gently, covered, until the vegetables are very soft, then squash them lightly with a fork.

CHICKEN FILLING

1 lb. cooked boned chicken	Salt, white pepper, and grated nutmeg
2½ tablespoons butter	
2½ tablespoons flour	1 egg
1¼ cups hot milk or chicken stock	

Use leftover chicken, if you like, and cut it into small pieces.

Make a thick sauce. Melt the butter in a thick saucepan or preferably in the top of a double boiler. Add flour and stir well. Cook gently over boiling water for 5 minutes, stirring constantly, until the flour is cooked through. Gradually add ½ cup hot milk or stock, beating well between each addition, and cook until the sauce thickens. Add the rest of the milk or stock slowly, stirring vigorously until it begins to bubble and thicken again. Season to taste with salt, pepper, and nutmeg, and simmer gently for 10 to 15 minutes.

Remove from the heat, break in an egg, and beat well. Add the pieces of chicken and mix well.

Sanbusak

At a banquet given by the Caliph Mustakfi of Baghdad in the tenth century, a member of the company recited a poem by Ishāq ibn Ibrāhīm of Mosul describing *sanbūsaj* (*sanbusak*) as follows.

> *If thou woulds't know what food gives most delight,*
> *Best let me tell, for none hath subtler sight.*
> *Take first the finest meat, red, soft to touch,*
> *And mince it with the fat, not overmuch;*
> *Then add an onion, cut in circles clean,*
> *A cabbage, very fresh, exceeding green,*
> *And season well with cinnamon and rue;*
> *Of coriander add a handful, too,*
> *And after that of cloves the very least,*
> *Of finest ginger, and of pepper best,*
> *Two handfuls of Palmyra salt; but haste,*
> *Good master haste to grind them small and strong.*
> *Then lay and light a blazing fire along;*
> *Put all in the pot, and water pour*
> *Upon it from above, and cover o'er*
> *But, when the water vanished is from sight*
> *And when the burning flames have dried it quite,*
> *Then, as thou wilt, in pastry wrap it round,*
> *And fasten well the edges, firm and sound;*
> *Or, if it please thee better, take some dough,*

Conveniently soft, and rubbed just so,
Then with the rolling pin let it be spread
And with the nails its edges docketed.
Pour in the frying-pan the choicest oil
And in that liquor let it finely broil.
Last, ladle out into a thin tureen
Where appetizing mustard smeared hath been,
And eat with pleasure, mustarded about,
This tastiest food for hurried diner-out.

(From Mas'ūdī's *Meadows of Gold*. Translated by Professor A. J. Arberry in *Islamic Culture*, 1939.)

Here is a modern recipe for sanbusak, popular in Syria, the Lebanon, and Egypt. The recipe for the dough has for centuries been explained as "one coffee cup of oil, one coffee cup of melted butter, one coffee cup of warm water, one teaspoon of salt. Add and work in as much flour as it takes." Translated into American weights and measures, it is:

DOUGH
½ cup oil
8 tablespoons (1 stick) butter
½ cup warm water
1 teaspoon salt
3½ cups all-purpose flour, sifted

Cheese Filling I or Meat Filling I
 (pages 85–6)
1 egg, beaten
Sesame seeds [optional]
Clarified butter for shallow frying
 or oil for deep frying

To make the dough: put the oil and butter together in a small heat-proof bowl, and heat over boiling water until the butter has melted. Mix with warm water and salt, and pour into a large mixing bowl.

Add flour gradually, stirring slowly with your hand, until the dough forms a soft, rather greasy ball. One or two tablespoons more flour may be required. The dough should be handled as little as possible, so stop mixing as soon as it holds together. Alternatively, work the oil and creamed butter into the flour, and add milk instead of water gradually until the dough becomes a ball and leaves the sides of the bowl. In this case, too, do not work the dough longer than necessary.

Traditionally, *sanbusak* are half-moon-shaped. Either roll the dough out thinly and cut into rounds about 3 inches in diameter with a pastry cutter, or take walnut-sized lumps and flatten them out as thinly as possible between the palms of your hands.

Put a heaping teaspoonful of filling in the center of one half of each circle. Fold the other half over to make a half-moon shape and seal by pinching the edges tightly. If you like, make the traditional festoon-type edge by pinching and folding over all along. Arrange on baking sheets, which need not be greased.

Brush the surface with beaten egg and, if you like, sprinkle lightly with sesame seeds. Bake in a preheated slow to moderate oven (350° to 375°) until they are a pale golden color, about 35 to 45 minutes. Alternatively, fry gently in clarified butter, or *samna*, until golden and well cooked inside, which takes only a few minutes, or deep-fry in oil. In this case, do not brush with the egg-and-water mixture.

Serve hot or cold, but preferably just out of the oven, when they are at their best. Depending on the size of the *sanbusak*, this quantity makes about 30 pastries.

Pasteles

These little pies are a Sephardic Jewish specialty, believed to have been brought by them from Spain to Turkey; but both the dough and one of the traditional fillings are similar to those of the Oriental *sanbusak*.

Their shape is that of a little covered pot, like a tiny English meat pie. Two fillings are traditional: either of the meat fillings on page 86, and the *khandrajo* (eggplant filling) on page 88.

Prepare the dough as in the recipe for *sanbusak*, using 3½ cups flour. Take walnut- or egg-sized balls and hollow them out with a finger. Shape them into little pots by pinching and smoothing up the sides. Fill the little pots with one of the fillings mentioned above, and cover with flat round lids of dough a little larger in diameter than the tops of the pots. Secure them firmly by pinching lid and pot edges together. Pinch and fold over the overlapping edges of each lid to make a festoon edge.

Paint the lids (and the sides as well if you like) with a mixture of egg beaten with 2 tablespoons water, and place on an ungreased baking tray. Bake in a preheated slow oven (350°) for 30 to 45 minutes, until the dough is well cooked and the *pasteles* are a warm golden color.

A modern labor-saving method for making *pasteles* is to use a muffin tin or individual tart tins. Use deep shapes if possible. Line them with thinly rolled dough, filled with one of the fillings and cover each one with a lid, pressing it on firmly. Brush with an egg and water mixture, and bake as above.

The number of pastries varies according to their size, but will be about 30.

Turkish Savory Börek

There are as many recipes for börek *as there are people who make this Turkish version of* sanbusak. *They range from bread and pie doughs to flaky pastry.*

1. PIE DOUGH

A very simple and particularly successful pie dough. Use any of the fillings described on pages 85–9.

3½ cups all-purpose flour
½ teaspoon salt
½ lb. (2 sticks) butter
2 eggs

About ¼ cup water
1 egg beaten with 1–2 tablespoons
   water, to glaze

Sift flour and salt into a large mixing bowl. Cream the cold butter and work it into the flour, first with your fingers, and then by rubbing the mixture lightly between the palms of your hands. Add 2 eggs and work them in lightly. Add water gradually, working it in gently until the dough forms a soft ball which comes away from the sides of the bowl. Stop kneading as soon as this happens. The dough is better for being worked as little as possible. Allow to rest in a cool place, covered with a damp cloth, for at least 1 hour.

Roll the dough out on a lightly floured board or marble top with a lightly floured rolling pin. Roll as thinly as possible from the center outwards, lifting up the roller and patching any tears as they occur. Cut out rounds about 3 inches in diameter with a pastry cutter. Alternatively, take walnut-sized lumps of dough, roll into a round ball and flatten out as thinly as possible between the palms of your hands.

Put a heaping teaspoonful of filling in the center of each circle. Fold the pastry over to make a half-moon shape and pinch the edges together to seal them. Pinch and fold over all around the edges to make a festoon effect. Arrange on ungreased baking trays.

Brush the tops with egg beaten with water, and bake in a preheated slow oven (350°) for about 45 minutes, or until a warm golden color.

Depending on the size of the pastries, this quantity makes about 30 *börek*.

II. BREAD DOUGH

This is a rather more uncommon type of *börek* made with a bread dough, rather like a miniature stuffed pizza.

Prepare the dough as in the recipe for *lahma bi ajeen* (page 105). Prepare one of the cheese fillings or either of the meat fillings on page 86.

Take walnut-sized lumps of dough after it has been well kneaded and allowed to rise to twice its size. Flour the board and rolling pin, and roll the dough out, but not quite as thinly as for *lahma bi ajeen*. Put a tablespoon of filling on each round and fold over into a half-moon shape. Seal edges by wetting them with water and pressing them together.

Arrange on greased baking sheets and brush the tops with 1 egg beaten with 1 or 2 tablespoons water. Leave in a warm place to rise again, then bake in a preheated fairly hot oven (425° F) for about

10 minutes only. Makes about 30, but this again depends on the size of the pastries.

III. FLAKY PASTRY

The most delightful *börek* are made with flaky or puff pastry. One recipe is similar to the French *pâte feuilletée*. It requires much time and application, but the results are extremely good and worth the trouble.

One condition necessary for the pastry to be successful is that the ingredients, your hands, the bowl, and any working surface should be kept cold throughout the preparation. So this precludes attempting the pastry in hot weather unless air conditioning is available.

3½ cups all-purpose flour
1 teaspoon salt
1 cup iced water
1 lb. unsalted butter

1 egg beaten with 1–2 tablespoons water, to glaze
Fillings: see pages 85–9

Sift the flour into a large bowl, or onto a pastry board. Make a well in the center. Dissolve the salt in the water and pour gradually into the well, working it into the flour as lightly and as quickly as possible. As soon as the dough forms a soft ball, stop mixing. Cover the bowl with a cloth and leave in the refrigerator for 15 minutes.

Work the butter with your hands to soften it, but dip it occasionally in cold water to prevent it from becoming warm.

Roll the dough out on a lightly floured board with a floured rolling pin into a neat rectangle three times as long as it is wide (about 8 inches wide) and about ¼ inch thick. Shape the prepared butter into an oblong smaller than half the size of the rectangle of dough, so that when it is placed over one half of the dough, it is surrounded by a 1-inch margin of dough. Fold the other half of the dough over the butter and pinch the edges together.

Roll the dough out lengthwise very evenly, taking great care not to break it or allow the butter to ooze out. If there is a break, patch it quickly. Fold the pastry in three, overlapping the sections. Chill in the refrigerator for 15 minutes.

Now roll the dough out transversely (sideways) into a long strip. Fold in three once again and chill for 15 minutes. Repeat this process until you have rolled and folded the dough six times in all. The more times it is rolled and folded, the flakier the pastry will be. After the final folding, let the dough rest for about ½ hour. It will keep well for a few days if stored in the refrigerator, wrapped in aluminum foil, but it is preferable to use it on the same day.

Roll it out as thinly as possible and cut into round or square shapes (3 inches or wider) with a sharp pastry cutter. Place a heaping teaspoon of the chosen filling in the center of each shape. Fold the round shapes in half over the filling to make a half-moon shape. Seal the edges by pinching firmly with your fingers and fold them over to make a festoon effect. Bring the corners of the square shapes together over the filling like an envelope and seal by pinching together the edges nearest to each other.

Place the shapes on baking sheets which have been sprinkled with a little cold water. Brush the tops with the egg-and-water mixture, being careful not to allow any of it to run onto the trays. Bake in a preheated very hot oven (500°) for 5 minutes, then reduce the temperature to 375° and continue to bake for about ½ hour, or until the pastries are well done and golden. Makes about 30 pastries.

These pastries are best eaten hot straight from the oven, when they are light, well puffed, crisp, and golden; and they are good cold. They are also excellent deep-fried in hot oil.

IV. ROUGH PUFF PASTRY

I was recently given a most ingenious and easy, if unconventional, way of preparing flaky pastry for *börek*. Margarine is used for its spreading quality.

¼ lb. (1 stick) plus ½ lb. (2 sticks) margarine	½ teaspoon salt
	½ cup iced water
3½ cups all-purpose flour, sifted	1 teaspoon lemon juice or vinegar

Rub ¼ lb. softened but cold margarine into the flour. Sprinkle in salt. Mix the water with the lemon juice or vinegar, and add it to the flour gradually, working it in quickly. Allow the pastry to rest overnight in a cool place, covered with a damp cloth.

Next day, roll the dough out as thinly as possible and spread the entire surface with the remaining ½ lb. margarine, softened but still cold. Roll up like a Swiss roll and chill for about 1 hour. Then roll out as thinly as possible.

Use this pastry to make square or half-moon *börek* as described in the previous recipe, using any of the fillings given on pages 85–9. Arrange on ungreased baking trays. Bake in a moderate oven (375°) for the first 10 minutes, then lower the heat to 325° and bake for 25 minutes longer, or until well done and lightly colored.

V. COMMERCIAL FLAKY PASTRY

I have found that good-quality, ready-made, commercial flaky pastry makes very acceptable *börek*. Use any of the fillings described on pages 85–9, and shape in the usual way.

FILA PASTRIES

Fila is a fine, paper-thin dough extremely popular throughout the Middle East (*phyllo* to the Greeks, *yufka* to the Turks, *brik* or *malsouka* to the Tunisians). It lends itself to an infinite variety of uses. It is also cheap and extremely easy to work with.

The dough itself is easy enough to make, a mixture of flour and water kneaded to a fine, firm, elastic mass. But the achievement of paper-thin sheets is extremely difficult and requires much skill. Expert pastry cooks knead the dough vigorously for a long time until it is very elastic, then allow it to rest for 2 or 3 hours. Next, it is divided into fist-sized balls, which are again kneaded, and then pulled and stretched as much as the dough will endure (until it becomes almost transparent).

I have watched this being done at the workshops of P.S.P. Confectioners Ltd. in London. The dough was pulled out over large canvas sheets which had been stretched on a large square frame and served as a table. Two sources of heat (electric heaters) placed underneath the canvas "set" the dough immediately. It was then cut into standard-sized sheets, 12 by 20 inches, and quickly wrapped and sealed in plastic in weights of ½ lb. and 1 lb. (1 lb. gives about 24 large sheets of pastry).

The pastry can also be bought ready-made in many Greek stores and pastry shops.‡ The sheets can be stored indefinitely in a freezer, but in this case they should be defrosted very slowly, as they will break if they are used while still hard. Once the packet has been unsealed, the sheets should be used as soon as possible, since they tend to dry up and will crumble when folded.

Fila sheets are used to make the casings for both large and small pies. They can also be folded into small triangles, cigar and snail shapes, envelopes and little nests—in fact, almost any shape you fancy.

Small Savory Fila Pastries

Light and delicate and delightful to eat, these splendid party and buffet savories come in various traditional shapes and sizes. Use 12 sheets (about ½ lb.) prepared *fila* and any of the fillings on pages 85–9.

The most common of the traditional shapes is the triangle. It is formed in the following manner.

Cut the standard sheets of *fila* lengthwise into 4 rectangular strips about 3 inches wide. Take one at a time and brush the whole length with melted butter. Put a teaspoon of filling near one end, about an inch from the short edge. Fold one corner over the filling, making a triangle, then fold the angle over again and again until the whole strip is folded. Tuck the loose end neatly into the triangular shape.

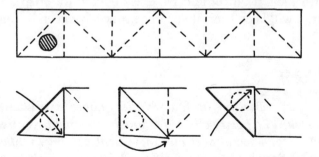

Repeat with the other strips of dough. Place the pastries on oiled baking sheets, brush them with melted butter, and bake in a preheated moderate to moderately hot oven (375° to 400°) for 30 to 45 minutes, or until crisp and golden.

Another common shape is the square. This is made by putting a heaping teaspoon of filling at one end of a similar strip of pastry brushed with melted butter, folding the upper and lower edges and the end edge over the filling. Then fold the pastry with the filling inside over and over until you come to the end of the strip. Bake as described above.

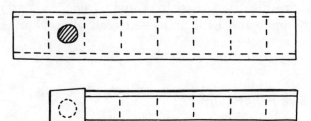

A long, thin cigar shape is made with a strip about 4 inches wide and 10 inches long. A cheese filling (page 84) is commonly used. Place a heaping teaspoonful lengthwise about ½ inch from the shorter edge. Fold this nearest edge over it, then fold the two longer edges inwards a little over the filling to prevent it from oozing out. Roll the strip up like a cigar. Bake as above.

The traditional shape for spinach-filled pastries is a spiral (although triangular shapes are also used). Roll into long thin cigars as described above, then curl into snail-like spirals. Pack the pastries tightly on an oiled baking sheet to prevent them from unrolling. Brush with melted butter and bake as above until crisp and golden. The pastries will keep their shape once they have been baked.

Brik à L'œuf

This Tunisian variation of fila savories makes a brilliant and delightful snack. The pastry allows for much personal inventiveness and individual taste, since almost any ingredient can be wrapped up in a thin sheet of dough (or even a different filling in each little pastry), deep-fried, and served immediately.

I feel that this dish would be a sure success for Western parties because of its versatility and the ease and rapidity with which it is made—a whole meal neatly wrapped in a delicate crisp casing, easily served and handled.

FILLING FOR 1 SERVING

2 tablespoons chopped onion, softened in oil or butter

4 tablespoons mashed canned tuna

1 teaspoon finely chopped parsley

Salt and black pepper

1 egg

AN ALTERNATIVE FILLING

4 tablespoons grated cheese

2–3 mushrooms, sliced and sautéed
lightly in butter or oil

1 teaspoon finely chopped parsley

Salt and black pepper

1 egg

Other fillings can be made with chopped spinach or eggplant lightly
fried with tomatoes and peppers (a sort of *ratatouille*).

Spread one sheet of *fila* out on a large plate or flat surface. If the
filling tends to be rather moist and you think that it may break the
pastry, lay two sheets together one on top of the other.

Lay the filling ingredients at one end of the sheet, breaking the
egg over the other ingredients last. (Do not mix them together.) Fold
the sheet over, rolling the filling up into a neat, firm packet, being
careful not to squash the ingredients.

Drop the packet or *brik* into deep but not too hot oil. Turn it
over as soon as it turns a light brown color and fry the other side.
Remove and drain on absorbent paper.

Serve hot immediately, or keep warm in the lowest of ovens until
ready to serve.

LARGE PIES

These larger versions of the small savories, made with the same doughs and similar fillings, are far less time-consuming and make an excellent first course or main dish.

Spanakopitta

A Greek favorite, this spinach pie has been adopted by many countries throughout the Middle East.

2 lbs. fresh spinach
Butter, about 10 tablespoons in all
Salt and black pepper
¼ teaspoon grated nutmeg [optional]

¼ lb. cheese [Gruyère, Parmesan, Cheddar, or feta], grated or mashed
8–10 sheets *fila* pastry

Wash spinach leaves and cut off any hard stems. Drain and chop. Stew gently with about 2 tablespoons butter, a sprinkling of salt and pepper, and grated nutmeg if liked, until tender. Drain off excess juice; add cheese and mix well.

Butter a large, deep, square or round baking pan or oven dish. Fit four or five sheets of pastry in it, one on top of the other, brushing each sheet with melted butter, and folding them up so that they overlap the sides of the dish. Spread the spinach and cheese mixture over this and cover with the remaining sheets of pastry, brushing melted butter between each layer as well as on top.

At this stage the pie is sometimes cut diagonally into lozenge shapes or squares with a sharp knife, but this is not really necessary. Put the pie into a preheated moderate oven (375°) and bake for about ¾ hour. Then increase the heat to 450° or 475° for 5 to 10 minutes, or until the top of the pie is crisp and golden, and all the inner leaves are well cooked.

Another version of the same pie can be made with flaky *börek* pastry (see the two recipes on pages 94–5, which are equally suitable).

The pastry is divided into two pieces, one slightly larger than the other, and rolled out thinly on a lightly floured board. One piece is cut 1½ inches wider all around than the pan or dish, to fold well up over the sides of the pan and to allow for shrinkage. The pan need not be greased. Ease the sheet of pastry into it loosely, then press it carefully into place, taking care not to trap any air underneath, which would form blisters in baking. Trim off excess pastry with a sharp knife.

If the filling is a little too moist, brush the pastry lightly with egg white to prevent it from becoming soggy. Spread the filling over the pastry and cover with another sheet of pastry, rolled out thinly and cut about ¾ inch wider all around than the pan. Press the edges together with those of the bottom sheet to seal them. If you like, pinch and fold them over to make a festoon-type edge, or tuck the top sheet under the bottom one. Prick the top of the pie with a fork to allow steam to escape.

Bake in a preheated very hot oven (500°) for 5 minutes, then reduce the heat to 375° and continue to bake for ½ hour longer, or until crisp and golden.

Short pastry is also sometimes used for this pie.

Tyropitta

Another traditional Greek cheese pie made with feta, the white Greek cheese available from most Greek stores. If you cannot find it, substitute your favorite cheese.

For 8 to 10 sheets of *fila* pastry, prepare the following filling:

1 lb. feta cheese	5 tablespoons finely chopped fresh
2 eggs	dill, chervil, chives, or any
White pepper	other herb of your choice

Crumble and mash the cheese with a fork. Beat in the eggs, and season to taste with pepper. Stir in herbs and mix well.

Prepare the pie as in either version of the recipe for *spanakopitta* above. It is also excellent made with flaky pastry.

AN ALTERNATIVE FILLING FOR TYROPITTA

1 lb. feta cheese	½ cup yogurt
2 small onions, finely chopped and softened with salt	White pepper
	3 eggs, well beaten

Mash the cheese with a fork. Add the onions, which have been softened by being sprinkled with salt and allowed to drain, the yogurt, white pepper, and eggs. Mix well.

Kotopitta

This is a Greek chicken pie prepared with the chicken filling on page 88 and sheets of *fila* pastry or either of the flaky pastries on pages 94–5.

Large Meat Pie

A rather splendid large meat pie can be made with either of the meat fillings on page 86 and *fila* or flaky pastry.

Bstilla

Pronounced "pastilla," this is one of the Moroccan dishes said to have been brought back by the "Moriscos" from Andalusia after the Reconquista.

"Food for the Gods," as it is described by Moroccans, this magnificent pigeon pie is baked on special occasions, such as when entertaining important guests. Its gentle harmony is achieved by contrasts—it is juicy and crisp, sweet and salty at the same time.

This pie is usually enormous and must be baked in a gigantic tray; even the very reduced quantities which I give below will feed 6 to 8 people generously. Traditionally, it is made with pigeons, but since English pigeons are of a different variety and taste, they would be inappropriate, and I suggest that you use broilers or a larger chicken instead.

The pastry for this pie is generally made at home in Morocco. The preparation of the dough requires much skill and an almost inherited experience. However, Moroccans who do not want to, or cannot, make the pastry themselves use the fila *pastry which is available ready-made in Greek grocery shops and bakeries.*

FILLING

2 broilers or 1 large chicken
2½ tablespoons butter
1 large onion, finely chopped or grated
Salt and black pepper
½ teaspoon ground ginger
¼ teaspoon powdered saffron [optional]
½ teaspoon ground cinnamon
½ teaspoon mixed spice or ground allspice
4 tablespoons finely chopped parsley

7–8 eggs
12 tablespoons butter, melted
16 sheets fila
1 tablespoon sugar
¼ teaspoon ground cinnamon
1 cup almonds, chopped and sautéed in butter
1 egg yolk, beaten, to glaze
A little cinnamon and sugar, to garnish

Wash the broilers or chicken. Quarter them, and simmer in a very little water with butter, onion, seasonings, and parsley for about 2 hours, or until the flesh is so tender that it falls off the bones. Add a little more water as required. The giblets and liver may be simmered with the birds. When cooked, drain off the stock and reserve. Skin and bone the chicken, and cut the meat into smallish pieces.

Take about ½ cup of the stock and beat it well with the eggs. Season to taste with salt and pepper, pour into a small pan, and stir over low heat until the mixture is creamy and nearly set. The eggs and chicken constitute the filling of the pie.

Brush a large round (or square) pie pan or oven dish about 13 inches in diameter and 1½ to 2 inches deep with melted butter. Fit a sheet of *fila* in the dish so that the ends fold well up and overlap the edges. If this is not possible, use overlapping sheets of *fila*. Lay 6 sheets of pastry on top of each other, brushing melted butter evenly between each layer. Sprinkle the top layer with sugar, cinnamon, and sautéed almonds. Spread more than half of the egg mixture over this, and sprinkle with a little of the remaining chicken stock. Cover with another 4 sheets of *fila*, each one brushed with melted butter. Lay the pieces of boned chicken neatly on top and cover with the rest of the egg mixture. Sprinkle with a little more chicken stock. Cover with the remaining *fila* sheets, brushing each layer with melted butter. Tuck the top *fila* sheets between the overlapping bottom sheets and the sides of the dish.

Paint the top with beaten egg yolk and bake in a slow to moderate oven (350° to 375°) for the first 40 minutes. Then raise the temperature to 425° and bake for a further 15 minutes, or until the pastry is crisp and the top a deep golden color.

Serve sprinkled with sugar mixed with cinnamon, and cut, if you like, in a crisscross pattern of lozenges.

Tagine Malsouka / Tunisian Meat Pie

1 lb. lean lamb, cubes
2½ tablespoons oil
¼ lb. dried white beans (navy, pea, or Great Northern), soaked overnight
Salt and black pepper
¼ teaspoon powdered saffron [optional]

½ teaspoon ground cinnamon
6 eggs
8 tablespoons (1 stick) butter, melted
12 sheets *fila*
Beaten egg yolk, to glaze

In a saucepan, brown the meat in 2 tablespoons oil. Add soaked and drained beans, cover with water, and season to taste with salt, pepper, saffron if used, and cinnamon. Bring to the boil and simmer slowly and gently, covered, for about 2 hours, or until the beans are soft, the meat tender, and the liquid very much reduced. Add a little water while the stew is simmering if it evaporates too quickly. Break the eggs into the pan and stir well. Taste and adjust seasoning. Keep stirring over low heat until the eggs have thickened a little and are creamy.

Brush a large baking dish with melted butter and fit 4 sheets of *fila* pastry into the dish, one on top of the other, so that the edges fold up over the sides of the dish, brushing melted butter between each layer. Spread half of the meat stew evenly over the top and cover with another 4 sheets of pastry, again brushing each one with melted butter. Cover with the rest of the stew and the remaining sheets of pastry, each one brushed with melted butter. Brush the top with beaten egg yolk and bake in a slow to moderate oven (350° to 375°) for the first 40 minutes. Then raise the heat to 425° or 450° and bake for 15 minutes longer, until the pastry is crisp and a deep golden color, and the eggs in the stew have set firmly.

A Sephardic Jewish dish for Passover makes use of sheets of matzos softened in water for a similar pie.

Lahma Bi Ajeen

A brilliant dish—an Arab type of pizza with a meat filling. Delicious, dainty, elegant to serve at a party, these savories are also very easy to prepare with a simple bread dough.

A few years ago, my brother met a well-known ex-restaurateur from Alexandria in a cinema queue in Paris. He brought back from this encounter detailed instructions on how to make lahma bi ajeen *—to our unanimous delight. My mother has made them on numerous occasions since, usually in large quantities. She uses a dough made with 2 lbs. flour and a filling based on 2½ to 3 lbs. meat to serve 20 people easily. I am giving smaller quantities to serve about 8 to 10.*

DOUGH

½ oz. (1 cake) fresh yeast or ¼ oz. (1 package) dried yeast
1 cup lukewarm water
Pinch of sugar

3½ cups all-purpose flour
1 teaspoon salt
2½ tablespoons oil

Dissolve the yeast with a pinch of sugar in about ½ cup of the lukewarm water specified above. Leave aside in a warm place for about 10 minutes, or until the mixture begins to bubble.

In the meantime, sift the flour and salt into a large warmed mixing bowl. Make a well in the center and add the oil and the yeast mixture. Work the dough vigorously, adding the remaining lukewarm water gradually to make a soft dough. Knead vigorously for about 15 minutes until the dough is pliable and elastic, and comes away from the sides of the bowl. Cover with a damp cloth and set aside in a warm, draft-free place for 2 to 3 hours, or until doubled in bulk. To prevent a dry crust from forming on the surface, put a very little oil in the bottom of the bowl and roll the ball of dough in it to coat the entire surface before leaving it to rest.

While waiting for the dough to rise, prepare the filling:

1 lb. onions, finely chopped
Oil
1½ lbs. lean lamb or beef, ground
1 lb. fresh tomatoes, skinned and chopped, or a 1-lb. can whole tomatoes
3 tablespoons tomato paste

1 teaspoon sugar
¾ teaspoon ground allspice
1–2 tablespoons lemon juice
Salt and black pepper
4 tablespoons finely chopped parsley [optional]
Pinch of cayenne pepper [optional]

Soften the onions in a little warm oil until they are transparent and have lost their water, taking care not to let them color. Mix the meat, tomatoes, and tomato paste in a large bowl. If you are using fresh tomatoes, get rid of as much of their juice and seeds as possible, and crush them to a pulp. If you are using a can of tomatoes, drain them well, as too much liquid will make the dough soggy. Add sugar, allspice, and lemon juice, and season to taste with salt and pepper. Drain the onions of oil and add them to the meat mixture. Knead well by hand. Some people like to add chopped parsley and a little cayenne pepper as well.

The filling is sometimes varied by omitting the tomatoes altogether, and adding ⅓ cup pine nuts and 2 to 3 tablespoons tamarind (page 443) instead.

Knead the risen dough a few times and divide it into many walnut-sized balls. Allow to rest for a few minutes, then roll each piece on a lightly floured board with a lightly floured rolling pin into a round flat shape 5 to 6 inches in diameter. Alternatively, oil your hands lightly, take smaller lumps of dough, and flatten each piece as much as possible with the palm of your hand on an oiled plate.

Spread the prepared filling very generously over each piece, covering the entire surface (otherwise the filling will look meager when the pastries are baked). Transfer each round to a lightly oiled baking sheet as you prepare it.

Bake in a preheated very hot oven (450° to 475°) for 8 to 10 minutes only. The pastries should be well done but still white and soft enough to roll up or fold in the hand to be eaten, as some people like to do.

Lahma bi ajeen can be reheated by putting them in a warm oven for a few minutes. They can also be warmed up in the top of a double boiler. Serve with various salads: cucumber and yogurt (page 64), *salade Rachèle* (page 70), or any other Arab salad.

Ataïf with Cheese

Ataïf (pancakes) are extremely popular served sweet, stuffed with nuts and doused with syrup (see page 407). A more uncommon but most excellent way of preparing them is to stuff them with cheese.

Prepare *ataïf*, following the recipe on page 409, and adding a little salt to the batter instead of sugar. Greek Halumi cheese is my favorite filling for savory *ataïf*.

Fill with a small slice of Halumi cheese or mozzarella; or make a filling with ½ lb. grated Gruyère, Wensleydale, Gouda, Edam, or Canadian Cheddar, 1 whole egg and black pepper to taste. Mix the ingredients thoroughly with a fork.

Put a heaping teaspoon of filling in the center of each little *ataïf* on the soft, unfried side. Fold the pancake over the filling to make a half-moon shape and seal the edges by pinching them together with your fingers. The soft, moist dough will stick together.

Deep-fry in hot oil until golden and drain on absorbent paper. Serve hot or cold, preferably hot.

An alternative cheese filling is made with feta, the white Greek cheese, crumbled with a fork, seasoned with white pepper, and mixed with a few finely chopped chives. Ordinary white cream cheeses will not do, since they invariably melt and ooze out.

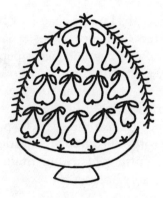

SOUPS
Shorbah

In the Middle East, soups are often eaten as a meal in themselves, accompanied by Arab bread, or *pitta* (page 364). Rich with vegetables, meat, legumes, and rice, they are sometimes indistinguishable from stews, except for the fact that they have very much more liquid. Some of the richer soups play a part in the rituals of religious festivals, and are called "festive" or "wedding" soups.

Calf's feet or sheep's feet are added for their gelatinous quality. Legumes—lentils, chickpeas, yellow split peas, dried green peas, and haricot and fava beans—lend themselves beautifully to make thick, creamy soups, delicately enhanced by spices, lemon, garlic, and fresh herbs. There are infinite combinations of spinach and lentils, spinach and meat balls, yogurt and barley, yogurt and spinach, and so on. Chicken stocks are sometimes thickened with beaten egg yolks and lemon, and fish stocks with egg yolks and vinegar, while meat stocks are made richer with a marrow bone.

Some of these soups and stews were branded as "servants' food" by the rich, Europeanized Egyptians, who preferred cosmopolitan food. Most of these families gave their servants a daily sum with which to buy themselves, say, 2 piasters' worth of meat and 1 piaster's worth of vegetables. These were put in a large pot and left to cook over a very low flame on a portable oil stove, or *fatayel*, on the rooftops of the luxury blocks of apartments, where the servants' quarters were usually situated. Sometimes all the servants of one block pooled their purchases or money to make one large, communal dish. The strong aromas enveloped the street below, drowning the limper, delicate perfumes of their masters' refined dishes.

The rich defended themselves from the accusation that they ate well while their servants had only cheap food, by saying that the latter *preferred* their own food. There was a great deal of truth in this, and I know many children of rich families who would sneak up to the roof terraces to share their servants' soups and stews.

I have discovered with some excitement that several of the soups I know are almost identical to dishes described in medieval texts. I am full of respect for the constancy of the people who continue to prepare them to this day, and for their dignified loyalty to their own past.

Hamud / Chicken Soup with Lemon

An Egyptian favorite, hamud *has a versatile nature. Although generally served as a sauce for rice, it often appears twice in the same meal, first as a soup, and then again as the sauce. It is basically a a chicken soup with celery, strongly flavored with lemon and garlic, but other green vegetables find their place in it when they are at hand.*

Carcass and giblets of 1 chicken
3–4 stalks celery with leaves, sliced
2 leeks, sliced [optional]
2–3 cloves garlic, slivered
Salt and black pepper

Juice of 1–2 lemons
2–3 zucchini, sliced [optional]
¾ cup rice, boiled [measure un-
 cooked]

Collect a chicken carcass, giblets, and bones to make a rich stock. The giblets must be very fresh, and the bones and carcass those of a chicken prepared the same day, otherwise any meat on them will be hard and dry, and the marrow in the bones very stale. Crack the bones slightly to release more flavor.

There are two ways of preparing this soup. The stock can be made beforehand and strained through a fine sieve, the vegetables then being cooked in the clear broth. However, I usually cook all the ingredients together in the following manner.

Put the carcass, bones, and giblets in a large pan. Add the celery and, if you like, sliced leeks. (The basic recipe is made with celery only.) Add the slivered garlic and cover with about 9 cups water. Bring to the boil and skim the scum off the surface. Season with salt and pepper, and squeeze the juice of 1 lemon into the pan. Simmer gently for about 1 hour. Remove the pan from the heat and discard all the bones, leaving only pieces of chicken in the broth. Add the zucchini, if using them, and cook for 15 minutes longer. Adjust seasoning, adding more lemon juice if necessary. The soup should have a distinctly lemony tang. It is this and the taste of garlic which give it an Oriental flavor.

Add cooked rice just before serving so as not to give it time to become sodden and mushy.

Beid Bi Lamoun / Egg and Lemon Soup

This is a great favorite all over the Middle East. It is the Greek avgolemono. Egg yolks alone or whole eggs are used as a thickening for this very lemony soup.

7½ cups chicken stock [see below]
Salt and white pepper
⅓ cup rice, washed, or ⅓ cup
    Italian pastina, or ¼ cup
    tapioca

3 egg yolks or 2 whole eggs
Juice of 1–2 lemons
2 tablespoons finely chopped parsley
    or chives [optional]

Make a rich chicken stock with leftover chicken bones or giblets. If it is not strong enough, add a stock cube. Season with salt and pepper.

Add the rice, pastina, or tapioca to the boiling stock and simmer until tender. Beat the egg yolks or whole eggs and add the lemon juice, beating constantly. Add a ladleful of the soup to the egg mixture and beat well. Pour this back into the pan slowly, still beating constantly. Keep the heat under the pan very low, and cook the soup gently, stirring all the time, until it thickens. On no account allow it to boil, or the eggs will curdle. Taste and adjust seasoning, adding more lemon juice if necessary.

Garnish, if you like, with chopped parsley or chives, and serve immediately.

In Greece, fish and meat stocks are also used to make the soup, but this is uncommon in the other countries of the Middle East.

Melokhia

Melokhia is one of Egypt's national dishes. It is an ancient peasant soup, the making of which is believed to be portrayed in Pharaonic tomb paintings. The medieval melokhia seems to have been a little richer, incorporating fried ground meat and chicken balls. Today, only a few families add these.

This soup has the qualities of the Egyptian peasant: his timelessness and his harmony with nature, the seasons, and the soil. The fellah *is virtually the same today as he was when he first appeared in known history. (At least, this was so until I left Egypt twelve years ago.) He wears the same clothes, uses the same tools, and daily repeats the same movements as did the peasants depicted in the Pharaonic tomb paintings and described in Coptic legends. In his present lies the past. The fellah gives himself entirely to the soil; in return, the soil yields to him his food. Every peasant, however poor, has a little patch of ground for his own use, and in summer this is reserved exclusively for the cultivation of the deep green* melokhia *leaf (Corchorus olitorius). The leaves can be eaten fresh, or dried and stored for the winter.*

Peasant women prepare this soup almost daily. Protein stock is too expensive, so they cook the leaves in water in which a few vegetables have been boiled. The leaves give the soup a glutinous texture. The women cook the soup in large pots, which they carry to the fields on their heads for the men to eat at midday. When the work is done and the men come home, they eat it again at dusk with equal pleasure.

Melohkia has recently acquired a symbolic and patriotic importance in Egypt, for it represents the national, popular taste as opposed to the more snobbish and cosmopolitan taste of the old regime. Most families have their own special way of preparing it, and the proportions vary according to the financial means, position, and preferences of the people who make it.

Since fresh melokhia *leaves are hard to find outside the Middle East, I suggest that you use the dried* melokhia, *readily available in most Greek shops, instead.‡ I find it very acceptable.*

Here is a traditional recipe.

7–10 cups chicken, rabbit, goose, duck, or meat stock [see below]
Salt and black pepper
2 lbs. fresh *melokhia* or ¼ lb. dried *melokhia* leaves
2–3 cloves garlic
Salt
2½ tablespoons butter or oil
1 tablespoon ground coriander
Cayenne pepper

To make the stock: boil a whole chicken or rabbit, half a goose, a duck, or a piece of lamb, beef, or veal (I suggest knuckle of beef or veal) for 2 to 3 hours, removing scum from time to time. Season with salt and pepper. You can do this before you cook the soup.

Remove the bird or piece of meat, bone it if necessary, and discard the bones.

If you are using fresh leaves, cut off the stalks. Wash and drain the leaves, and spread them out on a cloth to dry. With a *mezzaluna* chopper or whatever chopping knife you are used to, chop the leaves on a board until almost reduced to a purée.

If you are using dried *melokhia*, crush the leaves with your hands into a large bowl, or use an electric blender, and pour a little hot water over them. Let them swell until doubled in bulk, sprinkling with a little more water if necessary. (If the leaves are not brittle enough to be crushed, try drying them out by putting them, scattered over a large baking sheet, in a turned-off hot oven for 5 minutes.)

Strain the stock into a large saucepan and bring to the boil. Add the prepared *melokhia* leaves and stir well. Boil for 5 to 10 minutes if fresh, and 20 to 30 minutes if dried leaves have been used.

Prepare the *taklia* (garlic sauce). Crush the garlic with a little salt, using more or less garlic as you prefer. Fry it in butter or oil (in Egypt *samna*, a clarified butter, is used). When the garlic is golden brown, add the coriander and a good pinch of cayenne pepper. Mix thoroughly to a paste and fry a little longer.

Add this preparation to the soup, cover the pan tightly, and simmer for a further 2 minutes. Stir occasionally to prevent the leaves from falling to the bottom, and do not overcook for the same reason. The *melokhia* should stay suspended throughout the stock. Taste and adjust the seasoning.

This can be served on its own first, as a soup, then accompanied by plain rice (which can be cooked in some of the stock), and finally with pieces of the meat used for making the stock, cut into serving pieces and reheated.

I like to make a richer stock by adding 2 leeks, 2 turnips, 2 tomatoes, skinned and quartered, 1 onion, and a clove of garlic at the start. When the stock has cooked for a few hours, remove the vegetables together with the meat, and proceed as described above.

Havuç Çorbasi / Turkish Carrot Soup

1½ lbs. carrots	7½ cups chicken stock
5 tablespoons butter	2½ tablespoons flour
Salt and black pepper	½ cup milk
1 teaspoon sugar	3 egg yolks

Scrape, wash, and chop the carrots into small pieces. Sauté until lightly colored in 2 tablespoons butter, and add enough water to cover. Season to taste with salt, pepper, and a teaspoon of sugar. Bring to a boil, cover the pan, and simmer until the carrots are very soft. Drain and mash the carrots to a purée, or use an electric blender for a particularly smooth, creamy consistency. Combine the carrot purée and chicken stock in a saucepan. Bring to a boil and simmer gently for a little while until the purée has practically dissolved in the stock. (Alternatively, cook the chopped, sautéed carrots in the stock, and blend all together in an electric blender.)

Melt the remaining butter in a separate pan. Add the flour and blend well together, stirring for a few minutes over low heat. Gradually add the milk, stirring all the time, and cook until the mixture thickens. Remove from the heat. Add the egg yolks one by one, beating constantly. Then add to the soup a little at a time, mixing vigorously. Adjust the seasoning, bring just to boiling point again, and remove from the heat at once so as not to allow the egg yolks to curdle. Serve immediately.

Ful Nabed Soup

This soup, made with the same white fava beans as ta'amia *(page 47), is popular in Egypt, where sick and convalescing people are encouraged to eat it to regain their health. It is plain but delicate in flavor, and highly nutritious.*

1 lb. white dried skinless beans [ful nabed]
2½ tablespoons olive oil

Salt and white pepper
4 tablespoons finely chopped parsley
Juice of 1 lemon

Soak the beans for 2 days. Drain them and put them in a large saucepan with 7–10 cups water. Bring to a boil and simmer, covered, for 1 hour, or until they are very soft. Press the beans and liquid through a sieve, or blend in an electric blender. Alternatively, mash with a fork or potato masher.

Return the soup to the saucepan, add the oil, and season to taste with salt and pepper. Bring to the boil again and simmer for a few minutes, adding a little water if too thick.

Serve garnished with chopped parsley and squeeze a little lemon juice over each individual bowl. In Egypt, this soup is served with Arab bread to dip in it.

Lentil Soup

Lentil soup is one of the great Middle Eastern favorites and has several variations.

Red, yellow, green, or brown lentils can be used. Although, as with split peas, soaking is often recommended for brown lentils, I find that this is not really necessary.

The soup can be made with water, but a meat or bone stock will make it considerably richer and tastier.

4 tablespoons butter
1 large onion, chopped
1 stalk celery with leaves, chopped
1 carrot, chopped [optional]
1½ cups lentils
7½ cups water or meat stock

1 marrow bone, cracked
Salt and black pepper
Juice of ½–1 lemon [optional]
1 teaspoon ground cumin [optional]
Small garlic-flavored croutons [see below]

Melt the butter in a large saucepan and soften the onion, celery, and carrot if used. Add the lentils, water or stock, and the marrow bone which, if cracked, will release even more marrow; bring to the boil and skim if necessary. Simmer gently, covered, until the lentils are very soft. This will take ¾ to 1½ hours, the cooking time varying according to the quality and age of the lentils, and whether soaked or not. In a pressure cooker it is about 20 minutes. Small yellow or red lentils will disintegrate; brown ones will not.

When the lentils are cooked, season the soup with salt and pepper and, if you like, add a little lemon juice and cumin. Simmer for a few minutes longer, then remove the marrow bone. Rub the soup through a sieve, put it in an electric blender, or squash with a potato masher to make a smooth purée. Return the soup to the saucepan, bring to the boil again, and either add a little water if you want a lighter soup, or evaporate by simmering a little longer to reduce and thicken it.

Serve with small croutons of bread fried in oil to which a clove or two of crushed garlic has been added just as they begin to turn golden brown. Garlic is not always used, but I feel that, fried and aromatic, it enhances the taste of the lentil cream.

A good variation for a rather liquid soup is to add about ⅓ cup rice and simmer for about 15 minutes, or until the rice is just tender. An alternative flavoring to the cumin and lemon juice is to stir in, just before serving, a *taklia* (garlic) sauce, made with 2 or 3 cloves garlic, as described on page 113. A Turkish variation. To a similar lentil soup without the flavoring of cumin or coriander add a liaison of 2 tablespoons flour stirred into 2 tablespoons melted butter over low heat for 2 to 3 minutes. Add 1 cup warm milk gradually, stirring all the time until well blended. Cook gently for about 10 minutes, then add to the soup. Beat the yolks of 3 eggs. Beat in a ladleful of the hot soup, and pour back into the soup gradually, beating constantly. Reheat, but do not allow the soup to boil again. Bread sprinkled with grated cheese (Kephalotyri, Parmesan, or Gruyère) and toasted in the oven makes an excellent accompaniment to this version.

Spinach and Lentil Soup

1 cup large brown lentils
1 lb. fresh spinach or ½ lb. frozen
   leaf spinach
1 large onion, finely chopped
3 tablespoons oil

2 tablespoons tomato paste
   [optional]
Salt
Pinch of cayenne pepper

Soaking the lentils is not really necessary, but it reduces their cooking time.

Put the dry or soaked lentils in a large saucepan. Cover them with about 7½ cups water, bring to a boil, and simmer for ¾ to 1½ hours, according to their quality and size, and whether they have been soaked or not.

Meanwhile, wash fresh spinach carefully and drain well. Defrost frozen spinach in a colander. Cut into pieces or ribbons. Fry the chopped onion to a russet color in the oil. Add the prepared spinach and sauté over very low heat. It will release a considerable amount of juice. Let it stew in this liquor, covered, for a few minutes, then pour both into the pan with the cooked lentils. Stir in the tomato paste, if used, season to taste with salt and cayenne pepper, and simmer until the flavors and colors have blended.

Add a little more water if the soup is too thick, season to your liking, and serve.

Turkish Spinach Soup

The traditional Turkish egg and lemon thickening gives this soup a creamy texture and a delicate tang which is in harmony with the flavors of spinach, celery, dill, and parsley.

7½ cups meat or chicken stock
Salt and black pepper
1 lb. fresh spinach or ½ lb. frozen leaf spinach
1 large carrot
1 stalk celery
A few celery leaves

2½ tablespoons butter
2½ tablespoons flour
3 egg yolks
Juice of 1 lemon
2 tablespoons finely chopped parsley
1 tablespoon finely chopped fresh dill [optional]

Prepare a meat or chicken stock. Stock cubes can be used. Season to taste with salt and pepper.

Wash the spinach leaves very thoroughly in several changes of water. If frozen spinach is used, let it defrost thoroughly. Drain and chop the leaves finely. Wash and chop the carrot and celery stalk and leaves. For a prettier effect, cut the carrot into matchstick strips. Cook the carrot and celery in the stock until nearly done. Add the spinach and continue to simmer for about 15 minutes longer, until all the vegetables are quite soft and cooked.

Make the thickening. Melt the butter, blend in the flour, and stir well over very low heat for a few minutes. Add a ladleful of the soup, beating constantly. Then pour the mixture back into the soup gradually, mixing thoroughly. Simmer over low heat for about 15 minutes. Mix the egg yolks and lemon juice, and beat vigorously. Add a ladleful of the soup and beat well. Pour back into the soup gradually, stirring constantly. Bring the soup to just below boiling point. Sprinkle with parsley, and dill if available, and serve.

Yellow Split Pea Soup

1½–2 cups yellow split peas
1 stalk celery with leaves, finely chopped
7½ cups chicken or meat stock, or water
Salt and black pepper [optional]

1 teaspoon ground cumin [optional]
Juice of ½ lemon or more
2 tablespoons finely chopped parsley
Fried croutons

Wash the split peas if necessary. It is sometimes recommended to soak the peas overnight, but I find this unnecessary. The larger amount of peas will give a thick, creamy soup, a favorite consistency in the Middle East.

Add the split peas and celery to the stock or water, bring to the boil, remove the scum, and simmer gently, covered, until the peas are very soft and nearly disintegrating. The cooking time varies with the quality of the peas, where they were grown, and their age, but it should take from 1 to 1½ hours (after 25 minutes they are soft but still firm). Use a pressure cooker if one is available. In this case, 15 minutes should be sufficient.

When the peas are quite soft, season to taste with salt and pepper. A teaspoon of ground cumin and the juice of ½ lemon, or more, may also be added. Simmer for a few minutes longer to allow the peas to absorb the seasoning, then rub the soup through a sieve or blend in an electric blender to achieve a smooth cream. Return to the pan, bring to the boil again, and thin with a little water if necessary.

Garnish the soup with chopped parsley. Small fried croutons are often served with it and sprinkled over each individual bowl.

Dried White Bean Soup

2 leeks	7½ cups meat stock or water
4 tablespoons butter	Salt and black pepper
¾–1 lb. dried white beans (navy, pea, or Great Northern), soaked overnight	

Cut off and discard the green parts of the leeks and wash the rest well, particularly in between the leaves. Slice and sauté in butter in a large saucepan until soft. Add the drained beans and stock or water. Bring to the boil, remove the scum, cover, and simmer gently until the beans are very soft. Do not season until they are almost ready. This may take from 1 to 1½ hours or longer, according to the quality of the beans, but a pressure cooker will reduce the cooking time to about 30 minutes.

Season to taste with salt and pepper, and simmer for a few minutes longer. Rub the soup through a sieve or blend in an electric blender. (I also rather like it when the beans are left whole but practically disintegrating.) Return the purée to the saucepan and bring to the boil again. Add a little water if the soup is too thick, or reduce and thicken it by simmering a little longer, if it is too light. Adjust the seasoning and serve.

Another version of this soup adds 2 skinned and chopped tomatoes and a tablespoon of tomato paste at the start of cooking. This colors the soup a gentle pink. The juice of 1 lemon is also sometimes added, and chopped parsley sprinkled as a garnish over each individual bowl.

YOGURT SOUPS

Milk, both fresh and sour, and particularly in the form of yogurt, is a very ancient ingredient in the cooking of the Middle East in general. In certain soups, yogurt is added at the end of the cooking and just allowed to become hot, without boiling. In this case there is little danger of its curdling. However, when yogurt is called for in the actual cooking, precautions must be taken to "stabilize" it (see page 81).

It is good to prepare one's own yogurt (see page 79), especially if making dishes which call for more than a pint. Besides the quite different, fresher taste, the cost will be considerably reduced.

Labaneya / Spinach Soup with Yogurt

An Egyptian soup traditionally made with the leaves of a plant of the spinach family called silq *(beet); the French call it* blette. *The soup is equally delicious made with spinach, fresh if possible, but frozen leaf spinach will also do. (I often find silq in Greek stores.)*

1 lb. silq [beet greens] or fresh
    spinach, or ½ lb. frozen leaf
    spinach
1 onion
About 2 tablespoons oil
1 leek or 3–4 scallions, finely
    chopped

¾ cup rice
Salt and black pepper
2 cups yogurt
1 clove garlic, or more, crushed
½ teaspoon turmeric [optional]

Wash the beet greens or fresh spinach leaves in a bowlful of water. Drain and cut into large pieces or ribbons, but do not chop them.

Chop the onion and sauté in oil in a large saucepan until faintly colored and soft. Add the spinach, stir, and sauté gently. A finely chopped leek or a few scallions will add a delicate flavor to the soup. Add them to the saucepan, together with the washed and drained rice. Cover with 5 cups water, season with salt and pepper, bring to the boil, and simmer gently until the rice and spinach are cooked. This will take about 15 minutes, and the rice should not be allowed to get too soft or mushy.

In the meantime, beat the yogurt with one or more crushed cloves of garlic. When the rice and spinach are ready, add the yogurt mixture to the soup and beat well. Heat but do not let the soup boil again, or it will curdle.

A pinch of turmeric added to the spinach and rice while they are cooking will give the soup a pale yellow, Oriental tinge.

Cold Cucumber and Yogurt Soup

This is identical to the *cacik* salad on page 64, only more yogurt is used to give a liquid consistency.

A Persian variation includes chopped hard-boiled eggs, 2 tablespoons raisins, and about 1 tablespoon finely chopped fresh dill, mixed into the yogurt.

Turkish Yogurt Soups

Here are two more soups in which yogurt is added at the end of the cooking. In the third one the yogurt is cooked with the soup.

i. A soup based on a meat stock which is thickened with a liaison of butter and flour.

2½ cups meat stock	Salt and white pepper
2½ tablespoons butter	5 cups yogurt
2 tablespoons flour	2 tablespoons dried crushed mint

Bring the stock to the boil in a large saucepan. Melt the butter in a small pan, add flour, and blend it in well, stirring for about 5 minutes over very low heat. Pour in a ladleful of the stock and beat well. Pour this mixture back into the stock, stirring constantly, and bring back to the boil very slowly to avoid making lumps. Cook, stirring, for 15 to 20 minutes, until the soup thickens, is very smooth, and has lost the taste of flour. Season to taste with salt and pepper, and remove from the heat.

Beat the yogurt in a bowl and pour it into the soup gradually, beating vigorously. Return the pan to the heat and bring the soup to just below boiling point. Do not allow it to boil, or it will curdle.

Serve garnished with rubbed dried mint.

ii. A chicken and barley soup with yogurt.

1 large onion, chopped
2½ tablespoons butter
3¾ cups clear chicken stock
½ cup pearl barley, soaked over-
    night

2 tablespoons finely chopped
    parsley
Salt and white pepper
3¾ cups yogurt
2 tablespoons dried crushed mint

Fry the chopped onion in butter in a large saucepan until soft. Add the chicken stock (made with stock cubes if necessary) and bring to the boil.

Add the soaked and drained barley to the boiling stock and simmer over low heat for ¾ to 1 hour, or until the barley has swelled enormously and is soft. Add chopped parsley, and season to taste with salt and white pepper.

Beat the yogurt. Add a little of the soup and beat vigorously. Pour the yogurt mixture into the soup gradually, beating constantly, and heat to just below boiling point. Do not allow the soup to boil, or it will curdle.

Adjust the seasoning and serve, garnished with dried crushed mint.

iii. Chicken and yogurt soup with rice.

3¾ cups chicken stock
Salt and white pepper
⅓ cup rice, washed
3¾ cups yogurt
1 tablespoon cornstarch dissolved in
    ½ cup cold water

3 egg yolks, lightly beaten
2 tablespoons dried crushed mint
2½ tablespoons butter

Bring the stock, seasoned to taste, to the boil. Add the rice, reduce the heat, and let it simmer while you prepare the yogurt. In another saucepan, beat the yogurt well and add the cornstarch dissolved in water. Stir well. This will stabilize it. Add the lightly beaten egg yolks and beat again. Put the pan on the heat and bring to the boil slowly, stirring constantly in one direction. When the mixture thickens, add it slowly to the chicken and rice soup, stirring constantly, and continue to simmer gently until the rice is soft. Adjust the seasoning.

Fry the mint gently in hot butter and pour a little over each individual bowl when serving.

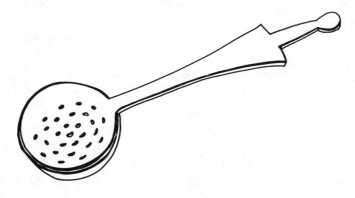

Tutmaj / Armenian Yogurt Soup

5 cups yogurt
2 eggs, beaten
4 oz. flat noodles, or some other form of small pasta

Salt and white pepper
1 large onion, finely chopped
4–6 tablespoons butter
3 tablespoons dried crushed mint

Beat the yogurt and eggs together in a large pan. Bring to the boil slowly, stirring constantly in the same direction. The eggs will prevent the yogurt from curdling. Stir in 2 cups water and add the noodles. Season to taste with salt and pepper. Bring to the boil again and simmer gently for 10 minutes, or until the noodles are well done.

In the meantime, fry the onion very gently in butter until soft and a pale golden color. Add the mint, stir well into the butter, and fry for a minute longer.

Pour the hot onion and mint butter over each individual bowl of soup as you serve it.

Eshkeneh Shirazi / Persian Yogurt Soup

A specialty of the city of Shiraz. This soup is given texture with chopped walnuts, and gains an unusual flavor from the herb fenugreek, called shanbalileh *in Iran.*

2½ tablespoons butter	2 tablespoons fresh fenugreek
1–2 onions, finely chopped	(or 1 teaspoon ground)
2½ tablespoons flour	5 cups hot water
½ cup walnuts, chopped	Salt and black pepper
	2½ cups yogurt

Melt the butter in a large pan. Fry the onions in it until they are a pale golden color. Add the flour and stir over very low heat for a few minutes until well blended. Add the walnuts and fenugreek. Pour in a ladleful of the hot water and beat vigorously, then add the rest of the water gradually, stirring constantly. Season to taste with salt and pepper, bring to the boil slowly, and simmer, covered, for 15 to 20 minutes, until the soup thickens a little and has lost its floury taste.

Beat the yogurt vigorously. Add a ladleful of the hot soup and beat well. Pour the mixture back into the soup gradually, stirring all the time. Leave over low heat until it comes to just below boiling point, but do not allow the soup to boil, or it will curdle. Serve immediately.

MEAT SOUPS

There exists in the Middle East an infinite variety of meat soups, almost as many soups as there are vegetables and legumes available. As with the repetitive and ornamental art of that part of the world, where motifs are taken and tried in every possible combination, so the ingredients for these soups are coupled, separated, and recoupled in various new combinations.

Below, I give a few of the basic soups. These can be varied by using different vegetables or legumes.

Although, in the past, lamb or mutton was always used, beef and veal are used extensively today for their different qualities. The more expensive cuts would, of course, be wasted, and it is generally stewing meat, lean or fat according to taste, which is used.

Shoulder, leg, breast, saddle, and shank of lamb will do beautifully. Rump of beef makes a marvelous soup, while shank gives a rich, gelatinous stock. If using veal, I recommend breast or shoulder, shank, end of loin or knuckle for its gelatinous quality. Marrow bones are always added. They are removed before serving, but the marrow is slipped into the soup, to be eaten with a piece of bread.

The meat is either left whole and allowed to soften and break up during the long cooking, or it is cubed beforehand. Meatballs, well kneaded and smooth, are often dropped into the soup toward the end of cooking.

Legumes, rice, and vegetables are added during the cooking, according to the time they require to become tender.

Chickpeas, beans, lentils, and whole wheat are soaked overnight and added to the soup at the start of cooking. Onions, leeks, tomatoes, celery, turnips, and carrots are cooked at the same time as the meat and bones. Zucchini and eggplant, spinach and beet greens are added a short while before serving, as they become tender very quickly and are not good overcooked.

Vermicelli and other pastas, and cereals such as rice which cook very quickly, are added just long enough before serving to give them time to soften. Small pastas and white rice take less than 20 minutes, but tapioca will take longer unless a quick-cooking variety is used.

These soups are sometimes seasoned very lightly with salt only; sometimes, depending on the region and the preference of the cook, they are seasoned gently or fiercely with allspice, cumin, coriander, ginger, or cinnamon, and black pepper, paprika, or cayenne. Some people add tomato purée, others prefer a little saffron. Garlic, lemon, and vinegar are also used for flavoring. In my own experience, meat soups have always been rich in meat and vegetables but rather gentle in seasoning.

Make them as a complete meal for the family, or as a first course before a light main dish. They can be exciting and delicious served at a late party with Arab bread, or *pitta* (page 364).

Rich Meat and Vegetable Soup

This soup and other similar ones in which the meat and vegetables are fried before being boiled are very rich and tasty, though heavier than they would be if they were only boiled.

1 lb. stewing beef, cubed
1–2 marrow bones, cracked
1 large onion, thinly sliced
2 stalks celery, chopped
2 leeks, trimmed and thinly sliced
3 tomatoes, chopped

2½ tablespoons oil or butter
Salt and black pepper
Pinch of cayenne pepper [optional]
1 large eggplant, chopped [optional]
2 zucchini, thinly sliced [optional]
2 tablespoons finely chopped parsley

Wash the meat and bones, put them in a large saucepan, and cover with 8 to 10 cups cold water. Bring to the boil and remove the scum.

Fry the onion, celery, leeks, and tomatoes lightly in oil or butter, adding the tomatoes last. Add the vegetables to the meat and bones. Season with salt and pepper and, if you like, a good pinch of cayenne; cover and simmer gently for about 2½ hours, or until the meat and vegetables are very soft. If you want to add the eggplant and zucchini, the former should first be sprinkled with salt and left to drain in a colander for at least ½ hour to get rid of its bitterness. Fry both the eggplant and zucchini gently, and add them to the soup about 20 minutes before serving. Simmer and adjust seasoning.

Add a little water to the soup if too thick. Crush the vegetables with a potato masher if you like them slightly mashed. Excess fat may be removed from the surface of the soup with absorbent paper or an ice cube wrapped in paper.

Remove the bones, garnish the soup with parsley, and serve with Arab bread or *pitta*.

An onion soup can be made in exactly the same way as above, substituting about 1 lb. onions for all the other vegetables. Another good combination consists of tomatoes, celery, and potatoes. Yet another uses potatoes and marrow.

Beef and Puréed Vegetable Soup

1 lb. stewing beef
2 marrow bones, cracked
2 stalks celery, chopped
2 carrots, chopped
3 leeks, trimmed and sliced
3 tomatoes, skinned and quartered
1 onion, chopped
Salt and black pepper

3 zucchini, sliced [optional]
1–2 eggplants, chopped, salted, and
    drained for ½ hour [optional]
¾ cup rice, boiled [weight
    uncooked]
5 tablespoons finely chopped
    parsley

Wash the meat and bones, and put them in a large pan. Cover with 8 to 10 cups water, bring to the boil over high heat, and remove all the scum. Add all the vegetables except the zucchini and eggplants. Season with salt and pepper, and simmer, covered, for about 2 hours, until the meat is very tender. Add the zucchini and/or eggplants if used, and cook for about 15 minutes longer.

Remove the bones and drop the marrow into the soup. Put aside the meat. Ladle off any excess fat, or skim the surface of the soup with absorbent paper. Purée the soup and vegetables through a sieve or in an electric blender. Return the puréed soup to the saucepan and add the meat and cooked rice. Bring to the boil again, adjust seasoning, and thin with a little water if necessary. (It is always better to start with less water than you need, since you can always add more later as it becomes reduced.)

Serve, giving a little meat to each portion, garnished with chopped parsley.

For a spicier soup, add paprika and cayenne to taste, and any other favorite spices, such as ground cumin, coriander, or cinnamon (about 1 teaspoon in all).

Meat Ball Soup

1 lb. stewing lamb or beef, cubed
2 marrow bones, cracked
Salt and black pepper
Ground cinnamon [optional]
1 lb. ground lamb or beef

½ teaspoon ground allspice
2½ tablespoons butter or oil
¾ cup rice
4 tablespoons finely chopped parsley

Wash the meat and bones, put them in a large pan, and cover with 7½ cups cold water. Bring to boil, remove the scum, and season with salt and pepper. A little cinnamon is said by some to "camouflage" the taste of the meat, by others to enhance it. I like to add ½ teaspoon. Simmer gently for about 2 hours, covered, until the meat is tender and the stock rich.

In the meantime, prepare little meat balls. Pound the ground meat to a paste with seasonings of allspice, salt, and pepper, grinding it at least twice or kneading vigorously with your hands to achieve a smooth texture. Wash your hands and roll the mixture into marble-sized balls. Fry gently in butter or oil until lightly colored all over.

Half an hour before the soup is ready, drop in the meat balls. A quarter of an hour before serving, add the raw rice, and simmer until tender. Alternatively, you can cook the rice separately, and add it to the soup just before serving.

Serve the soup sprinkled with chopped parsley and dusted with cinnamon.

This soup can also be colored lightly with 1 or 2 tablespoons of tomato paste.

Armenian Meat Soup with Burghul (Cracked Wheat)

1½ lbs. knuckle of veal [with bone]
1 carrot
1 onion
1 teaspoon ground cinnamon
    [optional]

Salt and black pepper
1 cup burghul
4 tablespoons finely chopped parsley

Wash the meat and bones, and bring them to the boil with 7½ cups cold water in a large saucepan. Remove the scum. Add the carrot and onion, both whole, and flavor with cinnamon if liked. Season with salt and pepper, and simmer gently, covered, for about 2 hours or until the meat is tender. Then remove the vegetables and bone, leaving the meat in the pan. Add the burghul and simmer for about 15 minutes longer until it is well cooked. Add more water if the mixture becomes too thick. The burghul will absorb a lot of liquid and expand considerably.

Adjust the seasoning and serve, garnished with parsley.

This soup is sometimes made with whole wheat kernels. In this case, buy the variety already husked. Soak overnight and cook with the meat until very tender. The cooking time varies, depending on the quality and age of the grain, but it generally takes about 2 hours.

WEDDING SONG *

Your father, O beautiful one!
Has so often screamed and shouted,
And lowered the price of your dowry,
And said, "My daughters are beautiful!"

Dügün Corbasi / Turkish Wedding Soup

Mutton is traditionally used for this soup, but it is advisable to use lamb.

1 lb. lean lamb, cubed	3 egg yolks
Flour	Juice of 1 lemon
4 tablespoons butter or oil	
1–2 marrow bones, cracked	GARNISH
1 carrot	4 tablespoons melted butter
1 onion	1 tablespoon paprika
Salt and black pepper	½ teaspoon ground cinnamon
Pinch of cayenne pepper [optional]	[optional]

Roll the cubed meat in flour and turn it in hot butter or oil in a large saucepan until lightly colored all over. Add 7½ cups water and the

* Maspéro, *Chansons populaires.*

marrow bones and bring to the boil. Skim off the scum and add the carrot, onion, and salt and pepper to taste. Add a pinch of cayenne as well if you like. Simmer gently, covered, for about 2 hours, or until the meat is very tender and the soup rich and full of flavor. Remove the bones and vegetables. The carrot may be sliced into thin sticks and used as a garnish.

Just before serving, beat the egg yolks. Add the lemon juice and beat again. Beat in a ladleful of hot soup and pour back into the soup slowly, beating constantly. Do not allow the soup to boil again, or it will curdle.

Decorate in the Turkish manner by dribbling melted butter mixed with paprika over the top of the soup tureen or individual soup bowls. Add the reserved carrot sticks, dust with cinnamon if liked, and serve immediately.

Fata

An Egyptian feast-day soup, traditionally eaten seventy days after Ramadan. It is made of the leftover meat and bones of a sacrificial lamb. The custom is to slay the lamb in the name of God, and to distribute the meat among the poor. However, the family of the donor must eat some of the lamb in order to benefit from the sacrifice; this soup is a good way of doing so.

1 lb. lean leg of lamb, cubed	2 or more cloves garlic, crushed
A few lamb bones, cracked	4 tablespoons butter
Salt and black pepper	4 tablespoons vinegar
⅓ cup rice, washed and drained	2 tablespoons finely chopped parsley
3 rounds Arab bread or 6 slices white bread, toasted	

Make a rich stock by boiling the meat and bones in 8 to 10 cups water. Bring to the boil, remove the scum, season with salt and pepper, and simmer until the meat is tender, about 2 hours.

Add the rice and continue to simmer for a further 15 minutes, until it is cooked but not mushy.

Arrange the toasted bread slices in the bottom of a large soup tureen. Fry the crushed garlic in hot butter until lightly colored and aromatic. Sprinkle with vinegar, bring to the boil, and pour over the toasted bread. Allow the toast to become well soaked; then pour the soup over it and serve, garnished with chopped parsley.

This method of serving soup over toasted and seasoned bread is a familiar one in the Middle East, and can also be used with stews. The toast swells and becomes imbued with the rich juices.

Shorbet el Samak / Fish Soup

Several Turkish fish soups recorded by Sidqi Effendi in the last century are on the following theme: a fish stock colored with saffron, flavored with vinegar, lemon, mint, and cinnamon, and thickened with egg yolks. Unfortunately, quantities are all given in piasters' worth and difficult to follow. However, here is a modern Turkish recipe with almost identical ingredients.

2 large onions, finely chopped
4 tablespoons olive oil
Several fish heads, bones, and tails *
4 tablespoons wine vinegar
2 tablespoons finely chopped parsley
Salt and black pepper
1–2 cloves garlic, crushed

¼ teaspoon saffron or 1 teaspoon turmeric [optional]
1 lb. white fish fillets: cod, haddock, halibut, etc., skinned if necessary
3 egg yolks
Juice of 1 lemon, or more
½ teaspoon ground cinnamon

Soften the onions in olive oil in a large saucepan. Add as many fish heads, bones, and tails as are available to make a good broth. Pour in 8 to 10 cups water and add vinegar, chopped parsley, salt and pepper to taste, the garlic, and if you like, a little powdered saffron or turmeric. Bring to a boil and simmer for about 1 hour, until a good rich broth is obtained. Strain through a fine sieve and return the clear stock to the pan. Bring to a boil again and poach the pieces of fish for about 20 minutes, until the flesh flakes easily with a fork.

Beat the egg yolks. Add lemon juice and beat again. Beat in a ladleful of the fish stock and return the mixture to the soup, beating vigorously. Heat the soup again to just below boiling point, but do not let it boil, or it will curdle.

* If you manage to get very large fish heads, you may find that they are so meaty that you do not need additional fish.

If you prefer to keep the fish slices whole, remove them while you beat in the egg and lemon mixture, and return them to the pan later.

Serve hot or cold, dusted with cinnamon.

Fresh Summer Fruit Soup

This fresh stewed fruit salad is eaten in Israel as a soup, sometimes accompanied by hot boiled potatoes. It is served hot in winter and cold in summer. Every few years some new fruit which has made its appearance on local soil for the first time is added, and most people have their favorite combinations. Here is one.

2 large cooking apples, peeled, cored, and thickly sliced

2 firm pears, peeled, cored, and thickly sliced

6 fresh apricots, pitted

6 fresh plums or greengages, pitted

A few black or red cherries or grapes, seeded

2 oranges, peeled, thinly sliced, and depipped

Juice of ½ lemon

Sugar

1 teaspoon ground cinnamon

Prepare the fruits and put them in a large saucepan with about 7 cups water, the lemon juice, and sugar to taste. Bring to the boil, cover, and simmer very gently for 10 to 15 minutes or until all the fruits are tender, removing the foam. You can keep the apples and pears separate and firm, or you can let them disintegrate, as you prefer.

Dust with cinnamon and serve accompanied by a bowl of boiled, or preferably steamed, potatoes, allowing one large or two medium ones per person. These can be eaten separately on a little plate, or crumbled into the soup.

This soup is sometimes thickened with a little gelatin or ground rice, dissolved or cooked in the syrup, and served cold. When individual fruits are in season and at their best, a soup can be made with one fruit only, such as apples or cherries.

EGG DISHES

Beid

Egg dishes are very popular throughout the Middle East. *Beid*, as they are called, receive the full Oriental treatment. Hard-boiled and colored yellow or brown, flavored with cumin, coriander, or cinnamon, they are sold in the streets with little cornets of rolled-up newspaper filled with a thimbleful of seasoning to dip them in. Fried or scrambled, they are enhanced with flavorings of garlic, onions and tomatoes, lemon, vinegar, or yogurt.

The Arab omelet, called *eggah*, is more like a cake. Thick and rich, with an infinite variety of vegetables, it is not unlike the Spanish *tortilla* to which it is undoubtedly related through the Moorish conquerors of Spain. Did the Moriscos introduce the omelet to Spain, or did they bring it back to North Africa after the *Reconquista*? It does not appear in early Arab culinary literature, so its origin is still a matter for speculation.

From very early times, however, eggs were used poached, hardboiled, or long-cooked in the *hamine* fashion (page 136), as a garnish for various types of dishes, especially stews. This custom has been continued to the present day. Eggs are still added in their shells (duly scrubbed) at the start of the lengthy cooking of a stew so that all the flavors and aromas of the other ingredients can penetrate the shells. They are usually peeled and returned to the pan before serving. They can also be opened over the stew just before serving to be "poached" in the sauce. This type of egg "garnish" was a feature of al-Baghdadi's medieval cooking, and it is still a feature of Moroccan cooking today.

Besides the thick *eggah*-type omelets, which make an excellent first course or main dish, a new type of light omelet, inspired by the French one, has recently been adopted in many Middle Eastern countries. It has, however, been adapted to local taste and acquired a Middle Eastern touch by the use of distinctively Middle Eastern flavorings.

Beid Masluq / Hard-boiled Eggs with Cumin

Prepare hard-boiled eggs in the usual way, packing several tightly in a pan to prevent them from moving about too much and cracking. Peel them. Cut in half and sprinkle with salt and ground cumin; or serve whole, accompanied by a small bowl of salt mixed with about twice as much cumin, to dip the eggs in. Serve as an appetizer.

In Morocco, vendors sell these eggs in the streets, sprinkled with the same seasoning.

Baid Mutajjan / Fried Hard-boiled Eggs

A medieval recipe from al-Baghdadi advises hard-boiling the eggs, then peeling them, frying them in oil, and sprinkling them with, or dipping them in, a mixture of dried ground coriander (1 teaspoon), cinnamon (½ teaspoon), cumin (1 teaspoon), and salt to taste. This type of egg is still sold in the streets in Egypt and Morocco today, and many families prepare these eggs (without the strong seasoning) as a garnish for meat and potato dishes.

Beid Hamine / Hamine Eggs

Great favorites of ancient origin.

Put the eggs and skins from several onions in a very large saucepan. Fill the pan with water, cover, and simmer very gently over the lowest heat possible for at least 6 hours, even overnight. A layer of oil poured over the surface is a good way of preventing the water from evaporating too quickly. This lengthy cooking produces deliciously creamy eggs. The whites acquire a soft beige color from the onion skins, and the yolks are very creamy and pale yellow. The flavor is delicate and excitingly different from eggs cooked in any other way.

Some people add ground coffee to the water, to obtain a slightly darker color.

My mother sometimes uses a pressure cooker to prepare *hamine* eggs in a hurry. In this case, it is advisable to hard-boil the eggs first, and then cook them under pressure with the onion skins. They will

be ready after about 1½ hours. Although this method produced reasonable results, the traditional way still provides better, creamier eggs.

Serve *hamine* eggs as an appetizer over a dish of *ful medames* (page 268), or as a garnish for meat stews.

Hard-boiled Eggs

During the numerous festivals, such as the *Mûlid el Nabi*, which celebrates the birth of the Prophet, the pilgrimage to the sacred well of Zemzem, or the *Cham el Nessim*, a festival in honor of nature originating in Ancient Egypt and signifying "breathing the new fresh air," people were in the habit of filling baskets with picnic food and spending the days and nights in public gardens or on pilgrimages to sacred places and the tombs of the saints. There, they would settle down to enjoy the contents of their baskets while they listened to reciters of romances recounting the tales of *Abou-Zeyd*, *El Zahir*, and *Alf leyleh wa-leyleh* (A Thousand and One Nights), and watched the antics of conjurers, buffoons, and dancers. Hard-boiled eggs have since time immemorial taken pride of place in these picnic baskets —beautifully flavored and sometimes colored, as described in the previous recipe.

In North Africa, ordinary hard-boiled eggs are sometimes peeled, then gently simmered in water in which a little saffron and salt have been dissolved. This gives them a brilliant yellow color. They make a good substitute for *hamine* eggs.

"When it has been proved that the evil eye has been given, steps may be taken to detect the guilty person. A common expedient is to hold an egg between the two palms and to press upon it as the name of

each suspect is spoken. At the name of the guilty one the egg will break." *—One of a large variety of beliefs and practices connected with the "evil eye."

Deep-fried Eggs

A fine way of preparing eggs is deep-fried in hot oil, garnished with a sprinkling of finely chopped fresh mint, dried *rigani* (wild marjoram) or oregano, and whole spring onions.

Baid Masus

A medieval recipe from al-Baghdadi for fried eggs, using vinegar.
"Take fresh sesame oil, place in the saucepan and heat: then put in celery. Add a little fine-brayed coriander, cumin, and cinnamon, and some mastic; then pour in vinegar as required, and color with a little saffron. When thoroughly boiling, break eggs, and drop in whole: when set, remove."

SUGGESTED QUANTITIES

3 tablespoons oil [any cooking oil will do]	3 tablespoons wine vinegar
1 stalk celery, chopped	Pinch of powdered saffron [optional]
Salt and black pepper	6 eggs
Pinch each of ground coriander, cumin, and cinnamon	

Scrambled Eggs with Vinegar

A splendid Arab way of making scrambled eggs.
Fry 1 or 2 cloves of crushed garlic slowly in plenty of butter until just golden, using a nonstick frying pan if possible. Beat 6 eggs very thoroughly, and season with salt and black pepper. Pour into the pan and cook over gentle heat, stirring constantly. As the eggs begin to thicken, add 3 tablespoons vinegar, one at a time, and keep stirring to a creamy consistency.

* Donaldson, *The Wild Rue.*

Beid bi Tom / Fried Eggs with Garlic and Lemon

2 cloves garlic
Salt
Juice of ½ lemon, or more

4 tablespoons butter
6 eggs
Dried crushed mint, to garnish

Crush the garlic cloves with salt and mix well with the lemon juice. Melt the butter in a large frying pan, or use two smaller ones. Add the garlic and lemon mixture. As the garlic begins to color, slide in the eggs, previously broken into a bowl, and continue to fry gently. Rub some dried mint in the palm of your hand, letting it sprinkle over the eggs. When the whites are set, remove the pan from the heat, sprinkle lightly with salt, and serve.

Beid bi Tamatem / Eggs with Tomatoes

1 large onion, finely chopped
2½ tablespoons butter
1–2 cloves garlic, crushed

5 tomatoes, skinned and sliced
Salt and black pepper
6 eggs

Soften the chopped onion in butter in a large frying pan. Add the crushed garlic. When it turns golden, add the tomato slices, season with salt and pepper, and continue to cook gently until they are soft, turning the slices once with a spatula.

Break the unbeaten eggs carefully into a bowl and slip them into the frying pan. Cook until set, season if necessary, and serve immediately with *pitta* (page 364) or other bread.

The eggs can also be stirred gently until creamy and thickened, but I prefer to leave them whole.

Beid bi Gebna Maqlia / Fried Eggs with Cheese

This dish is traditionally prepared in individual portions in two-handled frying pans and served in the same pans straight from the fire. You can, of course, use one large frying pan, or as many as are convenient.

In the Middle East, the hard, dry Greek cheeses Kashkaval, Kephalotyri, or Kasseri are used for frying, or Halumi, which is white and firm. The white cheese for which I have given a recipe on page 38 can also be fried once it has become dry and firm enough. As alternatives, Gouda, Cheddar, and especially Gruyère lend themselves well to frying.

PER PORTION

1 thick slice cheese	1 egg
Flour [optional]	Salt and pepper
1 tablespoon butter or oil	

Some people dip the slice of cheese in flour before frying it, but this is not really necessary.

Fry the cheese in hot butter or oil in a small frying pan just large enough to hold it. When it begins to melt and bubble, open the egg over it and continue to cook until the white has set. Sprinkle lightly with salt and pepper, and serve piping hot.

Fried Eggs with Chicken Livers

½ lb. chicken livers	½ teaspoon ground cinnamon
3 tablespoons butter or oil	6 eggs
Salt and black pepper	1 tablespoon finely chopped parsley

Toss the chicken livers in hot butter or oil in a large frying pan. Season with salt, pepper and cinnamon. Do not overcook the livers: their merit lies in their juiciness.

Break the eggs over the livers and fry until set. Season lightly with salt and black pepper, sprinkle with finely chopped parsley and serve immediately.

Chakchouka

This is a dish of Tunisian origin which today is eaten in most Middle Eastern countries. A similar Turkish west coast regional dish is called menemen.

1–3 green peppers, depending on size	Butter or olive oil
2 onions	Salt and black pepper
8 small tomatoes	6 eggs

Cut the peppers open and remove the cores and seeds. Cut them into strips. Slice the onions and cut the tomatoes in half.

Fry the onions and peppers in butter or oil in a large frying pan. Season to taste with salt and pepper, and let them stew gently in their own juices. When the peppers are soft, add the halved tomatoes and continue cooking until they, too, are soft. Taste the mixture, adding more seasoning if necessary. Drop the eggs in whole, and cook until set. Season again if necessary, and serve.

In some versions, the eggs are not left whole but stirred and blended with the vegetables to achieve a creamy texture.

Cilbir / Turkish Poached Eggs with Yogurt

6 eggs	1¼–2 cups yogurt
1 tablespoon vinegar	4 tablespoons butter
Salt	1 tablespoon paprika

Use fresh eggs. Poach them in the usual way.

A good method for poaching eggs is to dip them, still in their shells, in boiling water for a few seconds so as to set a thin layer of the white nearest the shell. This will prevent the egg white from spreading too much. Break each egg into a cup and slide into another pan of boiling water to which a tablespoon of vinegar and some salt have been added. Remove the pan from the heat and leave it, covered, for 4 minutes. Then remove the eggs with a perforated spoon. Do not attempt to poach more than 2 eggs at a time.

Arrange the poached eggs on a hot serving dish.

Beat the yogurt with salt to taste and pour some over each egg. Melt the butter and stir in the paprika. Dribble over the yogurt and serve.

EGGAH

I have classed the *eggah* as an egg dish or omelet, but this is misleading unless one describes its character further. The idea of an omelet, influenced by the image of the French version, implies extreme lightness, softness, creaminess, and a slight fluidity in texture. If one looked for these qualities in an Arab *eggah*, one could well feel disappointed and let down.

An *eggah* is firm and sound, rather like an egg cake. It is usually an inch or more thick, and generally bursting with a filling of vegetables, meat, chicken, and noodles, suspended like currants in a cake. The egg is used as a binding for the filling, rather than the filling being an adornment of the egg. For serving, the *eggah* is turned out onto a serving dish and cut into slices, as one would cut a cake. It is sometimes cooked in a rectangular dish, especially if baked in the oven. In this case, it is usually served cut into rectangular or square pieces.

These extremely popular dishes are used for several purposes. They are cut into very small pieces as hors d'œuvres or into larger ones as first courses, and they are also used as side dishes to accompany grilled meat and meatballs. Some are so rich with meat or chicken and noodles that they are a main dish in themselves, often served with yogurt and a salad.

An *eggah* can be eaten cold as well as hot, which makes it a good luncheon or party piece. It is a great favorite for picnics and pilgrimages during national holidays. The fact that a very large one can be prepared to serve several people, cooked in advance and warmed up or eaten cold, gives it a great advantage over the French type of omelet, which must be small, and eaten immediately after it is prepared to be successful.

As far as the pan is concerned, any large heavy frying pan which will assure an even distribution of heat can be used. One with its own lid, or any lid or plate which fits it tightly, is useful. If the dish is to be baked in the oven, any ovenproof dish will do, provided it has a lid.

When the dish is cooked on top of the stove, it requires from 15 to 30 minutes over very gentle heat, according to the number of eggs used and the type of filling, and depending on whether the filling has been cooked beforehand. It is usually cooked covered.

If it is cooked in the oven, the tray or dish must first be greased with butter. The cooking time in a 350° oven varies from ½ hour to 1 hour, again depending on the size of the dish and the type of filling. The dish should be covered to begin with, and then uncovered toward the end to allow the top to brown. When cooked, the *eggah* should be firm, even in the center.

I prefer the first method over heat.

Butter or *samna* (clarified butter) is commonly used to cook these omelets.

In Persia, the *eggah* is called a *kuku*, and plays a particularly impressive role in the cuisine. It is served on almost all occasions, as an appetizer, a first course, or a side dish.

Eggah bi Eish wa Kousa / Bread and Zucchini Eggah

½ lb. zucchini	6 eggs
Salt	3 slices bread, crusts removed,
1 medium-sized onion, finely	soaked in a little milk
chopped	4 tablespoons chopped parsley
Butter	Black pepper

Wash the zucchini and cut them into ¼-inch-thick slices. Sprinkle with salt and allow the water to drain off in a colander for about ½ hour. Pat dry with a clean cloth or kitchen paper.

Fry the chopped onion in hot butter until soft and just golden. Add the zucchini slices, and sauté until soft and lightly colored all over. Drain on absorbent paper.

Beat the eggs. Add the soaked bread, squeezed dry, crumbling it in your hand. Then add the onion and zucchini, and the chopped parsley, and season lightly with salt and pepper. Mix well.

Pour the mixture onto sizzling butter in a frying pan and cook gently over very low heat until the eggs are set, about 20 minutes. Dry and brown the top lightly under a broiler; or invert the omelet onto a plate of the same size and carefully slip it back into the frying pan for a few minutes longer.

If you wish to bake this *eggah,* pour the mixture into a buttered ovenproof dish and cook in a preheated slow oven (350°) for 40 to 45 minutes, or until well done. Cover the dish for the first 30 minutes, then remove it to allow the omelet to brown for the final 10 to 15 minutes.

Serve as a main dish with salads and yogurt.

Eggah bi Kousa / Zucchini Eggah

6 small zucchini	Butter or oil
Salt	Pinch of ground cinnamon
6 eggs	[optional]
Black pepper	

Wash the zucchini and scrape them if the skins are rough. Slice them. Boil in salted water until soft, and drain thoroughly. Beat the eggs, season to taste, and add the zucchini.

Cook as above, in a frying pan or in the oven.

A pinch of cinnamon, although uncommon, is liked by some people as a flavoring.

Eggah bi Ful Akhdar / Fresh Fava Bean Eggah

¾ lb. fresh or frozen fava beans	Butter
6 eggs	2 tablespoons chopped parsley
Salt and black pepper	

Boil the beans until they are tender, and drain them thoroughly. Beat the eggs and add the cooked beans. Mix well and season to taste with salt and pepper. Cook as above, in a frying pan or in the oven.

Turn out onto a heated serving dish and sprinkle with chopped parsley. Serve cut in wedges like a cake.

Eggah bi Betingan / Eggplant Eggah

2 eggplants
Salt
1 onion, finely chopped
Butter or oil

1–2 cloves garlic, crushed
6 eggs
Black pepper

Wash the eggplants and cube them. Sprinkle them with salt and leave in a colander for about 1 hour for their bitter juices to drain off. Squeeze, wash, and dry them lightly.

Fry the chopped onion in a little butter or oil until soft and yellow. Add the crushed garlic. When it begins to color and smells sweet, add the eggplant. Sauté with the garlic until cooked and gently colored all over. Then add the eggs, lightly beaten and seasoned with salt and pepper, and stir well. Cook over very low heat until the eggs are set, about 20 minutes. Dry and brown the top of the omelet under the broiler, or turn it over onto a plate and slip it back into the frying pan to cook the underside.

Eggah bi Korrat / Leek Eggah

1½ lbs. leeks
Butter
½ teaspoon sugar

Juice of ½ lemon
Salt and black pepper
6 eggs

Wash the leeks, trimming off the roots and removing the outer leaves. Cut off the tough tops of the leaves and wash the leeks again carefully. Cut into thinnish slices. Sauté in a little butter, then season with the sugar, lemon juice, and salt and pepper to taste. Let the leeks stew in their own juices until soft and lightly colored.

Alternatively, the leeks can be washed and trimmed as above, then boiled in salted water until just soft, drained, and chopped.

Beat the eggs lightly in a large bowl. Add the leek mixture, mix again and adjust seasoning. Cook as usual, in a frying pan or in the oven, and serve cut in slices.

Eggah bi Sabaneh / Spinach Eggah

1 lb. fresh spinach or ½ lb. frozen Salt and black pepper
   leaf spinach Butter
6 eggs

Wash spinach thoroughly, if fresh. Stew it in its own juice until tender. Drain well and chop. If you are using frozen spinach, allow to defrost, then drain it thoroughly and simmer in its own juice until tender.

Beat the eggs and add the chopped spinach. Mix well, and season with salt and pepper. Cook as usual, in a frying pan or in the oven.

Turn out onto a heated serving dish, and serve cut in slices like a cake. Accompany with yogurt and a salad if serving it as a main dish.

Eggah bi Lahma / Meat Eggah

6 eggs Salt and black pepper
1 lb. raw lamb or beef, ground Butter
A bunch of parsley, finely chopped

Beat the eggs lightly in a bowl. Add the meat, 1 tablespoon water, and the chopped parsley, and season to taste with salt and pepper. Mix well.

Heat some butter in a large frying pan. Before it has a chance to change color, pour in the egg and meat mixture. Cook, covered, over very low heat for about 20 minutes, or until the eggs are almost set. Then place a plate of suitable size over the frying pan, invert the omelet onto the plate, and slip it back carefully into the pan to cook and brown the other side. Alternatively, put the frying pan under the broiler to set and brown the top of the omelet.

This dish can also be baked in the oven in a buttered casserole or baking pan. It will take about ¾ to 1 hour in a slow oven (350°). Like others of its kind, it must be covered until nearly cooked and then allowed to brown for a few minutes.

Turn out onto a hot serving dish, and slice in portions like a cake. Serve as a main dish with yogurt and a mixed salad.

One modern variation uses veal instead of lamb or beef, which gives a more delicate dish. The ground veal is lightly fried in a little oil before being added to the eggs. Half a teaspoon of cinnamon may be added to give a light fragrance.

Eggah bi Ferakh wa Rishta / Chicken and Noodle Eggah

This magnificent eggah will do equally well as a first course or as a main dish. The cardamom gives a delicate and distinctively Arab flavor.

¼–½ chicken, cooked and boned, or ¾–1 lb. leftover cooked chicken
¾–1 lb. tagliatelle or flat noodles
Chicken stock, for cooking tagliatelle
4 eggs
2–3 cardamom pods, cracked
Salt and black pepper
Butter
2 tablespoons chopped parsley

Cut the cooked chicken into small pieces. Boil the tagliatelle or flat noodles in stock until just soft but not overdone. Use chicken stock left over from cooking the chicken, or one made by boiling the chicken bones for some time. A commercial stock cube will also do, though not as well.

Drain the noodles in a colander, discarding any which have stuck to the pan.

Beat the eggs in a large bowl. Add the chicken, noodles, cardamom pods, and salt and pepper to taste, and mix well. The eggs will act more as a binding medium than as the main feature.

Heat a little butter in a large frying pan. Add the egg mixture and cook over very low heat for about ½ hour, or until quite set. Dry and brown the top under the broiler. Unmold onto a heated serving dish, decorate with chopped parsley, and serve.

Ojja bil Mergaz / Tunisian Eggah with Sausages

4 tablespoons olive oil
4 medium potatoes, cubed or diced
2 tablespoons tomato paste
1 teaspoon–1 tablespoon Harissa *
3–4 cloves garlic
2 teaspoons caraway seed

2 teaspoons paprika
6 small, spicy sausages, sliced or
    halved †
6 eggs
Salt

Heat the olive oil in a large thick frying pan. Add the potatoes and sauté lightly. Add tomato paste, Harissa diluted in a little water, the garlic and caraway seed crushed together, and the paprika. Pour in just enough water to cover and cook over low heat for about ¾ hour. Add sausages and cook for a further 15 minutes.

Beat the eggs and pour them into the pan gradually, stirring constantly, until they set to a firm but creamy consistency. Season to taste with salt and serve immediately.

Eggah bi Mokh / Eggah with Brains

2 calf's brains or 4 lamb's brains
Vinegar
Salt

6 eggs
Black pepper
2 tablespoons butter

Soak the brains for about 1 hour in water to which you have added a tablespoon of vinegar. Remove the membranes under running water. Throw the brains into boiling salted water acidulated with a teaspoon of vinegar, and simmer for about 10 minutes, until cooked. Cut into slices.

Beat the eggs, and season to taste with salt and pepper. Take two frying pans and heat a tablespoon of butter in each. Pour half of the egg mixture into each pan and drop the sliced brains on top, spreading them evenly over the surface and letting them sink in. Cook over gentle heat until the eggs are just set, about 20 minutes. Then finish

* Harissa is a very strong, peppery preserve. ‡ It should be added with caution. Use a pinch of cayenne pepper if it is not available.
† Thin Yugoslav or Italian spiced sausages, obtainable in many delicatessens, can be used.

the cooking under the broiler; or, as usual, invert each *eggah* onto a plate, slip it back into its frying pan, and cook for a few minutes longer.

Kukuye Sabsi

The Persian eggah-*type omelets called* kuku *are generally baked in the oven.* Kukuye sabsi *is particularly Persian in flavor and texture. It is made with fresh green herbs and green vegetables, and sometimes with chopped walnuts as well.*

This is a traditional Iranian New Year's Day dish. Its greenness is believed to be a symbol of fruitfulness in the coming year, bringing prosperity and happiness.

Any favored herbs may be used in addition to the usual parsley, scallions, spinach, and leeks. (One may use either or both of the last two.) Dill, chervil, tarragon, chives, and fresh coriander are others. A few chopped walnuts may be included to add to the quality of the texture and flavor.

2 leeks	3 tablespoons mixed chopped fresh
¼ lb. spinach	herbs
4–5 scallions	A few walnuts, chopped [optional]
6–8 eggs	Salt and black pepper
3 tablespoons chopped parsley	4 tablespoons softened butter

Wash the vegetables, dry them, and chop them very finely. Beat the eggs in a large bowl, add the chopped vegetables, parsley, and mixed herbs, and a few chopped walnuts if liked. Season to taste with salt and pepper, and mix well.

Butter an ovenproof dish and pour in the egg mixture. Bake in a slow oven (350°) for 45 to 60 minutes, covering the dish for the first 30 minutes. The vegetables should be tender and the eggs set, with a golden crust on top. Alternatively, cook the *kuku* in a large frying pan like an *eggah*. When the eggs have almost set, brown the *kuku* under a hot broiler or turn out on a plate and slip back into the pan to color the underside.

Serve hot or cold as an appetizer or side dish, accompanied by yogurt.

Kuku Sibzamini / Persian Potato Omelet

2 medium-sized potatoes
3 tablespoons butter
6 eggs

4–5 scallions, chopped, or 1 bunch
chives, chopped
Salt and black pepper
2 tablespoons finely chopped parsley

Peel and boil the potatoes, and mash them to a smooth purée. Mix with about 2 tablespoons butter. Beat the eggs and add them to the potato purée gradually, beating all the time to achieve a smooth texture. Add onions or chives, and season to taste with salt and pepper.

Pour into a buttered baking dish and bake in a slow oven (325° to 350°) for about ¾ to 1 hour, or until set and colored. Alternatively, pour over hot butter in a large frying pan and cook over very low heat until the eggs have almost set, about 20 minutes. Then turn out onto a large plate and slip back into the pan to dry and color the underside.

Turn out onto a heated serving dish, garnish with finely chopped parsley, and serve cut in slices like a cake.

Another Middle Eastern potato omelet is made with thinly sliced potatoes, onions, and tomatoes. These ingredients are first sautéed in butter for 15 to 20 minutes. The beaten eggs are then poured over them and cooked over very low heat until they have set.

Omelets

A new type of omelet, inspired by the French example, has recently been adopted by many in the Middle East. It is nevertheless Middle Eastern in flavor, adapted to local taste by the addition of favorite regional fillings.

Make a plain French omelet, using not more than 4 eggs. Beat the eggs lightly in a bowl, and season only very mildly, to allow for the seasoning of the filling. Heat the frying pan. Add a tablespoon of butter and shake the pan to allow it to run all over the base. When it starts to sizzle, but before it has had a chance to brown, pour in the eggs, stir a little, and when they start to set on the bottom, lift the edge up with a fork and tip the pan to allow the liquid from the top to run underneath. As soon as the eggs are no longer liquid but still very moist on top remove the pan from the heat. Pour the prepared filling in a line across the center (only a little is required so as not to unbalance the omelet) and fold in three with a palette knife or fork. Slip the folded omelet onto a heated serving dish and garnish with a little of the filling.

The filling must always be prepared in advance.

Fillings for a 4-Egg Omelet

CHICKEN LIVERS

Chop 3 chicken livers finely, and cook gently in a little butter for 2 or 3 minutes. Season to taste with salt, black pepper, and a pinch of ground cinnamon.

ONIONS AND TOMATOES

Soften 2 tablespoons finely chopped onion in a little butter. Add ½ clove crushed garlic. When it is golden, add 2 skinned, chopped tomatoes. Season to taste with salt and black pepper, and cook gently until the tomatoes are almost reduced to a pulp.

SPINACH

Frozen spinach, either chopped or puréed, will do. Defrost ½ cup spinach and simmer it with a small knob of butter. Season with salt and black pepper. If you like, you can add a pinch of ground coriander fried with ½ clove crushed garlic.

Herb Omelet

4 eggs
1 tablespoon finely chopped parsley
1 tablespoon finely chopped fresh
    mint or 1 teaspoon dried
    crushed mint

4 scallions, finely chopped, or ½
    large mild onion, very finely
    chopped
Salt and black pepper
Butter

Break the eggs into a bowl and beat lightly. Add the herbs and onions, season lightly with salt and pepper, and mix well.

Cook in butter as above.

About 1 tablespoon chopped green fennel, coriander, or chervil may be substituted for the parsley.

FISH

Samak

"A remedy for a man who is 'tied' by his enemies, and made impotent. He must go to a quack, who will say: 'There is something written against you that has been eaten by a fish in the sea. I can release you from your trouble by obtaining the fish for a fee!' The quack finds a fish, writes a curse, perhaps on a piece of bread, puts it in the mouth of the fish and delivers it to the patient. The latter will be cured." *

In some parts of the Middle East fish is still believed to have magical properties. Tunisians in particular believe it to be highly beneficial. The day after their wedding, couples are encouraged to step over a large fish as an assurance of happiness and a protection from evil. Today, the shape of a fish has become a symbol. Embroidered on material and carved in metal, it is believed to ward off the evil eye. In Egypt, one felt compelled to eat fish for the first meal in a new home. In Persia, fish is eaten on New Year's Eve to cleanse the people from evil, while Jews display it in the center of the Passover table as a symbol of fertility, or as is done in some families, the head of the fish alone is placed on the table with bitter herbs, a boiled egg, a lamb bone, and *harosset* (page 434), in the hope that Jews will always be at the "head."

The medieval cooking manual of al-Baghdadi gives a few recipes for fish, both fresh and salted, but without specifying any varieties. Even today, recipes for fish can often be applied to any of a number of varieties. When asking which fish should be used for *cousbareia, sayyadiah,* or *blehat samak,* I was inevitably told "any fish you like" or "any fish will do." Nevertheless, certain fish are more suitable for a particular dish, if only because of their size and oiliness. Their distinctive flavors and affinities also make them natural favorites for certain methods of preparation; but it is always possible to substitute a similar one if a particular kind is unobtainable.

These recipes were, of course, originally evolved for fish from the Mediterranean and neighboring seas. Most popular are the red mullet, called *barbunya* by the Turks and *Sultan Ibrahim* by the Arabs; the

* From an ancient book of Egyptian folk medicine.

gray mullet; a fish called *morgan* or *arous*, which is the French *daurade*, and whose closest English equivalent is the sea bream; the sea bass, called *loukoz*; and the sole, called *samak Moussa* after Moses (because of its thinness it is said to have been cut in half when Moses separated the Red Sea). Turbot, cod, sardines, tuna, John Dory, gurnard, and swordfish abound in the seas of the region.

Of the freshwater fish, a type of trout called *chaboute* is fished in the Tigris and Euphrates rivers. It is usually smoked over a fire to make *masgouf*, a popular Iraqi specialty. Carp is a Turkish freshwater favorite, and shad is a popular fish found in the rivers of North Africa. However, fish from the Nile are considered hardly fit to eat, since they are impregnated with the strong taste and smell of the Nile mud.

Ever since ancient times, salted and dried fish has been known in all parts of the Middle East. This was originally done to preserve the fish so that it could be stored and taken on long journeys, or sent to regions far away from the coast. Today, it is prepared in this way primarily because people like it so much. Methods vary in detail but are basically the same. The fish is washed and cleaned and split open. It is salted inside and out and left to dry in the hot sun, or buried in the hot sand or mud for a few days to "mature." The result is called *fessih*.

Samak Meshwi / Charcoal-grilled Fish

One of the most excellent ways of eating fish is grilled over a charcoal fire. Swordfish *alla shish* or on skewers is a popular Middle Eastern dish. The fish is cubed, marinated in oil, vinegar, salt, and pepper, and threaded onto skewers together with slices of onion and tomato. It is then grilled over charcoal with frequent turning and basting with the marinade.

All types of fish, small, medium, and large, can be cooked over a fire. Large ones are usually sliced or filleted or fixed whole to the spit with a thin wire, and turned and basted continuously. For small or flat fish, fillets and slices, it is useful to have a double grill in which the two parts fold over each other, securing the fish between so that it can be turned without breaking its flesh or skin. The grill must be well oiled and preferably hot before the fish is placed on it, to prevent it from sticking. It should be placed about 2 inches from the heat.

Washed, cleaned, and scaled fish need only be sprinkled with salt and brushed with oil before grilling, but marinating enhances the flavor considerably. Marinades vary. The basic mixture includes oil and lemon or vinegar (preferably lemon), well mixed and seasoned with salt and pepper. Sometimes crushed chopped onions (pieces of onion squeezed in a garlic press to extract juice) and bay leaves are added, together with favorite herbs: marjoram, oregano, basil, tarragon, rosemary, fennel, thyme, and sage perfume the fish beautifully. The fish can also be slit open and stuffed with herbs for a more penetrating flavor. The skin should be slit in a few places to prevent it from breaking during grilling. Judge from the thickness of the fish how near it should be to the heat so that it does not dry out too quickly. Vary the distance from the fire if you like (and if possible) to achieve a soft, juicy interior and a crisp, brown skin.

Most of the fish available in England and elsewhere can be treated in this manner. Trout, sole, salmon, flounder, red and gray mullet, sea bream and sea bass, herring and mackerel are all very suitable. Sole should be skinned before grilling. Red mullet is particularly good grilled wrapped in aluminum foil together with its seasoning. Turks have a marvelous way of grilling sardines wrapped in vine leaves. Try this with other fish, but be careful not to let the leaves burn.

Finally, when it is not possible to grill over charcoal, an electric or gas broiler will also give excellent results, but make sure in this case, too, that the grid is well oiled.

Samak Maqli / Fried Fish

A popular way of preparing fish in the Middle East is to deep-fry them and serve them with a sauce or simply with lemon wedges.

Wash, clean, and scale the fish if necessary. Leave small fish whole but cut larger ones into thick slices. Pat dry with a cloth or paper towels and dredge with flour.

Fry in olive oil if possible (nut oil will also do) deep enough to cover the fish entirely. The oil must be very hot. Do not put too many pieces of fish in at a time, or the temperature will drop considerably and the fish will be soggy instead of crisp. As soon as the fish is in, turn the heat up to maximum for a short time to make up for the heat lost.

The pieces of fish take from 5 to 10 minutes' frying. Shake the pan occasionally to prevent them from sticking. Drain, sprinkle with salt, and garnish with chopped parsley and lemon wedges. Serve accompanied by one of the sauces for fried fish below, and a salad such as *baba ghanoush* (page 46) or thinly sliced eggplant or zucchini deep-fried until crisp (page 295).

Fried Fish with Cousbareia Sauce

This is an Egyptian regional specialty. Any fish that can be fried will do (small fish left whole, larger ones thickly sliced). Red mullet is often prepared in this way.

A fish weighing about 2 lbs.
Olive oil for deep frying
2 onions, thinly sliced
2 tablespoons oil
½ lb. tomatoes, sliced

1 cup hazelnuts, chopped
⅓ cup pine nuts
3 tablespoons finely chopped parsley
Salt and black pepper

Fry the fish as directed in the preceding recipe.

In a separate deep frying pan or sauté dish, fry the onions in oil until soft and just golden. Add the tomatoes and sauté gently until soft. Add the hazelnuts and pine nuts, and fry for only 2 minutes longer. Add just enough water to cover, stir in parsley, and season to taste with salt and pepper. Simmer for a few minutes longer.

Lower the pieces of fried fish in carefully and simmer again for about 15 minutes. At this stage the fish and sauce can also be cooked in the oven. Put the pieces of fish in a deep ovenproof dish, cover with the sauce, and bake for 15 to 20 minutes in a moderately hot oven (400°).

Beid bi Lamoun (Avgolemono Sauce) for Fried Fish

2 cups fish stock [see below]
Salt and black pepper
1 tablespoon cornstarch or flour

2–3 egg yolks
Juice of 1 lemon, or more

Strain the fish stock (made by boiling the discarded heads and tails of the fish with perhaps a celery stalk and a carrot) into the top of a double boiler or a thick-bottomed ordinary pan. Season to taste with salt and pepper. Mix the cornstarch or flour (I much prefer the former) with a little cold water, and introduce the paste gradually into the hot stock, mixing vigorously to avoid lumps. Cook gently, stirring constantly, until the sauce thickens and no longer tastes floury, about 15 to 20 minutes.

Beat the egg yolks in a bowl. Add the lemon juice and stir well. Add a little of the hot sauce, beating well, then return the mixture to the pan with the sauce gradually, stirring with a wooden spoon over low heat until the sauce thickens to a smooth, custard-like consistency. Do not let it come to a boil, or it will curdle. If you use cornstarch, the result will be more jelly-like and translucent.

Serve hot or cold, poured over the fish or in a separate bowl. This sauce is also delicious with poached or baked fish.

Khall Wa-Kardal

A medieval almond and vinegar sauce from al-Baghdadi which makes an excellent accompaniment to fried fish. Echoes of this sauce are found in the modern fish tarator *(page 166) and Turkish walnut* tarator *sauce (page 70).*

"Take sweet almonds, peel, and chop up fine: then moisten with sour vinegar until making a thin paste. Grind mustard fine, and mix in as required, together with a little *blattes de Bysance:* then serve."

SUGGESTED METHOD

Mix ¼ lb. (½ cup) ground almonds with wine vinegar and mustard to taste. Beat well and add enough water to make a smooth, thinnish sauce. Omit the *blattes de Bysance (Strombus lentiginosus)*.

This is equally good with deep-fried, poached, or baked fish.

Zemino Sauce for Fried Fish

A strongly flavored anchovy and garlic sauce—a Sephardic specialty.

2–3 cloves garlic, or more, crushed
2 tablespoons oil
1 small can anchovy fillets, or more,
   or 1½–2 tablespoons anchovy
   paste

1 tablespoon flour
½ cup wine vinegar
2 tablespoons tomato paste
Black pepper and salt

In a small thick-bottomed saucepan, fry the garlic in oil for a minute or two until it just begins to color. Add the anchovies, pounded if fillets are used, and flour, and stir well. Add the vinegar gradually, stirring vigorously to combine it smoothly with the flour paste, followed by the tomato paste diluted in about ½ cup water. Bring to the boil, stirring constantly, and simmer for about 20 minutes, or until the sauce is well cooked and thickened. Season to taste with black pepper, and salt if necessary, taking into account the saltiness of the anchovies. Pour into a bowl and serve cold.

A variation is to thicken the sauce with 3 tablespoons bread crumbs instead of the flour. Some people like to sweeten the sauce with a little sugar.

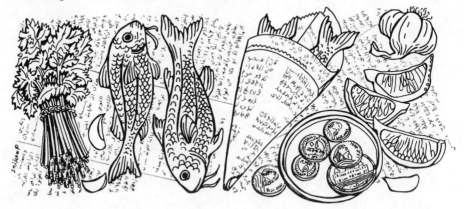

Fish Fried in Butter

Another, though less common way of frying fish in the Middle East is in *samna*, or clarified butter. This is made by melting butter in a cup over boiling water and passing it through cheesecloth to remove the impurities which cause the butter to burn and color. Small red mullet and Dover sole are particularly good fried in hot *samna*. They should be seasoned and dipped in flour just before they are gently fried on both sides.

Garnish with finely chopped parsley and lemon slices, and accompany with any of the sauces for fried fish above.

Sardines in the Algerian Manner

2 lbs. fresh sardines	Salt
4 teaspoons ground cumin	2 eggs, beaten
2–3 cloves garlic, crushed	Flour or fine dry bread crumbs
½ teaspoon cayenne pepper	Oil for deep frying

Wash the sardines and remove heads and tails. Slit them open down one side only, and remove their backbones. Dip the sardines, open side down, in a mixture of ground cumin, garlic, cayenne pepper, and salt. Stick the open sardines together in pairs, trapping the seasonings between them.

Dip the pairs in beaten egg, then in flour or bread crumbs. Deep-fry in hot oil, being very careful not to allow the pairs to separate.

I suppose a good alternative method would be simply to deep-fry the fish individually and not in pairs after they have been slit down one side, relieved of their backbones, flattened out and dipped in seasonings, then closed again.

You can try this recipe with other small fish, such as herring, smelts, or sardines. The dish also makes an excellent *mezze*.

Deep-Fried or Grilled Small Fish

Use small fish such as smelts, sardines, or herring. Remove the heads and gut the larger fish. (This is not necessary if using smelts.) Wash well in cold water and pat dry. Sprinkle the fish with salt. (Some people also like to rub them with a cut clove of garlic.)

Dip the prepared fish in seasoned flour or batter, and fry in deep hot oil, shaking the pan or basket to prevent the fish from sticking together.

Serve hot or cold, garnished with chopped parsley. If you like, serve one of the sauces for fried fish (above) with the morsels.

If an outdoor charcoal fire is available, arrange the fish in an oiled double grill and cook them over the fire, turning the grill over once.

Small Red Mullet with Garlic

A street vendor in Cairo used to sell these small red fish garnished with parsley and lemon wedges and wrapped in newspaper, to be eaten on the spot or carried home.

They were rubbed with crushed garlic, salt, and pepper, stuffed with finely chopped parsley mixed with a little crushed garlic, then lightly floured and deep-fried in very hot oil.

Blehat Samak / Fish Sticks

These make an excellent cold buffet dish or hors d'œuvre. They are also good served hot in a tomato sauce, accompanied by rice.

A few fish heads, tails, and bones
1 lb. fish: cod, haddock, halibut, sea
    bream, sea bass, or a mixture of
    any of these
2 small onions
2 bay leaves
1 stalk celery
Salt and black pepper
6 oz. white bread or 2 cups dry
    white bread crumbs

2 cloves garlic
2 tablespoons finely chopped parsley
1 teaspoon ground coriander
1 teaspoon ground cumin
1 egg
Flour
Butter or oil
Juice of ½ lemon, or more
Chopped parsley, to decorate

Ask the fish dealer to give you some heads, tails, and bones to make a stock.

Skin, bone, and mince the fish. Alternatively, boil whole pieces of fish until soft and mash them to a paste with a fork.

Boil the fish trimmings in about 5 cups water with a whole onion, the bay leaves, celery, and salt and pepper to taste. Simmer gently for about ½ hour; strain and reserve.

Slice the bread and remove the crusts. Soak in water and squeeze dry. Or if using dry bread crumbs, moisten them with water. Crush the garlic cloves with a little salt. Chop the remaining onion finely.

Put the minced (or mashed cooked) fish in a bowl. Add the chopped onion, garlic, parsley, coriander, cumin, and egg, and salt and pepper to taste. Mix and knead thoroughly by hand. Take walnut-sized lumps of the mixture and roll them into small finger shapes. Roll them in flour. Fry them in butter or deep-fry in oil until golden brown. Drain thoroughly; arrange in a large pan.

Pour in enough of the prepared fish stock to cover. Add lemon juice, bring to the boil and simmer gently for 20 minutes. Turn the fish into a large serving dish and cover with the sauce. Allow to cool. The sauce will become a jelly when cold. Serve sprinkled with parsley.

Some people like to color the *blehat* yellow by adding ½ teaspoon turmeric to the stock. A variation to this dish is to poach the fingers in a tomato sauce. Fry 1 onion, finely chopped, in a little oil. When it is golden brown, add 3 tablespoons tomato paste diluted with about 1 cup water. Throw in a bay leaf and season to taste with salt and pepper. Bring to the boil and simmer for 20 minutes. Add the fish sticks, previously fried in butter or oil as above, and simmer for a further 20 minutes. Serve cold, sprinkled with a little chopped parsley.

Fish in Olive Oil (Served Cold)

A Turkish specialty, popular throughout most of the Middle East. This makes a good first course or cold buffet dish. Sliced swordfish is generally used, but most fish are also excellent cooked in this manner.

2 lbs. fish: whole red mullet or
  mackerel, or a piece of a larger
  fish, sliced
Olive oil
2 large onions, sliced
2 green peppers, seeded and sliced
2 cloves garlic, crushed

1 lb. tomatoes, skinned and sliced,
  or a 1–lb. can whole tomatoes,
  drained and sliced
A bunch of parsley, finely chopped
1 tablespoon tomato paste
Salt and black pepper
About a dozen green or black olives,
  pitted [optional]

Scale and clean the fish. Fry it gently in a few tablespoons olive oil until lightly colored. Remove to a plate and reserve.

Fry the onions in the same oil until soft and golden. Add the sliced green peppers and fry until soft and sweet. Add the crushed garlic and fry for only about a minute more. Finally add the tomatoes, chopped parsley, and tomato paste diluted in about half a cup of water. Season to taste with salt and pepper, stir well, bring to a boil, and simmer for 10 minutes.

Lay the fish in the sauce carefully, making sure that the pieces are completely covered, and cook for a further 10 to 15 minutes until done, adding a little water if necessary. A few olives that have been blanched in boiling water to remove excess salt can also be added to the dish toward the end of the cooking.

Arrange the fish in a serving dish and pour the sauce over it. Serve cold.

Fish Plaki

—or poisson à la grecque, *as we used to call it in Egypt. Most fish can be cooked in this way: large fish such as gray mullet, sea bream, sea bass, and John Dory, as well as halibut, cod, or haddock.*

2 lbs. fish, cut into thickish slices
Olive oil
2 large onions, sliced
2–3 cloves garlic
1 lb. tomatoes, skinned and quartered, or a 1–lb. can whole
  tomatoes, quartered

Juice of ½ lemon
A bunch of parsley, finely chopped
Salt and black pepper

Fry the fish slices gently in olive oil in a frying pan until they are a pale golden brown color. Transfer to an ovenproof baking dish.

Fry sliced onions and whole garlic cloves until soft and golden. Add the tomatoes, lemon juice, and parsley, and season to taste with salt and pepper. Stir well and simmer for about 10 minutes. Dilute the sauce with a little water if too thick and pour it over the fish slices.

Bake in a slow oven (350°) for about 20 minutes, or until the fish is opaque and easily pierced with a fork.

The fish can also be left whole, in which case bake in a similar oven (350°) for 30 to 45 minutes. The flavor of this dish can be made richer by adding a teaspoon of dried oregano (or *rigani*, the Greek variety) ‡ and a bay leaf or two to the sauce.

Boiled or Poached Fish

Put the fish, whole or cut into steaks, in cold salted water. Bring to a boil slowly and simmer gently until it is cooked and its flesh flakes easily with a fork, about 10 minutes per lb. if whole. To avoid breaking a large fish when lifting it out of the pan, cook it wrapped tightly in cheesecloth. Use a baking pan large enough to hold it comfortably.

Alternatively, poach the fish in a *court-bouillon*—a stock made by boiling 5 cups water with ½ cup wine vinegar, a finely chopped onion, salt, a few peppercorns, a bay leaf, 3 tablespoons chopped parsley, and the juice of ½ lemon. Boil for 10 minutes before adding the fish.

Serve the fish hot or cold, garnished with lemon wedges and accompanied by "rice to accompany fish" (page 175) and a sauce: *avgolemono* sauce (page 158), one of the *tarator* sauces (pages 70 and 166), or the medieval *khall wa-kardal* (page 159).

Fish Baked in the Oven

Almost any fish can be baked in the oven, medium or large, whole or cut into thick slices, either in an open dish or wrapped in foil. Red mullet is a Middle Eastern favorite, but most other fish are treated in the same way.

Scale, clean, and wash the fish. Rub it generously with salt, pepper, and olive oil or *samna* (melted clarified butter—see page 160). The flavor of the fish can be enhanced by marinating for a few hours in a mixture of oil, lemon juice, onion juice (extracted by squeezing pieces of onion in a garlic press), and any favorite fresh herbs: bay leaves, oregano, marjoram, tarragon, and basil give a pleasant perfume. For those who like it, crushed garlic may be added for a faint aroma.

A few incisions should be made in the skin of the fish to prevent it from curling and, particularly if the skin is tough, to allow the heat to penetrate better.

The cooking time depends not only on the weight of the fish but also on its shape and whether it is whole or in pieces. The fish should be tested for doneness after the minimum cooking time specified. If done, its flesh should flake easily with a fork and no longer be translucent. Bake a 2- to 3-lb. fish in a preheated slow oven (325°) for 30 to 45 minutes, or until done, basting frequently with the oil.

A rather better way, to my taste, is to bake the fish in foil. Place the seasoned or marinated and well-oiled fish on a large piece of oiled foil. Wrap up and seal the edges of the foil firmly. Bake in a rather warmer oven (350°) and test for doneness after about 1 hour.

The baked fish is often smothered in a sauce at the end of cooking or when it is half-done. It can also be served more simply, accompanied by a sauce which is handed separately or poured over the fish just before serving.

Samak Tarator / Fish with Tarator Sauce

This is a great gala dish, particularly popular in Egypt, Syria, and the Lebanon. It is usually served lavishly decorated in a variety of brilliant colors and traditional designs according to local taste. Today it is sometimes replaced on special occasions by the French *poisson à la mayonnaise*, or decorated in a more European manner.

Choose a large fish such as sea bass or bream. Clean and wash it. Leave the head on, but remove the eyes. Rub all over with salt, pepper, and olive oil, and bake in an oiled baking dish or wrapped in foil as described above.

Serve the fish on a large dish on a bed of parsley or lettuce. Decorate it with lemon slices, sliced green pickles, black olives, radishes, fried pine nuts or almonds, and pieces of pimiento. Make an Oriental design, for example a crisscross pattern.

Serve cold, accompanied by bowls of *tarator* sauce made as follows:

2 slices white bread, crusts removed
1⅓ cup pine nuts [ground almonds will do if these are unobtainable or too expensive]

1–2 cloves garlic, crushed with salt
Juice of 1–2 lemons, or more
Fish stock left over in baking dish or foil, or water

Soak the bread in water and squeeze it dry. Pound the pine nuts. Add the bread and pound them together. Add crushed garlic, lemon juice, and enough fish stock or water to make a firm paste. Beat well and put through a sieve, or blend in an electric blender to a smooth creamy paste.

A delightful version of this dish is boned fish *tarator*. Prepare the fish and bake it in foil. Allow to cool. Cut off the head and tail neatly and set aside.

Skin the body of the fish and bone the flesh. Season to taste with salt and pepper. Place the boned fish on a large serving dish, patting it back into its original shape. Place the head and tail at each end and mask the whole body of the fish with *tarator* sauce.

Serve decorated with whole pine nuts or almonds, lightly fried, pickles, olives, and whatever else you like.

This method of boning and reassembling the fish is particularly useful if dealing with a very large fish that does not fit into the oven. It can be cut into manageable pieces instead, and then baked in foil as usual.

Samak Maqlu bi Khall wa Rahshi / Fish Fried with Vinegar and Sesame Meal Paste (Tahini)

A close relative of a modern Arab recipe appears in al-Baghdadi's thirteenth-century manuscript. It is made with salted fish. Try it with salt cod, or a smoked fish such as haddock, or with fresh fish. (I prefer it with the last-named.)

"Take salted fish, wash thoroughly in water, then dry, and fry in sesame oil. Put into the frying pan a good handful of whole dry coriander. Now take good vinegar as required, pour on top of sesame meal, and knead by hand, adding the vinegar little by little until the required consistency is obtained, not too light and not too heavy. If desired, some fine-ground mustard may be added, but this is not necessary. Take the salt fish out of the frying pan hot, put on top of the meal; then pour over it the sesame-oil remaining in the frying pan, together with the coriander. Sprinkle with fine-ground cumin, coriander and cinnamon, and also walnuts. It may be eaten either hot or old."

SUGGESTED METHOD

Al-Baghdadi has failed to describe the necessary process of desalting and "freshening" which must be done before salted fish is cooked.

To desalt about 2 lbs. salt cod, leave it in running cold water for 12 hours if possible, or soak for at least 24 hours in several changes of cold water. Put in a saucepan with a fresh portion of cold water to cover, bring to a boil, and simmer for 20 to 30 minutes. Drain well, skin, and bone. The fish is now ready for use.

Cut it into medium-sized cubes and fry in olive or other oil with 2 tablespoons whole dried coriander seed until colored and well done.

In the meantime prepare a *tahina* (sesame meal) sauce. Stir 6 tablespoons wine vinegar into ½ cup *tahina* paste (with a spoon rather than by hand). Thin to a creamy consistency with about ½ cup water. Add 1 tablespoon French mustard (or more, if you like) and mix well. Use an electric blender to achieve a smooth, creamy texture.

Just before serving, lay the pieces of fish over the sauce and sprinkle with the oil and coriander left in the frying pan. Garnish with a pinch each of ground cumin, coriander, and cinnamon, and 2 tablespoons chopped walnuts.

Uskumru Dolmasu / Stuffed Mackerel

A Turkish delicacy. A humble fish for a regal occasion. The skin of the fish is stuffed with its own flesh mixed with a rich filling. It is rolled in beaten egg, then in flour and bread crumbs, and deep-fried in olive or nut oil. It is delicious eaten hot or cold as an entrée or as a main dish.

6 small mackerel
2 eggs, lightly beaten
Fine dry bread crumbs
Oil

STUFFING
½ lb. onions, finely chopped
Olive oil
1 cup shelled walnuts, ground or
    pounded

½ cup shelled hazelnuts, ground or
    pounded
½ cup seedless raisins
2 teaspoons mixed spices [a mixture
    of allspice, cinnamon, nutmeg,
    cloves, and black pepper]
Salt
A bunch each of parsley and fresh
    dill or chervil, finely chopped

Clean the fish and cut off their heads. Snap the backbones off near the tail. Rub the skins to loosen them and to soften the flesh. Then, using your hands, rub and squeeze the fish, starting from the tail, forcing the flesh and bones out of the loosened skin as though emptying a tube of paste. This is quite easily done, as the skin is very strong. Any tears in the skin can be mended by sewing them up with a needle and thread. Another good method of emptying the fish skins is to loosen them as above, then, holding the backbone firmly where it shows at the head, to pull the skin down, turning it inside out. Proceed as above. Remove the bones carefully and use the flesh for the stuffing.

Prepare the stuffing. Fry the onions until soft and golden in 2 tablespoons oil. Add the nuts, raisins, spices, and salt to taste, and mix well. Add the boned fish and fry for 5 minutes longer. Stir in the chopped parsley and dill or chervil, and remove from the heat.

Fill the fish skins tightly with this mixture, closing the openings by sewing them up carefully. Dip in beaten egg and then in bread crumbs. Fry in hot oil until golden brown and cooked through. Serve hot or cold.

Sayyadiah / Fish with Rice

A popular Arab dish. Sea bass, bream, turbot, haddock, cod, or halibut can be used.

2 lbs. fish [see above]
Oil
2–3 medium-sized onions, finely
    chopped
Salt

1 teaspoon ground cumin or allspice
2 cups long-grain rice, washed
    [measure uncooked]
Lemon juice

Wash the fish and cut it into pieces. Heat 2 or 3 tablespoons oil in a large saucepan, and fry the onions gently until soft and transparent but still white. If you let them get dark brown you will have a brown *sayyadiah,* a good alternative. Add about 3 cups of water and simmer until the onions have nearly melted. You can leave the onions as they are or, if you like, reduce them to a pulp with a little of the liquid in an electric blender, or rub them through a sieve.

Return them to the pan, season with salt and cumin or allspice. Add the fish and simmer for about 15 minutes until well cooked but still firm. Skim off the scum as it rises to the surface.

Remove the fish and keep hot. Pour about 1½ cups of the stock into another pan and add lemon juice to taste to make a well-flavored sauce. Simmer to reduce it until richly flavored.

Add enough water to the remaining stock to make 4 cups of liquid. Bring to a boil and add the rice. Let it boil vigorously for a minute, then reduce the heat, cover the pan, and simmer gently, undisturbed, until the rice is tender, about 15 to 20 minutes. Allow to "rest" for 10 minutes.

Serve the rice heaped in a mound on a large heated serving dish. Arrange the pieces of fish over or around it, and pour the hot, lemony sauce over the whole dish.

Here is an Egyptian variation. Color and soften the onions, then fry the fish with the onions. Make a stock with the bones, head, and trimmings of the fish, simmered with 1 stalk celery, 1 onion, and 1 carrot. Strain through a fine strainer. Cook the rice as above, in its own volume of stock. Mix the cooked rice with the fish and onions in a baking dish. Garnish with lightly fried pine nuts and moisten with a little of the stock, considerably reduced. Bake in a slow oven (325°)

for about 20 minutes. Another way of preparing this dish is to make a fish stew and then cook the rice in it. Slice the onions into half-moon shapes and fry until golden. Add the pieces of fish and fry until colored all over. Add 4 cups of water and season to taste with salt, pepper, and ¼ teaspoon powdered saffron. This will give the dish a lovely pale golden color and a subtle aroma. Simmer until the fish is nearly done, then break it up into smallish pieces with a fork. Add 2 cups rice to the pan. Cover and simmer gently, undisturbed, until the rice is tender, about 15 to 20 minutes. Add a little more water if the mixture becomes dry before the rice is soft. Serve with a light salad.

Malih bi-Laban

A medieval recipe from al-Baghdadi for salted fish in milk.

"Take salted fish, wash and clean . . . then fry in sesame oil. Take out while hot, and drop into milk in which chopped garlic has been placed. Sprinkle with fine-ground cumin, coriander, and cinnamon. Eat either hot or cold."

SUGGESTED METHOD

Desalt and "freshen" 1 lb. salt cod as described on page 168. Drain and fry in olive or other cooking oil until golden. Cover with milk, add a clove or two of crushed garlic, and simmer for 10 to 15 minutes. Serve hot or cold, garnished with a pinch each of cumin, coriander, and cinnamon.

This recipe is particularly good when used for other smoked fish such as haddock which do not require the desalting process.

Malih bi Khall wa-Khardal

Another medieval dish for salted fish from al-Baghdadi, this time cooked in vinegar with mustard.

"Fry in sesame oil as described. Take out of the frying pan, and place in vinegar into which have been dropped fine-ground mustard and a little fine-ground coriander. Color the vinegar with a little saffron."

Desalt and "freshen" 1 lb. salt cod as described on page 168. Drain and fry in olive or other oil. When golden, remove and poach in ½ cup white wine vinegar with a little mustard to taste, ½ teaspoon ground coriander, and if you like, a pinch of saffron (although I don't feel this is necessary).

Smoked cod fillets and smoked haddock can be cooked successfully in the same way without the initial lengthy soaking in water.

Moroccan Shad Stuffed with Dates

This freshwater fish, found in the Sebou River, is popular in Morocco. It is fat but rather full of bones, and its delicate flesh is said to be at its best soon after spawning upriver. Boned shad can be found seasonally in America and is excellent. However, other oily fish such as mackerel can be prepared in the same way.

The dish requires rather lengthy preparation, which can be enjoyable from time to time. Dates are stuffed with rice and blanched almonds, and they, in turn, provide the stuffing for the fish.

A 3- to 4-lb. shad	Black pepper
½ lb. fresh dates [dried ones will do, but choose soft, juicy ones]	Ground ginger
	2 tablespoons butter
⅓ cup almonds, blanched and finely chopped	Oil
	Salt
3 tablespoons cooked rice	½ onion, finely chopped
1 teaspoon sugar	¼ teaspoon ground cinnamon, to garnish [optional]
½ teaspoon ground cinnamon	

If the fish has not been boned and prepared, wash and clean it. Slit open the belly, and remove as many of the bones as you can. If there are roes, leave them in, for they are a delicacy.

Remove pits from the dates and stuff them with a mixture of chopped almonds, rice, sugar, cinnamon, and a pinch each of pepper and ginger, kneaded with a little butter to hold it together.

Rub the fish all over with oil, salt, pepper, and a little ground ginger. Fill it with the stuffed dates. Place the fish on a large, well-oiled sheet of foil and sprinkle with the finely chopped onion. Wrap the fish up neatly and seal the edges of the foil firmly. (The foil allows you to omit the sewing up of the fish.) Lay the parcel on a large baking tray.

Bake in a preheated slow oven (350°), allowing about 15 minutes per lb. Then unwrap the foil and allow the fish to become crisply golden. Serve dusted with cinnamon if you like.

Ritza * / Sea Urchins

Hunting for *ritza* is a favorite pastime in Alexandria. It is a pleasure to swim out to the rocks, dive into the sea, and discover hosts of dark purple and black, spiky, jewel-like balls clinging fast to the rocks, a triumph to wrench them away, and a delight to cut a piece off the top, squeeze a little lemon over the soft, salmon-colored flesh, scoop it out with some bread, and savor the subtle iodized taste, lulled by the rhythm of the sea.

Poached Prawns or Shrimp

2½ lbs. fresh prawns or shrimp in their shells
Salt
3 celery stalks with leaves, sliced

A small bunch of scallions, sliced, or
1 onion, chopped
2 cloves garlic, slivered
Juice of ½–1 lemon
Salt and black pepper

Wash the prawns or shrimp well and poach in a stock made by simmering the remaining ingredients in 7 to 10 cups sea water or salted fresh water (no salt is required if sea water is used). Simmer the prawns or shrimp for about 5 minutes, or until pink. Do not overcook. Drain well and allow to cool.

Shell the prawns or shrimp or allow each person to shell his own: split along the back with a small pointed knife and remove the skin. Remove the head and pull away the shell from the tail.

Serve accompanied, if you like, by a dressing of olive oil, lemon juice, salt and black pepper, mixed to taste.

* After the Greek name.

Prawns or Shrimp with Rice

2½ lbs. prawns or shrimp, shelled, fresh, or frozen
1 onion, sliced into half-moon shapes
2 leeks, thinly sliced
1 celery stalk, thinly sliced
2–3 tomatoes, skinned and chopped
1 clove garlic, slivered
4 tablespoons butter or oil
1 6-oz. can tomato paste, or less
½ teaspoon sugar [optional]
Salt and black pepper
3 tablespoons finely chopped parsley
3 cups long-grain rice
2½ tablespoons butter

Shell, clean, and wash the prawns or shrimp carefully. If using frozen ones, defrost them slowly and thoroughly.

Soften the vegetables in butter or oil. Add tomato paste and season to taste with sugar, salt, and pepper. Add parsley and cover with 2 to 4 cups water (some people like to use white wine instead of water, though this is uncommon). Bring to the boil, reduce the heat, and simmer gently, covered, until the sauce is reduced and rich, about 45 minutes. Add the prawns or shrimp and simmer for 5 to 8 minutes longer (frozen ones need less time).

Pour this sauce into the center and over the crest of a ring of plain rice, prepared according to one of the recipes on pages 339–40, pressed into a mold and kept hot until ready to turn out into a hot dish.

Deep-Fried Prawns or Shrimp

Shell and devein the fresh prawns or shrimp. Wash in cold water. Poach in sea water or salted fresh water for 5 minutes, drain well, and pat dry. Season to taste with salt and pepper.

Roll in flour or dip first in lightly beaten egg and then roll in flour. Alternatively, use the batter given for mussels on page 55 to coat the prawns.

Deep-fry in hot oil until golden. Remove and drain on absorbent paper.

Serve garnished with lemon wedges and accompanied by a *tarator* sauce made with pine nuts or almonds (page 166), or with walnuts (page 70).

Boiled Lobster

Poach lobster in boiling sea water or the stock given for poached prawns or shrimp above.

Cook vigorously for 5 minutes, then reduce the heat and simmer about 3 minutes for each pound. Drain, and serve hot or cold.

Serve with lemon wedges and a dressing of olive oil, lemon juice, salt and pepper, mixed to taste.

Lobster with Rice

Prepare the sauce given in the recipe for prawns or shrimp with rice (page 174). When well cooked, add the meat of a freshly boiled lobster and simmer for a few minutes longer.

Serve with a ring of rice as described in the same recipe.

Rice to Accompany Fish

Most Middle Eastern fish dishes are accompanied by rice. The traditional Arab rice for fish is cooked with pine nuts and colored pale yellow with saffron.

Oil
¼–½ teaspoon powdered saffron
2½ cups long-grain rice
Salt and black pepper

⅓ cup pine nuts
2 onions, sliced into half-moon
    shapes

Heat 2 tablespoons oil in a heavy saucepan. Stir in the saffron and add the rice. Sprinkle with salt and pepper and stir well over high heat until the rice acquires a yellow, transparent glow. Add 5 cups boiling water. Bring to a vigorous boil, cover the pan, and simmer very gently, undisturbed, until the rice is tender and fluffy, and the water has been absorbed, about 20 minutes.

In the meantime, fry the pine nuts in a little oil for about 2 minutes until golden. Remove them and fry the onions in the same oil until very soft, and brown rather than golden.

Serve the rice in a mound, garnished with fried pine nuts and onions.

POULTRY

In the villages of most Middle Eastern countries, where it requires an *eid el kibir* or very important feast to kill a lamb, poultry is the usual festive dish. Geese, ducks, hens, or fat chickens are the festival queens.

Often they are boiled first to provide the legendary wedding or other festive soups, and in Egypt, the *melokhia* (see page 111). Sometimes they are filled with rich stuffings before they are boiled. At all times they are served beautifully decorated and flavored in an extraordinary variety of ways.

In his *Kitab al-ifadah wa'l-l'tibar*, written in 1204 after a visit to Egypt, Abd al-Latif al-Baghdadi gives a description of the food of the time:

"As for the stews of the Egyptians, those which are sour or ordinary have nothing in particular, or very little, different from those used elsewhere, but on the contrary, their sweet stews are of a singular kind, for they cook a chicken with all sorts of sweet substances. Here is how they prepare the food: they boil a fowl, then put it in a julep, place under it crushed hazelnuts or pistachio nuts, poppy seeds, or rose hips, and cook the whole until it thickens. Then they add spices and remove it from the fire.

"These stews are surnamed *fistakiyyeh* (pistachio), *bondokiyyeh* (hazelnut), *khashkhaschiyyeh* (poppy) or *wardiyeh* (rose hip) or *sitt alnoubeh* (purslane, called 'Nubian woman' because of its black colour). There are many skilful ways of preparing this kind of food which would entail too great detail to describe." *

Maxime Rodinson, in his description of the manuscript of the *Kitab al Wusla il al Habib*, which is believed to have been written in the twelfth century, notes more than 500 recipes for chicken, of which he has unfortunately fully translated and explained only a few. Among them are:

* Zand and Videan, *The Eastern Key.*

Minced chicken and lamb rissoles
Stuffed boned chicken
Chicken with vinegar
Chicken boiled with crushed chickpeas
Chicken with lemon or pomegranate sauce
Chicken with rhubarb or quinces
Chicken with hard-boiled egg yolks and herbs
Chicken with pistachio nuts; with hazelnuts, walnuts, almonds, or
   poppy seeds; with parsley, oranges, or rose jam; with plum jelly,
   yogurt, or mulberries
Chicken with chickpeas, onions and cinnamon, or spiced rice
Chicken with pistachios, perfumed with rose water and musk
A loaf of bread stuffed with chicken

Luscious ingredients for recipes which are echoed in the dishes of today—in the fruit stews of Morocco, the walnut and hazelnut sauces of Turkey and Syria, and the chickpeas, onions, and lemons of Egypt.

Every day, the streetcars and buses coming into the towns from the villages are crowded with peasants carrying crates of live, cackling poultry. The chickens are killed and plucked at the market or poultry shops. In Egypt, it is common practice for peasants and shopkeepers to push a large handful of corn down the birds' throats before killing them so that they weigh more.

Here is a little story of Goha, the folk hero, buffoon, and jester of the Middle East. In this story, Goha is a peasant coming to a strange and hostile town under Turkish rule to sell chickens at the *soukh* or market.

He was stopped at the gates of the town by the Turkish police, who asked what he fed his chickens. "Wheat," said Goha. The police then demanded to see his receipt for the taxes paid on the wheat he had used. Not having heard of, or paid, any taxes on wheat, Goha was dragged off to the *qadi* (magistrate) and forced to pay a fine of five piasters, more than half of what he expected to get for his chickens.

The next time he journeyed to the *soukh*, he declared that he had fed the chickens on barley, to escape the fine. It turned out that barley, too, was taxable and he was fined again.

The incident was repeated several times. Goha tried chickpeas, millet, and beans, but it turned out that all of these were taxable.

Finally, in desperation, having been stopped yet again by the police and asked what his chickens had been fed on, he replied, "Oh! I just give each one a *maleem* (farthing) a day and tell him to buy what he likes!"

Although many of the following recipes are for chicken "stews" and a boiling hen could be used, one doesn't find them in the market today. I therefore suggest using roasting chickens for all dishes.

Grilled Chicken

My favorite way of preparing chicken is to grill it over charcoal. It can also be grilled under an oven broiler, but then the delicious aroma of the charcoal is lost.

Only young chickens or broilers should be treated in this way. Cut into serving pieces and marinate for at least 1 hour (Persians always marinate overnight) in the marinade below. Some people, particularly the Turks, like to flavor it with a little cinnamon instead of the garlic and lemon.

MARINADE
Juice of 1 lemon
½ onion, chopped and crushed to extract juices

1–2 cloves garlic, crushed [optional]
3 tablespoons olive oil
Salt and black pepper

Place the marinated chicken pieces on an oiled grill over a charcoal fire that is already very hot and glowing, and no longer smoking. Grill until the pieces are golden brown all over but still pale and tender inside, basting with marinade and turning once.

A delicious variation is to marinate the chicken pieces for as long as possible in yogurt flavored with crushed garlic, salt, and pepper. Sometimes dried crushed mint is added, and a little paprika is mixed with the yogurt to give the chicken an appetizing red color. Yogurt used in this way does not contribute very much to the flavor, but serves to soften the flesh of the chicken, rather like the Indian manner of preparing *tandoori* chicken.

Tavuk Jölesi / Jellied Chicken

This modern Turkish way of preparing chicken makes a particularly attractive party dish. It is a clear chicken jelly with a layer of boned chicken pieces suspended in the middle.

1 large roasting chicken [4–5 lbs.]
1 carrot
1 onion
1 stalk celery
Salt and white pepper
Juice of ½ lemon, or more
1 egg white [plus a little crushed eggshell] to clarify stock

½ oz. (2 envelopes) powdered gelatin
4 tablespoons finely chopped parsley
2 tablespoons blanched flaked almonds

Put the cleaned chicken in a large saucepan and cover with about 7½ cups water. Add the vegetables, salt, pepper, and lemon juice, and bring to the boil. Skim off scum and simmer gently for ¾ to 1 hour, or until the chicken is very tender.

As soon as it is cool enough to handle, remove the chicken, bone it, and cut the meat into neat pieces. Cool stock a little, and remove the vegetables.

To clarify the stock, beat an egg white lightly, add to the stock, and heat very gently, beating with a wooden spoon. If possible, add a little crushed eggshell as well. Simmer for 10 minutes, but do not allow to come to a fast boil. Then remove from the heat and leave for a further 10 minutes. The egg white will collect all the impurities and rise to form a crust on the surface of the stock. Strain the stock through a sieve or colander lined with wet muslin.

Measure it. Reduce it if necessary to about 4 cups. Taste and adjust the seasoning. Add ¼ oz. powdered gelatin (soaked in a little water) for every 2 cups of stock. Beat vigorously until it has dissolved. Allow to cool.

Rinse a large, long mold with cold water and pour in half of the stock mixture. Chill until set. Lay the pieces of chicken over it and cover with a little of the stock mixture. (Not all, or some of the chicken will float to the top.) Chill until set. Add the remaining stock and chill again until firmly set.

To turn out, dip the bottom of the mold in hot water for a few seconds only. Run a knife around the sides. Place a large plate over the top of the mold and quickly turn upside down. Remove the mold carefully.

Serve attractively decorated with chopped parsley and blanched almonds.

An alternative method is to mix the parsley and almonds with the first portion of stock and gelatin before pouring it into the mold.

Chicken Awsat / Chicken in a Bread Loaf

This is a medieval recipe from the Kitab al Wusla il al Habib, *where it is also called "Egyptian chicken." It is a loaf of bread from which the soft inside has been removed to make room for a stuffing of boned chicken meat and livers.*

I am giving my own interpretation and quantities of ingredients as I have prepared them.

1 medium loaf bread with an attractive shape [rectangular or cottage]
1 medium chicken, boiled or sofrito [see next recipe]
½ lb. chicken livers
Oil [originally sesame oil, but corn or nut will do well]
Chicken stock
¼ teaspoon ground allspice
Salt and black pepper
1–2 oz. pistachio nuts, chopped
4 tablespoons finely chopped parsley
1 teaspoon dried crushed mint
Juice of ½ lemon
½ teaspoon rose water [optional]
Sprigs of parsley and other fresh herbs

Cut a slice off the top of the loaf and put it aside to serve as a lid. Carefully remove all the pith from the loaf, leaving the crust intact.

Bone and chop the cooked chicken. Clean the chicken livers and sauté gently in a little oil for 3 to 4 minutes. Add about ⅓ cup of the stock in which the chicken was cooked, and season to taste with allspice, salt, and pepper. (A little brandy or sherry could be used instead of chicken stock, but this does not, of course, appear in the original recipe.) Mash or pound the livers to a smooth paste, using an electric blender if you have one.

Mix the liver pâté with the chopped chicken in a large bowl. Add pistachio nuts, parsley, mint, and lemon juice. Mix well and taste for seasoning, adding more salt and pepper if necessary. Knead the mixture vigorously until well blended, and add a little more stock if too dry.

Moisten the bread shell with stock to make it soft and easy to cut. The original recipe recommends sprinkling with a few drops of rose water, but I do not care for its perfume in this particular dish. Fill the shell with the chicken and liver mixture, packing it tightly. Cover with the lid, which has also been sprinkled with stock to soften it.

Chill in the refrigerator until ready to serve.

This is a rather beautiful dish. Decorate it with sprigs of parsley and other fresh herbs. Serve cut in slices and accompanied by a light salad. An orange salad (page 67) will do well as a second salad.

Cold Chicken Sofrito

1 large roasting chicken [4–5 lbs.]	½ teaspoon turmeric
2½ tablespoons corn oil	Salt and white pepper
Juice of ½ lemon	1 cardamom pod, cracked

Wash the chicken and wipe it dry.

In a large saucepan or flameproof casserole put the oil, lemon juice, a cup of water, turmeric, salt and white pepper, and the cardamom pod. Bring to the boil, then place the chicken in the pan. Cover and cook over very low heat, turning the chicken over frequently and adding another cup of water as the juices are absorbed. Continue cooking until the chicken is very soft and tender. Adjust the seasoning. Remove the pan from the heat and allow to cool.

Divide the chicken into pieces, removing the larger bones, and arrange in a deep serving dish. Pour the sauce over it and allow it to become quite cold. On cooling, it will become a pale, lemony jelly and the chicken will be a very delicate off-white. If you prefer a clear jelly, simply skim any fat off the surface before pouring it over the chicken. Use absorbent paper to remove the last traces. It is unnecessary to clarify with egg whites.

This is a very simple and delicate way of cooking chicken. Serve as part of a cold buffet, or for a family meal in summer, accompanied by salads. The ground almond salad on page 77 does particularly well.

Chicken with Chickpeas

A Middle Eastern dish which is particularly popular in Morocco.

1 large roasting chicken [about 4 lbs.]
2½ tablespoons corn oil
1 onion, finely chopped
1 teaspoon turmeric

½ lb. (1½ cups) chickpeas, soaked overnight
Juice of 1 lemon, or more
2–4 cloves garlic, crushed
Salt
Black pepper or a pinch of cayenne

Wipe the chicken inside and out with a damp cloth.

Heat the oil in a saucepan or deep flameproof casserole (large enough to hold the chicken). Fry the chopped onion in the oil until soft and golden. Sprinkle with turmeric and mix well. Add the chicken and sauté gently, turning it until it is a dark yellow color all over. Add 2½ cups of water, the soaked and drained chickpeas, lemon juice, and garlic, and season with salt and pepper. Bring to the boil and simmer gently, covered, for 1 hour or longer, until the chicken is very tender, the chickpeas soft, yellow, and lemony, and the liquid very much reduced. Adjust seasoning and serve, cut up into pieces.

Moroccan Tagine T'faia

It is said in Morocco that this dish was brought back from Andalusia by the Moriscos after the Reconquista.

1 roasting chicken [about 4 lbs.], cut up
Butter or oil
Salt and black pepper
½ teaspoon ground ginger
About ¼ teaspoon saffron [optional]

2 onions, finely chopped
4 tablespoons finely chopped parsley
6 hard-boiled eggs
¾ cup blanched almonds, or more

Put the chicken in a large pan with 2½ tablespoons butter or oil, salt, pepper, ginger, saffron if used, onions and parsley. Cover with water, bring to a boil, and simmer gently, half-covered, for 1 hour, or until the chicken has absorbed the taste of the ginger and saffron and is well cooked, and the sauce is reduced.

Heat a little water to which you have added a pinch of saffron. Shell the hard-boiled eggs and roll them in the saffron water to color them all over. Fry the blanched almonds in butter.

Turn the chicken into a deep serving dish and pour the sauce over it. Arrange the eggs on top, placing them between the pieces of chicken, and garnish the dish with fried almonds.

A similar stew can be made using lamb instead of chicken.

Treya / Chicken with Pasta

A splendid dish described to me by an aunt in Paris, the origin of which I was thrilled to discover in al-Baghdadi's medieval cooking manual. In Egypt, spaghettini, which is thinner than spaghetti but not quite as thin as vermicelli, was used to prepare this dish, but spaghetti, tagliatelli, or other pasta can also be used.

1 large roasting chicken [4–5 lbs.], cooked [see method]	Juice of ½ lemon
	Corn oil
Salt and black pepper	1 lb. spaghettini or other pasta
1 cardamom pod	1 teaspoon ground cinnamon

Prepare the chicken according to the recipe for *sofrito* on page 182, seasoning it with salt and pepper, and flavoring with 1 cardamom pod (cracked to release the flavor from the seeds) and lemon juice. Simmer gently, covered, in a little oil and about ¾ cup water until very tender, turning it over occasionally. When cooked, bone the chicken, discarding the skin and tendons, and cut the meat into medium-sized pieces.

While the chicken is cooking, boil the spaghettini for about 7 minutes until almost but not quite tender. Drain in a colander.

Heat about ⅛ inch corn oil in a large ovenproof pan or sauté dish until very hot. Throw in the well-drained spahettini and sauté for a few minutes, stirring and tossing with a fork. Remove half the spaghettini and spread the remainder over the bottom of the pan. Arrange the chicken pieces in a layer over them, sprinkle with cinnamon and cover with the remaining spaghettini. Pour over the sauce in which the chicken was cooked and cover the pan with a lid.

Bake in a moderate oven (375°) for 20 to 30 minutes. Unmold onto a serving dish and serve either hot or cold.

Alternatively, make extra sauce by adding a little more water to the chicken while it is cooking. Remove the chicken when cooked; skin, bone, and chop it, and put the pieces back in the sauce. Boil the spaghettini until only half cooked as before; drain and add to the chicken. Continue to simmer the mixture until the spaghettini is well done and has absorbed the sauce, sprinkling with the cinnamon during cooking. It acquires a particularly delicious flavor.

Mishmisheya (a rich apricot sauce) is traditionally served with this dish: soak ½ lb. dried apricots overnight and simmer until soft in water or stock left over from cooking the chicken. Add a little sugar, and the juice of ½ lemon if you prefer a sharper taste. When the apricots are soft, crush them with a fork and continue to simmer until reduced to a soft purée. Serve cold in a separate bowl.

Çerkez Tavuğu / Circassian Chicken

This dish, popular throughout the Middle East, is part of a very old tradition in which nuts, ground fine, are used to thicken and enrich the sauce.

1 large roasting chicken [about 4 lbs.]
2 large onions, quartered
2 stalks celery
Salt and black pepper
1 cup shelled nuts [almonds, hazelnuts, or walnuts, or a mixture]

1 cup fine dry white bread crumbs [optional]
2 tablespoons oil
1 teaspoon paprika
3 cups long-grain rice
2½ tablespoons butter

Wash the chicken and put it in a large saucepan. Cover with water and add the quartered onions, celery stalks, salt, and pepper. Bring to a boil and simmer for about 1 hour, or until the chicken is tender, skimming off scum as it comes to the surface. Drain the chicken, reserving the stock; cut the bird into serving pieces and keep warm.

The sauce is traditionally made with walnuts only, but other nuts and bread crumbs are often added. Pound the nuts in a mortar or grind them in an electric blender. Strain 2 cups reserved stock into a clean pan, and stir in the nuts and bread crumbs. Bring to the boil and cook, stirring, until the mixture has thickened. Add more stock if it becomes too thick, and season to taste with salt and pepper.

Mix the oil with paprika until it becomes bright red.

Cook the rice with butter according to one of the methods given on pages 339–40, using some of the reserved chicken stock.

Arrange the chicken pieces in the center of a large serving dish. Surround them with a ring of cooked rice. Pour the nut sauce over both the chicken and the rice, and decorate with a dribble of red oil.

This dish is often served cold, with salads.

Ferique

A delicious Egyptian chicken dish with whole wheat and hard-boiled eggs. A few medieval recipes from al-Baghdadi are for dishes of chicken or meat cooked with whole wheat in a similar manner.

1 large roasting chicken [4–5 lbs.]
1 calf's foot
6 eggs in their shells
½ lb. husked whole wheat kernels,
    soaked overnight

1–2 teaspoons turmeric
3 tablespoons oil
Salt and black pepper

Wash the chicken. Scrape the calf's foot and blanch it in boiling water to clean it. Scrub the eggshells well.

Put all the ingredients in a large saucepan and cover with about 5 cups water. Bring to the boil and simmer gently for 3 to 4 hours, or until the chicken is practically falling apart, the calf's foot very tender, and the wheat well cooked.

Remove the eggs, shell them, and return them to the pan. The lengthy cooking will have given them a creamy texture and they will be colored pale yellow by the turmeric. Cook for a further 10 minutes. Taste and adjust seasoning.

Serve in deep bowls.

Chicken with Olives

This excellent Middle Eastern dish is a particularly Moroccan specialty.

1 large roasting chicken [about 4 lbs.]
2½ tablespoons oil
2 onions, sliced
Salt and black pepper

¼–½ teaspoon ground ginger
1 teaspoon paprika
1 onion, finely chopped
½ lb. green or black olives
Juice of ½ lemon, or more

Wash the chicken and wipe it with a damp cloth.

Heat the oil in a large saucepan. Add about ¾ cup water very gradually, stirring vigorously. Add onion slices, sprinkle with salt, pepper, ginger, and paprika, and lay the chicken on top. Cook over low heat, covered, for 1 hour, turning the chicken frequently. Add a little more salt if necessary, and the finely chopped onion, and cook for ½ hour longer.

Pit the olives. Put them in a pan, cover with cold water, bring to the boil, and leave for 1 minute. Drain off the water and repeat the process. This will remove excess salt. Add the olives to the pan and cook with the chicken for a few minutes only.

Just before serving, squeeze a little lemon juice over the dish. Sometimes a few pickled lemon slices (page 332) are added just before serving. Serve with plain boiled rice or *couscous* (page 277).

Riddle: Our Negress servant is green. Her children are born white and then grow black. Who is she?
Answer: An olive tree.

Moroccan Chicken Qdra

This is a tagine or stew, traditionally cooked with smen, the clarified butter called samna by other Arabs. Ordinary butter will also do.

1 large roasting chicken [about 4 lbs.], quartered
2½ tablespoons butter
¾–1 lb. onions
¼ teaspoon powdered saffron [optional]
1 teaspoon ground cinnamon, or more

Salt and black pepper
1½ cups chickpeas, soaked overnight
¾ cup almonds, blanched and peeled
A bunch of parsley, finely chopped
Juice of ½ lemon

As so often in Moroccan cooking, one onion is cooked first with the meat or chicken, and when these are nearly done, the remaining onions are added. This is because of the prolonged cooking. The first onion is used to add flavor to the meat, and it practically melts and disappears into the sauce. The onions added later keep their shape and add body to the sauce.

Put the chicken, butter, and 1 onion, finely chopped, in a large pan, and cover with water. Add a little saffron for color if liked, and season to taste with cinnamon, salt, and pepper. Bring to the boil, add the soaked chickpeas, and simmer for about 1½ hours, until the chickpeas are soft and the chicken well cooked, adding more water if necessary. The chicken should be cut up as soon as it is tender enough to pull apart.

Add the rest of the onions, finely chopped, the almonds and parsley, and simmer until the onions are soft and the sauce considerably reduced.

Arrange the chicken pieces on a serving dish and cover with chickpeas and almonds. Squeeze ½ lemon over the dish and serve.

Dried black-eyed peas or white beans can be substituted for the chickpeas, or all three can be cooked together. However, where dried beans are used, salt should not be added until they are soft, since it tends to keep them hard.

Tagine with Prunes

In the Kitab al Wusla il al Habib, *a medieval manuscript, there is a dish of chicken with prunes. Moroccans today cook a similar dish. Here is the recipe.*

1 large or 2 small chickens
1 onion, sliced
¼ teaspoon powdered saffron
¼–½ teaspoon ground ginger

Salt
2 onions, finely chopped or grated
1 lb. prunes, soaked overnight

Wash the chicken and put it in a large pan with the sliced onion. Sprinkle with saffron, ginger, and salt to taste, cover with water, and simmer gently, covered, until the chicken is tender and the stock is very much reduced. After about the first ¾ hour of cooking, add the finely chopped onions.

When the chicken is tender, add the prunes and continue cooking with the pan uncovered for about ½ hour longer, or until the prunes are soft and the sauce is considerably reduced.

Serve the chicken cut into pieces and covered with the sauce and prunes. Accompany with plain rice or *couscous* (page 277).

Moroccan Fruit Tagine

1 large roasting chicken [about 4 lbs.], cut up
2 onions, finely chopped
4 tablespoons finely chopped parsley
3 tablespoons butter

¼ teaspoon ground ginger [optional]
Salt and black pepper
1 lb. cooking or sharp eating apples, peeled, cored, and sliced

Put the chicken pieces, chopped onions, and parsley in a large saucepan. Cover with water, add butter, and the ginger if liked, and season with salt and pepper. Bring to the boil and simmer, covered, until the chicken is very tender and the onions have practically disintegrated, about 1 hour. The sauce should be reduced.

Add the sliced apples and continue to simmer until they are only just tender. The apples must not be allowed to disintegrate; eating apples will keep their shape better than cooking ones.

Serve with rice, *couscous* (page 277), or Arab bread to dip into the sauce.

Similar *touajen* (the plural of *tagine*) can be made with pears, quinces, fresh dates, raisins, or prunes which have first been soaked overnight.

Stuffed Chicken

1 large roasting chicken [about
    4 lbs.]
Salt and black pepper
Butter

STUFFING
1 lb. beef or lamb, ground
4 tablespoons oil or butter
Salt and black pepper
¾ cup blanched almonds, halved
⅓ cup pine nuts
¾ cup rice, cooked [weight
    uncooked]

Clean the chicken, burning off any stray feathers over a flame if necessary. Wash and wipe dry. Simmer in seasoned water for about ¾ hour, or until nearly tender, skimming away scum to begin with. Allow to cool a little.

Prepare the stuffing. Fry the ground meat in 3 tablespoons oil or butter until browned, and season to taste with salt and pepper. In a separate pan, melt the remaining tablespoon of oil or butter and fry the almonds for 2 or 3 minutes only. Mix the meat, almonds, and pine nuts with the cooked rice, and taste for seasoning. Stuff the chicken tightly with this mixture and skewer the openings. (If there is any stuffing left over, warm it up again and serve with the chicken.)

Roast the stuffed chicken, brushed with butter, in a preheated slow oven (350°) for 20 minutes, or until it is a beautiful golden color.

If you prefer, you can stuff the chicken raw and roast it in the usual manner, surrounded with butter shavings and wrapped in foil, in a fairly hot oven (400°) until tender, allowing about 20 minutes per lb. Or cook it uncovered, placed on a rack in an oven preheated to 450° and then reduced at once to 350° for about the same time. One or two peeled and chopped tomatoes can be included in the stuffing, which can also be flavored with ½ teaspoon ground cinnamon.

Boned Stuffed Chicken

A splendid party dish, similar to those featured in medieval manuals.

1 large roasting chicken [about 4 lbs.]	1½ lb. veal, ground
	⅓–½ cup pistachio nuts, coarsely chopped
Oil	
Salt and black pepper	Juice of ½ lemon

Clean and wash the chicken, and cut off the wing tips and leg ends to make the removal of the skin possible. Singe the chicken over a flame to "loosen" it and burn away any feathers. Loosen the skin from the flesh. Carefully pull the skin right off as though undressing the chicken, taking care not to tear it, starting from the neck and pulling it off the legs last. It will come right off. Wash the skin, turn it right side out, and put it aside.

Quarter the skinned chicken, put it in a saucepan and cover with water. Add 2 tablespoons oil, season to taste with salt and pepper, bring to the boil, and simmer gently until the chicken is very tender. Remove from the heat and let it cool in the stock. Drain and keep the stock.

Bone the chicken, discarding nerves and tendons, and grind or chop the meat finely. Put it in a large bowl and mix with the ground veal. Use extra veal if the chicken is not very meaty. Knead well. Add the pistachio nuts and knead them in. Season the mixture to taste with salt and pepper.

Using a needle and strong thread, sew up all but the largest vent in the chicken skin and "darn" any holes. Stuff the skin carefully with the chicken and veal mixture, and re-form as nearly as possible in its original shape. Sew the opening tightly.

Turn the stuffed chicken over in about 2 tablespoons warm oil in a pan until the skin is golden. Add the lemon juice and about half a ladleful of leftover stock and simmer gently, covered, for about 1 hour, adding more stock or water, half a ladleful at a time, if it becomes dry. At the end of cooking time, the veal should be well cooked and almost blended with the chicken, and the sauce much reduced. Remove from the heat and allow to cool overnight in its own sauce.

Traditionally, the chicken should be served in thick slices, but I think it looks rather beautiful with its subdued boneless shape, served whole and sliced at the table.

A variation of this dish, said to be for lazy cooks, is just as delicious though not as dramatic. Cook the chicken as in the recipe for *sofrito* (page 182), adding just a pinch of turmeric or none at all. When cool, skin it and remove the bones and tendons. Grind the flesh and mix it with the ground veal, 1 egg, and a handful of chopped pistachios. Knead thoroughly and shape or roll into a thick sausage. Sauté in 2 tablespoons hot oil until golden all over. Add water, a little at a time, as it becomes absorbed, and simmer gently, covered, until well cooked. Allow to cool in its sauce for several hours before serving. Serve cut in slices.

Arab saying: "Eat and praise your host."

Persian Chicken Stuffed with Dried Fruits

1 large roasting chicken [4–4½ lbs.]	½ lb. dried apricots, soaked and chopped
1 onion, finely chopped	½ cup seedless raisins
Butter	2 apples, peeled, cored, and chopped
½ lb. prunes, soaked, pitted, and chopped	Salt and black pepper
	1 teaspoon ground cinnamon

Clean and wash the chicken, and wipe it dry. Fry the chopped onion in 2 tablespoons hot butter until soft and golden. Add the chopped fruits and sauté gently for a few minutes. Season to taste with salt, pepper, and cinnamon.

Stuff the chicken with this mixture. Rub it with salt and pepper, truss, and place in a baking tin. Roast in a preheated slow oven (350°), allowing about 20 minutes per lb. Baste frequently with melted butter.

Alternatively, cover the chicken with butter shavings and wrap in foil before putting it in a hotter oven. It will be more tender and juicy. Place any leftover stuffing in the foil with the bird.

Serve the chicken surrounded with the extra stuffing and plain rice.

Faisinjan

An exquisite Persian dish, to be made with roast or fried duck or chicken. Pomegranate juice or sauce (a concentrate) should be used for this dish, but if this is not available lemon juice may be substituted.

1 duck or 1 chicken
Salt and black pepper
Butter

SAUCE
1 onion, grated or finely chopped
Butter
1 cup ground walnuts

½ cup fresh pomegranate juice [obtained from squeezing pomegranate seeds], or 3 tablespoons pomegranate sauce, or the juice of 2 lemons
2½ cups stock or water
Salt and black pepper
1 teaspoon sugar, or more

Divide the duck or chicken into pieces, season to taste with salt and pepper, and fry gently in butter until almost tender, turning to brown all over.

Make the sauce. In a large saucepan, fry the onion until soft and golden in about 2 tablespoons butter. Add the ground walnuts and stir well into the hot butter. Then add the pomegranate juice or sauce, or the juice of 1 or 2 lemons, and stock or water. Cook, stirring, until the sauce thickens. Season to taste with salt, pepper, and 1 teaspoon sugar, or more if too sour.

Add the pieces of duck or chicken and simmer gently, covered, for a further ½ hour. Serve with plain rice, or preferably rice steamed in the Persian manner (pages 340–1).

A variation is to stir 2 tablespoons tomato paste into the browned onion. One sliced, salted, and drained eggplant and/or sliced zucchini may also be added. Sauté in butter until well cooked, and add to the sauce together with the duck or chicken.

Koftit Ferakh I / Chicken Balls I

This delicious recipe for leftovers comes from the Kitab al Wusla il al Habib. *For 3 or 4 people.*

½ lb. cooked boned chicken
¼ lb. white bread, crusts removed
⅓ cup pistachio nuts, finely
    chopped

1 tablespoon olive or salad oil
Juice of ½ lemon
Salt and white pepper

Grind or chop the chicken finely. Soak the bread in water, squeeze dry, and crumble. Mix the chicken with the crumbled bread, pistachios, oil, lemon juice, and salt and pepper to taste, and knead vigorously. Shape and roll into marble-sized balls.

These can be served as they are, as a cold dish with salad; or they can be rolled in flour and fried, or poached in a chicken soup, and served hot.

Koftit Ferakh II / Chicken Balls II

Here is a modern version of the same dish. Yet another recipe is given on page 50.

½ lb. cooked boned chicken
    [preferably white meat]
1 slice white bread
½ lb. ground veal
2 tablespoons finely chopped
    parsley

1 egg
Salt and black pepper
About 2 tablespoons butter or oil
½ teaspoon turmeric [optional]
Juice of ½ lemon

Grind the chicken. Trim the bread of crusts, soak in water, and squeeze dry. In a large bowl, mix the ground chicken, crumbled bread, veal, parsley, and egg, and season to taste with salt and pepper. Knead well and roll into marble-sized balls.

Melt butter or oil in a large, deep frying pan, and fry the chicken balls, shaking the pan, until they are gently browned all over. Add a little turmeric if liked, sprinkle with lemon juice and a pinch of salt and pepper. Half-cover with water and simmer gently, uncovered, for about 20 minutes, until the *koftit* are very tender and well cooked.

Artichoke hearts are often stewed with the *koftit*. If fresh ones are not available, canned artichoke hearts make an excellent substitute. Add them 10 minutes before the dish is ready. In another variation, the fried chicken balls are simmered in a tomato sauce made with 5–10 tablespoons of tomato paste, diluted with water and seasoned with salt, pepper, and a little lemon juice. Ten minutes before the end of cooking time, throw in 1 lb. fried potatoes cut into squares, and let them absorb the sauce.

Stuffed Turkey

In the Middle East, turkeys range very freely and are small and tough, more like game birds. So they are usually stewed rather than roasted. This makes the flesh very juicy, and helps it to absorb the flavors of the stuffing as well as the seasonings in the stock. A very large pan is required to hold the bird.

A 10- to 12-lb. oven-ready turkey	2¼ cups long-grain rice
Lemon juice	½ cup raisins [optional]
Oil or butter	Salt and black pepper
2 lbs. beef, lamb, or veal, ground	1 teaspoon ground cinnamon
2 cups chopped mixed nuts:	¼ teaspoon ground allspice
blanched almonds, walnuts,	
pistachio nuts, and pine nuts	

Wash the turkey thoroughly and rub it both inside and out with a little lemon juice.

Prepare the stuffing. In a saucepan heat 2½ tablespoons butter or oil and fry the meat until it changes color, mixing with a fork. Stir in the nuts and fry for 2 or 3 minutes longer. Add the rice, and fry for another minute or so until well coated with fat. Add raisins if used. Season to taste with salt, pepper, cinnamon, and allspice. Mix well.

Stuff the turkey loosely with this mixture to allow the rice to expand, and sew the openings tightly with strong thread. Truss the bird.

Melt 6 tablespoons butter in a pan large enough to hold the turkey and brown it well, turning it to color it all over. Add enough water to cover and season to taste with salt and pepper. Bring to the boil and simmer gently, removing the scum to begin with, until the turkey is very tender. This will take 2 to 2½ hours, depending on the size of the bird.

The turkey may be either served whole or cut into pieces and arranged over the stuffing in a large platter.

The turkey can also be boned before stuffing: cut the skin and flesh of the bird along the spine all the way down from the neck. Starting from the neck, strip and cut away the flesh from the carcass as close to it as possible, using a very sharp knife, taking care not to damage the skin, and pushing the flesh back as you cut. Break the shoulder and leg joints. Carefully remove the carcass all in one piece. Pack with stuffing and sew up neatly, re-forming the bird as far as possible in its original shape. In this way it will take more stuffing and can be served in slices. The legs and wings remain unboned and help to keep the shape of the turkey firm. If a large enough pan is not available, roast the turkey in the oven in the usual manner, rubbed with either butter or chicken fat, and wrapped in foil or uncovered. Baste frequently. Begin roasting in an oven preheated to 450° and as soon as the bird is brown, reduce the heat to 350°. Allow 25 minutes to the lb. plus 25 minutes more. If roasting in foil, roast for the same time but keep the oven heat at a constant 400°.

Browned Duck

This is a Turkish recipe from Sidqui Effendi's nineteenth-century cooking manual.

A 5- to 6-lb. oven-ready duck
½ cup yogurt
Salt
2 medium-sized onions, chopped
Oil or butter
Liver and heart of the duck

Black pepper
⅓ cup mixed chopped almonds and pine nuts
½ cup raisins
2½ cups long-grain rice

Clean and wash the duck, and cut it in serving pieces. Marinate for several hours in yogurt seasoned with a little salt.

In a large pan, fry the onions in 2 tablespoons oil or butter until soft and golden. Add the well-drained pieces of duck and brown all over. Cover with a little water, season to taste with salt, bring to the boil and simmer gently, covered, for about 40 minutes, or until tender. Drain, reserving stock.

Cut the duck liver, heart, and other duck giblets if you like into small pieces. Fry these in oil or butter until soft, using another large saucepan, and season to taste with salt and pepper. Add the nuts, raisins, and rice, and mix well. Pour in 5 cups of duck stock and water, cover, and cook very gently, undisturbed, until the rice is tender and has absorbed the liquid. Taste for seasoning and adjust if necessary.

Serve very hot on a large, heated serving dish, alternating layers of the rice mixture and duck.

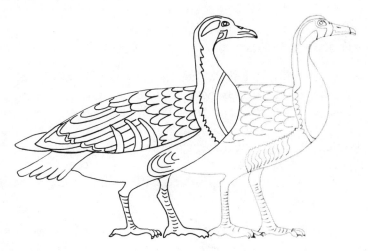

Duck with Orange Juice

This is a modern Lebanese favorite. It probably owes its inspiration to the French canard à l'orange—or perhaps the opposite is true. It is a sort of sofrito (see page 182) with orange.

1 duck [about 5–6 lbs.]	Juice of 1 sweet orange
1 large onion, chopped	Juice of 1 bitter or Seville orange
3 tablespoons butter	Salt and black pepper

Clean and wash the duck, and wipe it dry.

Fry the chopped onion in butter until soft and golden, using a pan large enough to hold the duck. Brown the duck in the same fat, turning it occasionally to color it all over. Add the juice of both oranges, and season to taste with salt and pepper. Simmer very gently, covered, for about 1 hour, adding a ladleful of water from time to time, and turning the bird over occasionally. Take the partially cooked duck, cut it into serving pieces, and return to the pan. Continue to simmer until the duck is very tender and has absorbed the flavor of the orange juice.

In a modern Israeli version, a cut-up and lightly fried chicken is placed in a casserole and covered with a mixture of orange juice, white wine, cognac, and chicken stock. The dish is baked for ¾ hour, and is served garnished with orange sections and blanched almonds.

Assafeer (Small Birds)

In parts of the Middle East where they are readily available, restaurants make a specialty of serving small birds as *mezze*.

The birds are plucked, and their beaks and legs cut off. They are then rubbed with salt and pepper, and their heads are tucked into their bodies. Finally, they are threaded onto skewers and grilled over glowing charcoal fires for 5 to 10 minutes, according to size; or they are fried in butter and sprinkled with lemon juice, to be served between two pieces of warm *pitta*.

Grilled Quail

Every year, a type of migrating quail flies over Alexandria. Hundreds of the small birds fall, exhausted, on the dunes of the beaches of Agami, to be caught in large nets and collected in baskets. They are marinated in a rich sauce flavored with cumin and coriander, and grilled on the beaches over numerous little fires.

The flesh of these birds is not as gamy as that of the usual wild quail, and the nearest equivalent available is a broiler or tiny spring chicken.

Clean and wash the birds. Rub the following sauce into them, and marinate for at least 1 hour before grilling over charcoal or under the broiler.

5 tablespoons olive oil
Salt
1 teaspoon ground cumin
1 teaspoon ground coriander

1 onion, cut in half and crushed in a
garlic press to extract juices
2 tablespoons finely chopped
parsley
Pinch of cayenne pepper

Hamam Meshwi / Grilled Pigeons

One of the happiest and most popular outings of my childhood in Cairo was to go for the day, in the company of several uncles, aunts, and cousins, to an old restaurant called Le Café des Pigeons, on the way to the Pyramids. There we would feast on charcoal-grilled pigeons shot in the neighborhood.

I cannot recollect a more delicious meal. Huge dishes piled high with halved pigeons, sprinkled with lemon juice and chopped chervil or parsley, were brought to us in the ancient gardens of the restaurant, overgrown with jasmine and bougainvillaea. We ate them all, even their small soft bones.

To my dismay, I found that, as with quail, the pigeons available in England are of a totally different variety. Again, the nearest in flavor that I can suggest (though still very far removed) is spring chicken or in the U.S. squab. Our pigeons were often just grilled over charcoal and sprinkled with salt, but if spring chickens are used, I suggest that you marinate them first in oil and lemon with salt and pepper to tenderize their flesh and enhance their flavor. Serve sprinkled with chopped fresh chervil or parsley.

MEAT DISHES

In Arabic literature and folklore, meat dishes have always been labeled the food of the rich and aristocratic, in contrast to the filling dishes of beans, lentils, and wheat which are the diet of the lowly poor. Many stories and proverbs illustrate this distinction. Here is an old Egyptian tale of the Mamluk period by Ahmad ibn al Hajjar, in which the various foods are personified and their status is defined:

A Book about the Pleasant War Between Mutton and the Refreshments of the Market*

King Mutton reigns over a large and powerful people, comprising mainly meats. He hears of the power of a rival, King Honey, who has been crowned by the poor, and who reigns over vegetables, fruits, sweets, fish, milk dishes, and particularly the refreshments of the market. King Mutton sends his ambassador, Mutton's Tail (*alya*), to King Honey, demanding that he surrender his kingdom and pay tribute. King Honey refuses and calls his troops together, but the ambassador has taken advantage of his stay in the kingdom to debauch and corrupt the officers of rank, in particular, the Sugar, the Syrup, the Clarified Fat, and others, to whom he has promised important positions at the court of his master. Thus, because of their treachery, the battle between the two armies is easily won by the troops of King Mutton, and even the reinforcements of fruits sent to help the broken army of King Honey are of no avail.

Most Middle Eastern meat recipes, both the medieval ones and more recent versions, simply state "meat"—meat with lentils, meat with yogurt, and so on—without specifying what kind of meat or any particular cut. This is because, in the past, only mutton and lamb were eaten, apart from an occasional gazelle, kid, or camel. Cattle were seldom bred, except for a type of buffalo mainly used for work in the fields. Those brought from elsewhere had to travel a long way, across whole countries, to reach the Middle East, and by the time they

* From the French translation by M. Rodinson.

got to their destination, their flesh was tough and inedible unless ground.

Today, however, beef and veal are gradually becoming more popular. Although mutton and lamb remain, from habit, the most widely used and favored, beef and veal quite often replace them, the recipes themselves remaining unchanged.

It is common in the Middle East for people to buy a live sheep at the market, and to keep it for a few days in their kitchen before killing it. A tale of Goha illustrates this custom.

One day, Goha took his small son to the market with him to buy a sheep. Now it is well known that the value of a sheep depends on the amount of fat which it stores in its tail. At the *soukh* (market), Goha proceeded to feel, and weigh in his hands, the tails of the sheep one after another, until his son asked:

"Father, why do you do that?"

"I must do so before I decide which sheep to buy," Goha replied.

A few days later, while sitting waiting for the evening meal, the little boy turned to his father and said:

"Father, our neighbor was here today. I think he wants to buy my mother!"

In the Middle East, as elsewhere, grilling, frying, grinding, and stewing are common ways of dealing with meats. For all grilled dishes, such as the shish kebabs well known in the West, buy the best and most tender cuts of meat: leg or loin of lamb, and fillet of beef or veal. Cut the meat preferably across the grain for extra tenderness. Clean it well, trim off the fat, and remove any tendons, tough membranes, and ligaments. Marinate for as long as possible (from 2 to 24 hours) to tenderize and flavor it.

MESHWI (GRILLS)

The word *meshwi* in Arabic covers all types of meat, whether large or smaller pieces, which are grilled or roasted over a fire. In North Africa, people light small fires in their courtyards and sit around them while a leg or other piece of lamb is turned on a spit, helping themselves to slices of the meat as it becomes deliciously brown.

In Turkey, *döner kebab* is a great favorite. Although veal cut from the leg is sometimes used, lamb is more popular. Tender meat, preferably boned leg, from which veins and tendons have been removed, is cut in slices about 1 inch thick and 4 to 5 inches wide and allowed to marinate in a refrigerator for 24 hours in a mixture of olive oil, salt, pepper, and onion juice with chopped parsley, *rigani*,* and fresh mint. Alternative marinades are given in the following recipe for shish kebab.

The meat is allowed to warm up to room temperature before it is threaded onto a rotating vertical spit, the larger slices being placed first, and the others pressed tightly over them in diminishing sizes with a few pieces of fat squeezed between them here and there to keep the meat moist and tender. The meat is packed tightly, pressed down, trimmed, and built up into a cone shape. A flat metal ring at the top holds the meat, which forms an almost solid shank.

The spit turns automatically and slowly close to a hot charcoal fire. Gas or electric heat may be used. Some spits are rotated manually. In restaurants this is often done in full view of the diners. Slices are cut off and the joint is allowed to continue turning on the spit so that the meat, left bare and pink by the sharp knife, can acquire the warm brown glow and characteristic aroma that only grilling can give it.

Rotisserie spits which are available as an attachment to oven cookers, or on their own, give excellent results.

Leg of lamb is ideal for spit roasting. Marinate it for 2 hours in any one of the marinades given below for shish kebab. Then set it over a charcoal fire which has stopped smoking. If gas or electric heat is used, preheat the grill very thoroughly. Turn the leg, basting or brushing with marinade occasionally. The cooking time will depend on the size and age of the meat. A small leg of young lamb should provide some cooked slices within 35 to 45 minutes, older meat in 1 hour. When these are cut off, the inside meat continues to cook, providing more slices within 10 to 15 minutes.

Lamb cutlets and chops lend themselves beautifully to the *meshwi*

---

* The Greek variety of wild marjoram, to be found in Greek and Cypriot stores. ‡ If not available, used dried oregano or thyme.

treatment. They should be placed on a hot oiled grid over an open fire which has stopped smoking, or under a thoroughly well-heated broiler.

Serve with plain rice, salads, both fresh and puréed or creamed, and *pitta*, or Arab bread (page 364).

Shish Kebab / Grilled Meat on Skewers

This is probably the most famous Turkish dish, and it undoubtedly lives up to its reputation. It is said by Turks to have been created during the splendid, conquering era of the Ottoman Empire, when Turkish soldiers, forced to camp out in tents for months on end, discovered the pleasure of eating meat grilled out of doors on open fires of charcoal or dry wood.

The meat grilled on its own is delicious. An added refinement is to marinate it first, and to perfume the flames over which it is grilled with herbs. In Greece and Turkey, quartered raw tomatoes and pieces of onion and sweet pepper are threaded onto the skewers between the cubes of meat.

Here are three popular marinades for seasoning the meat, enough for 2 lbs. leg of lamb or fillet of beef, cut into medium-sized cubes about ¾ inch square.

MARINADE I

½ cup olive oil
Juice of 1 lemon
2 onions, chopped and crushed to extract juices *

2 bay leaves, cut into small pieces
2 teaspoons dried rigani
Pulp of 2 tomatoes, sieved [optional]
Salt and black pepper

This is a particular favorite in Greece, where the distinctive flavor of *rigani* (see footnote page 203) is much appreciated.

Mix all the ingredients together in a large bowl. Marinate the cubed meat for at least 2 to 3 hours, longer if possible. Persian cooks marinate it for at least 12 hours, which makes it beautifully tender.

The method of cooking the meat for shish kebab is much the same, which ever marinade is used.

* Can be done in a garlic press or an electric blender.

Drain the cubes and thread them onto skewers, preferably the flat-edged "sword" type. Grill over charcoal or wood, or under a preheated gas or electric broiler, turning and basting them from time to time, or brushing them with the marinade. Make sure that the fire has stopped smoking before grilling. Cook the meat until the cubes are a rich brown color on the outside, but still pink and juicy within. This takes from 7 to 10 minutes, but the time depends on the type and degree of heat, how far the skewers are from the heat source, and the size of the cubes.

MARINADE II—from Sidqi Effendi's Turkish cooking manual.

½ cup olive oil   1 teaspoon ground cinnamon
Juice of 2 onions   Salt and black pepper

Prepare the marinade and proceed as above.

MARINADE III

½ cup yogurt   Salt and black pepper
Juice of 1 onion

Marinate the meat cubes for at least 3 hours in the well-mixed marinade ingredients. Serve sprinkled with a little ground cinnamon if you like.

The kebabs may be served in a flat, hollow Arab bread or *pitta*, which is often placed under them to catch the juices when they are grilled *under* the heat. These "hollow cups" can be served topped with a salad of finely chopped raw tomato and raw onion.

Alternatively, serve the skewers on a bed of parsley or chervil accompanied by various salads or, as is traditional in some countries, on a bed of plain white rice. In Persia, the rice is garnished with an egg yolk, presented on the half shell. The yolk is then stirred into the rice at the table.

"By reason of the sweet smiles of the salt cellar of her mouth, blood flows from the heart as from a salted kebab." (From the Kanju'l Ishtiha [The Treasure of the Appetite] by Abu Ishaq of Shiraz, the sixteenth-century Persian poet of food.)

Kofta Meshweya / Grilled Ground Meat on Skewers

Each country and each area in the Middle East has its favorite flavorings for kofta. *Here is a basic recipe, giving a few simple alternative seasonings.*

2 lbs. lamb, beef, or a mixture of both, ground
2 onions, grated
1–2 eggs
Salt and black pepper

Optional seasonings: 1 teaspoon ground cinnamon, or 1 teaspoon ground allspice, or ½ teaspoon ground cumin and ½ teaspoon ground coriander

Put the meat through the grinder two or three times, then mix together with the remaining ingredients in a bowl, and pound or knead until very, very smooth. The art of making this delicious meat dish lies in achieving an extremely soft and pasty texture.

Take smallish lumps of the mixture and pat them into sausage shapes around skewers (preferably the flat-edged "sword" type.) If grilling over a barbecue, wait until the charcoal has stopped smoking and glows dull red before you place the skewers over it. Try not to let the meat touch the metal, and make sure the grill is well oiled to prevent the meat from sticking to it. Turn the skewers until the *kofta* are cooked and browned all over.

Serve nestling in warm Arab bread or *pitta* to catch the juices, or with plain rice, and accompanied by salad.

Grill rows of shish kebab (above) and *kofta* together. Serve them on a bed of parsley or chervil, sprinkled with finely chopped onions. This is often served in cafés as *kofta wa kebab*.

Moroccan Brochettes

Moroccans call their diminutive kofta *"brochettes" in the French manner. The streets of Fez are dotted with little braziers of glowing charcoal over which turn many small skewers heavy with tiny pieces of meat, liver, or* kofta, *irresistibly enveloping passersby with their enticing aroma.*

More than any other Middle Eastern people, Moroccans have adopted and become intoxicated with every spice that has come their way en route to Europe from the Far East. But they use them so

discreetly that one should only just be able to guess what has gone into the rich combination. Moroccan kofta *are sometimes rich with every spice sold in the* attarin, *or market. Here is one of many variations.*

2 lbs. beef or lamb, finely ground
2 onions, grated
5 tablespoons finely chopped
    parsley
½ teaspoon dried sweet marjoram
    or oregano

¼ teaspoon ground cumin
¼ teaspoon ground coriander
½ teaspoon Harissa or Ras el
    Hanout ‡
Salt and black pepper
¼ teaspoon cayenne pepper
    [optional]

Mix finely ground meat with onions, herbs, and seasonings, and pound or knead vigorously until very smooth and pasty. Shape small lumps of the mixture around skewers, and grill as in the preceding recipe.

Another favorite brochette is made up of grilled pieces of lamb's liver sprinkled with salt, cayenne pepper, and cumin.

Riddle: It is red like blood. It burns like fire. What is it?
Answer: Red pimiento.

Whole Roast Lamb on a Spit

Whole roast lamb or sheep is a festive, ceremonial repast in the Middle East, prepared for parties, festivals, and family gatherings. Although the poor can rarely afford meat, there is one day at least when all are assured of eating it. This is at the *Eid-el-Kurban* (sometimes called *Eid-el-Kibir* in Egypt), on the tenth day of the last month of the Muhammadan year, a festival in commemoration of Abraham's sacrifice of Isma'il.*

By ancient custom, well-to-do families sacrifice a sheep or lamb on this day. The victim must be fat, young, and unblemished. The eyes of the animal are blackened, a piece of confectionery is placed in its mouth, and its head is turned toward Mecca. The words, "In the name of God," are spoken as the animal is slain. It is then usually roasted on a spit, and the meat is distributed to the poor. These offerings are also made after a death, a birth, and on other important occasions such as moving to a new house, the start or end of a long journey, or the arrival of an important guest.

In Cairo, our balcony overlooked a street where, on several occasions, I watched the roasting of a "ceremonial" lamb, accompanied by wailing and singing. The smell penetrated my bedclothes and wardrobe, and remained with me through the night.

A recipe written by Sidqi Effendi in the nineteenth century gives instructions for roasting a lamb in the open, a fabulous piece for a summer party.

Buy a baby lamb (see the following recipe) or a young lamb. Ask the butcher to clean it and remove the entrails. (You can keep the heart and liver to cook separately.) The head may be left on, but have the eyes removed.

* In Islamic lore, he offered Isma'il, not Isaac.

Rinse the lamb inside and out, and wipe it dry. Rub it well with salt and black pepper, and sprinkle it with onion juice, made by squeezing a few onions in a garlic press or puréeing them in an electric blender. Push a wooden or metal rod right through the lamb from breast to hindquarters, and truss its legs together.

If you do not have a large enough barbecue, it is not difficult to make one. In his recipe, Sidqi Effendi describes the fire and the spit used in his day—a hole dug in the ground and filled with charcoal.

In their booklet *Profitable Catering with New Zealand Lamb*, the New Zealand Meat Producers' Board gives a rather more detailed and accurate explanation for building a turnspit and fire:

"An outdoor fire must be red hot when starting to roast. The building of an efficient turnspit involves some considerations. The spit must be set on a level which turns the meat at the right distance from the fire. Air vents to the ash pit, dripping trays set low enough to prevent the drippings from being burnt, a fender barrier to prevent live pieces from the fire falling into the drippings—all these need close and careful attention.

"The fire is best raised on old furnace bars or a piece of an old iron fence placed at least 1 ft. off the ground, and the fire built up on this at least 2 ft. high so that the heat is radiated onto the carcass as it slowly revolves. A back brick wall and wings are needed—4 to 4½ ft. in height and supported by buttresses at the back and sides. The spit can consist of a long galvanized pipe about 1½ in. in diameter with a sturdy old cart wheel fixed to it for turning. This is then set in grooves on top of the side walls at not more than 3 ft. above the basting pans. The lamb carcass is then impaled on the pipe and rotated backwards and forwards by an operator standing on one side of the fire out of the direct line of the heat.

"Before a barbecue occasion, the fire should be lit and a complete test made of the arrangements for shielding the wind, the type of fuel being used, the efficiency of the turning wheel, and so on. The fire should be started early enough in the day to allow it to get well burnt through, so that an even flow of heat is available along the full length of the turnspit. Later, as the lamb is being roasted, the heat must be reduced at the forequarter end, or it will be done before the thicker hindquarter is cooked.

"The essential of good spit-roasting is constant basting. Use ladles or basting spoons firmly fastened to long poles for this purpose. The use of a shield with eye holes is also an advantage when basting a carcass.

"After 3 or 4 hours' roasting allow the carcass to rest for 20 to 30 minutes to enable top heat to escape, and for the meat to settle for clean carving. Serve from the spit or remove to a large tray."

Allow at least 3 hours to roast a 29- to 35-lb. lamb. Increase this to at least 4 hours for a lamb up to 50 lb. in weight. With the carved lamb serve mounds of rice cooked with pine nuts or almonds and raisins, and scented with spices (see the stuffing in the next recipe), and a selection of salads. Alternatively serve with Arab bread, which can be used to hold the meat and salads.

If a deep-frozen lamb is used, it must first be allowed to defrost for at least 24 hours before being prepared. Rub with salt, black pepper, and onion juice, and proceed as above.

A medieval cooking manual gives a method of barbecuing adopted from the Crusaders. The lamb was pierced with a rod and held between two poles. Fires were lit on either side, with the result (it was said) that roasting was quicker and more even.

Arab saying: "One's eating shows one's love."

Qouzi Mahshi aw Kharouf Mahshi / Roast Stuffed Kid or Baby Milk-fed Lamb

This is a Saudi Arabian specialty. It appears at every feast, be it royal or humble, served on a huge tray, surrounded by mountains of rice and decorated with hard-boiled eggs. Kid is traditionally used, but baby lamb is often substituted. The lamb is stuffed, then roasted outdoors over charcoal as in the preceding recipe. It can also be roasted in the oven if there is room for it.

Baby milk-fed lambs can be bought either from a specialist butcher or possibly from a farmer. They are most likely to be available in spring. At other times of the year they must be ordered in advance and are more expensive.

What is generally sold as young lamb, and readily available, is already weaned, usually weighing at least 24 lbs.

A 15- to 18-lb. baby lamb
2 tablespoons ground coriander
1 teaspoon ground ginger
Salt and black pepper
Juice of 1–2 onions

STUFFING
6 cups long-grain rice
¼–½ teaspoon saffron [optional]
2 onions, chopped

2 tablespoons oil
¾ cup almonds, chopped
⅔ cup pistachio nuts, chopped
1 cup walnuts, chopped
1–2 cups seedless raisins
Salt and black pepper

GARNISH
Sprigs of parsley
2–3 hard-boiled eggs, sliced
2 large onions, thinly sliced

Ask the butcher to prepare the lamb as in the preceding recipe.

Rinse the meat inside and out, and wipe it dry with a clean cloth. Rub inside and out with the seasonings and onion juice, and set aside while you prepare the stuffing.

To make the stuffing: boil the rice until tender, adding a little saffron if you like. Drain well. Sauté the chopped onions in the oil until transparent. Add them to the cooked rice and mix well with the nuts and raisins. Season to taste with salt and pepper.

Stuff the lamb tightly and sew the openings with strong thread. Put it in a large baking tray in an oven preheated to 450°, then reduce the heat to 325° to 350°. Roast the lamb, basting it occasionally with its own juices and turning it over once or twice if possible. Alternatively, you can wrap it in foil and roast it in a moderate oven (375°), uncovering it for the last ½ hour of cooking. Roast for approximately 2 hours for well-done meat, and 1½ hours if you prefer it slightly pink.

If using a 24-lb. lamb, prepare in the same manner, using about half as much again stuffing, and roast for about 4 hours, or until done to your liking.

Serve on a large tray or platter, lavishly decorated with parsley, sliced hard-boiled eggs, and sliced onions. Surround with a ring of rice prepared in the same way as the stuffing.

This magnificent dish serves 15 to 18 people, if you prepare the smaller lamb.

The lamb can also be boned before it is stuffed. I have seen baby lambs served at weddings, made to look like miniature camels, their boneless backs shaped into a hump.

Whole Roast Leg of Lamb

Here is another traditional dish which, in the past, would probably have been sent to the local baker's oven for cooking.

1 large leg of lamb
3–4 cloves garlic, slivered
Salt and black pepper
1½ lbs. potatoes, thickly sliced
2 large onions, sliced

1 lb. tomatoes, sliced
1 teaspoon dried rigani ‡ or oregano
    [optional]
1–2 eggplants, sliced [optional]

Wipe the leg of lamb clean. Pierce it all over with the point of a sharp knife and insert the slivers of garlic at different depths. Rub generously with salt and pepper.

Put the prepared lamb, fat side up, in a large baking pan, and surround it with the sliced potatoes, onions, and tomatoes. Sprinkle if you like with a little *rigani* or oregano. If eggplants are to be used, sprinkle the slices with salt and leave them in a sieve or colander for at least ½ hour to allow the bitter juices to drain away. Do not add them at this stage.

Have the oven preheated to 450°. Put in the leg of lamb, reduce the heat to 350°, and roast for about 2½ hours, or until done to your liking—only about 1½ hours if you prefer the meat very rare. Baste occasionally with the pan juices.

Squeeze the moisture from the eggplant slices and add them after the first ¾ hour. Turn the vegetables over once during the cooking so that they cook evenly in the juices from the meat, and pour off excess fat.

The meat should be very tender, juicy and sweet, and the vegetables quite soft. I like them practically disintegrating, but if you prefer them to be rather more firm, add them to the meat after about 1 hour's cooking, when it has already released some fat. Baste the vegetables when you baste the meat, and moisten occasionally with a little water if necessary.

Leg of Lamb Sofrito

An alternative way of cooking a leg of lamb is by the method called *sofrito*. Page 215 gives detailed directions for this cooking method, under the recipe for veal *sofrito*. Breifly, it consists of cooking the meat, seasoned and flavored to taste, in a large, covered pan over very low heat, with only about ½ cup water and a few tablespoons of oil or other fat. The meat simmers gently and is turned occasionally, with a few more tablespoons of water added as necessary. It is cooked until almost falling apart. This takes about 3 hours for an average-sized leg of lamb of, say, 4½ to 6 lbs.

Thickly sliced potatoes, tomatoes, and onions are sometimes added to the pan in the same way as in the preceding recipe for roast leg of lamb. Eggplants may also be included, added about ½ hour before the end of cooking time.

Dala' Mahshi / Stuffed Breast of Lamb

This is an extremely cheap dish. It is exquisite served with vegetables or accompanied by a pyramid of extra stuffing, and a great favorite in our family.

This is one of the Middle Eastern fruit and meat dishes, possibly inspired by ancient Persia. A quince sauce, stewed apples, black cherry jam, or cranberry sauce may be substituted for the apricots.

2 whole large breasts of lamb
Oil
Salt and black pepper
½ lb. dried apricots, soaked
    overnight
1 tablespoon sugar

STUFFING
2½ cups long-grain rice
2 medium-sized onions, chopped
3 tablespoons oil
½ lb. beef, ground
4 tablespoons finely chopped
    parsley
Salt and black pepper
⅔ cup pine nuts or walnuts
1 cup small seedless raisins
    [optional]

Ask the butcher to chine the meat and to cut a pouch between the skin and the ribs—or do the latter yourself with a long, sharp knife. Wipe clean with a damp cloth.

Prepare the stuffing. Fry the chopped onions in oil until golden brown, using a large saucepan. Add the ground beef and fry until browned. Add the rice and continue to fry for a few minutes until well coated. Sprinkle with parsley and pour in 5 cups of boiling water. Season to taste with salt and pepper, cover the pan tightly, and simmer undisturbed over low heat for 20 minutes, or until the water has been absorbed and the rice is tender but still firm. Remove from the heat and, when cool, add the nuts and, if you wish, raisins. Sometimes the stuffing is colored with ½ teaspoon saffron or turmeric, or perfumed with a tablespoon of orange blossom water, but I do not personally care for these additions.

Stuff the pouches with the rice mixture. Rub the meat with oil, salt, and pepper, and roast, uncovered, in an oven preheated to 450°, then reduced to 350°. Roast for about 1 hour, or until the meat is well cooked and browned on the outside.

Put the apricots in a small saucepan with 1 tablespoon sugar and their soaking water. Bring to the boil and simmer, uncovered, for about 20 minutes. By this time the apricots will be soft and the liquid reduced.

A few minutes before serving, pour off the excess fat from the roasting pan. Turn the oven up to 475°. Pour the apricot sauce over the lamb and glaze in the oven for 5 to 7 minutes. Do not leave in the oven too long, as the apricots burn easily.

Instead of being roasted, the lamb may be braised on top of the stove. It is first seared in hot fat to brown it all over, then simmered until quite tender. The apricots and their water are added after searing, and the lamb simmers with them gently for about ¾ to 1 hour. In this method, there is no need to simmer the apricots separately first. They need only be soaked.

Kuzu Kapama / Turkish Lamb with Scallions and Herbs

1 tender leg of lamb
2 large bunches scallions, chopped
1 bunch fresh dill or chervil, finely chopped
1 large onion, quartered
¾ cup water
2½ tablespoons oil
Salt and black pepper

Clean the leg of lamb and remove excess fat. Put it in a saucepan or casserole with the scallions, herbs, and onion. Add water and oil, and season with salt and pepper. Cover and simmer gently for 2 to 3 hours, or until very tender, turning the meat over occasionally, and adding a little more water when necessary.

Choua / Moroccan Steamed Lamb

Besides favoring rich stews, Moroccans also appreciate tender steamed meat, gently flavored with cumin alone. The Turks also eat steamed lamb, not usually alone as in the recipe below, but accompanied by vegetables such as tomatoes, shallots, and sliced eggplants (the last sprinkled with salt and allowed to drain before being added), and flavored with a little tomato paste and a sprinkling of sage.

2 lbs. leg or shoulder of lamb   1 teaspoon cumin
Salt

Cut the meat into ¾-inch cubes. Sprinkle lightly with salt and cumin. Steam over boiling water for about 2 hours, or until the meat is tender and juicy. In the past, steaming was done in a pot sealed with paste, but today a hermetically sealed double steamer can be used instead.

Serve with plain rice or *couscous* (page 277).

Veal Sofrito

Sofrito, *the name our community in Egypt used to describe a method of cooking halfway between roasting and stewing in oil with very little water, is, predictably, a Spanish name. For a sofrito of lamb, see page 212.*

The cooking fat in this method varies according to the country and the community in which it is practiced. Butter can be used, but I prefer corn or nut oil.

A 2- to 3-lb. piece of veal, leg or loin   Juice of ½ lemon
4 tablespoons corn or nut oil   1 teaspoon powdered turmeric
Salt and black pepper

Turn the meat in hot oil in a large pan until it is browned all over. Sprinkle with salt and pepper, lemon juice, and turmeric, and moisten with ⅓ cup of water. Cover the pan and cook over very low heat for about 2 hours, turning it over once, or until the meat is very tender. It will cook in its own juices, released by the salt, so add only very little more water at a time, about ¾ cup in all, as it becomes absorbed.

Serve hot with potatoes or rice, or cold with salad.

Yoğurtlu Kebab / Kebabs with Yogurt

A Turkish meat and yogurt dish with bread.

1½ lbs. lean tender lamb or beef
Oil
Butter
Salt and black pepper

6 thick slices bread
4 tomatoes, skinned and chopped
1¼–2 cups yogurt
1 tablespoon paprika

Cut the meat into 1-inch cubes and sauté gently in oil or butter until tender but juicy. Season to taste with salt and pepper. (Some people like to marinate the cubes first in a mixture of oil, onion juice, salt, and pepper, or in seasoned yogurt, for at least an hour to tenderize them.)

Remove the crusts from the bread and cut the slices into 1-inch squares. Toast lightly or fry in butter. Arrange at the bottom of a shallow serving dish.

Sauté tomatoes in a very little butter until they are very soft, and season to taste with salt and pepper. Beat the yogurt and season to taste.

Just before serving, spread the puréed tomatoes over the squares of toast, pour the yogurt over the tomatoes, arrange the meat cubes on top, and dribble 2 tablespoons butter mixed with the paprika over the entire dish.

Serve immediately.

A rather good party snack is made keeping the bread slices whole. Fry or toast them and arrange them in individual plates. Then cover them just before serving with the respective layers of puréed tomatoes, yogurt, and fried kebabs, and decorate with paprika butter.

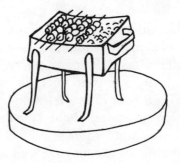

Lamb or Veal Chops in Tomato Sauce

6–8 large lamb or veal chops
About 2 tablespoons butter
1 large onion, sliced
2–3 whole cloves garlic
½ lb. ripe tomatoes, skinned and
    chopped, or about 1 cup
    canned whole tomatoes,
    drained and chopped

Salt and black pepper
2 tablespoons chopped parsley
½ teaspoon ground cinnamon
    [optional]

Trim as much fat from the chops as possible and flatten them lightly. Sauté the chops in hot butter for a few minutes on both sides until just colored. Remove them from the frying pan and arrange in a large pan. Keep hot.

Fry the onion and garlic cloves in the same butter until they are golden and the garlic is sweet and aromatic. Add the tomatoes, season to taste with salt and pepper, and sprinkle with parsley and cinnamon if liked. Cook for a few minutes longer, then add about ½ cup water. Mix well and pour the sauce over the chops. Simmer gently, uncovered, until the chops are tender and the sauce is rich and aromatic, adding more water if necessary. Taste and adjust seasoning, and serve on plain rice (pages 339–40) or burghul pilav (page 276), or with sautéed or mashed potatoes.

The garlic may be removed at the end of cooking time, and the sauce strained or put through an electric blender. I prefer to leave it as it is.

GROUND MEAT DISHES

Behind the seemingly inexhaustible range of subtly varying and intriguing ground meatballs, one can discern the creative spirit responsible for the luscious designs which decorate Arab pottery, carpets, and minarets. It inspired in cookery a rhythmic and prolific repetition as it did the floral and geometric patterns, endless variations on a theme. Each district and each town has striven to offer its own particular specialty for a meatball. I give here only a few, and leave the reader to imagine the rest.

One thing they all have in common is a perfectly smooth texture. To achieve this, the meat is usually ground two or three times, then pounded, sometimes with a little grated onion, until it becomes extremely soft and pasty. I find that this smoothness can best be achieved by pounding the meat against the sides of a bowl with a wooden spoon, or by kneading vigorously by hand. Another excellent and very simple way recently suggested to me is to use an electric blender. First blend the chopped onion until practically liquefied, then add the meat, egg or eggs (if used), and seasonings, and blend at high speed until pasty. Other ingredients should then be added and blended for a short time until thoroughly mixed.

Use ground lamb, beef, or veal, or a combination of lamb and beef, according to your taste—beef and lamb give a rich, strongly flavored dish, veal a paler, more delicate one. Always pound or knead it for as long as possible. The delightful smoothness of the texture is well worth the effort.

Seasonings vary within the Middle East from gentle cinnamon to allspice, cumin, coriander, and, of course, salt and either mild or strong pepper. Season mildly to begin with and keep on adding spices, salt, and pepper until you achieve the flavor you desire.

Kofta Bil Roz / Ground Meat Fingers with Ground Rice

2 lbs. lean beef, ground	2 onions, finely chopped
3 tablespoons ground rice ‡	2 cloves garlic, crushed [optional]
4 tablespoons finely chopped parsley	Salt and black pepper
	Oil or butter

Put the meat through the grinder two or three times if possible. Turn it into a large bowl. Add the ground rice, chopped parsley, onions, and garlic (if used). Work to a fine smooth paste by squashing with a wooden spoon and kneading vigorously by hand. If you have an electric blender, use it as described above. Season to taste with salt and pepper.

Take large, walnut-sized lumps and shape them into long fingers. Fry them gently in oil or butter, turning them until they are brown all over and well cooked inside. This should take about 10 minutes.

. . .

Quite often, Middle Eastern cooks drop the lightly fried fingers into a tomato sauce similar to the one suggested for *koukla* (following recipe).

Koukla

From the Greek word for doll.

3 slices white bread, crusts removed
2 lbs. lamb or beef, a mixture of these, or veal
3 eggs

¾ teaspoon ground allspice or 1 teaspoon ground cinnamon
Salt and black pepper
Oil for deep frying

Soak the bread in water, squeeze dry, and crumble. Grind the meat two or three times if possible, then add the soaked bread, eggs, and allspice or cinnamon. Knead vigorously to work the mixture to a smooth paste. If you have an electric blender, drop in the eggs first and beat for 10 seconds; add the bread and beat for another 10 seconds. Add the meat and seasonings gradually, beating between each addition. This gives a beautiful paste. Season to taste with salt and pepper.

Roll the mixture into marble-sized balls and deep-fry in hot oil for a few minutes until cooked through and a rich brown color.

Alternatively, you can stew the *koukla* in a tomato sauce made by blending 1 tablespoon flour with 1 tablespoon melted butter in a large pan, and stirring for a few minutes over low heat. Gradually add a 6-oz. can of tomato paste diluted in about 2 cups water, stirring constantly. Bring to a boil and season generously with salt and pepper. Drop in the meatballs and simmer them for about ½ hour, or until they are well done and the rich sauce is thick and reduced. (In this case the frying of the meatballs is best omitted, since the sauce would otherwise become very rich indeed.)

Kadin Budu / or "Lady's Thighs" (Turkish Meatballs)

This interesting recipe with the enticing name reverses the usual procedure of frying the meatballs before simmering them in sauce. Its virtue lies in producing a juicy, tender combination, and then trapping it in a crisp, dry shell.

1 lb. lamb or beef, ground	1 teaspoon finely chopped fresh dill
1 tablespoon rice	[if available]
3 eggs	Salt and black pepper
1 teaspoon olive or other cooking oil	Flour
1 small onion, grated	2½ tablespoons butter
1 teaspoon finely chopped parsley	

Work the meat to a smooth paste (see the recipe for *koukla* above). Put it in a bowl with the rice, 2 eggs, the oil, grated onion, parsley, and dill if available, and season with salt and pepper. Mix well and knead to a smooth paste. Shape into walnut-sized balls, rinsing your hands with water to prevent the meat from sticking to them, and arrange them in a pan with a little water—about ½ cup. Cover and simmer gently for about 20 minutes, or until the water has been absorbed and the meat and rice are cooked. Drain the meatballs and cool them.

Beat the remaining egg. Dip the meatballs in the beaten egg and roll them in flour. Melt the butter in a frying pan. When it is sizzling, add the meatballs and fry them until crisp and golden brown all over.

Terbiyeli Köfte

Here is a Turkish way of cooking meatballs also popular in Greece.

Prepare the meat mixture for either *kofta bil roz* (page 218) or *koukla* (page 219), and shape it into marble-sized balls. Poach them in lightly salted water for about 20 minutes until soft and tender.

Prepare the following sauce. Beat 3 egg yolks until light. Add the juice of 1 or 2 lemons (2 for a strong, lemony flavor) and ¾ cup of water, and continue beating until well blended. Season to taste with salt and pepper. Heat very gently over water, using a double boiler if you have one, to just below boiling point. Do not on any account let the mixture boil, or the eggs will curdle.

Lift the meatballs out of the poaching water, using a slotted spoon. Drain them well. Then drop them into the egg-and-lemon sauce and heat them through.

This is delicious served with plain rice.

Kofta Bil Sania / Ground Meat Loaf in a Tray

2 lbs. lamb, beef, or veal, ground
2 onions, grated
Salt and black pepper
1 teaspoon ground cinnamon or
    allspice

Oil or butter
4 tablespoons tomato paste
5 tablespoons finely chopped parsley

Have the meat ground two or three times if possible. Add the grated onions and work them together to a very smooth, soft paste, as for all *kofta* mixtures. Season to taste with salt, pepper, and cinnamon or allspice, and mix these spices in thoroughly.

Spread the meat mixture evenly over the bottom of a large oiled or buttered baking tray, flattening it out with a wooden spoon. The meat should be ¾ to 1 inch thick. Dot with butter shavings and bake in a moderate oven (375°) until the surface of the meat is browned and gives off a roasted aroma—about 40 minutes.

Mix the tomato paste with 1¼ cups water and pour it over the meat. Return the loaf to the oven, and continue to bake for about 10 minutes, or until the tomato sauce has become absorbed and the meat is well cooked. It will shrink away from the sides of the tray.

Turn the loaf out onto a large serving dish and cut it into squares or lozenges; or, if you are using a round baking tray, cut it into wedges like a cake. Garnish with chopped parsley, and serve with mashed or roast potatoes or a selection of salads.

Some people prefer to flavor the meat with a teaspoon each of ground cumin and coriander instead of cinnamon or allspice.

Armenian Kofta

1 lb. potatoes, boiled and mashed
1½ lbs. lean lamb or veal, ground
1 egg, beaten
Salt and black pepper
¼–⅓ cup pine nuts

Butter
¼–½ cup small seedless raisins
Flour
Oil for deep frying

Mix the potatoes and ground meat together in a bowl. Add beaten egg, and salt and pepper to taste, and knead vigorously by hand until the mixture is very smooth and soft. Fry the pine nuts in butter for a minute or two to color them lightly. Drain and knead them into the meat and potato mixture, together with the raisins.

Shape into walnut-sized balls. Roll them in flour and deep-fry in hot oil until crisp and brown on the outside and well done inside.

Blehat Lahma bi Beid / Meat Rolls Stuffed with Hard-boiled Eggs

2 lbs. lean beef or lamb, ground
3 slices white bread, crusts removed
1 onion, finely chopped
2 egg whites
1 teaspoon ground cinnamon
½ teaspoon grated nutmeg
Salt and black pepper

2 tablespoons finely chopped parsley
   [optional]
4 hard-boiled eggs, shelled
Flour
Butter or oil
4 tablespoons tomato paste
1 bay leaf
1 celery stalk with leaves

Grind the meat two or three times if possible, then pound it to a very smooth paste as described in the preceding recipes. Soak the bread in water, squeeze it dry, and crumble it into the meat. Add the onion, egg whites, spices, salt, and pepper to taste, and chopped parsley if used. Mix well to a light paste.

Divide the mixture into four equal parts and shape each portion around a hard-boiled egg, making four oval rolls. Pat and press the meat firmly around the eggs so that the rolls do not come apart during cooking. Alternatively, you can make one fat, long roll and stuff it with all four eggs.

Flour the rolls and fry in hot butter or oil until colored all over.

Make a sauce with the tomato paste, bay leaf, celery, about 1 cup water, and salt and pepper. Bring it to the boil and simmer for a few minutes. Drop in the meat rolls and simmer them gently until they are well done, and the sauce has reduced and thickened.

Lift the rolls out very carefully. Serve them hot with the sauce, accompanied by rice or sautéed potatoes; or serve them cold, also in their sauce. Thinly sliced, they make a fine appetizer or a cold main course.

Persians vary this dish by adding about ¼ cup yellow split peas, boiled until soft, to the ground meat mixture, and imbedding a few soaked and stoned prunes next to the hard-boiled eggs. It is a delight to encounter them, sweet and soft, in the midst of the beautifully spiced and flavored meat. A splendid variation.

Daoud Pasha / Meatballs with Pine Nuts and Tomato Sauce

2 lbs. lamb, beef, or veal, ground
Salt and black pepper
Seasonings: 1 teaspoon ground cinnamon or allspice, or ¾ teaspoon each ground cumin and coriander *

2 largish onions, cut in half-moon slices
Oil or butter
⅓ cup pine nuts
6-oz. can tomato paste
Juice of ½ lemon
2 tablespoons finely chopped parsley

Grind, pound, or knead the meat to a smooth paste as described in the preceding recipes. Add salt, pepper, and seasoning (I prefer cinnamon for this dish). Knead well and roll into marble-sized balls.

In a saucepan or deep frying pan, fry the onion slices gently in a little oil or butter until golden and transparent. Add the meatballs and sauté over low heat, shaking the pan and rolling the balls about almost constantly to color them all over. Add the pine nuts and fry gently for 2 minutes longer. Mix the tomato paste with a little water and add it to the pan. Add more water, enough to cover the balls; flavor with lemon juice and season with salt and pepper. Stir well and simmer over low heat until the balls are well done and the sauce is reduced; add more water from time to time if the sauce reduces too quickly.

A few minutes before serving, adjust the seasoning and sprinkle the dish with finely chopped parsley.

An attractive way of serving this dish is to fry extra pine nuts in butter for about 2 minutes until lightly colored. When the meatballs are cooked, decorate each one by sticking a pine nut into the top. Serve with plain white rice. A popular variation is to knead the same quantity of pine nuts into the meatball mixture instead of having them as part of the sauce.

* These quantities will give a rather highly flavored dish—reduce them for a more delicate aroma.

Kofta Mabrouma / Meat Rolls with Pine Nuts

This is a specialty of Aleppo in Syria, where it is traditionally baked in a round tray and served on a round dish, with the rolls arranged in diminishing circles.

2 medium-sized onions	5 tablespoons pine nuts
2 eggs	4 tablespoons butter or margarine
2 lbs. lean lamb or beef, ground	Chopped parsley and slices of
Salt and black pepper	lemon, to garnish

Peel and grate the onions. Beat the eggs with a fork. Have the meat ground two or three times if possible, and mix it with the grated onions and eggs. Season with salt and pepper, and mix well. Squash against the sides of the bowl with a wooden spoon and knead vigorously by hand, in the old Middle Eastern style—or use an electric blender to make the mixture very soft and pasty.

Flatten the meat mixture on a board or large plate into six thin rectangular shapes. Put a row of pine nuts about ¼ inch in from one of the longer sides of each rectangle and roll up into a fat sausage shape, starting from the edge lined with pine nuts.

Take an oven tray or dish, square or round, which will just hold the six rolls, and arrange them in it side by side. Dot with butter or margarine shavings, or melt the butter and brush it over each roll. Sprinkle with about 4 tablespoons water and bake in a moderate oven (375°) for about ¾ hour or longer, depending on the thickness of the rolls, until cooked and well browned.

Turn out onto a hot serving dish, garnish with chopped parsley and slices of lemon, and serve hot with rice or sautéed potatoes.

Zucchini or Eggplant Meatballs

This dish is a specialty of Smyrna.

2 lbs. zucchini or peeled eggplant	2 oz. Parmesan or Cheddar cheese,
Salt	grated (½ cup)
Oil	2 large eggs, beaten
2 onions, chopped	Black pepper
1 lb. beef, lamb, or veal, ground	Flour

Slice zucchini or eggplant. Sprinkle with salt and leave to drain in a colander for at least ½ hour. If zucchini are used, boil them until tender. Otherwise, fry the eggplant in a little oil until soft, and drain on absorbent paper. Fry the chopped onions until soft and golden.

Chop the zucchini or eggplant finely, and mix with the meat, which has been squashed with a wooden spoon and kneaded or blended to a smooth paste. Add the cheese, onions, and beaten eggs, and season to taste with salt and pepper. Mix well.

Shape the mixture into walnut-sized balls. Roll them in flour and fry or sauté them gently over very low heat so that they are well cooked inside before they become too brown on the surface.

These vegetable meatballs can be eaten hot with potatoes or rice, or cold with salad. Both ways are delicious.

A variation given to me by an Egyptian uses 1 lb. chopped artichoke hearts mixed with 1¼ lbs. minced meat which has been worked to a paste.

Leek Meatballs

This dish is a specialty of Salonika.

2 lbs. leeks	Black pepper
Salt	Oil
1 lb. beef, ground	Juice of 2 lemons
1 cup dry white bread crumbs	1 tablespoon butter
2–3 eggs	

Wash the leeks very carefully. Remove their tough outer leaves and trim both ends. Boil in lightly salted water until just tender. Drain and grind or chop very finely.

Turn the meat into a very smooth paste in the usual way. Mix it with the ground leeks, bread crumbs, and eggs, and season with salt and pepper. Mix well. Shape into walnut-sized balls and fry in oil until colored all over.

Put the lemon juice, butter, and a little water (about ¾ cup) in a large pan. Sprinkle with salt and pepper, and bring to the boil. Drop in the meatballs and simmer, covered, for 15 to 20 minutes, or until they are soft and well cooked, and the lemony sauce has been absorbed, shaking the pan occasionally and adding a little more water if the sauce reduces too quickly. The combination of leek and lemon with meat is unusual and delicious.

An excellent version of these vegetable and meatballs is made with spinach. Substitute 1½ lbs. fresh spinach for the leeks. Wash the leaves carefully and stew them for a few minutes without additional water. Put through a mincer or chop finely, and add to the meat mixture.

KIBBEH

Kibbeh is the great love of the Syrians and the Lebanese—their national dish and glory. The daily life of the people revolves around its preparation, a dramatic ritual. The pounding of the meat and wheat in a stone or metal mortar with a heavy metal pestle is a sound that wakens one in the morning and lulls one to sleep in the afternoon, a sound instantly provoked by the arrival of an unexpected guest or a ring of the doorbell.

I know of no other dish whose preparation is enveloped by such a mystique. Some women are known to have a special "hand" or "finger" for making *kibbeh*. This knack is envied by other women and especially by their husbands. One is said to be favored by the gods if one is born with a long finger, which makes the shaping of *kibbeh* easier.

Today, one can use a very fine grinder to save some of the pounding (or an electric blender as suggested for meatball mixtures), and a machine has recently been developed in the Lebanon which takes care of the whole process.

There are countless variations of *kibbeh*, some widely known throughout the Middle East, others less common or belonging to one particular community. I shall give as many as I know, for I think that they are really worth trying.

The most common *kibbeh* is a mixture of fine cracked wheat or burghul, grated onion, and ground lamb pounded to a paste. Eaten raw, it is called *kibbeh nayé*. The same paste can be fried or grilled. In *kibbeh bil sanieh*, a layer of minced meat filling is sandwiched between two layers of *kibbeh* and baked in the oven. Stuffed *kibbeh* are hollow, oval or long torpedo-shaped shells of the same paste, filled with a minced meat mixture and deep-fried. This last type has innumerable variations: the outer *kibbeh* shell is sometimes made with seasoned cracked wheat alone. Jews have a variation made with matzo meal (called *massa* by Sephardic Jews), evolved for Passover but prepared throughout the year because of its particular lightness. Another *kibbeh*, popular in Egypt, is made with ground rice instead of cracked wheat and is stewed in a lemony stock or *hamud*. We called it *kibbeh hamda* (page 232).

Small *kibbeh* are often added to eggplant and other vegetable stews, or are cooked in yogurt, pomegranate juice, or sesame meal mixed with orange juice.

Kibbeh Nayé / Raw Kibbeh

1 lb. lean tender lamb, cubed [leg is good]	1 large onion
Salt	Black pepper
	1 cup fine burghul [cracked wheat]

Pound the meat rhythmically and vigorously with a little salt in a stone mortar until it is smooth and pasty. Alternatively, if a grinder is available, put the meat through it several times. Grate and pound the onion with salt and pepper, or grind it a few times. Mix the onion and meat together and grind or pound again, adding 1 or 2 tablespoons cold water or 1 or 2 ice cubes to achieve a soft and smooth texture.

Rinse the burghul in a strainer and quickly squeeze out the moisture. Add to the meat and onion mixture, and knead vigorously by hand. Adjust seasoning and pound in the mortar for as long as possible, about ½ hour; or grind together several times, then pound and knead again until smooth and moist.

This dish is traditionally served on a decorative glass or china plate, accompanied by a bowl of lettuce leaves. It is passed around as an appetizer or at the start of a meal. Each guest selects a lettuce leaf and, using it as a spoon, scoops up a small portion of *kibbeh* which is eaten together with the lettuce. Some people also like a squeeze of lemon over it.

Another way of serving *kibbeh nayé* is to roll the meat mixture into small thin fingers, pile them on a bed of lettuce leaves and accompany them with a bowlful of young lettuce. Romaine or cos lettuce is used in the Middle East.

The quantities of meat and burghul are sometimes reversed (4 cups burghul to ¼ lb. meat). The paste is shaped as above, and the rolls are sprinkled with a dressing of olive oil and lemon juice or tamarind, and garnished with cayenne pepper and a few finely chopped scallions.

Kibbeh Nayé with Sauce

Another popular way of serving raw kibbeh *is accompanied by a minced meat sauce—in this case, veal is a favorite.*

1 lb. onions, finely chopped	⅓ cup pine nuts
4 tablespoons butter	Salt and black pepper
1 lb. lean veal, ground	Juice of 1 lemon

Fry the onions in hot butter until golden. Add the ground veal and continue to fry until the meat changes color. Add the pine nuts. Season to taste with salt and pepper, and add water to cover. Bring to the boil and simmer gently until the meat is well cooked and soft, and the sauce is reduced. Some people prefer to fry the pine nuts lightly on their own, and add them just before serving. Sprinkle with lemon juice and serve in a separate bowl with the *kibbeh nayé.*

Grilled or Fried Kibbeh

1 lb. lean tender lamb, cubed	Black pepper
Salt	2 cups fine burghul [cracked wheat]
1 large onion, finely grated	Oil

Prepare the basic mixture as in the recipe for *kibbeh nayé* but using double the quantity of burghul, as given above. Pat into round, flat, biscuit shapes. Grill over charcoal or under a grill, or fry in hot oil until crisp and golden.

Kibbeh bil Sanieh / Kibbeh on a Tray

Prepare kibbeh *mixture as above, using 1 lb. meat to 2 cups burghul, and following the method described for* kibbeh nayé *on page 227.*

1 medium-sized onion, finely chopped	Salt and black pepper
2½ tablespoons oil	½ teaspoon ground cinnamon
½ lb. lamb, veal, or beef, ground	A few tablespoons stock
⅓ cup pine nuts	Butter

Fry the onion in hot oil until golden and soft. Add the meat and pine nuts, and continue to cook until the meat has changed color. Add a few tablespoons of water to soften the meat, season, and add the cinnamon.

Butter a baking tray and smooth half of the *kibbeh* over the bottom. Spread the filling over this evenly and cover with a second layer of *kibbeh*. Cut diagonal lines over the top to make lozenge shapes.

Melt 8 tablespoons (1 stick) butter and pour this all over the top of the *kibbeh*. Bake in a moderate oven (375°) for ¾ to 1 hour. It should be well done, and beautifully brown and crisp on top. Basting occasionally with a few tablespoons of stock makes the inside moist and even better.

This is equally delicious hot or cold. Serve with yogurt and salads.

Syrian Stuffed Kibbeh

This is the most popular as well as the most intriguing of *kibbeh*. The preparation of these small *kibbeh* requires all the talent of *kibbeh* making. Syrian women measure their art and make their reputations by their craftsmanship and finesse when making this dish. The art lies in making the outer shells as long, as thin, and as even as possible. The crisp, light, tasty shells should crack to divulge a juicy, aromatic meat filling.

Prepare the *kibbeh* meat mixture as for raw *kibbeh* on page 227, using 1 lb. meat to 2 cups burghul, and the filling as for *kibbeh bil sanieh* (above).

Wet your hands with cold water. Take a small lump of *kibbeh* mixture the size of an egg. Holding it in your left hand, make a hole in it with a finger of the right hand and use the left hand to pat the paste around the finger and work it into a long, slim, oval shape, pressing it up the finger, widening it and slipping it around and around. This is rather reminiscent of pottery making. If the paste cracks, dip a finger in cold water and use it to stick the shell together again. There must be no holes in the shell. British soldiers in the Middle East during the Second World War used to call these *kibbeh* "Syrian torpedoes," and I think that this describes their shape rather well.

Fill the shell with about a tablespoon of filling. Close the opening by wetting the rim with cold water and sticking the edges together. Pat and smooth into a thin end to achieve a slim, oval shape. If you find all this too difficult, make a small round or oval shape. This seems easier to achieve.

Deep-fry the "torpedoes" in oil to a rich, dark brown color. Drain. Serve hot or cold with a selection of salads: ground almond (page 43), a *tahina* cream salad (pages 42–4), or a mixed fresh vegetable salad.

These *kibbeh* can be prepared ahead and fried just before serving, or fried and warmed up again in a covered dish in the oven. Smaller versions are cooked for the last ½ hour in eggplant, zucchini, and meat stews.

Plain Burghul Kibbeh

This variation of the preceding kibbeh *is a much easier one which does not require the long preparation of mincing and pounding. It is equally delicious and rather lighter, although the shell has a tendency to break as it is handled, and must be carefully patched if it does.*

KIBBEH SHELL
2 cups fine burghul [cracked wheat]
¾ cup plain flour
1 tablespoon oil
1 teaspoon salt
Black pepper

Filling: as for *Kibbeh bil Sanieh*
   [page 229]
Oil for deep frying

Make the shell. Wash the burghul in a fine-meshed strainer and squeeze it dry. Put it in a large bowl with the other shell ingredients and knead vigorously for at least 15 minutes to achieve a smooth paste.

Shape and fill the shells as in the preceding recipe. Deep-fry and serve with salads.

Kibbeh made with Matzo Meal (Massa)

This is a Sephardic Jewish recipe. It is easy to make and quite exquisite.

½ lb. matzo meal
2½ tablespoons ground rice ‡
½ onion, crushed in a garlic press
½ teaspoon ground cumin

Salt and black pepper
Warm water
Oil for deep frying

Mix all the ingredients together. Add a little warm water gradually, working it in by hand, enough to make a firm, stiff paste. Use this paste to make the outer shells as described in the recipe for Syrian stuffed *kibbeh* (page 229).

Fill with the filling (top page 229). Prick with a skewer to prevent the occasional one from bursting. Deep-fry until crisp and golden.

Kibbeh with Matzo Meal (Massa) and Meat

Here is a variation for the outer shell in the recipe above.

¼ lb. lamb or beef, ground
½ lb. matzo meal

Salt and black pepper
Warm water

Pound the ground meat or knead it vigorously by hand to a smooth paste. Add the matzo meal and season to taste with salt and pepper. Add a little warm water gradually, a little at a time, and keep kneading until the mixture is smooth again.

Use this to make the outer shells as for Syrian stuffed *kibbeh* (page 229). Fill with the filling (top page 229), and deep-fry until crisp and golden.

Stuffed Kibbeh in Yogurt

Prepare stuffed *kibbeh*, using burghul and meat (Syrian stuffed *kibbeh*, page 229), or burghul alone.

YOGURT SAUCE
5 cups yogurt
1 tablespoon cornstarch or 1 egg
    white

Salt
3–4 cloves garlic, crushed
2 tablespoons dried crushed mint
4 tablespoons butter

Stabilize the yogurt with cornstarch or egg white and salt to taste as described on page 80, to allow it to be cooked without curdling. Add the *kibbeh* and continue to simmer for about 20 minutes. (You can equally well deep-fry the *kibbeh* first, and then cook them in the yogurt for a few minutes only.)

Fry the crushed garlic and dried crushed mint in hot butter with salt to taste. Pour over the yogurt and stir well.

Alternatively, add the crushed garlic raw to the yogurt and garnish the dish with dried crushed mint.

Serve hot or cold, with plain rice.

Cooked rice is sometimes added to the yogurt in the pan and simmered for a few minutes before serving.

Kibbeh Hamda / Kibbeh of Ground Rice Cooked in Hamud

This is my mother's recipe for an unusual kibbeh. It is very easy to prepare and does not require so much time. This dish is always served in a hamud *sauce or soup as an accompaniment to rice.*

FILLING
3 oz. lamb or beef, ground
1 oz. fat [from the meat], finely
    chopped
2 tablespoons finely chopped parsley
Pinch of ground allspice
Salt and black pepper

KIBBEH SHELL
6 oz. lamb or beef, ground
½ lb. ground rice ‡
Salt and pepper

Oil
1 recipe *Hamud* [page 110]

Mix the filling ingredients well together in their raw state.

Make the *kibbeh* shell. Pound the ground meat and ground rice with a little seasoning. Gradually add a little water (a few tablespoons should be enough) and knead to a smooth paste. You can either pound the mixture in a mortar or use an electric blender to achieve a soft, homogenous paste.

Put a little oil on your hands to prevent the paste from sticking to them and roll the mixture into walnut-sized balls. Hollow each ball with your finger, and fill with about a teaspoon of filling. Close the openings by pinching them together firmly.

Drop the balls into boiling *hamud* and simmer gently for about 1 hour.

The little raw *kibbeh* can also be fried in hot oil and then cooked in an eggplant, fava bean, artichoke, or plain meat stew. They are quite delightful.

MEAT AND VEGETABLE STEWS

Yakhnie to the Syrians and Lebanese, *touagen* to the North Africans, and *abgusht* to the Persians, stews are one of the finest features of Middle Eastern food. In his *Işret Nāme*, the sixteenth-century Turkish poet Rēvanī describes a stew as "a saint who makes his prayer rug float upon the water," comparing the pieces of meat floating in the rich sauce to the prayer rugs on which the saints of old were wont to traverse rivers.

The earliest recipes that have been found, written in Baghdad in the year 1226, were for the most part descriptions of the stews, dishes otherwise known only by name—extraordinary and breathtaking dishes in which the art of blending flavors, of balancing and composing textures and aromas, is manifested in wonderful array. In many ways, it is similar to the art of the painter who builds up his canvas, knowing when one stroke of his brush demands another one, sharper or more subtle, larger or smaller; feeling his way toward a harmony of shapes and surfaces, color and tension; trying to achieve a balance between a small, sharp, acid yellow and a large, soft, pastel mauve; supporting the one with a cooler, sweeter red and piercing the other with an orange dart.

It is this subtle, sensuous feeling for the balance of ingredients, the harmony of flavors and aromas (sometimes achieved by a sharp contrast), which produced the recipes recorded by Muhammad ibn Hasan ibn Muhammad ibn al-Karim al-Katib al-Baghdadi, who "loved eating above all pleasures." The same talent is responsible for the stews of today, some originating in, and extraordinarily similar to, the ancient ones, using the same contrasts of sweet and sour, spicy and sweet, or the peace of equals. Some stews are earthly and simple, others are complicated and intoxicating, using fascinating combinations of meat with fruits, nuts, and vegetables. Persians have brought this luxurious cooking to its peak, as their recipes below will show. It is interesting to note the influence of the rich period of the Persian Empire on the food of all the Middle East, stretching as far as the North African Maghreb.

To return to the stews. Either they should be simmered very gently for a long time on top of the stove or they can be baked in the oven after the ingredients have been fried. The second method is less common and, to my mind, less successful. The use of a pressure cooker does, of course, reduce the cooking time considerably, but much of the richness and delicate blending of flavors is, I fear, lost. The usual accompaniment is *couscous* (page 277), plain rice, or burghul, but some people prefer to eat the stew simply with large quantities of bread, breaking pieces from it and dipping them into the sauce.

These stews can be served as party and family dishes alike, and they can always be extended for the unexpected guest simply by adding water. Nineteenth-century cooking manuals often remark that the amounts given will serve a certain number of people, but that you can add water if a friend should arrive.

Finally, to those who are afraid of trying new symphonies and harmonies of taste, may I remind them that not so long ago discordant colors such as pinks and oranges, blues and greens, were painful to Western eyes. The taste for them having been acquired, they have revolutionized design and fashion; and wherever colors are used today, it is the discords that stimulate, excite, and give the greatest pleasure.

When making these stews, use lean or fat meat, as you wish. Cheaper cuts are good enough, as the lengthy cooking ensures that the meat becomes tender. Clean the meat carefully, removing membranes, tendons, etc. Wash it or wipe it with a damp cloth, and cut into cubes ¾ to 1 inch square. Then sear the meat in oil or butter until lightly colored before stewing it. This adds richness and a deeper color to the dish, and keeps the meat juices within the meat. If you want a pale, light stew, simmer the meat in water without frying it first, removing any scum as it comes to the surface.

Marrow bones are often added to Middle Eastern stews for richness; they are cracked to allow as much of the marrow to escape as possible.

Use very small amounts of spices to begin with, and then add more to your taste after the stew has been cooking for some time. Add herbs, onions, garlic, celery, and scallions for flavoring. Introduce vegetables to enrich and vary the flavor, and yellow split peas, beans, lentils, or chickpeas to give weight, to bind, or to create extra texture. Use saffron to color the dish yellow, tomatoes to make it red, and pomegranate sauce to give it a brown color. Pour in a little wine vinegar where you would usually add wine, and balance it with sugar for a sweet-and-sour sauce. Use chopped or ground almonds, walnuts, pistachios, or hazelnuts to thicken the sauce, and raisins and fresh or dried fruits to sweeten it.

In the Middle East, stews are cooked for several hours over very low heat; quite often they are sent to the local communal oven to be cooked. Cook a stew gently for several hours on top of the stove, with a lid on the pan. Alternatively, you *can* put it in a slow oven (325°) in a covered dish; but in this case, you should use less liquid—only half that suggested in the following recipes.

Meat Stew with Eggplants

3 small eggplants or 2 medium ones
Salt
1 large onion, finely chopped
Oil
1½ lbs. lean or fat lamb, or veal,
    cut into 1-inch cubes

2–3 tomatoes, skinned and quartered
1 tablespoon tomato paste
Juice of ½ lemon
½ teaspoon ground cumin
½ teaspoon ground allspice [op-
    tional]

Slice the eggplants and sprinkle them with salt. Allow them to drain in a colander for at least ½ hour.

Fry the onion in about 2 tablespoons oil until soft and golden. Add the meat and brown it well. Add the tomatoes and squash them with a fork. Stir in the tomato paste and lemon juice thoroughly. Season to taste with salt, pepper, and cumin, and if you like, allspice. Cover with water, bring to the boil, and simmer gently, covered, for about 1½ hours.

Wash the eggplant slices and pat them dry. Fry them in hot oil for a few minutes to color them all over. Drain and add them to the stew, and simmer, covered, for a further ½ hour.

Turkish Meatballs with Eggplant Purée

4–6 eggplants, depending on size
2 lbs. beef, ground
2 eggs
4 tablespoons dry white bread
    crumbs
1 teaspoon ground cumin

1 teaspoon ground allspice
Salt and black pepper
Flour
About 4 tablespoons oil
1 large onion, sliced
2 tablespoons tomato paste

Grill the eggplants under a broiler or over a flame until the skins are blackened and blister away from the flesh. Cool, and rub the skins off under cold running water, taking care to remove every charred particle. Squeeze out as much of the bitter juices as possible; drain well and mash the flesh with a fork.

Grind the beef two or three times if possible, and knead by hand to a very smooth, soft paste (or use an electric blender as suggested on page 218). Add the eggs, bread crumbs, and seasonings (less if you want a blander mixture—this is rather strong). Knead again. Shape the mixture into small balls, roll them in flour, and fry in oil over fairly gentle heat until they are cooked through and colored all over. Remove and drain.

In the same oil, fry the sliced onion until soft and golden; add the eggplant purée and tomato paste, season to taste with salt and pepper, and cook gently for another 10 minutes. Drop in the meatballs and simmer for a final 10 minutes.

Serve with plain rice or bread, and with one or two salads.

Mefarka

A great delicacy of ancient origin, mefarka *was always prepared by my paternal grandmother and several of my aunts on Jewish feast days for the men to relish on their return from the synagogue. It is a very unusual cold dish of minced meat, fresh fava beans, and eggs, lightly perfumed with thyme and spices.*

Oil	1½ teaspoons mixed spices: nut-
2 lbs. fresh fava beans, shelled, or	meg, cinnamon, cayenne pep-
1 lb. shelled frozen fava beans	per, ground cloves
Salt and black pepper	3 eggs
½ teaspoon dried thyme, or more	Juice of ½ lemon [optional]
1½ lbs. lean beef, ground	

Mix 4 tablespoons oil with a little water (about ½ cup) in a saucepan. Add fava beans, sprinkle with salt and pepper to taste, and perfume with a little thyme. Simmer gently until the beans are tender, adding water, a little at a time, as it becomes absorbed.

In the meantime prepare the meat mixture, called *tatbila*. Heat 2 tablespoons oil in a deep frying pan or heavy, flameproof casserole. Add the ground beef when it is just warm—if the oil is too hot, the meat will dry up. Add also the mixed spices, salt and pepper to taste, and just enough water to cover. Simmer the whole until the meat is well cooked, soft, and moist and has absorbed the water as well as the aroma of the spices. The mixture should now be dryish.

Add the meat mixture to the beans and stir well, crushing lightly with a fork. Break the eggs into the pan and stir. Cook, stirring constantly, until they set. Turn out onto a serving dish and allow to cool. Taste and correct seasoning—the balance and degree of flavoring alters with the change in temperature.

Serve cold, sprinkled with a little lemon juice.

Lahma bi Ma'ala / Meat in the Frying Pan

2 lbs. best stewing beef, round or
    rump
3 tablespoons oil
1 lb. onions, coarsely chopped
Salt and black pepper
1 teaspoon ground allspice [or more
    for a spicy dish]

2 oz. parsley, chopped
1 lb. tomatoes, skinned and
    chopped, or a 1-lb. can
    whole tomatoes
4 tablespoons tomato paste

Cut the beef into 1-inch cubes. Fry in hot oil in a large frying pan, stirring and shaking the pan to brown the cubes all over. Remove from the pan. In the same oil, fry the onions to a dark golden color. Return the meat and add salt, pepper, allspice, parsley, tomatoes, and tomato paste, and about 5 tablespoons water. Simmer gently for 2 hours, uncovered. Add a very little water from time to time, but only if necessary. If using canned tomatoes, the liquid should be enough and no water need be added, except at the start.

The large quantity of onions and parsley and the allspice give this dish a distinctively Middle Eastern flavor.

Serve with rice or sautéed potatoes.

A similar Moroccan *tagine*, a specialty of Fez, varies in that the ingredients are not fried first but covered with cold water and simmered gently for 2½ hours with a little oil and a variety of seasonings: cumin, ginger, allspice, salt, black pepper, paprika, and cayenne are all used, though with a light hand, so that the effect is gentle rather than fiery. This *tagine* is sometimes colored with ¼ teaspoon turmeric. Another similar stew is the Tunisian *mirmiz*, which includes a sliced sweet green pepper, and possibly a hot dried chili pod or two. Chickpeas or dried white beans, soaked overnight, are sometimes added at the start of cooking as well.

String Bean and Meat Stew

This is a popular family meal in Egypt, Syria, and the Lebanon.

2 lbs. fresh string beans	2 lbs. stewing lamb or beef, cubed
2 large onions, finely chopped	3 tablespoons tomato paste
4 tablespoons butter or oil	Salt and black pepper

String the beans if necessary, and cut in half. Fry the onions in butter or oil in a large, thick-bottomed saucepan until transparent and golden. Add the meat and brown it all over to seal it. Add the beans and fry very gently until slightly softened. Stir in the tomato paste, blending it well into the fat. Cover with water, season with salt and pepper, and bring to the boil. Cover the pan and simmer gently for about 1½ hours, or until the meat and vegetables are very tender and the sauce is quite thick. Add more water if necessary during the cooking time. Adjust seasoning and serve.

This dish can also be flavored with ¼ teaspoon grated nutmeg, ½ teaspoon ground cinnamon, and the juice of 1 lemon.

Mozaat / Shin of Veal Stew

The particular quality of this dish (which I used to hate as a child) lies in its texture. The connective tissue of the shin softens in the cooking process and turns into gelatin, while the meat becomes extremely tender and soft.

2 lbs. shin of veal in large pieces	Salt and black pepper
6 potatoes, peeled and sliced	½ teaspoon turmeric [optional]
3 tablespoons oil	Juice of ½ lemon

In a large pan, sauté the meat and sliced potatoes gently in hot oil, turning them to brown them all over. Season with salt and pepper, and add the turmeric if you wish to give the stew a yellowish color. Half-cover with water. Simmer, covered, for about 2 hours, or until the meat is very soft and the sauce reduced, adding a little more water during this time if necessary, and turning the meat over occasionally. Adjust the seasoning and squeeze a little lemon juice over the pan just before serving.

This dish is particularly delicious if about a dozen little *kibbeh hamda* (page 232) are simmered in it instead of some of the potatoes. In other variations, about 6 artichoke hearts or 2 sliced, salted, and drained eggplants are added. In this case one again uses fewer potatoes; and, if using eggplants, one omits the turmeric.

Arab proverb: "God loveth those who are content."

Jellied Shin of Veal

2 lbs. shin of veal and 1 shin bone, cracked	6 hard-boiled eggs, shelled and quartered
3 tablespoons oil	2 tablespoons boiled green peas
Salt and black pepper	1 boiled carrot, cut into thin sticks
½ teaspoon turmeric [optional]	A little chopped parsley
Juice of ½ lemon	Thin slices of lemon

Sauté the meat and bone (well scrubbed and cracked to release the marrow) in hot oil in a large pan until colored all over. Season with salt and pepper, and sprinkle with turmeric if used. (This gives a fine taste and a delicate color.) Cover with water. Bring to the boil and simmer gently, covered, for about 2½ hours. The meat will be quite soft and the sauce rich and gelatinous. Remove any excess fat by drawing absorbent paper across the surface. Stir in the lemon juice and adjust the seasoning.

Remove the bone and cut up any largish pieces of meat. Rinse out a large mold and arrange the meat and hard-boiled eggs in it in a decorative pattern. Boiled green peas, thin sticks of cooked carrot, and chopped parsley can be used to brighten the dish. Strain the pan juices into the mold through a fine strainer, and leave the dish in the refrigerator for a few hours or overnight until the liquid has set to a jelly.

Turn out onto a large serving dish and decorate with thin slices of lemon.

The addition of a calf's foot at the start of the preparation or 1 teaspoon softened gelatin at the end will give a much firmer jelly.

Lissan al Assfour / Birds' Tongues

This is a lamb stew made with pasta, and I am assured that it tastes right only if small Italian pastine called graniamo (which look like tiny birds' tongues or largish grains of rice) are used. During the last war, when this Italian import was not available, families who loved the dish used to make the pasta themselves with flour and water, rolling it into the correct, tiny thin ovals between their fingers. A friend recalls spending hours with her brother every Sunday as a small child, rolling the little bits of dough.

2–3 onions, sliced
4 tablespoons butter or oil
2 lbs. lean lamb [e.g., leg], cubed
Salt and black pepper

1 teaspoon ground cinnamon [optional]
2½ cups meat stock or water
½–1 lb. *graniamo* pasta
Grated Parmesan cheese

Fry the sliced onions in the hot butter or oil until soft and golden, using a large pan. Add the cubed meat and brown it on all sides. Season with salt, pepper, and a little cinnamon if liked; cover the pan, and let the onions and meat cook very slowly in their own juice until nearly ready, about 1½ hours. Pour in the stock or water, and simmer for ½ hour longer.

Add the pasta and cook for a further 20 minutes, or until the meat is very tender and the pasta has swelled to double its bulk. Add more water if and as required. Some sauce must be left at the end of cooking time. Taste and adjust seasoning.

Serve with grated Parmesan cheese—a recent innovation in Egypt, owing to the Italian influence of the last century.

Meatballs with Spinach and Chickpeas

One of the dishes inspired by the ancient Persian tradition.

1½ lbs. beef, lamb, or veal, ground
1 onion, finely chopped
Salt and black pepper
Oil
¾ cup chickpeas, soaked overnight

1 lb. fresh spinach
1 tablespoon butter
2 cloves garlic, crushed
1 teaspoon ground coriander

Make small meatballs in the usual way (see page 218) with the minced meat, onion, and a little salt and pepper. Fry them lightly in oil until brown all over.

Boil the soaked and drained chickpeas in water until soft. Wash the spinach leaves thoroughly, removing any thick stems. Drain well and chop the leaves finely on a board. Stew them in their own juice and the butter until tender. Add the drained, cooked chickpeas and the meatballs, cover, and continue simmering for a further ½ hour, or until the meatballs are well done, adding a little water if necessary.

The particular refinement of this dish comes from a fried mixture called *taklia*, a great Arab favorite for flavoring stews and soups. It is made by crushing the 2 cloves garlic with a little salt, then frying them with the ground coriander until the mixture smells sweet. This should be added to the other ingredients at the end of the cooking and stirred in well.

Serve with rice.

A rather delicious Turkish way of eating this dish is to smother it in yogurt mixed with crushed garlic, seasoned with salt, pepper, and dried crushed mint. The whole is decorated with a sprinkling of scarlet paprika. In this case, omit the *taklia*. Another interesting variation from modern Persia is *khoresh sak*, a spinach and orange sauce served with rice. The juice of 1 lemon and 2 oranges is mixed with 1 tablespoon flour and cooked with the meat and spinach for the last ½ hour. In this case, add only crushed garlic fried in butter instead of the complete *taklia*.

Meat and Okra (Bamia) Stew

This is a great Egyptian favorite. Lamb was always used in the past, but today many families prefer to make it with beef or veal. In Egypt, the meat and vegetables are usually fried in samna, *or rich clarified butter, in which case rather less fat is needed than the amount of fresh butter given below. However, the Middle Eastern tendency today is to cook more and more with oil or ordinary butter.*

If using canned okra, add it to the stew toward the end of cooking time; otherwise it will disintegrate.

2 lbs. fresh okra [bamia] or 1 large can okra
2 large onions, finely chopped
2 large cloves garlic
4 tablespoons butter or oil
2 lbs. stewing beef, lamb, or veal, cubed
½ lb. ripe tomatoes, sliced
1–2 tablespoons tomato paste
Salt and black pepper
Juice of 1 lemon [optional]
1 teaspoon ground coriander [optional]

Wash fresh okra and cut off the stems. Fry the chopped onions and whole garlic cloves in butter or oil until both are golden and the garlic is aromatic. Add the cubed meat and brown all over. Then add the prepared okra and fry gently for a little while longer. Add the tomatoes, continue to cook for a few more minutes, and cover with water in which you have diluted the tomato paste. Season with salt and pepper, and stir well. Bring to a boil and simmer over low heat for 1½ hours or more, until the meat and vegetables are very tender and the rich sauce is reduced, adding a little more water if necessary. Taste and adjust seasoning.

The juice of a lemon may be added to the sauce, and a teaspoon of ground coriander can be fried with the garlic and onion before adding the meat, for those who like its distinctive taste.

Beef Stew with Fresh Fava Beans

2 lbs. lean stewing beef, cubed
4 tablespoons oil
1 lb. fresh or frozen green fava
    beans

2 whole cloves garlic
1 teaspoon ground coriander
Salt and black pepper

Sauté the meat in hot oil in a large pan until well browned. Add the remaining ingredients and cover with water. (If frozen beans are used, they should be defrosted and added only about ½ hour before the end of cooking time.) Bring to the boil and simmer gently, covered, for about 2 hours, or until the meat is very tender.

Meat with Zucchini and Chickpeas

Another Egyptian favorite.

2 onions, chopped
2 whole cloves garlic [optional]
4 tablespoons butter or oil
2 lbs. lean stewing lamb or beef,
    cubed
3 tablespoons tomato paste

⅓ cup chickpeas, soaked overnight
Salt and black pepper
1 teaspoon ground allspice [op-
    tional]
2 lbs. zucchini, sliced

Fry the chopped onions and whole garlic cloves, if used, in hot butter or oil until golden. Add the meat cubes and brown them all over to seal in the juices. Stir in the tomato paste, add the soaked and drained chickpeas, and cover with water. Season to taste with salt, pepper, and ground allspice if liked. Bring to the boil, stir well, and cover the pan. Simmer gently for about 1½ hours. Add the zucchini and simmer for a further ½ hour, or until the meat, chickpeas, and vegetables are very tender and the liquid has been absorbed, adding a little more water during cooking if necessary. Adjust seasoning and serve.

Khashkhashiya

A medieval recipe from al-Baghdadi, of doubtful ingredients (khashkhash is the poppy from which the drug opium is made) not to be recommended. I am including it only as a curiosity.

"Cut red meat into small slices: melt fresh tail and throw the meat in to fry lightly. Drop in half a *dirham;* and the same quantity of brayed [ground] dried coriander. Then cover with lukewarm water, boil and skim. Add fine-chipped cinnamon-bark and a little fine ground ginger. Make a broth with 1½ *ratls* of hot water, and add 150 *dirhams* of sugar and honey. When the sugar is dissolved, sprinkle in a handful of poppy-flour. Stir well until cooked and set. Then throw in 30 *dirhams* of fresh poppy: or, if this be not procurable, of dry poppy soaked and ground. Stir until well mixed. Color with saffron and spray with a little rose-water. Wipe the sides of the saucepan with a clean rag, and leave to settle over a slow fire for an hour; then remove."

Tagine of Kofta and Eggs

A Moroccan dish which may have been inspired by the medieval ones of meat and eggs described by al-Baghdadi.

1½ lbs. lamb or beef, ground	½ teaspoon ground cumin
4 tablespoons finely chopped parsley	¼ teaspoon paprika
1 tablespoon finely chopped fresh mint or 1 teaspoon dried crushed mint	Pinch of cayenne pepper
	Salt
½ teaspoon dried sweet marjoram	3 tablespoons butter
½ teaspoon ground allspice	6 eggs

Have the meat ground two or three times if possible. Pound or squash it with a wooden spoon, and knead vigorously by hand to achieve a smooth, pasty texture. (Or use an electric blender if you have one.) Combine with the herbs and spices, add salt to taste, and knead well. Roll into marble-sized balls. Sauté in butter in a large, deep frying pan, shaking the pan to color them all over. Cover them with water, add a pinch of salt, and simmer for about 20 minutes, or until the meatballs are very tender and the liquid reduced.

Break the eggs carefully into the pan over the mixture and cook over low heat until set. Leave them whole or scramble them lightly with a fork. Serve with plain boiled rice or mashed potatoes.

MEAT STEWS WITH FRUIT

I have found many Moroccan *touajen* (the plural form of *tagine*) incredibly like al-Baghdadi's medieval stews—a mysterious culinary bond between ancient Persia and modern Morocco.

Many Moroccans originate from the regions of the Yemen, Iraq, and Saudi Arabia. They came there at different times: first in the pre-Christian era, then with the Arab Islamic invasion in the seventh century, and then again in the twelfth, thirteenth, and fourteenth centuries. I suspect that the Arabs of the Abbassid period (the time of al-Baghdadi) brought these dishes with them. They were then adopted and perpetuated through the ephemeral Almovarid dynasty, the brilliant Moroccan period of the dynasty of the Almohads which diffused Moorish civilization throughout a vast empire, and again during the Sharifian dynasty of the descendants of Fatima, daughter of the Prophet, who came from Arabia at the end of the fourteenth century.

The same fruits—apples, prunes, quinces, and currants—and to a large extent the same spices are used by Moroccans today as were used by the ancient Persians and the Arabs of the Abbassid period. Al-Baghdadi's recipes recommended mashing the fruits to a pulp, but Moroccans leave them whole or sliced and add them toward the end of cooking, to prevent their disintegrating. Fasis (inhabitants of Fez) stew their ingredients, as al-Baghdadi did, without preliminary frying, as they consider that frying would add heaviness to otherwise delicate dishes.

Every Moroccan family prizes its own very special *touajen* which generations of their cooks have prepared for them, keeping the recipes fiercely secret, and I realize that I have been able to include only a few from a vast culinary treasury.

Modern Persian stews (*khoreshtha*) have developed them and changed them a little, remaining true to their own early traditions. I have included these in the chapter on rice, as today they are intended as sauces for rice.

Curiously, countries around the region of Baghdad, now the capital of Iraq, where al-Baghdadi lived, have not perpetuated this particular tradition.

Mishmishiya

A splendid meat and apricot dish which derives its name from the Arabic word for the fruit, mishmish. Lamb seems to have special affinity for apricots, and a similar dish was a great favorite in our family.
   From al-Baghdadi's cooking manual.

"Cut fat meat small, put into the saucepan with a little salt, and cover with water. Boil and remove the scum. Cut up onions, wash, and throw in on top of the meat. Add seasonings, coriander, cumin, mastic, cinnamon, pepper and ginger, well ground. Take dry apricots, soak in hot water, then wash and put in a separate saucepan, and boil lightly: take out, wipe in the hands, and strain through a sieve. Take the juice, and add it to the saucepan to form a broth. Take sweet almonds, grind fine, moisten with a little apricot juice and throw in. Some color with a trifle of saffron. Spray the saucepan with a little rose water, wipe its sides with a clean rag, and leave to settle over the fire: then remove."

SUGGESTED QUANTITIES

2 lbs. lean lamb, cubed	Black pepper
Salt	¼ teaspoon ground ginger
1–2 onions, finely chopped	½ lb. dried apricots, soaked and
½–1 teaspoon ground coriander	passed through a food mill
½–1 teaspoon ground cumin	⅓ cup ground almonds
¼ teaspoon pulverized mastic ‡	¼ teaspoon saffron [optional]
¼–½ teaspoon ground cinnamon	1 teaspoon rose water

This is one of the dishes in which the meat is not fried before stewing. It may seem dull at first, but the apricot sauce thickened with the ground almonds gives it a particular richness which makes frying superfluous.
   The stew requires about 2 hours of gentle cooking, preferably on an

asbestos mat. Leave out the mastic and saffron if you wish—I do not think they are at all necessary.

A modern Persian version consists of a lamb and apricot pilav, or *polo* as it is called in Persia. I have included it in the rice chapter (page 348).

SONG TO A GIRL *

Good night, O watermelon, O red wheat waiting in a sack,
I have waited beneath your window for the past four nights
Without food or drink, listening for the sound of your voice.
Good night, O fresh ripening apricot,
I want you for my wife, yet I am too shy to say it.

Moroccan Tagine with Quince

2 lbs. fat or lean stewing lamb, cubed
2 onions, finely chopped
Salt and pepper [black, cayenne, and paprika] †
1 bunch fresh coriander or parsley, finely chopped

¼ teaspoon powdered saffron [optional]
½ teaspoon ground ginger
½–1½ lbs. quinces, cut in half and cored but not peeled ‡
4 tablespoons butter [optional]

Put the cubed meat and 1 chopped onion in a large saucepan. Cover with water and season to taste with salt and pepper. (Moroccans use a variety of peppers, including paprika and cayenne, adding them with a light hand.) Add fresh coriander or parsley, saffron if used, and ginger, bring to the boil and simmer gently, covered, until the

---

* Maspéro, *Chansons populaires.*
† Use in moderation, to taste.
‡ You may prefer to use less fruit the first time you try this dish. Increase the amount once you have become accustomed to the taste of the meat flavored with the sweet aromas of the fruit, and the sharp shock of quince with ginger. Some people prefer to soften the taste of quince with a little sugar.

meat is tender and the onion has practically disintegrated in the sauce. This takes about an hour.

Now add the other chopped onion and cook until soft. Half an hour before serving, add the quinces and cook until only just tender. The quinces may be sautéed in butter first for a richer flavor.

Pears or apples (peeled and cored), dates and raisins or prunes (soaked overnight) may be used instead of the quinces, sometimes in combinations. They all make rather luxurious dishes. Chicken is also delicious cooked in this way.

Arab proverb: "A guest is the captive of the whole quarter." (Said to a guest who declines the invitation of his host's friends.)

Persian Lamb with Apples and Sour Cherries

2 lbs. lean lamb, cubed
2½ tablespoons butter or oil
½ cup yellow split peas
Salt and black pepper

1 lb. sour or morello cherries, pitted,* or 1 cup sour cherry jam †
1 apple, peeled, cored, and diced
Lemon juice [optional]

Turn the meat in hot butter or oil in a large saucepan until lightly colored all over. Add the split peas and water to cover, and season to taste with salt and black pepper. Bring to a boil and skim off any scum. Cover the pan and simmer for about 2 hours, or until the meat is very tender.

Add the cherries, or jam, diced apple, and a little more water if necessary. Adjust seasoning. If you are using cherry jam you may like to counterbalance its sweetness with a little lemon juice. Cook for a further ½ hour.

This stew is usually served as a sauce with plain rice.

* Fresh or canned.
† You may prefer to use less fruit the first time you try this dish. Increase the amount once you have become accustomed to the combination of meat and fruit.

Moroccan Tagine with Fruit and Honey

This fragrant dish, a specialty of Fez, can be prepared with various fruits—apples, pears, or quinces, for example. Below is a version using prunes, a local favorite, particularly good as a winter dish. Honey is used in this dish in rather an unexpected way, its sweetness sometimes threatened with a little ginger and much pepper. Saffron is traditionally added, but its taste is almost lost among the rich flavors and its high cost therefore makes it, in my opinion, optional.

2 lbs. lean lamb, preferably leg, cubed
3 tablespoons oil
¼ teaspoon ground ginger
¼ teaspoon saffron [optional]
Salt and black pepper
½ teaspoon ground coriander

1 teaspoon ground cinnamon
1 onion, finely chopped
½ lb. prunes, soaked overnight
2 tablespoons honey, or to taste
1 teaspoon orange blossom water
Roasted or broiled sesame seeds, to garnish [optional]

In this recipe the meat is not fried first. Put the meat in a large saucepan, cover with water, and add oil, ginger, saffron if used, salt and pepper to taste, coriander, cinnamon, and the finely chopped onion. Bring to the boil, cover the pan, and simmer very gently until the meat is tender and the water has become a rich sauce. This will take about 2 hours.

Add the prunes and simmer for 20 minutes longer. Stir the honey into the sauce, blending it in well, and cook for a further 15 minutes. Sprinkle with orange blossom water. The dish is sometimes served garnished with roasted or broiled sesame seeds.

This dish is similar to a modern Persian prune sauce or *khoresh*, made with prunes, meat, and spinach. I have given the recipe on page 358, in the rice chapter.

Rutabiya

A regal medieval dish of meatballs stuffed with almonds and garnished with dates, "rutab" being the Arabic word for dates. From al-Baghdadi.

"Cut red meat into small, long, thin slices: melt fresh tail, and throw out the sediment, then put the meat into the oil, adding half a *dirham* of salt and the same quantity of fine brayed [ground] dry coriander. Stir until browned. Then cover with lukewarm water, and when boiling, skim. Put in a handful of almonds and pistachios, peeled and ground coarsely, and color with a little saffron. Throw in fine-ground cumin, coriander, cinnamon and mastic, about 2½ *dirhams* in all. Take red meat as required, mince fine, and make into long cabobs [meat rolls], placing inside each a peeled, sweet almond: put into the saucepan. Take sugar candy dates, or Medina dates, as required: extract the pit from the bottom with a needle, and put in its place a peeled sweet almond. When the meat is cooked and the liquor all evaporated so that only the oils remain, garnish with these dates. Sprinkle with about ten *dirhams* of scented sugar, and a *danaq* of camphor: spray with a little rose water. Wipe the sides of the saucepan with a clean rag, and leave to settle over the fire for an hour: then remove."

SUGGESTED QUANTITIES

1 lb. lean lamb or beef, cubed
2 tablespoons oil
Salt and black pepper
1 teaspoon ground coriander
⅓ cup blanched almonds or pistachio nuts, chopped
¼ teaspoon saffron [optional, but not really necessary]
1 teaspoon ground cumin
1 teaspoon ground cinnamon
¼ teaspoon pulverized mastic [gum arabic] ‡
1 lb. minced lamb, beef, or veal
¾ cup whole blanched almonds [to stuff the meat rolls and dates]
½–¾ lb. dried dates
2 teaspoons sugar [optional]
[leave out camphor]
1 teaspoon rose water ‡

Add the meat rolls to the pan after the stew has been cooking for 1½ hours.

Dfeena

A very rich and filling Egyptian specialty. It was particularly popular as a Sabbath meal in Jewish circles, since it could be left cooking gently from early on Friday.

2 lbs. lean or fat stewing beef	½–1 lb. chickpeas or dried white
1 calf's foot [optional]	beans (navy, pea, or Great
6 small potatoes	Northern), soaked overnight
6 eggs in their shells	2 cloves garlic, crushed
2 large onions, finely chopped	1 teaspoon ground allspice
Oil	Salt and black pepper

Cut the meat into cubes. Blanch the calf's foot in boiling water. Peel the potatoes, and scrub the eggshells thoroughly. Fry the chopped onions in oil until soft and golden.

Put all these ingredients together with the drained chickpeas or white beans (less commonly used for this dish than chickpeas) in a large ovenproof pot or casserole with a tight-fitting lid. Cover with water and add the garlic and seasonings. If using white beans, it is preferable to add salt only after they have become tender, as it seems to prevent their softening. Cover the pot and bake in a moderate oven (375°) for 1 hour, then lower the temperature to the lowest setting and continue to simmer for several hours longer or overnight. Alternatively, you can leave the stew *barely* simmering over extremely low heat for several hours.

The meat will be extremely tender and practically falling apart, and the chickpeas or beans will be very soft and impregnated with the rich calf's foot stock. The eggs will have become creamy, like the *hamine* eggs described on page 136.

A variation is to boil about 2¼ cups long-grain rice, washed first, until just tender, then lower it into the casserole tied up in a cloth bag. This will allow it to absorb the rich sauce without being lost among the other ingredients. Serve with the *dfeena*.

Immos—meaning 'his mother's milk'

Recipes for meat cooked in milk or yogurt abound in early cooking manuals. Today, they are still a great favorite throughout most of the Middle East, as well as in the Balkans and India.

The name of this particular version, a Lebanese one, implies that the meat of a young animal is cooked in its own mother's milk, a vivid and rather tragic image which, of course, makes this and other similar dishes prohibited by Jewish dietary laws: "Thou shalt not cook the kid in his mother's milk."

2 lbs. lean lamb, preferably leg, cubed
2 medium onions, sliced
Salt and black pepper
2½ cups yogurt

1 egg white or 1 tablespoon corn-starch
1 teaspoon salt
2 cloves garlic, crushed
1 teaspoon ground coriander
2½ tablespoons butter

Steam the meat with the onions, and salt and pepper to taste, for about 1½ hours. Alternatively, boil it or cook it under pressure with very little water. It should be extremely soft and tender. Reduce the liquid if necessary by boiling vigorously, uncovered, for the last few minutes.

Prepare the yogurt with egg white or cornstarch dissolved in water and salt, according to the directions for stabilizing yogurt on page 81, to prevent it from curdling during cooking. Add it to the cooked meat, and simmer gently for 10 to 15 minutes longer.

Fry the crushed garlic and coriander in butter until the garlic just turns golden. Pour the mixture over the meat and yogurt, and serve accompanied by plain or saffron rice (pages 339–40).

LIVER, KIDNEYS, ETC.

Albanian-Style Liver

2 lbs. calf's or lamb's liver, sliced
2 tablespoons paprika
Flour
Olive or other oil

Salt
3 tablespoons finely chopped parsley
½ onion, thinly sliced

Wash the liver and cut it into small pieces about 1 inch square, removing any tough pieces or skin. Drain and dry on absorbent paper. Sprinkle with 1 tablespoon paprika and toss well, then roll in flour, shaking to separate each piece of liver.

Heat some oil in a frying pan and fry the liver, stirring and turning the pieces until well browned all over. They should be pink and juicy inside. Remove from the pan and drain well. Sprinkle with a little salt.

Mix the remaining tablespoon paprika with a little of the frying oil and dribble over the liver. Serve garnished with chopped parsley, and slices of onion which have been sprinkled with salt and left for at least an hour to soften and become mellow.

Calf's or Lamb's Liver with Vinegar I, II

Here are two equally delicious recipes for liver, both using vinegar. This is often substituted for wine which is, of course, taboo to Muslims, and as a matter of fact vinegar is better than wine in this case. For both recipes, the liver is tenderized and enhanced if marinated first in a mixture of oil, vinegar, salt, and pepper. Seasoned milk is sometimes used, though not by Jews. Drain well on absorbent paper before cooking.

i. A dish called higado con vinagre *by some in our Sephardic community.*

1–1½ cups dry white bread crumbs	Salt and black pepper
2–3 cloves garlic, crushed	½ teaspoon sugar
3 tablespoons oil	1½ lbs. calf's or lamb's liver, sliced
½ cup wine vinegar	2 tablespoons finely chopped parsley

Fry the bread crumbs and crushed garlic in hot oil until they are slightly colored, and the garlic becomes aromatic and sweet. Add vinegar, salt and pepper to taste, and sugar, and bring to the boil.

Poach the slices of liver in this mixture, simmering gently for 10 to 15 minutes, until just cooked. They must not be overdone.

Serve garnished with chopped parsley.

ii. This is a Lebanese recipe flavored with mint, a favorite Lebanese herb. Samna, or clarified butter, is generally used for frying in the Lebanon, but butter is a perfectly adequate alternative.

1½ lbs. calf's or lamb's liver, sliced	2–3 cloves garlic, crushed
Salt and black pepper	1 tablespoon dried crushed mint
2½ tablespoons butter	1 teaspoon flour
1 large onion, finely chopped	½ cup wine vinegar

Sprinkle the liver with salt and pepper. Brown it lightly and quickly on both sides in butter; remove from the pan, and put aside.

Fry the onions gently in the same pan until golden and soft. Add crushed garlic, mint, and flour, and blend well into the hot butter. Stir in vinegar and a little water, and season with salt and pepper. Bring to the boil slowly, stirring, and cook for 5 minutes. Add the fried liver and a little more water if necessary to cover. Simmer gently until the liver is just cooked but not overdone, about 10 minutes.

Kidneys with Lemon

1½ lbs. calf's or lamb's kidneys
1–2 tablespoons wine vinegar
2½ tablespoons butter

Salt and black pepper
Juice of 1 lemon, or more
4 tablespoons finely chopped parsley

Wash the kidneys. Remove the outer skins and cut out the fat cores. Soak them for 1 hour in water acidulated with a little vinegar and, if you like, blanch then for 2 to 3 minutes in a fresh portion of acidulated water.

Drain the kidneys and slice them in half lengthwise. Sauté in hot butter for a few minutes until firm and colored all over but tender inside. Season to taste with salt and pepper, sprinkle with lemon juice, and serve garnished with chopped parsley.

Kidneys in Tomato Sauce

2 onions, sliced
1 clove garlic, finely chopped
3 tablespoons oil or butter
6 calf's kidneys or 12 lamb's kidneys

1–2 tablespoons wine vinegar [optional]
2 tomatoes, skinned and chopped
4 tablespoons tomato paste
Salt and black pepper

Fry the onions and garlic in hot oil or butter until soft and golden. Wash the kidneys, remove the outer skins and fat cores, and, if you like, soak and blanch them in acidulated water as described in the preceding recipe.

Drain the kidneys and slice them in half lengthwise. Add them to the onions and garlic, and sauté until colored all over. Add the tomatoes and the tomato paste, season to taste with salt and pepper, and moisten with 3 tablespoons water. Cover and cook gently for about 20 minutes, taking care not to overcook the kidneys, as they will become tough and hard if you do.

Yoğurtlu Paça / Sheep's Feet with Yogurt

A delicious Turkish dish. The earthy richness of the meat is matched with the coolness of the yogurt.

6 sheep's feet [or 2 calf's feet]	GARNISH
Rind of ½ lemon	2 cups yogurt
2 large cloves garlic	Stock
Salt and black pepper	2 cloves garlic, crushed
6 thin slices bread, crusts removed	Salt and white pepper
Butter	4 tablespoons butter
	1 teaspoon paprika

Scrub the feet thoroughly, blanch them in boiling water for 5 minutes, and drain. Cover with fresh water in a saucepan, and add lemon rind, garlic, and salt and pepper to taste. Bring to a boil and simmer for 3 to 4 hours, or 1 hour in a pressure cooker.

Fry the slices of bread in butter until very brown and crisp. Lay the slices in one layer in a large, shallow, ovenproof dish and moisten well with stock from the meat. Drain the feet and bone them, arranging the meat on top of the bread slices. Sprinkle with more stock if the dish seems too dry, cover it, and keep it warm in a low oven.

Prepare the garnish. Beat the yogurt with a few tablespoons of stock, the crushed garlic, and salt and white pepper to taste. Melt the butter in a small saucepan and color it bright red with paprika.

Serve the meat on the bread, smothered with the yogurt mixture and decorated with a trickle of red paprika butter.

Brains Sofrito

3 calf's brains or 6 lamb's brains	½ teaspoon turmeric
1 tablespoon wine vinegar	Juice of ½ lemon, or more
3 tablespoons oil	Salt and black pepper
2 cloves garlic, crushed or halved	4 tablespoons finely chopped parsley
1 stalk celery, thinly sliced [optional]	

Soak the brains in water acidulated with a little vinegar for 1 hour. Remove the thin outer membranes and wash under cold running water. Drain well. Separate each brain into two or four parts, depending on whether calf's or lamb's brains are used.

In a pan, heat the oil with ⅓ cup water, the garlic, sliced celery if used, turmeric, and lemon juice. Add salt and pepper to taste. Simmer for a few minutes—for about 15 minutes if celery is used, to allow it to soften, but otherwise for only 2 to 3 minutes.

Poach the brains gently in this barely simmering mixture for 10 to 15 minutes, taking care not to break them. They will be tinged a beautiful yellow by the turmeric. Add a little water if the sauce evaporates too quickly.

Serve the brains in their sauce, sprinkled with finely chopped parsley, and accompanied by artichoke hearts stewed in oil (canned ones will do) and rice.

A variation is to add 1 teaspoon ground cumin to the sauce.

Kawareh bi Hummus / Calf's Feet and Chickpeas

This dish is loved all over the Middle East, in the Balkans, and in Spain and Portugal. Non-Muslims, and Muslims who are lax about their prohibitions, sometimes use pig's feet instead of calf's feet. The dish is sometimes served as a soup, prepared with only 1 calf's foot, and more water.

2 calf's feet	1½ cups chickpeas, soaked over-
4 tablespoons oil	night
Salt and black pepper	2 hard-boiled eggs, sliced
1 teaspoon turmeric	

Wash and scrape the feet thoroughly. Blanch them in boiling water until a scum has formed. Throw out the water. Heat the oil in a large saucepan and fry the feet in it for a few minutes until colored all over. Add salt and pepper to taste, turmeric, and the soaked and drained chickpeas. Cover with water, bring to the boil, and simmer gently until the meat is practically falling off the bones, about 4 hours. The time can be reduced to about ¾ hour with a pressure cooker. Bone the feet if you wish and return the meat to the pan.

Serve with a light salad and, if you like, garnished with hard-boiled eggs.

A variation to this dish uses cubed or thickly sliced potatoes instead of the chickpeas. They should be added only about 20 minutes before the end of cooking time, as prolonged cooking would make them disintegrate. *Hergma*, a Moroccan variation, is spiced with ½ teaspoon ground ginger, 1 teaspoon paprika, and ½ teaspoon cayenne, instead of turmeric, and 1 cup cooked rice is added at the end of the cooking time.

Fasulyeli Paça

Here is a Turkish variation of kawareh, *identical to a Spanish dish in which calf's feet are cooked with white beans.*

2 calf's feet	¾ lb. dried white beans (navy, pea,
2 tablespoons oil	or Great Northern), soaked
1 large onion, finely chopped	overnight
	Salt and black pepper

Wash and scrape the feet thoroughly, and blanch them in boiling water until a scum forms on the surface. Drain.

Heat the oil in a large saucepan and slowly fry the onion to a rich brown color. This will give the beans a deep, earthy color. Add the feet and fry them for a few minutes until colored all over. Add the beans and cover with water. Do not season with salt at this stage, as it will prevent the beans from softening. Bring to the boil and simmer gently, covered, for 3 to 4 hours, or until the meat falls away from the bones and the beans are very soft. The time can be reduced to ¾ hour by using a pressure cooker.

Season to taste with salt and pepper. Bone the feet, return the meat to the pan, heat through, and serve.

It is customary to cook eggs in their shells (well scrubbed) in the stew, adding them with the beans. They will become creamy and brown inside (see *hamine* eggs on page 136).

Sheep's Head

This is a popular Middle Eastern dish which, I have been told, was quite well known in England and Scotland in the past, particularly during the last war when meat was scarce.

Ask the butcher to remove the part around the sheep's nose altogether, as this is extremely hard to clean. Clean the sheep's head carefully, singeing off any hairs and scraping with a sharp knife.

One way of preparing it after this is to split it in half lengthwise and remove the brains. (These can be cleaned and cooked separately —see the recipes for brains.) Blanch the head in boiling water until a scum has formed on the surface, and drain. Rub with a little rose water or lemon juice.

Put the two halves in a pot with an onion, water to cover, and salt and pepper to taste. Bring to the boil and simmer until the meat is very tender, about 3 hours; or cook in a pressure cooker for about 1 hour. Serve as it is, or bone it and serve the meat separately.

Another, rather tastier way is to clean the head as above and roast it whole in the oven. Rub it with salt and pepper, and brush with melted butter. Roast until well done in a moderately hot oven (400°), turning it occasionally and basting generously with more melted butter. It will take from 1 to 2½ hours, depending on the age of the animal.

Serve the head whole on a platter, or if you wish, remove the meat and serve it garnished with paprika.

Serve with salads.

SUBSTANTIAL
DISHES

Since ancient times, dishes based on chickpeas, beans, lentils, and cereals have been looked down on as the food of the poor. In literature, proverbs, and songs they are constantly referred to as "the food of the poor." or "the food of the mean." They have even been included as such in the *Kitab al Buhala* (Book of Misers).*

Regardless of this stigma, these dishes are nevertheless loved by rich and poor alike. Numerous jokes are told about Arab dignitaries, who, when served with French *haute cuisine* or cosmopolitan food in hotels or at banquets, long for the *ful medames* (page 268) or chickpeas and spinach which they can tell that the servants are eating from the aromas wafting up from the kitchens.

A little dull at times, but more often rich and splendidly vulgar, seasoned with spices, garlic, onions, and herbs, or used in exciting combinations with other ingredients, legumes are also important for their nutritive value. By themselves, they can be eaten cold as salads or hot as vegetables. Cooked with meat, vegetables, rice, and pasta, they add body and texture to many dishes.

Generally, legumes have to be washed and picked clean of impurities, although the majority of the packaged varieties are prepared and already quite clean. Most, however, need soaking in cold water for a number of hours, except for the small yellow and red lentils, which cook and disintegrate very quickly. The soaking helps to tenderize the dried vegetables and shorten their cooking time. With brown and green lentils and yellow split peas, soaking helps to shorten this time only slightly. Dried white beans, such as navy, pea, and Great Northern beans, and dried white or brown fava beans require lengthy soaking, but again, some varieties are pretreated and need only be cooked. When soaking legumes, cover them with a large quantity of cold water, since they will quickly swell and absorb a great deal of it.

The time required to cook each variety varies widely according to the soil in which they were grown and their age since drying. However, varieties are constantly being improved and it seems that each new season's production requires less cooking time than the last.

* By Jahiz, Damascus, 1938.

Always cook in fresh, cold water. Generally, brown and green lentils take between ¾ and 1½ hours to become tender. Dried white beans may take any time between 1½ and 3 hours. Black-eyed peas can take as little as ½ hour. Egyptian brown beans require longer soaking than the others and very long, slow simmering.

Dried white beans and white and brown fava beans must not be salted at the start of cooking, or they will never become soft. They must be seasoned only when already tender.

Dried vegetables can also be pressure-cooked, but there is always the danger of overcooking, since the exact time is so often a matter of guesswork, and you may end up with a purée—except in the case of chickpeas and yellow split peas, which never disintegrate. Unless pressed for time, therefore, it is preferable not to use this method. It is far better to cook them in advance to ensure that they are ready when needed, since they keep and reheat well.

Cooking time in a pressure cooker at 15-lb. pressure is (roughly, and depending on their quality):

10 minutes for black-eyed peas and some chickpeas,
20 minutes for lentils,
½ to 1 hour for dried white beans and dried white fava beans.

Besides legumes, other substantial dishes are those based on burghul (cracked wheat), called *bulgur* by the Turks, and whole wheat kernels. These earthy peasant dishes are particularly popular among the Armenian communities scattered all over the world. *Couscous*, a cracked, uncooked wheat resembling semolina, makes the superb North African dishes which, together with the magnificent stews and broths over which the *couscous* is steamed, make ideal substantial one-course meals.

I have also included in this chapter dishes made with *rishta*, which is similar to Italian pasta. In the last century, Italian pasta dishes have become increasingly popular throughout the Middle East. Spaghetti and tagliatelli *alla bolognese*, *al aglio e olio*, and *al pomidoro* as well as *maccheroni al forno con besciamella* are common, everyday dishes in Turkey, Syria, the Lebanon, Egypt, and North Africa. I have been told that these dishes are often prepared in Cairo today by people wishing to impress their village or Bedouin friends visiting town—they are Oriental enough to please and yet have a foreign snob value.

Rishta, however, is of ancient Oriental origin. It was known in ancient Persia and is featured in medieval cooking manuals. Like rice, it has escaped the stigma of being a filling dish for the poor. Instead, it is considered rather grand, and is served on special occasions.

The preparation of the *rishta* dough is identical to that of any Italian pasta dough, and the cheese-filled pasta called *calsones* by the Jews is very similar to cheese ravioli. I have included these pasta dishes here since they are truly Oriental and do not owe their inspiration to Italian dishes, although they may sometimes share a certain flavor.

Recipes for dried vegetables served cold with olive oil are to be found in the chapters on *mezze* and salads. Recipes for stews with dried vegetables are given in the meat chapter.

THE YOUNG GIRL'S SONG *

By my father's life! By my father's life!
I will not have the poor man!
He wakes me in the morning and says,
He wakes me in the morning and says,
"Pound the lentils early!"

By my father's life! By my father's life!
I will have the rich man!
He wakes me in the morning and says,
He wakes me in the morning and says,
"Pound the pastry with fat!"

Lentils in Butter

1½ cups brown lentils
1 onion, finely chopped
1 clove garlic
6 tablespoons butter

Salt and black pepper
1 teaspoon ground cumin
Juice of ½ lemon [optional]

Clean and wash the lentils, and soak them in cold water for a few hours if possible. Drain well.

In a large saucepan, fry the onion and garlic in 3 tablespoons hot butter until the onion is soft and golden. Add the lentils and stir with the butter in the pan for a minute or two. Pour in about 2½ cups of water, bring to a boil, and remove scum. Season to taste with salt and pepper, and a teaspoon of ground cumin. Cover the pan and simmer gently for ½ to 1½ hours according to the quantity, adding more water as it becomes absorbed, until the lentils are tender but not too soft.

* Maspéro, *Chansons populaires.*

Serve with the remaining butter stirred in until melted, and a squeeze of lemon if you like.

This is particularly good as a partner to omelets or little spicy fried sausages, and any lean meat dish. Served with fried eggplant slices and boiled *rishta*, it also makes an excellent dish.

Lentil and Vegetable Stew

1 cup lentils, soaked overnight if
    necessary
2 medium potatoes, peeled and
    coarsely diced
½ lb. zucchini, sliced or cubed
½ lb. leeks, trimmed and sliced
1 stalk celery, sliced

Salt and black pepper
1 onion, finely chopped
Oil
2 cloves garlic, crushed
2 tablespoons finely chopped parsley
Juice of 2 lemons

Drain soaked lentils and simmer in a large pan in 2½ cups water for about ¾ to 1¼ hours, or until nearly soft. Add the potatoes, zucchini, leeks, and celery, season to taste with salt and pepper, and continue cooking for 15 to 20 minutes longer, or until the vegetables are cooked, adding more water if necessary. Only a little liquid should be left at the end of cooking.

Fry the onion in oil until soft and golden. Add garlic and fry for a minute or two longer until colored. Drain and add to the lentils and vegetables, together with parsley and lemon juice. Simmer for a few minutes longer, adjust seasoning and serve hot or cold.

A TALE OF GOHA

Goha invited a friend to his house. No sooner had he placed a plate piled high with food before him than the man had eaten it all up. Several times he rushed to fetch more beans, more rice, and more chickpeas, which he had prepared for his own lunch and for next day's as well. Each time the man emptied the plate and waited for more. Finally, there was nothing left in the house to eat. Then the man remarked that he was on his way to the doctor because he was suffering from loss of appetite. Appalled, Goha begged him to stay away when he had recovered it!

Shula Kalambar

A lentil and spinach dish prepared in medieval Persia to heal the sick. For the cure to be effective, the ingredients, so it was said, had to be bought with money begged in the streets.

Here are my quantities for the dish.

1 cup large brown lentils, soaked if required
1 lb. fresh spinach or ½ lb. frozen spinach
½ teaspoon ground coriander
½ teaspoon ground cumin
1 clove garlic, crushed
Salt and black pepper
2 tablespoons butter

Boil the lentils until very tender, about ¾ to 1½ hours. Wash the spinach carefully. If using frozen spinach, defrost and drain well. Chop spinach leaves finely and stew gently in their own juices until tender. Drain the cooked lentils and add them to the spinach. Season with coriander, cumin and garlic, and salt and pepper to taste. Stir well.

Add butter, let it melt into the vegetables, and serve.

Lentils with Rishta (Noodles)

A splendid dish. Use brown lentils if you want to leave them whole, red and yellow ones if you prefer a purée. Make this by rubbing them through a strainer or by puréeing them in an electric blender before the noodles are added. I prefer brown lentils left whole.

1–1½ cups lentils, soaked if required
Salt
2 onions, finely chopped
Oil
2–3 cloves garlic, crushed
1 teaspoon ground coriander
Black pepper
¾ lb. *rishta* [page 270], noodles, or tagliatelli
2 tablespoons butter

Drain soaked lentils and boil in a fresh portion of salted water to cover (about 2½ cups) for about ¾ to 1½ hours, or until the lentils are soft and the water has been absorbed. Use a large pan which will accommodate the noodles as well. Drain the cooked lentils thoroughly.

Fry the onions in 2 tablespoons oil until soft and golden. Add the garlic and coriander, and continue to fry gently for about 2 minutes, until golden. Add this mixture to the cooked lentils, and season to taste with salt and pepper. Throw the noodles into boiling salted water and cook until just tender (about 10 minutes if using the dried commercial variety). Drain well and add to the lentils. Stir in butter and mix well.

Serve very hot.

Puréed Chickpeas with Garlic and Onion

A young Lebanese chemistry student in London who translated some old Turkish recipes for me, nearly fainting with longing and hunger as he described the dishes, urged me to include his favorite recipe, which he cooked twice a week in large quantities in his bed-sitting room. He ate it daily, often twice a day, in the morning and in the evening.

Although a "peasant" and "poor" dish, it is extremely popular with all Lebanese.

2¼ cups chickpeas, soaked overnight
2–4 cloves garlic, crushed
Salt
Olive oil

½ lb. Arab bread, toasted, or any other white bread, sliced and toasted
Paprika, to garnish

Boil the soaked chickpeas in about 4 cups water until tender. Varieties available in most shops today require only about ½ hour's cooking. A pressure cooker will reduce this time even further, to a few minutes. When the chickpeas are soft, pour the reduced cooking water into a glass.

Flavor the chickpeas with crushed garlic and salt, and crush them to a paste with a potato masher. Stir in olive oil to taste.

Break the toasted bread and arrange the pieces in the bottom of a shallow serving dish. Sprinkle with the chickpea water until well soaked. Cover with the puréed chickpeas, sprinkle with a little more oil, and garnish with scarlet paprika. Serve hot.

A splendid variation is to pour yogurt flavored with crushed garlic and mint over the hot chickpeas just before serving. Paprika can be dusted over the top or mixed with a little olive oil and dribbled over the yogurt in an attractive pattern. In another variation 2 tablespoons pine nuts are fried in butter and mixed with the puréed chickpeas. This makes a rather more expensive dish.

Ful Medames / Egyptian Brown Beans

An Egyptian dish which has become "the" national dish. Ful medames is pre-Ottoman and pre-Islamic, claimed by the Copts, and probably as old as the Pharaohs. According to an Arab saying: "Beans have satisfied even the Pharaohs."

Although basically a peasant dish, the rich and the middle classes also delight in these small dark beans. Since time immemorial, they have faithfully been served in the same manner: seasoned with oil, lemon, and garlic, sprinkled with chopped parsley and accompanied by hamine *(hard-boiled) eggs, and since time immemorial people have adored them.*

Ful medames is eaten in the fields and in village mud houses, in luxury restaurants and on town terraces by masters and servants alike. It is sold in the streets, sometimes buried in Arab bread, garnished with tahina *salad and accompanied by a tomato and onion salad.*

The broad brown beans can be bought in all Greek stores and some delicatessens.‡ Ready-cooked, canned beans can also be found.‡

2 lbs. *ful medames,* soaked over-night	Finely chopped parsley
	Olive oil
2–4 cloves garlic, crushed [optional]	Quartered lemons
6 hamine eggs [page 136] or hard-boiled eggs	Salt and freshly ground black pepper

Boil the soaked beans in a fresh portion of unsalted water in a large saucepan until tender. In the past this took at least 7 hours (the beans were sometimes even left to cook overnight), but the quality which I buy in London are soft after 2 to 2½ hours of gentle simmering. A pressure cooker will reduce the time considerably—to 30 to 45 minutes—but care must be taken not to overcook the beans.

When the beans are soft, drain them and add crushed garlic to taste, or instead pass some around with the other garnishes for people to take as much as they want.

Serve in soup bowls. Put a hard-boiled *hamine* egg in each bowl on top of the beans, and sprinkle with chopped parsley. Pass around olive oil, quartered lemons, salt, and black pepper for each person to season as he wishes. Most people like to break the egg up with a fork and crush the pieces together with the beans to allow the seasonings to penetrate.

An unusual way of serving *ful medames* is to smother it in a tomato sauce flavored with garlic (see page 334).

Riddle: It is divided into two equal parts and covered by a strong skin. Praised be God who made it! And how do Arabs call it? Answer: El ful.

Dried White Beans with Onions and Tomatoes

¾ lb. dried white beans (navy, pea, or Great Northern), soaked overnight	4 tablespoons tomato paste
	Salt
	1 teaspoon paprika
2 onions, sliced	Pinch of cayenne
2½ tablespoons oil	1 bay leaf
2 cloves garlic, sliced	2 tablespoons finely chopped parsley
2 tomatoes, skinned and chopped	[optional]

Drain the soaked beans and boil them in a fresh portion of unsalted water to cover until almost tender. The time will vary from 1½ to 3 hours, depending on their age and quality. Use a pressure cooker to reduce this to 35 or 45 minutes.

Fry the sliced onions in oil until soft and golden. Add garlic and fry for 2 minutes longer. Then add tomatoes and sauté gently until well cooked and almost reduced to a pulp. Stir in tomato paste and add the beans, together with some of their cooking water (about ½ cup). Season to taste with salt, paprika, and cayenne. Add a bay leaf and a little chopped parsley if liked.

Mix well and simmer for 15 to 20 minutes longer, until the beans are very soft and colored a faint salmon pink. Serve hot or cold.

Dried White Bean Stew with Meat

1 lb. dried white beans (navy, pea, or Great Northern), soaked overnight
2 onions, finely chopped
6 tablespoons butter
2–3 cloves garlic

1½ lbs. stewing beef or lamb, lean or fat, cubed
2 tomatoes, skinned and chopped
2–4 tablespoons tomato paste
Salt and strong pepper

Drain the beans and boil them in a fresh portion of unsalted water to cover for ½ hour. Drain and reserve.

In a large saucepan fry the onions in butter until soft and golden. Add the garlic cloves and fry until lightly colored. Add meat and brown all over. Add tomatoes and sauté gently. Stir in tomato paste and the drained beans, and cover with water. Bring to the boil and simmer gently until the meat is very tender, and the beans are soft and well flavored with the tomato sauce. Do not add seasoning before this, since salt will prevent the beans from softening.

Rishta / Fresh Noodles

Recipes for rishta, an Italian-type pasta, appeared in the early Arab manuscripts. The word itself means "thread" in Persian. Today pastas of all kinds are becoming increasingly popular all over the Middle East.

Here is the basic recipe for plain rishta.

3½ cups plain flour
2 large eggs, beaten

1 teaspoon salt
5–6 tablespoons water

Sift the flour onto a large board or marble slab and make a little well in the center to hold the beaten eggs, salt, and 5 tablespoons water. Bury these in the flour. Mix well and knead vigorously until all the ingredients are thoroughly blended, adding the remaining tablespoon of water only if necessary. The dough should be firm and not sticky. Work it well for about 10 minutes until smooth and elastic, sprinkling a little flour over the board and your hands occasionally to prevent the dough from sticking. Divide the dough into 2 or 3 pieces.

Roll each piece out as thinly as possible, working from the center and sprinkling both the surface it is rolled on and the rolling pin with flour to prevent the dough from sticking or tearing. Continue until it is extremely thin, like a very fine, elastic cloth. Lay the sheet aside and roll out the remaining pieces of dough in the same way. Let the pastry sheets rest and dry out for 40 minutes.

Roll each sheet up tightly like a Swiss roll and cut into thin slices, making ribbons of pastry. Spread these out on a floured cloth and leave them to rest for a little while longer.

Five minutes before they are to be served, throw them into boiling salted water and simmer for about 5 minutes, stirring occasionally to prevent them from sticking to the pan.

Drain and serve immediately with salt, pepper, and a generous amount of butter.

This pasta is similar to Italian tagliatelli, but commercial dried varieties will require longer cooking, usually at least 10 minutes.

In all the following recipes, the amounts of fresh and dried pasta required are the same, but double the cooking time given if using dried pasta of any kind.

Rishta with Meat and Tomato Sauce

This dish can be made equally well with Italian spaghetti, macaroni, or tagliatelli. The sauce is rich enough to make a main dish and has a particularly Arab flavor.

2 onions, finely chopped	4 tablespoons tomato paste
1 clove garlic	½ teaspoon ground cumin [optional]
Oil	
¾ lb. lean stewing lamb, cut into small cubes	1½ lbs. *rishta*, spaghetti, tagliatelli, or macaroni
Salt and black pepper	Grated Parmesan or Gruyère [optional]
¾ teaspoon ground allspice	
1 lb. ripe tomatoes, skinned, or a 1-lb. can whole tomatoes	

Fry the onions and garlic in 2½ tablespoons oil in a saucepan until golden. Add meat and brown it all over. Season with salt, pepper, and allspice. Add tomatoes and tomato paste, stir well, and simmer gently in the tomato juice, covered, adding a little water if necessary. Cook for 1½ hours, or longer, until the meat is very tender and the sauce rich in texture and aromatic, adding water if necessary. Adjust seasoning. Some people like to flavor the sauce with a little ground cumin as well as the allspice.

Boil the *rishta* vigorously in a large pan of salted water for about 5 minutes, or until tender but not too soft—*al dente*. Drain and turn into a serving bowl. Pour the meat sauce over the pasta and serve, sprinkle with grated cheese if you like.

An attractive and particularly Oriental variation is to serve the pasta with its sauce in a casing of *fila* pastry (see pages 96–8).

Prepare the sauce as above but let it reduce rather more. Boil 1 lb. pasta until just tender. Line a large buttered oven dish or tray with a sheet of *fila* pastry and brush it with melted butter. Lay another sheet on top and brush again with butter. Repeat with three more sheets, arranging them so that they overlap the sides of the dish, folding them back neatly where necessary. Fill this pastry shell with the pasta and sauce mixed together, and sprinkle very generously with grated cheese. Cover with 5 sheets of *fila*, each one brushed with melted butter, including the top one. Fold the edges of the sheets neatly, tucking them down the sides of the dish.

Bake in a hot oven (450°) for 15 minutes, then reduce the heat to 325° and continue to bake for about 30 minutes longer, until all the sheets of *fila* are well-cooked and the top is crisp and golden.

Serve in the dish, or unmold and turn over onto a serving platter so that the golden side is on top. Serve cut in slices like a cake.

Baked Rishta (Noodles) with Eggplant I

3 large eggplants, sliced	Black pepper
Salt	1½ lbs. *rishta* or spaghetti
1 onion, finely chopped	Butter
Oil	4 hard-boiled eggs, thinly sliced
A 1–lb. can whole tomatoes	½ cup grated Parmesan
1 teaspoon dried oregano	

Sprinkle the eggplant slices with salt and leave them in a colander for at least ½ hour to allow the bitter juices to drain away.

Prepare a tomato sauce in the following manner. Fry the onion in 2 tablespoons oil until soft and golden. Add tomatoes and oregano, and season to taste with salt and pepper. Moisten with a little water and simmer, covered, for at least ½ hour.

Drain the eggplant slices and pat them dry. Fry them in a little oil until very tender, turning them once. Drain on absorbent paper.

Cook the pasta in vigorously boiling, salted water until al dente—just tender. Drain; mix with the tomato sauce and 2½ tablespoons butter.

Butter a large oven tray or dish. Spread a layer of pasta and sauce over the bottom of the dish; cover with a layer of fried eggplant and one of thinly sliced hard-boiled eggs, and sprinkle with a quarter of the grated Parmesan. Repeat all the layers twice more, so that there are three sets of layers in all. Cover with a thin layer of pasta and sprinkle with the remaining cheese.

Bake in a moderate oven (375°) for about 30 minutes, or until a warm golden color on top.

The dish can be prepared a day ahead and baked just before serving.

Baked Rishta (Noodles) with Eggplant II

1½ lbs. eggplant, sliced
Salt
1½ lbs. *rishta*, spaghetti, or tagliatelli
1 large onion, chopped
1 clove garlic
Oil
2 tomatoes, skinned and chopped

2½ tablespoons tomato paste
½ teaspoon ground cinnamon
¼ teaspoon grated nutmeg
Cayenne pepper
Butter
Grated Parmesan or Gruyère [optional]

Sprinkle eggplant slices with salt and leave them in a colander for at least ½ hour to allow the bitter juices to drain away. Squeeze the slices and wash them in cold water. Pat dry with a clean cloth or kitchen paper.

Boil the noodles in salted water until still slightly underdone. Drain and keep warm.

Fry onion and garlic in 4 tablespoons oil until soft and golden. Add eggplant slices and fry until lightly colored on both sides, using a little more oil if necessary. Stir in chopped tomatoes and tomato paste, and season to taste with spices, salt, and a generous amount of cayenne. Moisten with a little water and simmer gently until the eggplant is soft and the sauce is reduced.

Butter a large baking dish. Fill it with alternating layers of pasta and the eggplant mixture, starting and finishing with a layer of pasta. End by pouring all the sauce from the eggplant over the entire dish. Sometimes grated cheese is sprinkled over the top.

Bake in a moderate oven (375°) for about 30 minutes.

As a variation, fried kidneys and chicken livers can be added to the eggplant and tomato sauce.

Calsones

This is a Sephardic pasta similar to cheese ravioli.

Prepare the *rishta* dough on page 370. Roll it out into very thin, long sheets, but do not cut it into ribbons. Along one of the longer edges and about 1 inch from the edge, put a row of little mounds of filling made as follows.

Mix ¼ lb. grated Parmesan or Greek Kashkaval with ¾ lb. grated Greek Halumi, Gruyère, or mild Cheddar, and work it into a paste with 3 egg yolks, beaten, and a little salt and white pepper.

Alternatively, make a filling with the homemade curd cheese on page 38. I also use Italian ricotta, available in all Italian groceries. Crumble ¾ lb. cheese with a fork. Add 3 tablespoons cold milk, ¼ lb. grated Parmesan, 2 tablespoons finely chopped parsley, a pinch of nutmeg, and a little pepper if you like, and mix well.

Set the mounds of filling about 1 inch apart on the sheet of dough, and continue with rows of mounds until nearly half of the sheet is covered. Fold the other half of the sheet over to cover the mounds of filling and press gently with your finger between each one to seal it completely. Then cut little squares out with a sharp knife. Continue with the remaining dough and filling until all are used up.

Throw the *calsones* into boiling salted water and boil gently for about 10 to 15 minutes, or until well cooked.

Drain and serve with a generous amount of butter.

. . .

The boiled and drained *calsones* can also be put in a lightly buttered baking dish, dotted with butter, sprinkled with grated cheese, and baked in a moderate oven (375°) until the top is faintly golden, about 15 minutes.

Megadarra

Here is a modern version of a medieval dish called mujadarra, *described by al-Baghdadi as a dish of the poor, and still known today as Esau's favorite. In fact, it is such a great favorite that although said to be for misers, it is a compliment to serve it.*

An aunt of mine used to present it regularly to guests with the comment: "Excuse the food of the poor!"—to which the unanimous reply always was: "Keep your food of kings and give us megadarra *every day!"*

The proportions for this lentil and rice dish vary with every family. Here is my family recipe for rather a large quantity. Whereas I have used twice the weight of rice to lentils, many other people use equal amounts. Today, meat is not included as it was in the medieval recipe.

2 cups large brown lentils, soaked if required
1 onion, finely chopped
Oil
Salt and black pepper
1 cup long-grain rice, washed
2 onions, sliced into half-moon shapes

Boil lentils in a fresh portion of water to cover for ¾ to 1½ hours, or until tender. Fry the chopped onion in 2 tablespoons oil until soft and golden. Add it to the lentils and season to taste with salt and pepper. Mix well and add rice, together with enough water to make the liquid in the pan up to 2 cups. Season again and simmer gently, covered, for about 20 minutes until the rice is soft and well cooked, adding a little more water if it becomes absorbed too quickly.

Fry the sliced onions in 2 tablespoons very hot oil until they are dark brown and sweet, almost caramelized.

Serve the rice and lentils on a large shallow dish, garnished with fried onion slices.

This dish is delicious served either hot or cold, and accompanied by yogurt.

Burghul Pilav

A Turkish specialty also favored by Armenians.

12–16 tablespoons butter
1 large onion, finely chopped
4 cups burghul [cracked wheat]

Salt
About 2½ cups meat or chicken
   stock or water

Melt 8 tablespoons (1 stick) butter in a large, heavy saucepan and fry the chopped onion until soft and a pale golden color. Add the burghul and fry lightly for 10 minutes, stirring all the time. Season to taste with salt and pour in stock or water to cover the burghul by about ½ inch. Mix well and simmer over low heat for 10 minutes, covered, until all the liquid is absorbed. Add a little more water if it seems too dry. The total quantity used is usually just under 2½ cups.

Melt the remaining butter and pour it over the burghul. Stretch a clean cloth over the top of the pan, put on the lid again, and leave on an asbestos mat if you have one, over the lowest possible heat for ½ hour longer. The burghul will swell and become very soft.

Serve instead of plain rice with stews, meat, chicken, etc.

A variation is to stir 3 tablespoons pine nuts, fried in butter or oil for a minute or two, into the burghul before steaming it. In yet another, particularly delicious pilav, cheese cubes are added (Cheddar, Gruyère, or Halumi). Stir into the cooked burghul and cook for a few minutes longer until the cheese melts. Fried eggplant cubes or slices can be mixed in at the end. In another very popular variation, the burghul is boiled in 2½ cups stock, then mixed with ½ lb. crushed or broken vermicelli which has been lightly colored in a mixture of 2½ tablespoons each butter and oil, and steamed as above.

Burghul Pilav with Lamb

2–3 onions, finely chopped
½ lb. butter
1½ lbs. lean stewing lamb, cubed
Salt and black pepper

3 tomatoes, skinned and chopped
4 tablespoons tomato paste
4 cups burghul [cracked wheat]

Fry onions in a saucepan in about 8 tablespoons (1 stick) butter until soft and a pale golden color. Add the meat and turn it over moderate heat for a few minutes to color the cubes all over. Season to taste with salt and pepper. Add the tomatoes and tomato paste, cover with water, and simmer gently for about 2 hours, or until the meat is tender, adding more water as required.

In another pan, fry the burghul in the remaining butter for 10 minutes, stirring constantly. Add salt to taste, then pour in the meat mixture together with its sauce, which should measure about 2½ cups. Stir well and cover. Simmer gently for 10 minutes, or until all the liquid has been absorbed. Then steam for a further ½ hour on an asbestos mat over very low heat, with a cloth stretched under the lid to absorb the steam. The burghul should be plump and soft.

Burghul pilav with chicken can be made simply by substituting chicken pieces for lamb. Cook for about 30 minutes, depending on the size of the pieces.

COUSCOUS

Couscous is the national dish of the Maghreb, the North African countries of Morocco, Tunisia, and Algeria. Of Berber origin, this is a truly local dish. A *couscous* has been adopted by other Arab countries, who call it *maghrebia*, but this is very different from the one eaten in North Africa.

Couscous itself is a type of fine semolina made from wheat grain. Until very recently, every family would send its wheat to the local mill to be ground to the degree of fineness they preferred. Back home, the grain went through a process of rubbing with fine flour. It was put in a large wooden bowl. Gradually, flour was sprinkled over it, while the women rolled it into the *couscous* with their hands so as to coat each grain with a fine film of flour. This was in order to keep each grain separate when it was steamed. Today, most people buy their *couscous* ready-made for the sake of expediency.

There are infinite regional and family variations of this dish. It is eaten practically every evening, and every evening the dish is slightly different, the women putting all their expertise into varying it and yet keeping to the traditional form.

The basic process for the preparation of *couscous* is the steaming of the grain over a stew or broth. This is generally made with meat, usually lamb or chicken, and a variety of vegetables. Chickpeas are usually added, and sometimes raisins as well. The broth is often colored red with tomato purée or yellow with saffron. Many spices are used but so sparingly that one can hardly define each individual aroma. Often a sauce is prepared separately with some of the broth and made strong and fiery with cayenne or chili pepper and a concentrate of red pimiento called *harissa* (see page 149). This sauce is served beside the *couscous* for those who wish to be "inflamed and intoxicated."

In the Moroccan town of Fez, the stews or broths are generally lighter. The ingredients are boiled and delicately blended and perfumed.

In Tunisia and Algeria, they are richer and heavier. The meat and sometimes the vegetables as well are first braised in oil. Tunisians seem to prefer the stronger, spicier broths with cayenne and chili. Algerians like to add tomato purée, while Moroccans prefer the aroma and color given by a pinch of saffron.

A strong French influence on Algerian food has led to the adoption by the younger generation of more European vegetables such as string beans, peas, and carrots for their stews.

The actual process of cooking the *couscous* is very simple, but calls for a subtle handling of the grain. The aim is to make it swell and become extremely light, each grain soft, delicate, velvety, and separate from its neighbor. Bad handling of the grain will result in a lumpy and rather stodgy *couscous*. The grain must never cook *in* the broth or sauce, but only in the steam. It must not even touch the broth throughout the steaming. The *couscoussière*, the pot traditionally used, is in two parts, made from glazed earthenware or copper, and, more recently, aluminum. The bottom part is a large round pan in which the stew is cooked. The top consists of a strainer with widish holes. This holds the *couscous*. If you cannot get hold of an authentic *couscoussière*, you can improvise with a double boiler or a metal strainer or colander which fits exactly over a large pan.

The treatment of the grain is always the same, whatever the sauce. Moisten the *couscous* slightly with a little cold water, working it in with the fingers to prevent lumps from forming. Turn it into the strainer part of the *couscoussière*. This should be done after the stew below has already been cooking for some time and the ingredients are nearly ready. Rake the grains with your fingers to air them and help them to swell better. Do not cover the strainer. Steam over the simmering sauce for 30 minutes.

Now turn the *couscous* into a large bowl. Sprinkle generously with cold water and stir well with a wooden spoon to break up any lumps and to separate and air the grains. Add a little salt at this point if you like. The water will make the grains swell very much. (A tablespoon of oil is sometimes added at the same time.) Return to the top container and steam for a further 30 minutes.

Some people like to steam the *couscous* over boiling water, and then serve it with a stew prepared separately.

Moroccan Couscous

Here is a basic Moroccan couscous around which you can improvise.

2 lbs. lean stewing lamb or 1 lb. lamb, ½ lb. beef, and ½ chicken	¼ teaspoon saffron [optional]
	1 lb. or more *couscous*
2 onions, chopped	¼–½ cup raisins
⅓ cup chickpeas, soaked overnight	3 zucchini, sliced
2 turnips, quartered	¼ lb. fresh shelled or frozen fava
2 large carrots, sliced	beans
2½ tablespoons olive oil	2 tomatoes
Salt and black pepper	5 tablespoons finely chopped parsley
¼ teaspoon ground ginger [optional]	Cayenne or chili pepper
	1 teaspoon paprika
	2½ tablespoons butter

Use a *couscoussière*, or improvise one as described above.

Put the meat, chicken if used, onions, chickpeas, turnips, and carrots—all the ingredients which require longer cooking—in the bottom part of the pan. Cover with water, add the oil, and salt and pepper. Add ginger and saffron if you like, bring to a boil, and simmer for about 1 hour.

Now moisten the *couscous* as described in the introduction, put it in the top part of the *couscoussière* or whatever you are using, and steam for ½ hour. Remove the strainer. Moisten the grain and treat it as described. Before fitting the strainer over the pan again, add raisins, zucchini, fava beans, tomatoes, and parsley to the simmering stew. Cook for a further ½ hour.

Take a cupful of sauce from the stew and stir in cayenne or chili pepper, enough to make it very strong and fiery, and a little paprika.

To serve, pile the *couscous* onto a large dish, preferably a wooden or earthenware one. Add butter and work it into the grains as it melts. Arrange the meat and vegetables over the *couscous* and pour the broth over it. Pass the hot, peppery sauce around separately in a little bowl.

Alternatively, serve the *couscous*, the meat and vegetables, the broth, and the peppery sauce in separate bowls.

This dish can be varied indefinitely. Fry the meat and chopped onions in oil before adding the other ingredients if you like. Add baby onions, sliced green peppers, and a slice of pumpkin, or, as Algerians sometimes do, string beans and peas. Color the stew with tomato paste and paprika, and make it fiery with cayenne or *harissa* (see page 452). Or add a little cinnamon and rose water to the butter when you melt it into the *couscous*.

A *couscous* served with yogurt is steamed over water, seasoned with salt and pepper, allowed to cool and thoroughly mixed with yogurt. It is eaten cold.

In Algeria, a sweet *couscous* is served as an entrée. It is steamed over water and served with butter, sugar, and a few raisins. Milk is drunk at the same time. Some people like to pour milk over the *couscous* as well.

Couscous with Fish

A couscous favored by Tunisians. Any type of fish can be used, but generally red or gray mullet is preferred.

¾ cup chickpeas, soaked overnight
Fish tails and heads to make a rich
    stock
3 carrots, sliced
3 turnips, quartered
1 onion, quartered, or a few baby
    onions
1 sweet green pepper, seeded, cored,
    and sliced

Salt and black pepper
Cayenne pepper
¼ teaspoon saffron
1–1½ lbs. couscous
1½–2 lbs. fish [see above]
2–3 quinces, peeled, cored, and
    sliced

In a large pan, make a rich fish soup. Boil the fish tails and heads with all the vegetables, salt, black and cayenne pepper, and saffron in 5–7 cups water. Remove the scum as it rises to the surface. Simmer for an hour until the stock is rich and the vegetables are soft.

Prepare the *couscous* as described on page 277. Put it in the strainer and steam it over the simmering fish stock for 30 minutes. Remove the *couscous* and treat it as previously described.

Remove the fish tails and heads from the stock, and if you like strain through a fine sieve, then return the vegetables to the stock. Lower in the whole fish, sliced if too large. Add the sliced quinces. Return the *couscous* to the sieve and steam it over the simmering fish for a further 30 minutes, less if the pieces of fish are not large. Adjust the seasoning of the reduced fish stock.

Serve the fish and its sauce over the *couscous* in a large dish, or in separate dishes. The strong-tasting quinces give this dish a very distinctive flavor.

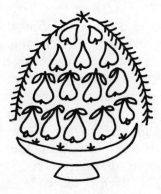

VEGETABLES

Khodar

Vegetables in the Middle East do not play second fiddle as do the "two veg" to meat in England and the United States. They hold a dignified, sometimes splendid position in the hierarchy of food. They are, in turn, *mezze*, pickles, and salads. They can be stuffed and ranked as a main dish, an adornment to meat in a stew, or deep-fried, sautéed, or steamed. In cooking, their nature is taken into account, and their flavor, texture, and color are treated with respect. They are expected to give of their best.

They do not come in plastic bags or packed tightly in little boxes, synthetically remote from their buyers. They are hunted, eyed covetously, handled, and smelled, chosen and bargained for, and at last brought home in triumph.

Early in the morning, people leave their houses to do their shopping at the market stalls spilling over with vegetables and fruits fresh from the villages. Men often do this pleasant task before going to work or on the way home.

To look for eggplants for one's *Imam Bayildi* or for zucchini for one's *kousa bi gebna* is a pleasure. Will the zucchini be good for stuffing? Or will they be too small? Will the eggplant be round today, or thin and long? Which stall will have the best tomatoes, and at what price? It is a challenge and a triumph to find a truly good, unblemished vegetable at a good price.

There is also the pleasure of bargaining, an ancient ritual. How dull it would be to have fixed prices and not to indulge in this game which daily sharpens the wits and brings shopping to a personal, human level! Practically all the vegetables used in the Middle East are easily available. A good number are available frozen or canned, and although these cannot equal fresh vegetables, they are sometimes an excellent alternative.

The basic vegetables, such as tomatoes, lemons, cucumbers, garlic, fava beans, zucchini, celery, onions, sweet peppers, leeks, and spinach are common.

ZUCCHINI   When buying zucchini squash, choose medium-sized or largish ones for stuffing, small or very large ones for slicing and deep frying, or for use in omelets, stews, etc.

EGGPLANT   Often called "poor man's meat" and, in one form, "poor man's caviar," the eggplant is one of the staple foods of the Middle East. It is extremely versatile.

There are different types of eggplant: small and round, large and round, long and thin, and small and thin. The color varies from mauve with sparks of violet, to blue-black, and one variety is opaline white. All should be shiny and firm.

The type of eggplant often determines the dish that can be made with it. Pick the smaller ones, preferably the longer type, for stuffing. The larger ones can be sliced or cubed, and deep-fried, sautéed, or stewed.

CUCUMBERS   The variety to be found in the Middle East is small and stubby in appearance, rather like a gherkin. It is sweeter than the larger variety, and has fewer seeds. I have sometimes found them in Greek shops in London.

TOMATOES are usually large and knobbly, and very flavorful.

SWEET PEPPERS vary in color from olive, pale or dark green, to bright green, or vivid yellow or red. When buying them, pick an odd scarlet one to place among the green ones to bring out their brilliance.

Peppers have a sweet, piquant flavor, but their seeds are usually very strong and should be removed. One in forty will be truly fiery, so it is advisable to taste a small piece from every pepper before using it.

ONIONS are usually very pale-skinned and white-fleshed. A favorite variety in the Middle East is the Italian onion, which has a cherry-red skin and a mauve-tinged, sweet, mild flesh, excellent raw in salads. Spanish onions are a good alternative.

GARLIC in the Middle East is of a variety with large cloves. Where a clove of garlic is indicated in a recipe, a largish one or 2 or 3 very small ones should be used.

LEMONS are small and round, with very thin skins and sharp, generous juice. This type can be found in most Indian and Greek food shops, but the usual variety available will do. You can also use limes.

LETTUCE in the Middle East is the long, crisp, romaine or cos variety. It is grown abundantly and is a great favorite. In Egypt, discarded leaves are found scattered about all the public gardens at the end of festival days.

ARTICHOKES occur in several varieties, both large and small. All are generally very tender. They are usually expensive; but the better qualities of canned artichokes keep their flavor and make an excellent substitute.

PARSLEY in the Middle East is rather like chervil in appearance, and has a much stronger flavor.

OKRA, or *bamia* as it is called in Arabic, is also called "ladies' fingers" in England, a very evocative name for this long, green, pointed vegetable. Fresh okra is available seasonally in most parts of the U.S. and it can also be bought frozen. Okra has a glutinous texture when cooked, and keeps its flavor well when canned.

FAVA BEANS are similar to those found elsewhere. When fresh ones are not available, frozen ones make an excellent substitute. Some canned qualities are also very good.

Middle Eastern SPINACH has the small tender leaves attached in bunches growing out of one root.

SWISS CHARD (*blette* in French) is a type of spinach with rather longer leaves.

SWEET POTATOES are generally available. Bake them in their jackets like ordinary potatoes, but for a bit longer. Cut open and eat with butter but no salt. They are deliciously sweet.

PLAIN AND MIXED
VEGETABLE DISHES

Potatoes with Chickpeas and Tomatoes

This dish is eaten cold in the Middle East. The hot version is the same, except that it uses butter or samna *(clarified butter) instead of oil.*

2 lbs. potatoes
3 onions, thickly sliced
6–7 tablespoons oil
⅓ cup chickpeas, soaked overnight

2–3 cloves garlic
1 lb. tomatoes, skinned and chopped
2½ tablespoons tomato paste
Salt and black pepper

Peel and slice the potatoes thickly. Fry the onions in oil until golden, using a large saucepan. Add the soaked and drained chickpeas and the whole garlic cloves, and fry until colored. Add the potato slices and turn them until they too are slightly colored. Add tomatoes, and water to cover mixed with tomato paste. Season to taste with salt and pepper.

Bring to the boil and simmer gently until the potatoes and chickpeas are soft. The chickpeas available today will need only about ½ to ¾ hour's cooking, if first soaked.

Serve cold.

Eggplant or Zucchini with Tomatoes

This dish can be prepared with either one kind of vegetable or both; in the second case, reduce the quantity of each vegetable.

1½ lbs. eggplant or zucchini
Salt
1 clove garlic, crushed
6–8 tablespoons oil [use olive oil if
    serving cold]

¾ lb. tomatoes, skinned and
    chopped
2 tablespoons chopped parsley
Salt and black pepper

Cut the eggplants or zucchini into moderately thick rounds. Sprinkle with salt and leave to drain in a colander for at least ½ hour. Squeeze eggplant dry.

Sauté gently with the crushed garlic in olive oil, turning the slices over once, until they are soft. Add the tomatoes and squash them gently in the pan. Sprinkle with parsley, season to taste with salt and pepper, and simmer until the vegetables are well done.

Serve hot to accompany meat dishes, or cold as an hors d'œuvre.

Okra (Bamia) with Tomatoes and Onions

This popular dish is often flavored with garlic and coriander, a favorite Arab combination. It is customarily served cold, and for this reason it is cooked in oil. However, it is equally delicious hot, served with rice or as a side dish with meat or chicken.

2 lbs. fresh young okra or a 28-oz. can okra with liquid
¾ lb. tiny white button onions or large onions
6–7 tablespoons olive oil

2–3 cloves garlic, halved
1 lb. tomatoes, skinned and sliced
Salt and black pepper
Juice of 1 lemon

Wash the fresh okra. Cut off any hard stems and dry the okra thoroughly. Peel the button onions but leave them whole. If using large onions, slice them thickly.

Heat the oil in a large saucepan and fry the onions with the halved garlic cloves until slightly soft, transparent, and golden. Add okra and continue to fry until slightly softened. Add the sliced tomatoes and sauté for a few minutes longer. Season to taste with salt and pepper. Cover with water, bring to a boil, and simmer until the okra is very tender, usually about 1 hour. Squeeze in the lemon juice and cook for a further 15 minutes. (Canned okra requires a much shorter time.)

Serve hot or cold. If to be served cold, allow to cool in the saucepan before turning out into a serving dish.

If you wish to flavor the dish with coriander, add a teaspoon of ground coriander together with the garlic cloves, which should in this case be crushed and not halved.

Eggplant, Tomatoes, and Green Peppers in Oil

This dish, similar to the French ratatouille, *is usually served cold, although it is also good hot. It makes a splendid hors d'œuvre.*

2 eggplants, sliced
Salt
1 onion, sliced
½ cup olive oil

1–2 green peppers, sliced, seeded, and cored
4 tomatoes, skinned and sliced
Black pepper

Sprinkle the eggplant slices with salt and let them drain in a colander for at least ½ hour to get rid of their bitter juices. Squeeze, wash, and dry the slices.

Fry the onion in olive oil until soft and a pale golden color. Add the sliced peppers and eggplant, and fry gently for 10 minutes longer. Add the tomatoes and season to taste with salt and pepper. As they cook, the vegetables will give out a great deal of water. Simmer for 30 minutes until they are tender and the liquid in the pan is considerably reduced. Allow to cool in the pan.

Turks serve this with beaten yogurt, sometimes flavored with crushed garlic and salt, and poured over the entire dish.

Turlu / Turkish Mixed Vegetables in Olive Oil

1 onion, sliced
¾ cup olive oil
½ lb. white dried beans (navy, pea, or Great Northern), soaked overnight
2 small potatoes, peeled and sliced
1 medium celeriac, peeled and sliced

1 large carrot, scraped and sliced
5 spring onions, chopped
2–4 large cloves garlic, or more
Salt and black pepper
1 teaspoon superfine sugar
4 tablespoons finely chopped parsley

Fry the onion in half the oil until soft and a pale golden color, using a large saucepan. Add the drained beans and about 2½ cups of water, but no salt. Bring to the boil and simmer for 1 to 3 hours, according to quality, until the beans are practically tender. A pressure cooker will reduce this time considerably.

Add remaining vegetables and garlic, and more water if necessary.

Simmer until all the vegetables and the beans are well cooked. Season to taste with salt and pepper, add sugar and the remaining olive oil, and cook for a further 10 minutes.

Serve hot, garnished with chopped parsley.

Moussaka

A splendid meal in itself, this dish is a favorite throughout the Middle East. Although it is claimed by the Greeks as their own, its name is an Arabic one. It is possible, however, that the Turks adopted the dish from the Greeks and gave it its present name. Numerous variations exist. In Greece it is made somewhat drier than in the following recipe.

3 eggplants
Salt
Oil
1–2 onions, thinly sliced or chopped
1½ lbs. lamb or beef, ground
Black pepper
½ teaspoon ground allspice or 1 teaspoon ground cinnamon [optional]

1 tomato, skinned and chopped
3 tablespoons tomato paste
3 tablespoons chopped parsley
2½ tablespoons butter
2½ tablespoons flour
1¼ cups hot milk
Pinch of grated nutmeg
1 egg yolk

Peel and slice the eggplants thinly, or slice them unpeeled. Sprinkle the slices generously with salt and allow their bitter juices to drain away in a colander for at least ½ hour. Squeeze, wash in cold water, and pat dry. Fry lightly in oil, turning the slices once. Remove and drain on absorbent paper.

Fry the onions in 2 tablespoons oil until pale golden. Add the ground meat and fry until well browned. Season to taste with salt and pepper, and flavor with allspice or cinnamon if you like. Add the chopped tomato, tomato paste, and parsley. Stir well, moisten with a few tablespoons of water, and simmer for about 15 minutes, or until the meat is well cooked and the water is absorbed.

Put alternate layers of eggplant slices and meat and onion mixture in a deep baking dish, starting and ending with a layer of eggplant.

Prepare the Béchamel sauce. Melt butter in a saucepan. Add flour and stir over low heat for a few minutes until well blended. Add the hot milk gradually, stirring until it boils, taking care not to allow lumps to form. Season to taste with salt, pepper, and a pinch of nutmeg. Simmer until the sauce thickens. Beat the egg yolk. Stir in a little of the sauce and beat well. Pour back into the pan slowly, stirring constantly. Do not allow the sauce to boil again.

Pour the sauce over the minced meat and eggplant and bake, uncovered, in a preheated moderate oven (375°) for about 45 minutes,

until a brown crust has formed on the top and the layers have fused and blended. This looks interesting and attractive in a transparent baking dish.

Serve hot, straight from the dish. *Moussaka* makes a splendid party or family dish served with salad and yogurt. It can also be cooked in small individual bowls, the layers repeated in exactly the same way.

A variation popular in England makes use of seasoned mashed potatoes. A layer is spread over the top of the dish and covered with the sauce. Potatoes can also be sliced and sautéed and arranged on top before the sauce is poured over the whole. Zucchini are sometimes used instead of, or at the same time as, eggplants. A very rich *moussaka* can be made by sprinkling grated Kephalotyri or Parmesan cheese (or by adding layers of thinly sliced Gruyère) over each layer of eggplant.

Kousa Bi Gebna / Zucchini with Cheese

A perfect vegetable dish. Use a good melting cheese such as Gruyère or Cheddar, mixed with a little Parmesan.

1 large onion, chopped	3 eggs
2½ tablespoons butter or oil	½ lb. (about 2 cups) grated cheese
2 lbs. zucchini	White pepper
Salt	

Soften the onion in butter or oil. Wash the zucchini. Scrape skins lightly if necessary. Trim the zucchini ends and cut into ½-inch slices. Poach in salted water for a few minutes until tender, or steam if you prefer. Drain well. Put into an ovenproof dish in which they can be served.

Beat the eggs, add the grated cheese and pepper to taste, and mix well. Pour over the vegetables.

Bake in a preheated moderate oven (375°) for about 20 minutes. Allow the top to color delicately.

Excellent served with yogurt.

Hünkâr Beğendi / Sultan's Delight

A delicious eggplant cream, pale and delicate, with the distinctive flavor of grilled eggplant.

2 lbs. eggplant	Salt
1 tablespoon lemon juice	2 oz. (½ cup) grated Parmesan or
5 tablespoons butter	dry Cheddar
5 tablespoons flour	Finely chopped parsley
2–2½ cups hot milk	

Grill the eggplants over a naked flame or under a broiler until their skins are black and blistered all over. Peel carefully, removing all charred particles.

Leave them covered with water acidulated with 1 tablespoon lemon juice for 15 minutes. This will keep them white.

Melt the butter in a saucepan. Add the flour and stir over very low heat for about 2 minutes until well blended. Remove from the heat.

Drain the eggplants and squeeze out as much of the water as possible. Mash well. Add to the butter and flour mixture. Mash with a fork or a potato masher, and beat vigorously until well blended. Return to the heat. Add the milk gradually, beating vigorously all the time. Season to taste with salt. Cook until the mixture thickens and the taste of flour has disappeared, about 15 minutes. Add the grated cheese, stir until melted, and turn into a serving dish. Sprinkle with finely chopped parsley.

Serve with steamed kebabs, stewed meat, or chicken cooked in a tomato sauce. The eggplant cream serves as a bed for the meat or chicken.

Artichoke Hearts and Fava Beans in Oil

The Copts observe a long and arduous fast during Lent (El Soum el Kibir), when they abstain from every kind of animal food, such as meat, eggs, milk, butter, and cheese, and eat only bread and vegetables (chiefly beans), and dukkah (see page 51).

Here is a favorite Lenten dish, also popular with the Greeks of Egypt, and a general favorite throughout the Middle East.

6 artichokes [or good-quality can-
  ned artichoke hearts] *
Juice of 1 lemon, or more
3 tablespoons olive oil
1 clove garlic, crushed, or more

1 teaspoon sugar
1 lb. fresh shelled or frozen fava
  beans
Salt and black pepper
1 tablespoon flour or cornstarch

Buy young artichokes. Remove the leaves, stems, and chokes, and use only the hearts. Rub with lemon juice and drop in ½ cup water acidulated with lemon to prevent discoloration.

* If canned artichokes and frozen beans are used, the cooking time will, of course, be much shorter.

Put the olive oil, garlic, sugar, and the acidulated water in a large pan with the artichoke hearts. Add the fava beans, and season to taste with salt and pepper. Add more water to cover if necessary. Simmer gently over low heat for about ¾ hour, until the artichoke hearts and beans are very tender and the liquid is considerably reduced.

Mix the flour or cornstarch to a smooth paste with a little cold water. Add a little of the hot liquid and stir well. Then add this to the pan gradually, stirring constantly. Simmer gently, stirring occasionally, until the sauce thickens and has lost the taste of flour (about 15 minutes). Pour into a dish.

Serve hot to accompany main dishes, or cold as an hors d'œuvre. The sauce will be gelatinous if cornstarch is used.

Bemuelos / Sephardic Potato Cakes

These potato cakes are traditionally prepared during Passover by many Jews in the Middle East, as they no doubt also are in Europe. Flour is used instead of matzo meal at times other than Passover.

2 lbs. potatoes	Salt and black pepper
2–3 eggs	Matzo meal
¼ lb. Parmesan or Cheddar cheese, grated (1 cup)	Oil for deep frying
	Chopped parsley [optional]

Boil and drain the potatoes and mash them, keeping them as dry as possible. Beat the eggs and mix with the potatoes, together with the grated cheese, and salt and pepper to taste. Knead well to a pasty consistency, adding a little matzo meal if necessary. Take tablespoonfuls of the mixture at a time and pat into round, flat shapes. Dip them in matzo meal and deep-fry until golden.

You can add a little chopped parsley to the potato mixture if you like.

Tartoufa / Jerusalem Artichokes

A delightful vegetable whose knobbly texture makes it difficult to peel, a disadvantage which rather limits its appeal.

Peel and wash them. Simmer in salted water, chicken, or meat stock to cover for just under ½ hour, adding more liquid if necessary. They should be tender and the liquid practically all absorbed. Finish with a tablespoon of butter or the juice of ½ lemon.

Tartoufa in Tomato Sauce

2½ lbs. Jerusalem artichokes
1 onion, finely chopped
1 clove garlic, halved
4 tablespoons olive oil
3 tomatoes, skinned and chopped

2 tablespoons tomato paste
2 tablespoons finely chopped parsley
Salt and black pepper
Juice of ½ lemon [optional]

Wash and peel the artichokes. Fry the onion and garlic in olive oil until soft and golden. Add the artichokes and roll them in the oil by shaking the pan. Add the tomatoes and squash them into the oil. Add tomato paste, parsley, seasoning, and lemon juice if used. Stir well and cover with water. Simmer gently for ½ hour, or until the artichokes are tender and the sauce is rich and reduced. Add more water during cooking if necessary.

Celeriac in Olive Oil

2 large celeriacs
4 tablespoons oil

Juice of 1 lemon, or more
Salt and black pepper

Peel the celeriacs and cut into ¾-inch cubes. Fry gently in olive oil until lightly colored. Add a little water to cover, lemon juice to taste, and salt and pepper. Simmer until the vegetables are tender and the liquid is considerably reduced, about ½ hour.
    Eat hot or cold.

Deep-fried Eggplant or Zucchini

Thinly slice the vegetables, lengthwise or crosswise. Sprinkle them with salt and leave them to drain in a colander for at least ½ hour. A plate with a weight on top will help to squeeze the juices out. Or squeeze with your hands after they have been left for some time.

This will get rid of their bitterness and will also make them lose their capacity for drinking oil.

Pat the slices dry, roll them in flour, and deep-fry a few at a time for 2 to 3 minutes in very hot oil. Remove and drain when golden brown.

Alternatively, dip the vegetable slices in a light batter. This is made by gradually adding ½ cup water to ¾ cup plain flour mixed with 4 tablespoons oil, leaving it to rest for 2 hours, and folding in a stiffly beaten egg white just before use. Another batter is made by beating the flour and water mixture with 1 whole egg. Fry as above, turning over once, remove with a perforated spoon and drain.

Garnish with roughly chopped parsley, deep-fried in the same oil. Serve with lemon wedges as an appetizer or side dish.

Deep-fried Cauliflower

Wash the cauliflower and separate into flowerets. Boil in salted water until only just tender. Drain and allow to dry well.

Roll the flowerets in beaten egg, and then in flour or bread crumbs. Deep-fry in very hot oil until crisp and golden. Drain on absorbent paper.

Alternatively, dip in one of the batter mixtures given in the preceding recipe, and deep-fry until golden, turning over once. Drain well.

Serve with yogurt or Turkish walnut *tarator* sauce (page 70).

Egyptian Cauliflower

Wash, boil, and deep-fry a cauliflower as directed above. Both the egg and flour and the batter methods are equally suitable.

Prepare a tomato sauce in a large saucepan. Fry 2 cloves garlic in about 2 tablespoons oil until golden. Add 4 tablespoons tomato paste diluted in ½ cup water, 4 tablespoons chopped parsley, and salt and black pepper to taste. Simmer for 10 to 15 minutes.

Drain the deep-fried flowerets, and drop them into the tomato sauce. Simmer for about ½ hour until the cauliflower is very tender and the sauce is reduced and rich.

Cauliflower with Lemon Juice

Wash, boil, or steam a young white cauliflower for about 10 to 15 minutes, until just tender. Acidulating the salted water in which it is boiled with a little lemon juice helps to keep it white.

Drain the tender head well. Break into flowerets. Heat 1 tablespoon butter with 1 tablespoon or more olive oil in a pan, add the juice of 1 lemon, and sprinkle with a little salt and pepper. Roll the cauliflower in this and keep over very low heat until it is heated through and has absorbed the lemon juice. Some people also like to add a little crushed garlic.

Grilled Corn on the Cob

Walking along the *corniche* or waterfront in Alexandria, one is irresistibly lured by the smell of corn grilled over charcoal. Vendors sit at the braziers, fanning the flames vigorously, or letting the sea breeze do it for them.

Remove the outer leaves or husks from the corn. Place the cobs on a charcoal grill, not too close to the fire. Turn them constantly. They will become flecked with black, charred spots, but inside they will be soft and milky.

Riddle: Beaded, her head is high and she sleeps in a shawl. Guess who she is.
Answer: A corn cob.

STUFFED VEGETABLES

Mahshi Khodar

Dolma to the Turks, *dolmathes* to the Greeks, *dolmeh* to the Persians, and *mahshi* to the Arabs, stuffed vegetables are the great family favorites, the party pieces and festive dishes of the Turks, the Uzbeks, the Azerbaijanis, Armenians, Greeks, Egyptians, Persians, Syrians, Lebanese, Saudi Arabians, and North Africans. Each country has developed its own variations.

Their origin is not certain, though both the Turks and the Greeks claim them as their creation. They do not appear in the very early Persian and Arab manuscripts, but seem to have been known at the time of the Ottoman Empire, and were served at the lavish banquets of the Sultans. Perhaps they were developed at this time; but they may equally well have been adopted from the vanquished Greeks, who claim a rich culinary tradition stemming from their early civilization.

However, stuffed vegetables were obviously developed as a "court cuisine," invented and prepared for a rich and powerful leisured class to excite their curiosity and titillate their palates, as well as to satisfy their desire for ostentation. The long, elaborate preparation required for these dishes and the experienced and delicate handiwork that goes into the making of them are proof of the number of dedicated cooks employed in the huge kitchens, while the subtle harmony of the vegetables and their fillings demonstrates the refined taste and deep culinary knowledge of their masters.

Today, poorer people can usually afford vine leaves, zucchini, onions, and eggplant; and although they have had to make the fillings simpler and cheaper, they count their own time as cheap as their masters deemed it, and spend it lavishly on rolling and filling their beloved *mahshi*.

As well as the love for different, subtle flavors, for the exciting fusion of vegetables and their fillings, the traditional wish to take pains and give of oneself is satisfied by the trouble one takes in making these dishes. So is the wish to impress by one's culinary expertise. And how the guest loves to be surprised by an intriguing parcel, the contents of which are always slightly unpredictable.

In the past, Arabs have been—and in certain places still are—obsessed by their belief in the existence of numerous spirits or *djinns*, several *djinns* per person in fact, who inhabit both things and people whenever they get a chance. Their tales give a fascinating picture of vegetables inhabited by *djinns*—rice *djinns*, meat *djinns*, chickpea *djinns*—seasoned and spiced, and given piquant, naughty, or gentle personalities, like the *djinns* who inhabit humans.

A very common filling for any stuffed vegetable is a mixture of chopped onion, ground meat, rice, and chopped parsley, sometimes with chopped tomatoes as well, seasoned with salt and pepper. Sometimes raisins, pine nuts, and chopped walnuts are added to the mixture. Persians favor the addition of well-cooked yellow split peas. An Armenian filling is made with burghul (cracked wheat) flavored with aniseed and garlic.

In the past, stuffed vegetables were customarily fried gently in oil or *samna* (clarified butter) before being stewed. Today, since the tendency is to make dishes lighter and less rich, this step, though an enhancement to the flavor of the dish, is omitted.

Almost any vegetable can be, and is, stuffed.

A man carried seven eggs in the fold (pocket) of his robe. He met another man in the street and said to him: "If you can guess what I have in the fold of my robe, I will give you these eggs, and if you can tell me how many there are, I will give you all seven."

The other thought for a while and said: "I don't understand, give me another clue."

The man said: "It is white with yellow in the middle."

"Now I understand," exclaimed the other. "It is a white radish that has been hollowed and stuffed with a carrot!"

A man told this anecdote to a group of people. When he had finished, one of his audience asked, "But tell us, what was there in the fold of his robe?" *

* Christensen, *Contes persans*.

What is more natural than a white radish stuffed with a carrot?

Fillings for Vegetables

From the great variety of fillings, I am giving the ones which are most widely used and the general favorites. They can also be flavored with different spices and herbs. The quantities given are enough to stuff about 2¼ lbs. vegetables, but this varies a little according to the size of the vegetables to be filled, and the amount of pulp scooped out of them.

FILLING I

Sheikh el Mahshi filling, also called tatbila. *The word "sheikh" implies that it is the grandest, since it is all meat.*

2½ tablespoons butter or oil
1 medium-sized onion, finely
    chopped
¾ lb. lean lamb or beef, ground
Salt and black pepper

½ teaspoon ground cinnamon or
    ¼ teaspoon ground allspice
⅓ cup pine nuts [optional]

Heat the butter or oil in a frying pan. Add the onion and fry gently until soft and transparent. Add the meat and fry it, tossing it and squashing with a fork, until it changes color. Season to taste with salt and pepper, sprinkle with spices, and stir in pine nuts if used. Moisten with a few tablespoons of water, and cook gently, covered, until the meat is very tender.

FILLING II

Meat and rice filling (the most common one).

½ lb. lean lamb or beef, ground
½ cup rice, washed and drained
1 tomato, skinned and chopped
    [optional]

2 tablespoons finely chopped parsley
    [optional]
Salt and black pepper
½ teaspoon ground cinnamon or
    ¼ teaspoon ground allspice

Put all the ingredients together in a bowl. Knead well by hand until thoroughly blended. One or two tablespoons of raisins and/or pine nuts may be added to this filling, an agreeable though uncommon variation. An alternative flavoring is ½ teaspoon dried basil or marjoram, more if the fresh herb is used.

Do not fill the vegetables more than three-quarters full, to allow for the expansion of the rice. Use cooked rice if the vegetables are to be baked.

FILLING III

A Persian filling of meat and rice with yellow split peas.

⅓ cup yellow split peas
1 medium-sized onion, finely
    chopped
2½ tablespoons butter or oil
½ lb. lean lamb or beef, ground
⅓ cup rice, cooked [measure un-
    cooked]

3 tablespoons finely chopped parsley
2–3 scallions, finely chopped [op-
    tional]
Salt and black pepper
½ teaspoon ground cinnamon
Pinch of grated nutmeg

Cook the yellow split peas in unsalted water for about 25 minutes, or until soft. Soften the onion in butter or oil. Put all the ingredients together in a bowl, including the split peas and onions. Mix well and knead by hand until thoroughly blended.

FILLING IV

A rice filling for vegetables to be eaten cold.

1 cup rice, washed and drained
6 oz. tomatoes, skinned, seeded, and
    finely chopped
1 large onion, finely chopped
A small bunch of parsley, finely
    chopped

Salt and black pepper
½ teaspoon ground cinnamon or
    ¼ teaspoon ground allspice
    [optional]

Mix all the ingredients together in a bowl, kneading well by hand until thoroughly blended. This filling is sometimes flavored with about 2 teaspoons finely chopped fresh dill or mint—1 teaspoon only if dried.

When filling the vegetables, allow room for the rice to expand. Use cooked rice and pack the vegetables tightly if they are to be baked.

FILLING V

A rice and chickpea filling for vegetables to be eaten cold.

⅓ cup chickpeas, soaked overnight
¾ cup rice, washed and drained
6 oz. tomatoes, skinned, seeded, and finely chopped
1 large onion, finely chopped

Salt and black pepper
½ teaspoon ground cinnamon or ¼ teaspoon ground allspice [optional]

Prepare and use as above.

FILLING VI

For vegetables prepared à la Imam Bayildi, *to be eaten cold, and sometimes called* yalangi dolma, *or "false dolma," because of the lack of meat. A very popular filling in Turkey.*

¾ lb. onions
4 tablespoons olive oil
2–3 large cloves garlic, crushed
A bunch of parsley, finely chopped

¾ lb. tomatoes, skinned, seeded, and chopped
Salt

Slice the onions thinly. Soften them gently in olive oil, but do not let them color. Add garlic and stir for a minute or two until aromatic. Remove from the heat and stir in parsley and tomatoes. Season to taste with salt, and mix well.

FILLING VII

A Turkish filling for eggplants.

2 small onions, finely chopped
2½ tablespoons oil
½ lb. lamb or beef, ground
Salt and black pepper

2 tomatoes, skinned and chopped
¼ lb. Gruyère or hard Cheddar, grated

Sauté the onions in oil until soft and a pale golden color. Add the minced meat and fry, squashing well with a fork, until it changes color. Season to taste with salt and pepper, add the tomatoes, and moisten with a few tablespoons of water. Cook until the tomatoes are reduced to a purée. Stir in the grated cheese and remove from the heat.

Stuffed Eggplants

Eggplants are available in abundance throughout the year all over the Middle East, either home-grown or imported from a neighboring country where the seasonal crop comes at a different time. They are therefore as common and as cheap as cabbages are in England.

The appearance of the vegetable, shiny, at times subtle and gentle in color, but more often fierce and blue-black, has stirred the imagination of the people, who have given it, in turn, gentle virtues and malicious magical powers. It is recommended in some parts not to grow eggplants in one's garden in case an evil one might spring up bearing the curse of female infertility. This same dark and shiny aspect, however, makes the eggplant a particularly attractive vegetable to serve.

Eggplants can be stuffed in an infinite variety of ways, but two slightly awkward characteristics must be dealt with before they can be cooked successfully. The first is their bitter juice, which is sometimes unpleasant in flavor; the second is their amazing power of absorbing large quantities of oil when frying. Both these disadvantages are corrected by sprinkling the peeled flesh with salt and placing the slit, sliced, chopped, or emptied-out eggplants in a colander to drain until much of the juices is lost. This takes at least ½ hour, occasionally much longer. A weighted plate can be placed over the vegetables to speed the process; or you can squeeze them gently by hand.

Another way of removing the bitter juice from eggplants is to soak them, scooped out or sliced, in salted water for about 1 hour. The vegetables, thus lightened of their juices, are softer and ready to use. They should then be rinsed in cold water and lightly patted dry with a towel or absorbent paper.

Various methods are used to prepare the eggplants for filling. Here are a few of the more common ones.

METHOD I

Cut a slice off just below the stem and hull. Peel strips off the eggplant lengthwise, leaving alternating strips of flesh and shiny peel. This is in order to bare the flesh, allowing salt sprinkled over it to draw the juices out. Drain in a colander. Rinse and pat dry.

Make a lengthwise slit in each eggplant without cutting right through the vegetable. Stuff the slits with the prepared filling, pressing a few teaspoonfuls into each one. Place the stuffed eggplants in the pan or oven dish with their slits facing upward.

METHOD II

Cut a slice off the stem end of the eggplants just below the hull, which may be removed. Keep the slices to use as "corks." Scoop out the pulp with a small knife or a pointed spoon, taking care not to break their skins, and reserve the pulp for a stew or salad. Sprinkle the inside of each shell with salt, and leave them inverted in a colander for at least ½ hour to allow the bitter juices to drain away.

Rinse the softened shells and stuff them with the prepared filling. Close them with the reserved "corks," and place them upright in a large saucepan or deep oven dish with the corked ends facing upward. Pack them tightly if they are small. If they are medium-sized, they can be laid sideways, but again closely packed to prevent the filling from falling out.

METHOD III

Leave about ½ inch of the stalks on, but remove the hulls. Peel off ½-inch-wide strips lengthwise, leaving alternating strips of bare flesh and shiny peel, as in Method I. This ensures that the eggplants keep their shape, while the peeled strips allow the bitter juices to escape. Sprinkle them wth salt and leave them in a colander for ½ hour. Rinse and pat dry.

Make a slash along the center, right through the eggplant, to within ½ inch of each end. Press the filling well into this slash.

METHOD IV

Cut the eggplants in half lengthwise. They may be peeled or not, as you prefer. Scoop out the centers. Sprinkle the hollowed-out vegetables with salt, and leave to drain for at least ½ hour. Then rinse with cold water and pat dry.

Fill each hollowed-out half with filling and proceed according to the recipe.

Syrian saying: "The woman killed herself with work, yet the feast lasted only one day."

Imam Bayildi / "The Imam Fainted"

This is a Turkish specialty. Widely conflicting stories are told about the origins of its name. Some say that the dish acquired it when an imam, or Turkish priest, fainted with pleasure on being served these stuffed eggplants by his wife. Others believe that the imam fainted when he heard how expensive the ingredients were, and how much olive oil had gone into the making of the dish.

The dish is delightful and, in fact, not very expensive. It makes a splendid first course.

6 long medium-sized eggplants
Filling VI [page 302]
½ cup olive oil
1 teaspoon sugar, or more
Salt
Juice of 1 lemon

Prepare the eggplants for filling by any of the methods described on page 303. Stuff them with Filling VI.

Arrange the eggplants side by side in a large pan. Pour over them the oil and enough water to cover (about ½ cup) mixed with a little sugar, salt to taste, and the lemon juice.

Cover the pan and simmer gently until the eggplants are very soft, about 1 hour. Remove from the heat and allow to cool. Turn out onto a serving dish. Serve cold.

Sheikh El Mahshi Betingan / Eggplants Stuffed with Meat and Pine Nuts

12 small long eggplants or 6 me-
    dium-sized ones
Butter or oil
Filling I [page 300]
3 tablespoons tomato paste
Juice of 1 lemon [optional]
Salt and black pepper

Prepare the eggplants for filling according to Method I, II, or III (pages 303–4). You can fry them lightly in butter or oil *after* they have been prepared but *before* filling. The flavor of the eggplants is enhanced, but the dish becomes rather heavier. I prefer to omit this step.

Stuff the vegetables with the prepared filling and place them in an ovenproof dish.

Mix the tomato paste with enough water to come halfway up the eggplants in the dish. Pour into the dish with about 5 tablespoons oil (omit the oil if the vegetables have been fried), lemon juice, and a little salt and pepper. Bake for 15 minutes in a hot oven (425° to 450°), then reduce the heat to 325° and bake until well done, about 45 minutes.

Alternatively, arrange the stuffed eggplants in a large saucepan, cover, and simmer gently for about ¾ hour until cooked, adding more water if necessary.

Serve hot with plain rice.

Another version is to stew the stuffed eggplants in a little water until they are soft. Then transfer them to a baking dish, and pour over them a Béchamel sauce (about 2 cups). Put the dish in a hot oven (425°) until the top is browned.

Eggplants Stuffed with Rice and Meat

12 small long eggplants or 6 me-
    dium-sized ones
Filling II or III [pages 300–1]
⅓ cup pine nuts or chopped wal-
    nuts [optional]

5 tablespoons olive oil
Salt and black pepper
Juice of 1 lemon

Prepare the eggplants for filling according to Method II.

Prepare Filling II or III in a bowl. Add the nuts if you wish, lightly fried for 1 or 2 minutes beforehand.

Stuff the eggplant shells three-quarters full with the filling, to allow room for the rice to expand. Close them with the reserved "corks."

Heat the olive oil in a large saucepan. Place the eggplants in it, arranged close to each other, and add enough water to come halfway up them. Season with salt and pepper, and squeeze a whole lemon over them. Cover and cook over very gentle heat for ¾ to 1 hour, adding more water if necessary. By the end of the cooking, the water should be almost completely absorbed.

A delicious variation and an attractive way of serving this dish is to cook the stuffed eggplants in an eggplant stew. Take the eggplant centers and about 1 lb. sliced or cubed additional eggplants, sprinkle with salt, and let them drain in a colander for 1 hour. Squeeze them as dry as possible, then fry them in oil or butter in a large saucepan, together with 2 large onions, sliced, until soft and golden. Add 4 or 5 tomatoes, skinned and sliced, 3 or 4 whole cloves garlic, and salt and pepper. Simmer, covered, over low heat until half-cooked, adding a little water if necessary. Place the stuffed eggplants in the stew and simmer gently, covered, for ½ to ¾ hour longer, until the eggplants are soft and the rice is well cooked, adding a little water if the whole becomes too dry. In an unusual Persian variation using Filling III, the eggplants are cooked in a sweet-and-sour sauce made with vinegar and sugar and colored with a little saffron. Half-cover the eggplants with water to which you have added 4 tablespoons oil, and simmer gently, covered, for about ½ hour. Mix ½ cup wine vinegar with about ½ cup sugar and ¼ teaspoon powdered saffron. Pour over the vegetables and continue to cook gently, covered, for another ½ hour. Serve hot with plain rice.

Eggplants Stuffed with Rice—Served Cold

12 small long eggplants
Filling IV or V [page 301]
½ cup chopped walnuts [optional]

¼ cup olive oil
½ lb. tomatoes, thinly sliced

Prepare the eggplants for filling according to Method II.

Prepare Filling IV or V. If using Filling V, the chickpeas may be replaced by chopped walnuts.

Stuff the eggplants only three-quarters full, to allow the rice to expand. Close the openings with the reserved "corks."

Heat the olive oil in a large saucepan. Cover the bottom of the pan with a layer of sliced tomatoes and arrange the stuffed eggplants in layers on top. Cover with another layer of tomato slices and pour over the remaining olive oil. Add water to cover the vegetables and simmer over very low heat, covered, for 30 to 45 minutes, or until the eggplants and their filling are cooked through, adding a little more water if necessary. The liquid should be very much reduced by the end of cooking time.

Allow to cool in the saucepan and turn out onto a serving dish. Serve cold. This dish makes an excellent first course. Use the left-over centers for a stew or salad.

Eggplants Medias

6 eggplants

2 eggs

½ lb. cheese, grated [Greek Halumi, Parmesan, or Cheddar]

Oil for deep frying

Salt

TOMATO SAUCE (optional)

3 tablespoons tomato paste

About 1 cup water

Salt and black pepper

Pinch of sugar [optional]

Prepare the eggplants for filling according to Method IV (page 304).

Beat the eggs and mix well with the grated cheese. Fill each hollowed-out eggplant half with the egg-and-cheese mixture. Then lower each half, cheese side up, into very hot, deep oil, one at a time. Fry for only a few minutes, until slightly browned. Remove from the oil and drain on absorbent paper.

Place the eggplants side by side in a saucepan, add just enough water to come halfway up them, sprinkle with salt, bring to the boil, and simmer gently, covered, for ½ hour, or until well cooked. Add a little more water during the cooking time if necessary.

Serve hot with yogurt and cucumber salad.

A popular variation is to cook the eggplants in a tomato sauce instead of water. Dilute the tomato paste with water, add a little salt and pepper, pour into the saucepan, and continue cooking as above.

Stuffed Zucchini

As with eggplants, there is an infinite number of variations for stuffed zucchini, all slightly different, each preferred by a certain region or town. I have chosen some of the more popular ones. The recipe below was given to me by a Syrian lady. It will serve 6 people generously.

24 small zucchini or 18 medium-
    sized ones
Salt
Filling II [page 300]
4–5 tablespoons butter [optional]

1–2 tomatoes, sliced
2 tablespoons tomato paste
Juice of 1½ lemons
2–4 cloves garlic
1 teaspoon dried crushed mint

Wash the zucchini well. Sprinkle them with salt and leave them to drain for at least ½ hour. This will soften them. Using a narrow apple corer, make a hole at the stem end of each zucchini and scoop out the pulp, being careful not to break the skin. The other end must remain closed. Keep the pulp for a stew or salad.

Prepare the filling in a bowl. Make a larger quantity if the size and weight of the vegetables require it. Fill each zucchini half-full only, to allow room for the rice to swell. There is no need to block the openings.

In the past, it was customary to fry the stuffed zucchini in butter until lightly colored before stewing them, but the tendency today is for lighter food, and many people prefer to omit the preliminary frying. However, if you wish to make the dish richer, fry the stuffed zucchini lightly in the butter.

Lay a few thin slices of tomato in the bottom of a large, deep saucepan. Place the stuffed zucchini side by side in layers on top of the tomatoes. In a small saucepan, mix the tomato paste with 1 cup water and the juice of 1 lemon. Bring to a boil and simmer for a little while. Pour the tomato sauce over the zucchini, cover the saucepan, and simmer very gently for about 1 hour, or until the zucchini are soft and the filling cooked, adding a little more water if necessary.

Crush the garlic cloves with a little salt. Mix with the mint and the remaining lemon juice, sprinkle over the zucchini, and continue cooking for a few minutes longer. The mint is added at the end, since prolonged cooking tends to spoil its taste.

Persians favor Filling III with yellow split peas (page 301), and serve the dish topped with yogurt. The stuffed zucchini are particularly good cooked in a much richer tomato sauce or stew. Fry 1 large chopped onion in 2 tablespoons butter or oil until soft and golden. Add 2 cloves crushed garlic, and fry until golden and aromatic. Add 1 lb. tomatoes, skinned and finely sliced, and sauté gently. Add a little water, season to taste with salt and pepper, and simmer gently until soft. Finally, add about 12 small stuffed zucchini and water to cover, and simmer until well done.

Stuffed Zucchini in Yogurt

This is a marvelous variation.

Stuff 18 small zucchini as described in the previous recipe. Arrange them in a saucepan and pour in about 2½ cups water, or enough to cover. Bring to the boil and simmer gently, covered, for about 35 minutes, until the water is absorbed and the zucchini are nearly done. Add a little more water during the cooking time if necessary.

Prepare about 3½ cups yogurt for cooking (page 79). Pour this over the zucchini and simmer, covered, for about 20 minutes longer, or until the zucchini are very tender.

Crush 3 garlic cloves with a little salt. Add about 1 teaspoon dried crushed mint, and mix well. Fry this mixture in 1 tablespoon butter for a minute or two, and mix with the yogurt. Stir and taste, adding more salt if necessary.

Serve hot with plain rice or *roz bil shaghria* (page 342).

Stuffed Zucchini with Apricots

Although a family favorite, this is not an Egyptian dish. It may have drawn its inspiration from medieval Persian dishes in which apricots were cooked together with meat and vegetables. However, Persians today do not seem to know this most excellent variation of stuffed zucchini.

Soak ½ to ¾ lb. dried apricots in cold water to cover overnight.

Prepare and stuff the same number of zucchini as in the basic recipe on page 308, using Filling II (page 300).

Drain the apricots, reserving the soaking water. Cut them open without separating the halves completely. Arrange a layer of fruit halves over the bottom of a large saucepan. Place a layer of stuffed zucchini side by side over the apricots, and cover them with a second layer of apricots. Continue with alternate layers of vegetables and fruit, ending with a layer of fruit.

Mix the water in which the apricots have been soaked with 4 tablespoons olive oil, and pour into the pan. Squeeze the juice of 2 lemons over the whole. Cook, covered, over very low heat for about 1 hour, until the stuffed zucchini are soft; add water, a ladleful at a time, as the liquid in the pan becomes absorbed.

Mock Stuffed Zucchini or Eggplant

This recipe, contributed by a Turkish lady, is a modern one sup-posedly devised to save time, which it does not. It is nevertheless a delightful dish.

3 zucchini or small thin eggplants	1 egg
Salt	Black pepper
Oil for deep frying	¾ teaspoon ground cinnamon [op-
1 lb. beef, ground	tional]
1 slice bread, crusts removed	2½ tablespoons olive oil

Slice the vegetables lengthwise into very thin slices. Sprinkle the slices with salt and leave them in a colander to drain for at least ½ hour. Wash in cold water and pat dry. Fry in deep, hot oil until soft and a little bronzed. Remove and drain on absorbent paper.

Mix the ground beef, the bread soaked in water and squeezed dry, the egg, salt, pepper, and cinnamon if used, and knead thoroughly. Shape into walnut-sized balls and deep-fry until slightly brown. Remove and drain on absorbent paper.

Roll the zucchini or eggplant slices around the little meatballs and secure them with toothpicks. Put 2½ tablespoons olive oil and about ½ cup water in a large pan. Add the "stuffed" vegetables, sprinkle with salt, and cook over very gentle heat until they are soft and well done. The liquid should all be absorbed by the end of cooking time, but add more water if the pan becomes dry too soon.

These vegetable rolls can also be simmered in a tomato sauce made with 3 tablespoons tomato paste diluted with a little water and seasoned with salt and pepper.

Zucchini Imam Bayildi

A zucchini version of the famous Turkish eggplant dish on page 305.

Filling VI [page 302]
2 lbs. zucchini
2 tomatoes, sliced

Olive oil
1 teaspoon sugar, or more
Salt

Prepare the filling.

Prepare the zucchini for stuffing as described on page 309. Scoop out their centers from the stem end, using an apple corer, and taking care not to pierce them right through.

Stuff the zucchini tightly with the onion and tomato filling. Lay them in layers side by side in a large pan on a bed of tomato slices, and pour over them about ½ cup olive oil mixed with 1 cup water, a teaspoon of sugar, and a little salt. Cover the pan tightly and simmer gently over low heat for about 1½ hours, or until soft. Serve cold as a first course or buffet dish.

Whole Stuffed Onions

6 large onions or 12 smaller ones
Filling II [page 300]

TOMATO SAUCE (optional)
1 tablespoon butter
1 tablespoon flour
3 tablespoons tomato paste
Salt and black pepper
1 cup water

Skin the onions and boil them in water for 15 minutes until they are fairly tender. Drain and cool. Cut a thin slice off the root ends and carefully scoop out the centers, leaving a thick shell.

Prepare the filling. Stuff the onions with this mixture, only three-quarters full to allow room for the rice to expand. Place side by side, open ends upward, in a large pan. Pour in water to half-cover them. Cover the pan and cook gently for about ¾ hour, or until the onions and the filling are well cooked. Add more water during cooking time if necessary.

An alternative is to pour the following tomato sauce over the onions instead of water. Melt the butter in a pan and blend in the flour. Add the tomato paste and stir well. Gradually add water, stirring constantly, and season to taste with salt and pepper. Bring to the boil and simmer for a few minutes. Pour over the onions and continue cooking as above, adding water if necessary.

An ancient Persian remedy: "A cold may be cured by throwing an onion on a neighbor's house—the neighbor will get the cold."

*It was also believed that "a person must not eat a raw onion on Friday, or the angels will not remain with him." Nevertheless, "he who eats onions for forty-one days will become a hadji, or pilgrim, to Mecca." ***

Saudi Arabian Stuffed Onions

2 large onions	3 tablespoons butter
Filling II [page 300]	2 tablespoons vinegar

Peel the onions. With a sharp knife, make a cut from top to bottom on one side of each onion through to the center. Put into boiling water and cook until the onions are soft and start to open so that each layer can be detached (about 10 to 15 minutes). Drain and cool. Separate each layer carefully.

Make the filling. Put a tablespoon in each hollow onion layer and roll up tightly, securing the bundles with thread if necessary.

Heat butter in a frying pan. Sauté stuffed onion rolls gently, turning them until they acquire a slightly golden haze. Pack closely in a wide, shallow pan. Pour in water to cover, sprinkle with vinegar, and continue to cook, covered, over gentle heat until well done (about ¾ hour).

* Donaldson, *The Wild Rue.*

Stuffed Cabbage Leaves

This particular stuffed vegetable dish is very easy to make, and a welcome change from the usual boiled cabbage.

1 medium-sized head white cab-   Black pepper
    bage   Juice of 1 lemon
Salt
Filling II [page 300]

Carefully strip off the leaves from the cabbage and wash them. Dip them in boiling salted water, a few at a time, until they become wilted and pliable. Trim the hard central veins flat. Cut very large leaves in half, but leave small ones whole.

Prepare the filling. Put a tablespoon of filling at one end of each cabbage leaf. Fold the sides of the leaf toward the center and roll up, making a neat little finger shape. Continue until all the filling is used up.

Line a large saucepan with torn or unused leaves to prevent the stuffed leaves from sticking to the bottom. Lay the stuffed leaves on top of them in layers, packing them tightly. Cover with water and lemon juice mixed with a little salt. Cover the pan and cook very gently for about 1 hour. Serve hot.

In some parts of the Middle East as many as 6 or 7 whole cloves of garlic are tucked in between the stuffed leaves to give a very strong aroma. In the Lebanon, dried mint (about 1 teaspoon) or chopped fresh dill (1 tablespoon) is often added to the sauce toward the end of cooking time. A good variation to this dish is made by cooking the stuffed leaves in a rich tomato sauce. Prepare and stuff the leaves as above, and pack them in a cabbage-lined saucepan. Then dilute 5 tablespoons tomato paste in some water and pour this over the stuffed vegetables. Add the lemon juice, salt, and pepper. Continue cooking as above. A modern, labor-saving variation is to prepare the same filling, but to make a sort of tart or pie with the cabbage leaves instead of rolling them into individual parcels. First separate and soften the leaves as described above. Then arrange alternate layers of leaves and seasoned meat filling in a deep oven dish, starting and ending with cabbage leaves. Mix 5 tablespoons tomato paste with about ½ cup water. Add a little salt and pepper. Pour this sauce over the dish. Bake in a moderate oven (375°) for about 1 hour, or until the leaves are very soft and the filling is well cooked. Add water during the cooking if the dish dries out too quickly.

Stuffed Potatoes

12 largish potatoes
4 tablespoons butter
Filling I [page 300], including pine nuts and, if you like, raisins

4 tablespoons tomato paste
Salt and black pepper
6 tablespoons oil

Choose a type of potato which does not disintegrate easily. Peel the potatoes and hollow them out with an apple corer or a small pointed knife. Turn them in hot butter for a few minutes until they are slightly colored.

Prepare the filling. Stuff the potatoes with it and pack them tightly side by side in a large oven dish. Dilute the tomato paste with enough water to half-cover the potatoes. Season to taste with salt and pepper, add oil, and mix well. Pour over the potatoes.

Bake, uncovered, in a preheated moderate oven (375°) until the potatoes have browned a little. Then cover with a lid or a large piece of foil, and continue to bake for ¾ hour longer, or until the potatoes are soft but do not fall apart, and most of the sauce has been absorbed.

Iraqi Stuffed Potato Balls

2 lbs. potatoes
1 large egg
2 tablespoons flour
Salt and black pepper

Filling I [page 300]
Fine dry bread crumbs or flour
Oil for deep or shallow frying, or butter

Peel, boil, drain, and mash the potatoes, keeping them as dry as possible. Add 1 egg, 2 tablespoons flour, and salt and pepper to taste; knead thoroughly until well blended.

Prepare the filling.

Take lumps of the mashed potato mixture the size of a small egg. Shape into balls. Hollow them out with your finger and stuff with the filling. Close the openings over the filling and pat into ball shapes again.

Roll the potato balls in bread crumbs or flour. Deep-fry, one at a time, or fry in shallow oil or hot butter, turning the balls to brown them all over. Keep them hot in a warm oven until they are all prepared.

Stuffed Sweet Peppers and Tomatoes

A dish popular throughout the Middle East and along the Mediterranean, where peppers and tomatoes are often cooked and served together. They seem to achieve a harmony and balance, in both color and flavor. So, although you can serve each vegetable separately, the two combined (perhaps with a few other stuffed vegetables such as zucchini and eggplant) will make a more perfect dish.

6 medium-sized sweet green peppers [add a red one if you like]
6 large firm tomatoes
Filling II if to be served hot, or
    Filling IV if to be served cold
    [pages 300–1]

Oil [olive oil is desirable if serving cold]
Salt and black pepper

Wash the peppers and tomatoes. Cut a thin slice off the stem end of each vegetable and reserve. Remove the cores and seeds from the peppers. Scoop out the tomato pulp and reserve.

Prepare the ingredients for either filling. They can be used raw, but one should preferably half-cook them to avoid their still being a little uncooked when the vegetable shells are already very soft.

For Filling II, fry the onion in 2 tablespoons oil until soft. Add the ground meat and fry gently until it changes color. Then add the rest of the ingredients (pine nuts and raisins may be included if liked). Moisten with water, using twice as much water as the amount of rice. Bring to the boil, cover, and simmer gently for 10 minutes. Cool.

If using Filling IV, fry the onion in 2 tablespoons olive oil, add the rice, the other ingredients, and twice as much water as the amount of rice. Cook gently, covered, for 10 minutes. Cool.

Stuff the vegetables with either filling, moistening with a little extra olive oil. Cover with the reserved tops. Arrange the stuffed vegetables in one layer in a wide baking dish into which you have poured a few tablespoons of oil. Chop the tomato pulp, add about ½ cup water, season with a little salt and pepper, and pour over the vegetables. Add enough extra water to come halfway up the vegetables.

Cover the dish with a lid or a sheet of foil, and bake in a preheated moderate oven (375°) for 40 minutes; then uncover, add a little more water if it has all been absorbed, and bake for a further 20 minutes, or until the vegetables are colored and well done.

Serve hot or cold as a first course, or hot as a main dish, accompanied by various salads and rice.

In the past, it was usual to deep-fry or sauté the vegetables before stewing them gently in a sauce or baking them in a slow oven. Today, this is still done by some cooks who prefer the richer taste. You can also cook the vegetables on top of the stove. Arrange them in a large heavy pan, half-cover with water mixed with a few tablespoons of oil, and simmer, covered, for about 1 hour over very low heat, adding water if necessary, a little at a time. Sprinkle with a little lemon juice toward the end of cooking. In this case, the filling need not be precooked, but do not fill the vegetables too tightly to allow room for the rice to expand.

Stuffed Tomatoes

12 large firm tomatoes	5 tablespoons oil
Filling I [page 300] with pine nuts if available	2 tablespoons tomato paste
	Salt and black pepper

Wash the tomatoes. Cut a thin slice off the tops; scoop out the pulp and reserve.

Prepare Filling I, preferably with pine nuts. Raisins, too, may be added for an unusual flavor, as well as some of the tomato pulp. Stuff the tomatoes and cover with their own tops. Arrange the stuffed vegetables close to each other in a baking pan to which you have added a thin layer of oil.

Dilute the tomato paste with about ½ cup water. Season to taste with salt and pepper, and add the strained tomato pulp. Pour over the stuffed tomatoes.

Bake in a preheated moderate oven (375°) until the tomatoes are very soft, ½ hour or longer.

Serve as a first course or a main dish, accompanied by plain rice, *roz bil shaghria* (page 342), or burghul pilav (page 276) and yogurt.

Stuffed Leeks with Tamarind

2 lbs. large fat leeks	1 tablespoon finely chopped parsley
Salt	Oil
Filling II [page 300] omitting to-matoes, and using only ¼–⅓ cup rice	3 tablespoons tamarind syrup *

Cut off the hard green part of the leek leaves and trim off the root ends. Throw the leeks into boiling salted water and poach until only just softened.

Cut a slice off the root end, thus freeing the layers from each other. Make a slit very carefully with a sharp knife along one side of each leek, through to the center. You will have wide, rectangular leaves. Separate them from each other.

Add parsley and 2 tablespoons oil to the filling. Mix well.

Put a little of the filling (about 1 tablespoon) in the center of each leaf. Roll up tightly like a cigarette. When you come to the narrow leaves, lay two together, side by side and overlapping, to achieve a roll as with the bigger ones. The ends of the rolls are open, but the filling will not spill out, because it has been placed in the center.

Arrange in a wide, heavy pan in which you have heated ⅓ cup oil. Sauté gently in this oil for a few minutes. Then pour water in which you have diluted some tamarind syrup over the vegetables to cover.

Cover the pan and cook on a very low heat for about 1 hour, adding water as it becomes absorbed, until the leeks are very tender.

---

* If tamarind syrup is not available, add the juice of 1 lemon and 1 tablespoon sugar to the water, or the juice of 1 pomegranate (a sour one) and 1 tablespoon sugar.

Stuffed Artichokes

*The winning recipe in the 1964 National Queen of the Kitchen
contest, held in Israel. It was submitted by Mrs. Abla Mazawie, a
well-known restaurant owner in Nazareth. It is also an old Arab dish.*

3 lbs. artichokes	2 large onions
¾ lb. (3 sticks) margarine	⅓ cup pine nuts
1 lb. lamb, plus a piece of lamb's	1 tablespoon salt
tail or other lamb fat	1 teaspoon black pepper
½ lb. beef, ground	1 teaspoon ground cinnamon

Peel the artichokes to the hearts. Pierce and remove the chokes. Soak
the artichokes in cold water acidulated with the juice of ½ lemon.

Meanwhile, melt the margarine in a frying pan and fry the artichokes on all sides. Remove to a platter.

Grind the meat and onion together. Fry in the margarine in which
the artichokes were fried. Add the pine nuts, salt, pepper, and
cinnamon.

Fill the artichokes with the meat mixture. Add water to cover and
simmer on top of the stove or in a moderate oven (375°) for 1
hour.

Serve hot as a first course or main dish. If the latter, accompany
with rice with *hamud* (page 354).

Stuffed Artichoke Hearts

If fresh artichokes are out of season, try this recipe with good-quality canned artichoke hearts. These are not like the fresh ones, but nevertheless acceptable.

12 artichokes	½–1 teaspoon dried thyme
Salt	¼–½ teaspoon grated nutmeg
2 lemons	Oil for deep frying
1 lb. lean beef, ground	1 tablespoon olive oil
1 egg	½ teaspoon turmeric
2 slices bread, crusts removed	1 bay leaf
Black pepper	

Remove the stems, leaves, and chokes of the artichokes, leaving only the hearts. Dip them in a little salted water acidulated with the juice of 1 lemon, to prevent them from discoloring.

Mix the ground beef, egg, bread soaked in water and squeezed dry, salt and pepper, thyme, and grated nutmeg, and knead well.

Fill the artichoke hearts, shaping the mixture into a mound. Deep-fry one at a time in hot oil, using a perforated spoon to lower them in and lift them out again. Take care the filling does not become dislodged. Remove and drain on absorbent paper.

Place the fried artichoke hearts in a large saucepan. Mix olive oil with about ½ cup water, the turmeric, salt and pepper, and the juice of the remaining lemon. Pour over the artichoke hearts and bury a bay leaf between them.

Bring to the boil and simmer over very low heat for about 1 hour, until the artichokes are tender, adding water when necessary.

SWEET-AND-SOUR DISHES

Reading quite recently about ancient pre-Islamic Persia of the Sassanid period and its Zoroastrian dualist religion, which is based on the confrontation of the two enemy forces of good and evil, I was struck by the similarity between the early philosophy of the Persians and the principles of harmony which they apply to their food.

The Zoroastrian belief is that their god Ahouramazda created the world. The spirit of creation which pulled matter out of nothing awoke a force of resistance, giving birth to a spirit of evil, Angromainyous, whose creative and malicious urge was to destroy the harmony of the universe. In this religion, creation could exist only in the equilibrium of the opposing forces which it had aroused.

It is this same equilibrium, poised between the vinegar and the sugar, the quince and the meat, which the Persians of the Sassanid period reflected in their dishes. Both ancient and modern Persian dishes blend opposite flavors and textures, coupling sweet with sour or spicy, strong with mild. These dishes were adopted by the Caliphs of Baghdad, and some were taken further afield to Morocco. (Other Middle Eastern countries have not, however, adopted the more markedly sweet-and-sour dishes, although they have welcomed most others.)

During the same period, parts of India adopted a version of the Zoroastrian religion, the Parsees of today, but with one god of creation, and without a necessary enemy or evil force. North Indian food is not unlike Persian food, but, strangely enough, it seems to lack the particular harmony through opposites which the Persian dishes have.

It is also interesting to compare the Middle Eastern "sweet and sour" with that of China. The Chinese have a predilection for sweet and sour, and harmony through opposites, and their early religion was also one based on opposing forces of good and evil.

Leeks with Lemon and Sugar

This is a particularly delicious sweet-and-sour way of preparing leeks.

2 lbs. leeks	4 tablespoons corn or nut oil
2–3 cloves garlic, crushed	Juice of 1–2 lemons
1 tablespoon sugar	

Wash the leeks carefully, removing any soil nestling between the leaves. Cut off the tough green part of the leaves. Cut the rest into longish slices.

Fry the garlic and sugar in hot oil until the sugar becomes slightly caramelized. Add the leeks and turn them a little over moderate heat to color them lightly. Sprinkle with lemon juice. Stew gently, covered, in this and the vegetables' own juices over very low heat until tender.

Serve hot or cold.

Dolmeh Sib / Persian Stuffed Apples

Persians have produced two dishes (and maybe more) of fruit stuffed with meat, one of apples and the other of quinces, which are exciting and very pleasing.

Either cooking or eating apples do equally well for this dish, although there is less danger that eating apples will disintegrate.

12 large tart apples	Salt and black pepper
Butter	½ teaspoon ground cinnamon

FILLING	SAUCE
¼–⅓ cup yellow split peas	½ cup water
1 onion, finely chopped	7–8 tablespoons wine vinegar
2½ tablespoons oil	2 tablespoons sugar
1 lb. beef, ground	

Make the filling. Boil the yellow split peas for about ½ hour until soft. Drain. Fry the chopped onion in oil until soft and only just golden. Add the meat and fry gently until it changes color. Season to taste with salt, pepper, and the cinnamon, and mix in the cooked split peas.

Wash the apples. Core them with an apple corer to within ½ inch of the bottoms, and remove some of the pulp to make room for the filling. Chop the pulp and reserve.

Stuff the apples with the split pea mixture and arrange them side by side in a large baking dish, on a bed of chopped apple pulp. It will disintegrate and form a sauce. (Alternatively, mix the chopped pulp with the prepared filling.) Put a shaving of butter on top of each apple and pour 2 cups of water into the dish. Bake in a preheated moderate oven (375°), covered, for about ½ hour, or until the apples are almost done.

Boil the water, vinegar, and sugar together, and pour a little into each apple. Return to the oven and cook for a further 15 minutes, or until done. The apples must be tender but not mushy, and their skins should not be broken.

Serve two per person: alone as a first course, or as part of a main dish.

Persian Stuffed Quince

This dish is similar to that of stuffed apples above, but the strong aroma of the fruit demands a slightly different flavoring. Serve one quince per person, two if they are very small.

Core and prepare the fruit as in the preceding recipe. Prepare the same filling, omitting the cinnamon. Pack it into the quinces. Arrange them side by side to fit tightly in a pan (or two pans if one is not large enough). Pour in water to come halfway up the fruit. Add a few butter shavings and a pinch of sugar. Cover the pan and simmer gently for about 30 minutes, until the fruit is tender.

This can be served on its own as a first course, or with grilled or plain steamed meat and a rice dish, or with a selection of salads.

PICKLES

Mekhalel

Food preservation is a particularly important problem in hot countries, especially in isolated, nonagricultural areas. The processes used today by Middle Eastern families, grocers, and street vendors are those inherited from their ancestors of the ancient Oriental and classical civilizations, who had an even greater need for careful preservation in the days before easy transport, refrigerators, and canned food.

Although pickling was originally devised as a method of preservation, the result is so delicious that pickles are now prepared for their own sake—for their flavor and texture—to be served as *mezze* or to accompany many main dishes. They are prepared in large quantities in their season, and often throughout the year, since even when the vegetables are not in season in one area, it is now generally possible to import them from a neighboring country. Every home has its *martaban*, or jars, filled with various pickles, ready to be eaten at all times of the day.

My father has told me that when he was a child visiting relatives in Syria he remembers that the women of the family devoted their time to pickling and to making jams and syrups whenever they had no parties, feasts, or other household activities to occupy them. Large glass jars were filled with turnips, onions, cucumbers, lemons, cauliflowers, eggplants, and peppers. The family could hardly wait to start eating them, and often did so before the pickles were quite ready. A visit to the cellar or store cupboard to see how they were maturing and mellowing to soft pinks, saffrons, mauves, and pale greens was a mouth-watering expedition.

Grocers in the Middle East prepare their own pickles. It was customary in the past, and still is today in many places, for them to offer customers a taste of their newly mellowed pickles as well as a sample of their cheeses and jams. This custom may, of course, have been motivated by the hope that, having tasted them, the customer would not be able to resist the urge to take some home; but any ulterior motive was well concealed behind a heartwarming affability and generosity. Some Greek, or "*Roumi*," grocers in Egypt would even insist on offering a second helping regardless of whether there appeared to be any intention on the customer's part to buy.

A relative of my father's was known to go from one grocer to another, tasting here and there, a little of everything, dipping a large finger into a new batch of jam or honey, until he had satisfied his appetite. No shopkeeper ever begrudged him, since they all regarded "tasting" as a traditional and obligatory duty. They may even have been secretly flattered that this fat man visited them so often.

Restaurants like to display a vividly colorful assortment of pickles, sometimes placing them on their windowsills to lure customers in. Pickle jars are also a colorful feature of Middle Eastern streets. Squatting on the pavements of busy streets, vendors sell homemade pickled turnips swimming in a pink solution, or eggplants looking fiercely black and shiny in the enormous jars. Passersby dip their hands in the liquor, searching for the tastiest and largest pieces, and savor them with Arab bread provided by the vendor, soaking it in the pink salt and vinegar solution or seasoned oil. The poor can afford only to dip their bread in the pickling liquor. They sit in the sun, rapturously savoring this modest treat. And when the pickles are finished, the vendor sometimes sells the precious, flavorsome liquor as a sauce for rice.

METHODS OF PICKLING

The Middle Eastern method of pickling is simple. Raw or lightly poached vegetables are left to soak in a salty acidulated solution (usually vinegar) in a warm place for a certain length of time, depending on their age and quality. The salt draws the moisture from the vegetables, preventing the growth of the microorganisms which cause decay. The salt and acid bath allows the vegetables to ferment and mature to mellowness, and also stops the entry of microorganisms into the jar, as well as preventing the growth of those already in it. For pickling to be successful, it is most important to keep out the air in which microorganisms flourish. In ancient times, jars were filled, sealed with a flour-and-water paste, and buried in the earth. Today, people drive away the air bubbles trapped between the vegetables by prodding them with a skewer or fork. Then they fill the jars with liquid, covering the vegetables entirely, and seal them tightly.

Choose very fresh, unblemished vegetables. Clean and wash them carefully, and peel or scrub them if they need it. Use perfectly clean or sterilized glass jars with tightly fitting glass tops. Quarter or slice the vegetables, or leave them whole, and pack them tightly in the jars. Mix the pickling salt and vinegar solution in a clean glass or china container and pour it over the vegetables, filling the jars to the top; cover and seal tightly.

The proportion of salt to water and vinegar can vary slightly according to personal taste. More or less salt can be used, but the quantities are generally near enough to 4 tablespoons salt for every 2½ cups of water. Too little salt will cause the vegetables to decay, too much would be unpleasant.

The proportion of vinegar to water varies more widely. Some people use as much vinegar as water, some pickle in vinegar alone. Others recommend half as much vinegar as water, while others again pickle in a salt-and-water brine, leaving out vinegar altogether. To my taste, the most successful combination to use is approximately three parts salted water to one part vinegar. This is what our family uses.

It is possible to adjust the degree of concentration during and after the process of pickling by adding more water, salt, or vinegar, thus changing the balance if it is not agreeable.

The solution can also be flavored according to individual taste with garlic, celery leaves, small hot dried chili pepper pods, and dill. To satisfy the Middle Eastern passion for color, the pickles are tinted pink or red with raw beets, or purple with red cabbage.

In Egypt, the solution is usually poured warm or cold over the tightly packed vegetables in the jar, but in some countries, such as the Lebanon, it is more common to use it boiling hot.

The U.S. Government advises Americans to boil bottled pickles for at least ½ hour. To my knowledge this has never been done in the Middle East, and although pickles are not generally made to last, and are usually opened as soon as they are ready, certain types, such as those pickled in vinegar only or in oil, can safely be kept for more than a year.

Torshi Left / Pickled Turnips

These are great favorites. They have a very distinctive taste which is enjoyed by most people even when first encountered. The turnips are traditionally colored pink by adding sliced raw beets. The rich, cherry-

colored juices penetrate the white turnips, coloring them bright red or soft pink, according to how much is used, and giving them a delicious taste.

Huge jars of these torshi adorn the streets and decorate the windows and counters of most cafés and restaurants.

2 lbs. small white turnips	6–7 level tablespoons salt
A few celery leaves	3½ cups water
2–4 cloves garlic [optional]	1¼ cups white wine vinegar
1 raw beet, peeled and sliced or cut	
into medium-sized pieces	

Choose small white turnips. Peel and wash them, and cut them in halves or quarters, depending on their size. Pack the pieces in a clean glass jar with celery leaves and garlic cloves if liked, placing pieces of raw beet between the layers at regular intervals.

Dissolve salt in water and stir in vinegar. Cover the vegetables with this solution and seal the jar tightly with a glass top if possible.

Store in a warm place. The turnips should mellow and be ready in about 10 days. Then transfer the jar to a cool spot.

This pickle should be eaten within a month to 6 weeks of making.

A medieval recipe for *lift mukhalal muhalla* (turnips in vinegar, sweetened) from al-Baghdadi gives directions for turnips pickled in vinegar, sweetened with honey, perfumed with aromatic herbs, and tinted with saffron.

Lebanese saying: "Her face is whiter than the inside of a turnip."

Torshi Arnabeet wa Koromb / Pickled Cauliflower and Red Cabbage

A popular pickle, stained deep purple by red cabbage. If using white cabbage, color the pickle with a few slices of raw beet.

1 young white cauliflower	1¼ cups white wine vinegar
½ red or white cabbage	1 small dried chili pepper pod
6–7 level tablespoons salt	[optional]
3½ cups water	

Wash the cauliflower and separate it into flowerets. Cut the cabbage into thick slices in one direction, and then again thickly in the other direction. Leave it in chunks; do not shred it or take the leaves apart. Pack into a large glass jar, arranging alternate layers of cauliflower and cabbage chunks.

Mix salt, water, and vinegar in a glass or china container. Pour the liquid over the vegetables, and bury a chili pepper pod in the jar if you like. Close tightly with a glass top if possible, and store in a warm place for about 10 days, by which time the vegetables will be mellow and ready to eat.

This pickle, like the first, should be eaten within a month or 6 weeks of making.

Torshi Basal / Pickled Onions

Choose small, perfect button onions. Peel them and poach them for about 3 minutes in boiling white wine vinegar seasoned to taste with a little salt and sugar. Pack the slightly softened onions in a glass jar and cover with the poaching vinegar. Close tightly. Leave for about 10 days before using.

This pickle will keep indefinitely.

Torshi Felfel / Pickled Sweet Peppers

2 lbs. sweet peppers	6–7 level tablespoons salt
1 small dried chili pepper pod [optional]	3½ cups water
	1¼ cups white wine vinegar

Rinse the sweet peppers and cut off the stems. The peppers can be either sliced or cut into large pieces or, if small, left whole. If slicing or cutting them, discard the cores and seeds. If leaving them whole, make small holes all over to allow the pickling solution to penetrate to their hollow centers and bathe them entirely.

Pack tightly in a large glass jar, with a chili pepper pod buried in the middle if you like. Cover with the salt, water, and vinegar solution, mixed in a china or glass container, and make sure that no air is left trapped inside the peppers or between the layers. Seal the jar tightly with a glass top if possible, and store in a warm place for about 2 weeks. By this time the peppers will be soft and mellow.

Do not keep this pickle longer than 2 months, unless stored under refrigeration.

Torshi Khiar / Pickled Cucumbers

2 lbs. small pickling cucumbers
4 cloves garlic
A few celery leaves, or a few sprigs
    fresh dill, or 1 teaspoon dill
    seed

3–4 black peppercorns
3–4 whole coriander seeds
6–7 level tablespoons salt
3½ cups water
1¼ cups white wine vinegar

Scrub the cucumbers well and pack them in a large glass jar with the whole garlic cloves, celery leaves, sprigs of dill or dill seed, peppercorns, and coriander seeds distributed at regular intervals.

Mix the salt, water, and vinegar solution in a glass or china container, and pour over the vegetables. Close the jar tightly with a glass top if possible, and leave in a warm place to soften and mellow. The pickle should be ready in 10 days to 2 weeks.

Do not keep for longer than about 6 weeks unless stored under refrigeration.

Torshi Betingan / Pickled Eggplant

There is a superstitious belief in some Middle Eastern countries that certain types of eggplant bring on one the curse of infertility. Women are sometimes afraid to use a particularly black one or an oddly mauve one. On the other hand, a walk through a field of eggplants is sometimes prescribed as a cure for female sterility. For many years the head gardener at the Ezbekieh Gardens in Cairo derived a small income from a patch of eggplants by charging women a fee to walk through it.

2 lbs. very small, long, thin eggplants
Salt
4 cloves garlic, finely chopped
1–2 small dried chili pepper pods,
   finely chopped

A few celery leaves and stalks, finely
   chopped
2½ cups water
4 tablespoons salt
1¼–2 cups white wine vinegar

Wash the eggplants. Do not peel them, but make a small incision in each one. Poach them in boiling, salted water for 5 to 10 minutes until just slightly softened. Drain well. This will make them lose their bitterness.

Mix the chopped garlic, pepper pods, and celery. Stuff the eggplants with this mixture through the incisions. Arrange them in layers in a glass jar. Mix the water, salt, and vinegar solution in a glass or china bowl as usual, and pour it over the eggplants. Close the jar tightly with a glass top if possible, and leave it for about 4 days before using.

Do not keep this pickle longer than 6 weeks to 2 months unless it is stored under refrigeration.

Arab saying: "Give what is in your pocket. God will give you what is absent."

Marinated Eggplant

2 lbs. eggplant
Salt
1¼ cups white wine vinegar

4–6 cloves garlic, crushed
1 tablespoon dried crushed oregano
Olive, corn, or nut oil

Peel and slice the eggplant. Arrange slices in a strainer or colander, sprinkling each layer with salt. Leave them for 2 to 4 hours, shaking occasionally, to allow the bitter juices to drain away. Poach the slices for 5 minutes in about 1¼ cups vinegar and a little water to cover.

Drain well and arrange the eggplant slices in layers in a large glass jar, putting a little crushed garlic and oregano between each layer. Fill the jar with oil and close it tightly.

The eggplant will be mellowed after about a week, but it will keep indefinitely. An excellent pickle.

Lamoun Makbouss / Pickled Lemons

A delicacy which is also magnificent made with fresh limes.

Scrub lemons well and slice them. Sprinkle the slices generously with salt and leave for at least 24 hours on a large plate set at an angle, or in a colander. They will become soft and limp, and lose their bitterness. Arrange the slices in layers in a glass jar, sprinkling a little paprika between each layer. Cover with corn or nut oil. Sometimes olive oil is used, but its taste is rather strong and may slightly overpower the lemons.

Close the jar tightly. After about 3 weeks the lemons should be ready to eat—soft, mellow, and a beautiful orange color.

My mother accidentally discovered a way of speeding the process when left with dozens of lemon wedges which had been used to garnish a large party dish. She put them in the freezing compartment of her refrigerator to keep them until she was ready to pickle them. When she sprinkled the frozen lemons with salt, she found that they shed a large quantity of water and softened in just over an hour. They were ready for eating after only a few days in oil and paprika.

Pickled Artichoke Hearts

3–4 lemons   12 artichokes
Salt   Corn or nut oil

Squeeze the lemons into a bowl and add salt to taste. Prepare the artichokes by removing the tough outer leaves and chokes, and trimming the leaves close to the hearts. Cut them in half if they are large. As each one is prepared, rub it with a squeezed-out lemon half and drop it into the salted lemon juice.

When all the artichokes have been prepared, arrange them in a large glass jar. Add oil to the remaining lemon juice and beat well with a wooden spoon. Pour over the artichoke hearts, adding more oil if necessary to cover them completely. Seal the jar tightly.

The artichokes will be ready in about 4 weeks, and will last indefinitely.

Torshi Meshakel / Mixed Pickles

½ lb. small, whole pickling cucumbers

2 large carrots, thickly sliced

1 small cauliflower, separated into flowerets

1 sweet green pepper, thickly sliced, seeded, and cored

½ lb. small white turnips, peeled and quartered

½ raw beet, peeled and cut into medium-sized pieces [optional]

A few raw green beans, if available, cut in pieces

3 cloves garlic

1 small dried chili pepper pod

A few sprigs fresh dill and 2 teaspoons dill seed

3½ cups water

1¼ cups white wine vinegar

6–7 level tablespoons salt

Prepare the vegetables and pack them tightly in glass jars together with the garlic cloves, a hot pepper pod divided between them, and dill.

Mix the water, vinegar, and salt solution in a glass or china bowl, and pour over the vegetables. Prepare and add more liquid if this is not enough. Seal tightly and store in a warm place. The pickle should be ready in about 2 weeks. The vegetables will be soft and mellow, and tinted pink by the beet. However, the beet can be omitted if you prefer the vegetables in their natural colors.

Do not keep longer than 2 months unless stored under refrigeration.

Tomato Sauce

Although this is not a pickle, I am including the recipe in this chapter since it is a very useful sauce to have on hand when required, and it can be prepared in advance and stored in jars.

2 lbs. tomatoes	Salt and black pepper
Olive oil	1 teaspoon sugar [optional]
1 large onion, finely chopped	2 tablespoons finely chopped parsley
4 cloves garlic	2 teaspoons dried crushed oregano

Skin the tomatoes by throwing them into boiling water for a minute or two to loosen their skins. Alternatively, hold them on a fork over an open flame until the skin bursts and blisters. They can then be skinned easily. Quarter them.

Heat 4 tablespoons oil in a large saucepan. Fry the chopped onion until soft and golden. Add the whole garlic cloves and fry for a few minutes longer until lightly colored. Add the tomatoes. Season to taste with salt and pepper, and a teaspoon of sugar if you like. Sprinkle with parsley and oregano, and sauté gently, squashing the tomatoes lightly with a wooden spoon, until softened. Then cover the pan and simmer very gently for at least an hour. The tomatoes should be stewed in their own juice as far as possible, and a little water should be added only if really necessary.

Remove the garlic cloves and pour the sauce into a glass jar. Pour a thin layer of oil over the surface, cover the jar tightly and store in a cool place until required. This sauce keeps for many months if the surface remains completely covered with a film of oil.

RICE

Roz

Rice is a basic dish in most parts of the Middle East, present in some form at practically every meal, except in Morocco, where its place is taken by *couscous*. It is *roz* to the Arabs, *pirinç*, or *pilav* when cooked with other ingredients, to the Turks. Persians call it *chilau* when it is plain, and *polo* when cooked with other ingredients.

Cooked plainly with water, salt, and a little oil or butter, it serves as an accompaniment to stews or grilled meats and salads, or is itself accompanied by rich sauces. It can also be cooked together with other ingredients, added to the sauce of a meat stew when the meat is already tender, or partially cooked and added to other cooked ingredients to finish cooking together. In this form it is known in the West as *pilav*.

Rice is sometimes colored yellow with saffron or turmeric, or red with tomatoes. It is molded into various shapes, the favorite one being a ring, and often garnished with nuts and sauces.

Following Middle Eastern tradition, it is served at the same time as all the other dishes, to be chosen first or last to each individual's taste. Some people claim that they cannot taste anything without eating rice at the same time as a sort of background and basic measure of taste. In families where the Western style of serving three courses has been adopted, rice is often served at the end of the meal, accompanied by a special sauce or by part of the main dish which has been set aside to be savored with it.

An Egyptian riddle describes this manner of serving:

Question: Why is rice like a chaouiche *(policeman)?*
Answer: It is brilliantly white like the chaouiche's *uniform in the summer, and it arrives at the end like the* chaouiche *when everything (i.e., the trouble) is over.*

HOW TO COOK RICE

Throughout the Middle East, the preparation of rice is enveloped by a certain ritualistic mystique. Although an extremely simple dish, various ways of cooking it exist. Each family cherishes a particular method and is skeptical about all others, refusing to believe that it is possible to achieve successful results in any way other than their own. Generally speaking, however, each country seems to prefer one method above all others. I have given four which are the most commonly followed.

Long-grain rice is always used as opposed to pudding, Italian, or Spanish rice. Its particular qualities lie in its fluffiness, and its ability to remain firm and separate. If well cooked, it is tender but firm, not too soft, and never mushy.

Basically, plain rice is cooked in water with salt and some fat—usually butter, clarified butter, oil, or margarine. The quantity of water necessary varies slightly according to the quality of the rice and the size and thickness of the saucepan, but generally twice as much water is required as the amount of dry rice to be cooked.

The rice is almost always cooked in a pan with a tightly fitting lid, but a few people prefer to leave the lid only half on. In this case, more water must be used to make up for the rapid evaporation.

In the past, rice in the Middle East was sold in large Hessian sacks, and had to be cleaned of stones and roughage (and sometimes small insects too) and washed many times before it was ready for cooking. Today, the prepacked rice available is perfectly clean and needs only to be rid of the starchy powder which causes it to be less separate and slightly sticky when cooked. Some people do not object to this and find the result of rice cooked without preliminary washing very acceptable, maintaining that the zeal of excessive washing is a hangover from the "Hessian sack" era.

A special word about Persian rice. As with her art of miniature painting and poetry, Persia has carried the preparation of rice to extraordinary heights of refinement and purity. It is a base or accompaniment for practically every dish and it is said that no other Middle Eastern country prepares rice in the same perfectionist manner. Its preparation is often started a day before it is to be eaten.

At least six different qualities of rice are cultivated in Persia. The best, "royal" rice, called *domsiah*, grows in rare conditions, and is very expensive. The next best is *darbori* rice; then come *sadri* and *champâ*. *Basmati* rice is the nearest to the third quality of rice and the best substitute to use.‡

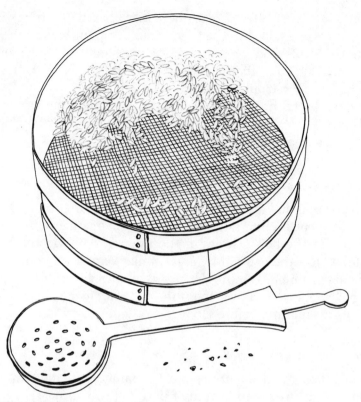

Four Ways of Cooking Plain Rice

One pound of rice is usually sufficient for 6 people. A chicken or meat stock left over from a soup or stew, used instead of water, will make a magnificent rice. If you are using commercial long-grain American rice that comes in a box or bag, there is no need whatever to wash it first. However, if you use one of the imported rices that come in sacks, be sure to wash by pouring water over it in a bowl and stirring well for a few seconds; then rinse under cold running water until the water runs clear, and drain thoroughly.

1. A SYRIAN WAY

2 cups long-grain rice   Salt
4 cups water   4–6 tablespoons butter or margarine

Bring 4 cups water to the boil in a pan with a little salt to taste. Throw in the washed and drained rice, bring to the boil again, and boil vigorously for 2 minutes. Cover the pan with a tight-fitting lid and simmer very gently, undisturbed, for about 20 minutes, until the water has been absorbed and the rice is cooked. It should be tender and separate, with little holes all over the surface. Turn off the heat, and allow the rice to rest for about 10 minutes.

Melt the butter or margarine in a saucepan and pour it evenly all over the rice. Let it rest again, covered, for 3 minutes longer, until the melted fat has been absorbed by the rice.

2. A LEBANESE WAY

The ingredients and quantities are the same as above.

Put the 4 cups water, salt, and butter or margarine in a saucepan, and bring to the boil. Throw in the rice and boil vigorously for 2 minutes. Cover the pan tightly and simmer very gently, undisturbed, for about 20 minutes, until the rice is tender and fluffy, and little holes have appeared all over the surface. Turn off the heat and allow to rest for 10 minutes before serving.

3. AN EGYPTIAN WAY

The ingredients and quantities are the same as in the first recipe, but oil is sometimes used instead of butter or margarine.

Heat the butter or oil in a saucepan. Throw in the rice and fry it gently for a minute or so, until the grains are translucent and well coated with fat. Add the water and salt to taste. Bring to the boil and boil vigorously for 2 minutes, then simmer gently, tightly covered and undisturbed, for about 20 minutes, until the rice is tender and the characteristic little holes have appeared on the surface. Never stir while it is cooking. Allow to rest for 10 minutes before serving.

4. A PERSIAN WAY and a particularly excellent one—*Chilau* or Steamed Rice

Use *basmati* rice.‡ Wash it well in boiling water, and then leave to soak in a bowl of well-salted water for 5 hours or overnight. An hour before it is due to be served, drain well and rinse with cold water. Throw into a pan of boiling water with 2 tablespoons salt. The salt helps the grains to remain separate but does not penetrate the grains and is lost with the water.

Boil the rice vigorously until it is slightly undercooked. The grains should, however, be cut easily with your teeth or a fingernail without presenting a hard inner core. The cooking time will be between 8 and 10 minutes. Strain the rice immediately and rinse with lukewarm water to remove excess salt. Drain thoroughly.

The rice must now be steamed with 4 to 6 tablespoons oil or melted butter. Put half the oil or butter at the bottom of a thick pan with 1 or 2 tablespoons of water. Heat gently and add the rice, then pour over the rest of the melted butter or oil. Place a clean cloth over the pan. Put the lid on, folding the corners of the cloth over it to keep them away from the flame. The cloth will capture and absorb the steam as it rises from the rice, leaving it white, light, and fluffy, each grain separate from its neighbor. Leave over low heat for 15 to 20 minutes.

The rice at the bottom of the pan will be crisp and golden. It is generally scraped and served at the side of the rice dish. Its texture is considered a delicacy, to be offered first to guests. It is called *dig*.

Some people like to put thin slices of fried bread or raw potato at the bottom of the pan when steaming the rice, and serve them in the same way as the crisp rice.

Although this preparation may sound rather complicated, it is not so. The result is so exquisite that it is well worth trying. You will then understand its importance in Persian life and the national pride in this dish.

Chilau is served with various sauces or *khoreshtha* (see pages 357–61)—aromatic and textual symphonies, the result of centuries of traditional harmonizing, creating, and enjoying.

Served without a sauce, for example as an accompaniment to shish kebab, it is eaten with a generous lump of butter and, traditionally, with a raw egg yolk served in an eggshell. The yolk is poured over each individual portion of rice and then stirred into it, making a glistening, creamy sauce.

Saffron Rice

Prepare rice according to the Egyptian way (page 340), adding ¼ to ½ teaspoon powdered saffron to the rice as it is frying.

The cooked rice will become a beautiful yellow.

In the Middle East it is prepared in this manner for its delicate flavor, especially for its decorative quality, and in the hope that its yellow color will bring joy and happiness.

You can substitute ¾ teaspoon turmeric (sometimes called "Oriental saffron") for a cheaper version.

Roz bil Shaghria / Rice with Vermicelli

A rice and vermicelli dish, eaten in many countries on the second night of the New Year "so that one's employment may be prolonged and multiplied" like the vermicelli, or, as some say, "so that one may be prolific and beget many children."

2 cups long-grain rice
¾ cup chickpeas, soaked overnight
1 onion, finely chopped
6 tablespoons butter
2½ tablespoons oil

6–8 oz. vermicelli, broken into
    smallish pieces
4 cups water
Salt

Wash the rice in boiling water, then rinse in cold water and drain well. Boil the soaked chickpeas in a fresh portion of water until very tender (about 30 minutes or more, according to their age and quality).

Fry the onion in butter mixed with oil (or in 4 tablespoons clarified butter), using a large, heavy saucepan. When the onion is golden and transparent, add the vermicelli and fry until lightly colored. Add the rice, and stir over moderate heat until the grains are transparent and well coated with oil. Add water and salt to taste. Bring to the boil and simmer gently, tightly covered, until the water has been absorbed and the rice is cooked and fluffy, about 20 minutes.

Mix in the cooked and drained chickpeas, and heat again until all the ingredients are very hot.

Serve with yogurt and cucumber salad.

Roz bi Dfeen / Rice with Meat and Chickpeas

1 lb. lean beef or lamb, cubed [op-
    tional]
6–8 tablespoons butter
1 lb. button onions
⅓ cup chickpeas, soaked overnight

Salt and black pepper
1 teaspoon ground cumin or cin-
    namon
2 cups long-grain rice

If you are using meat, brown it in hot butter in a large heavy saucepan at the same time as the onions. Let the onions become golden and the meat a rich brown color all over. Add the soaked and drained chickpeas, and cover with water. Season generously with salt and pepper to taste, add cumin or cinnamon, and simmer gently, covered, until the meat is very tender and the chickpeas are soft, about 2 hours.

If there is less than 4 cups liquid left in the pan, make it up to this amount with water. If there is more, reduce it by cooking uncovered, or pour some out. Bring to the boil again, add the rice, mix well, and simmer, covered and undisturbed, for about 20 minutes. Add a little water and cook further if the rice seems undercooked. Turn off the heat and allow to rest for a few minutes before serving.

If you are not using meat, fry the onions and then cook with the chickpeas in a meat stock. When the chickpeas are tender, make the liquid up to 4 cups with water, add rice, and continue cooking as above.

Rice with Meat, Pine Nuts, and Almonds

Here is a most delicious and decorative way of serving rice, an excellent party piece.

2 cups long-grain rice, cooked according to a method p. 339 [measured before cooking]	Oil or butter
	Salt and black pepper
½ lb. lamb, beef, or veal, ground	½ teaspoon ground cinnamon or ¼ teaspoon ground allspice [optional]
⅓ cup pine nuts	
⅓ cup almonds, peeled and chopped	¼–½ cup seedless raisins [optional]

Prepare 2 cups long-grain rice.

Fry the meat and the mixed nuts separately in oil or butter. The nuts require only 2 or 3 minutes' frying. Cook the meat longer, adding a few tablespoons water and crushing it with a fork until it has changed color and become soft, light, and crumbly. Mix the meat with the nuts; season to taste with salt and pepper, and other spices if you like. An exquisite variation is to add a few seedless raisins to the meat and nut mixture.

Pat or mold the hot rice into a pyramid or ring shape in a heated serving dish, and crown with the meat and nut mixture. Alternatively, spread half of the meat and nuts over the bottom of an oiled ring mold. Press the rice over it tightly to fill the mold and turn out onto a heated serving dish. Put the rest of the meat and nuts in the hollow in the center.

"Honor to rice; let burghul go hang itself!"—an old Lebanese saying originating from the time when rice was a delicacy and was rapidly eclipsing burghul, until then considered the staple food of the Lebanon.

Rice with Fava Beans

Nut oil
1 large onion, finely chopped
1 lb. fresh shelled or frozen fava
    beans

Salt and black pepper
2 cloves garlic, crushed
½–1 teaspoon ground coriander
2 cups long-grain rice

Heat 2 tablespoons oil in a large, heavy pan and fry the onion until soft and golden. Add the fava beans and sauté a little, turning them over and stirring. Cover with a little water and season to taste with salt and pepper. Simmer until the beans are tender.

Fry the garlic and coriander in 2 tablespoons oil in a large frying pan. Add the washed and drained rice, and fry until transparent but not browned. Add all this to the cooked fava beans together with enough water to make the liquid in the pan up to 4 cups. Bring to the boil and simmer very gently, covered and undisturbed, for about 20 minutes, or until the rice is tender.

Serve hot as an accompaniment to meat, or cold with yogurt and a salad.

Sometimes the rice is cooked separately as in one of the recipes for plain rice (pages 339–41). The fried garlic and coriander are added to the fava bean stew. Just before serving, the beans and rice are mixed together.

Rice with Fresh Herbs

Persians have a predilection for fresh herbs. A traditional New Year's dish consists of rice cooked with a variety of fresh herbs, their greenness believed to ensure a happy and "green" year ahead.

The herbs are chosen according to individual taste and mood, and to what is available at that time of year. Favorite Persian herbs include *tare* (tarragon), chives, parsley, and dill, and others, including fresh fenugreek and *"gishnise,"* both rather hard to find. Use whichever you prefer, but try to use fresh ones.

Wash and chop the herbs finely. Prepare 2 cups *basmati* rice according to the recipe for *chilau* (page 340). Boil it vigorously, and when it is nearly cooked, throw in the herbs. As soon as the rice is tender but not too soft—after 8 to 10 minutes—drain in a strainer or colander. The herbs will cling to the rice. Steam with oil or butter as directed in the basic recipe, with a cloth stretched under the lid to absorb vapor.

A splendid rice dish, often served with fried fish.

Rice with Pine Nuts, Pistachios, and Almonds

This is a rather elegant and highly decorative way of serving rice, a perfect party dish.

Prepare plain or saffron rice, or cook it in a chicken stock, following one of the recipes at the beginning of this chapter.

Chop ⅓ cup mixed pistachios and almonds coarsely, and fry them with the same quantity of pine nuts in a little oil until just golden. (Use only one or two kinds of nuts if you like.)

Just before serving, spread the nuts evenly over the bottom of an oiled ring mold large enough to hold all the rice. Press the rice over the nuts tightly and turn out onto a heated serving dish. This traditional round shape is particularly attractive for serving rice. In this case, it will be crowned by the assortment of fried nuts.

If more convenient, you can pack the rice and nuts into the oiled mold in advance and keep it warm in a low oven, ready to be unmolded just before serving.

Turkish Eggplant Pilav—Served Cold

1 lb. eggplants	¾ cup olive oil
Salt	3 cups long-grain rice

Cut the eggplants into smallish chunks and put them in a large strainer or colander. Sprinkle with salt and leave to drain for at least 30 minutes to rid them of their bitter juices. Squeeze out as much of the juices as possible, rinse in cold water, and pat dry with a clean cloth or paper towels.

Fry the eggplant pieces gently in half the oil until colored and tender; they do not require any additional salt.

Prepare plain rice according to one of the recipes on pages 339–40, using the rest of the oil instead of butter, and salt to taste. Let the rice cook for 15 minutes, then bury the eggplants in it. Steam for 20 minutes over low heat as directed for *chilau* (page 340), stretching a cloth under the lid to absorb the steam.

Serve cold with yogurt.

Arab saying: "Rather than eat rice with eggplants, buy something to cover your hind part." (Until very recently rice was considered an expensive dish and only for the rich. A poor man buying rice and eggplants too was therefore thought to be unnecessarily extravagant.)

Tomato Pilav

½ lb. onions, chopped	Salt and black pepper
4 tablespoons nut or olive oil	1 teaspoon sugar [optional]
1 clove garlic [optional]	1 bay leaf [optional]
1½–2 lbs. ripe tomatoes, skinned, or 2 one-lb. cans whole tomatoes	1 teaspoon dried oregano [optional]
	2 cups long-grain rice

In a large, heavy saucepan, fry the onions in hot oil until soft and golden. A whole clove of garlic may be added to the onions if liked. Add the tomatoes and season to taste with salt, pepper, and a little sugar if needed. Sauté lightly, squashing the tomatoes a little with a fork, until they acquire a "fried" taste. Cover with water and allow to simmer gently for about ¾ hour. This sauce may be perfumed with a bay leaf or oregano, but it is also good plain. Add more water while cooking if required. Sometimes small pieces of leftover meat or a little minced raw meat are cooked with the tomatoes for a richer dish.

When the sauce has become rich in flavor and texture, add water to the pan to make up the liquid to 4 cups. Add the rice, bring to the boil, and simmer gently, covered and undisturbed, for about 20 minutes, until the rice is tender. It will have acquired a pale, salmon pink color and will be impregnated with the flavor of the tomatoes.

Kuzu Pilav / Turkish Lamb Pilav

1 large onion, finely chopped	¾ teaspoon ground cinnamon
4 tablespoons butter or oil	3 tablespoons tomato paste
¾–1 lb. lean lamb, cut into small pieces	4 tablespoons finely chopped parsley
	2 cups long-grain rice
Salt and black pepper	

In a large, heavy saucepan, fry the onion in hot butter or oil until soft and golden. Add meat and brown it gently all over. Season to taste with salt, pepper, and cinnamon. Cover the pan, and cook the meat and onions in their own juices for about 10 minutes. Dilute the tomato paste in a little cold water, pour into the meat mixture, and stir well. Add more water to cover, sprinkle with finely chopped parsley, bring to the boil, and simmer gently for about 1½ hours until the meat is very tender and the sauce thick and reduced.

Make the liquid left in the stew up to 4 cups. Add the rice, bring to a vigorous boil, then simmer gently, covered and undisturbed, for about 20 minutes, or until rice is soft, adding more water if necessary.

An exquisite variation is to add about a tablespoon each of pine nuts and raisins to the simmering stew. Another is to cook a sliced sweet pepper and 2 ripe tomatoes, skinned and cut into pieces, in the stew.

A pinch of saffron may be added to give a subtle coloring (in this case the tomato paste is left out). Alternatively, chopped parsley and celery leaves can be used.

In each case, the rice is added and the cooking completed in the same way as described in the main recipe.

Persian Lamb and Apricot Polo

The apricot has a special affinity for lamb. Its sweet acidity blends with, and seems to bring out, the mild sweetness of the meat. The early Arab Abbassid dynasty, centered in Persia, greatly favored the combination and created a series of dishes on this theme which they called mishmishiya *(see page 247),* mishmish *being the Arab word for apricot. It is still a great favorite as a partner to lamb in modern Persia. The rest of the Middle East has adopted it to a much lesser degree.*

8 tablespoons (1 stick) butter	½ teaspoon ground cinnamon
1 onion, finely chopped	2½ tablespoons seedless raisins
1 lb. lean lamb, cubed	4 oz. dried apricots, halved
Salt and black pepper	2 cups long-grain rice

Heat 4 tablespoons butter in a large, heavy saucepan and fry the onion until soft and golden. Add the meat and fry gently, turning the pieces to brown them all over. Season with salt, pepper, and cinnamon. Add raisins and apricots, and sauté lightly. Cover with water and simmer gently, covered, for about 1½ hours, until the meat is very tender and has absorbed the sweet and acid flavors of the fruit. If the stew is still rather liquid by the end of cooking time, reduce it by fast boiling.

Cook the rice as in the recipe for *chilau* (page 340) or plain rice (page 339), using the remaining 4 tablespoons butter. If using the *chilau* method, boil the rice but do not steam it. If using the recipe for plain rice, simmer the rice until half cooked, i.e., for 10 to 15 minutes only.

Arrange alternate layers of rice and meat with sauce in a large heavy saucepan, starting and ending with a layer of rice. Cover and steam gently for 20 minutes longer, until the rice is tender and has absorbed some of the sauce. A cloth stretched underneath the lid will absorb the steam and make the rice lighter.

Seleq / Lamb with Rice Cooked in Milk

Here is a popular Saudi Arabian specialty which is similar to a medieval al-Baghdadi dish.

This makes rather a large quantity suitable for a party. Reduce it by half to serve 6 people.

1 large leg of lamb	4 cups milk
2 onions, finely chopped	4 cups long-grain rice
Salt and black pepper	12–16 tablespoons butter, melted

Simmer the lamb whole or cut into pieces for 2 hours, or until tender, together with the chopped onions and water to cover, seasoned to taste with salt and pepper. When cooked, remove the meat and keep warm. Add water if necessary to make the volume of stock up to 6 cups. Add the milk and bring to the boil. Then add the rice and cook very gently, covered, until it is so soft it is almost a purée. Adjust seasoning.

Serve in a large tray with melted butter poured over the rice and the pieces of meat arranged on top. This dish is served with a cucumber, lettuce, and tomato salad. Some people like to accompany it with clear, pure honey, to be stirred into each portion separately.

Tavuklu Pilav / Plain Turkish Chicken Pilav

1 large [4-lb.] roasting chicken	1 teaspoon dried herbs
2½ tablespoons oil	2 cups long-grain rice
Salt and black pepper	

Clean and wash a large fat chicken. Color it gently in hot oil, turning it so that it becomes golden all over. Add water to cover, and season to taste with salt, pepper, and a teaspoon of your favorite herbs. Bring to a boil and simmer until the chicken is very tender (usually about 1 hour). Let the chicken cool a little before taking it out of the stock.

When it is cool enough to handle, cut the large pieces into serving pieces and keep warm in a little of the stock to prevent them from becoming dry. Cut the rest of the meat into small pieces. Measure the stock, and add water to bring it up to 4 cups. Return the small chicken pieces to the stock. Throw in the rice, stir, and bring to a boil, then reduce the heat and simmer gently, covered and undisturbed, for about 20 minutes until the rice is tender.

Heap the rice on a large, flat serving dish. Arrange the reserved chicken pieces over it and serve.

In a Lebanese version of chicken pilav, the chicken stock is perfumed with a teaspoon of ground cinnamon. The rice is cooked in the broth with small pieces of chicken, as described above. One-third cup blanched almonds and about ¼ cup pine nuts are lightly fried in butter and arranged at the bottom of an oiled mold. The cooked rice is pressed over them, then the mold is turned out onto a heated serving dish and garnished with portions of chicken.

Persian Chicken Polo

Two of the most delicious chicken dishes are versions of Persian morg polo. *Both are meant, understandably, for great occasions such as the New Year, weddings, and saints' days.*

2 cups *basmati* rice	Salt and black pepper
1 onion, finely chopped	1 tablespoon raisins, or more
6 tablespoons butter or oil	4–6 oz. dried apricots, chopped
1 large [4-lb.] roasting chicken, cut up	½–1 teaspoon ground cinnamon

Boil the rice according to the recipe for *chilau* (page 340), but do not steam it. Alternatively, half-cook according to one of the recipes for plain rice on page 339.

Fry the onion gently in 4 tablespoons butter or oil until golden, using a saucepan or a deep frying pan. Add the chicken pieces and brown on all sides. Season to taste with salt and pepper, add raisins and apricots, and continue to cook for a minute or two longer, turning the fruit in the fat. Sprinkle with cinnamon, cover with water, and simmer gently, covered, until the chicken is very tender and the sauce reduced. Bone the chicken if you like.

Put 2 tablespoons melted butter or oil at the bottom of a large, heavy saucepan. Spread half of the partly cooked rice over this, cover with the chicken pieces, pour the rich, fruity sauce over them, and cover with remaining rice. Cover the pan with a cloth, put the lid on tightly, and steam over very low heat for 20 to 30 minutes. The cloth will capture the steam rising from the rice and help to make it fluffy. Serve all mixed together.

Shirini Polo

3–4 oz. candied tangerine or orange peel [see method below]
Sugar
1 large [4-lb.] roasting chicken, cut up
Salt and black pepper

½ teaspoon powdered saffron
¾ cup blanched almonds or pistachio nuts, chopped
3 cups long-grain rice, preferably *basmati*, washed and drained
Butter or oil

To prepare the candied peel: use peel with as much of the white pith removed as possible. Slice it into thin strips and make a note of the weight. Simmer without sugar in about ⅓ cup water until soft. Then add sugar equal to the original weight and cook until the water is reduced and the strips of peel are sweet. Bitter peel is particularly good prepared in this manner. (The candied peel available in shops can also be used.)

Boil the chicken pieces in water to cover with salt and pepper to taste and ¼ teaspoon saffron until the chicken is tender and the stock greatly reduced. Bone the chicken and cut the flesh into small pieces. Return the pieces to the pan with the remaining stock, add the peel and almonds or pistachios, and continue to simmer for 15 to 20 minutes, uncovered only if the sauce needs reducing to suit the rice.

Boil the rice according to the recipe for *chilau* (page 340), adding the remaining ¼ teaspoon saffron. Do not steam it yet. First, melt 2 tablespoons butter or oil in the bottom of a large, heavy saucepan. Put alternate layers of rice and chicken with peel and nuts in the pan, starting and ending with a layer of rice.

Now, stretch a clean cloth over the top of the pan, put on the lid and steam over very low heat for 20 to 30 minutes, until the sweet juices of the chicken sauce have penetrated the rice. The cloth will absorb the steam and help the rice to retain its fluffiness.

Havij Polo / Rice with Carrots

This is an excellent sweet Persian polo, usually served with minced lamb meatballs, or as an accompaniment to a whole leg of lamb which has been rubbed with salt, pepper, and paprika and roasted in the oven (see page 212).

1 onion, finely chopped	½ teaspoon ground cinnamon
Butter or oil	[optional]
1–1½ lbs. carrots, coarsely grated	2 cups long-grain rice
2 tablespoons sugar, or more [optional]	Salt
	1 tablespoon rose water ‡

Fry the onion in 3 tablespoons butter or oil until soft and golden. Add the grated carrots and sauté gently for 10 minutes. Sugar and cinnamon may be added at this stage if desired.

Boil plain rice separately, preferably according to the recipe for Persian *chilau* (page 340). Before steaming, put a little butter or oil at the bottom of a large, heavy pan, then spread alternate layers of rice and sautéed carrots in the pan, starting and ending with a layer of rice. Sprinkle rose water over the top and cook over very low heat for about 30 minutes, with a cloth stretched over the top of the pan underneath the lid. The rose water, a relic of early medieval times, gives a subtle perfume to the dish.

Surround a roast joint of lamb with the rice mixture. If you prefer meatballs instead, knead 1½ to 2 lbs. ground lean lamb until smooth and pasty, and season to taste with salt, pepper, and a teaspoon of ground cinnamon. Shape into marble-sized balls. Fry them lightly in oil or butter until cooked through and colored all over, and bury them in the middle of the rice and carrots before steaming.

One day Goha went to the market. He stopped to gaze into the window of a restaurant where pilavs, stews, chickens, fish, and other appetizing dishes were displayed. As he stood there enjoying the delicious aromas which reached him through the open door, the head cook hailed him: "Come in, sir, and make yourself at home!"

Believing that he was being invited as a guest, Goha accepted. He sat down and ate as much as he could of all the dishes, filling his pockets with pilav to take home to his son. But as he got up to leave, the head cook called out: "Pay me! You have eaten ten piasters' worth of food!"

"But I haven't any money," Goha replied. "I thought I was your guest."

The head cook dragged Goha before the Emir, who ordered him to be driven through the streets sitting backwards on a donkey as a punishment. As he proceeded through the town in this manner, followed by a train of jeering onlookers, some of them even playing music on pipes and drums, a friend saw him and exclaimed: "What are you doing, Goha? Why are they treating you in this manner?"

"I was served good pilav for nothing, with extra thrown in for my son," replied Goha. "And now I am having a free donkey ride with free music as well!"

Rice with Dates and Almonds

An Arab dish, said to be of Bedouin origin.

2 cups long-grain rice	½ cup raisins
Salt	¼ lb. dates, chopped [dried dates
¾ cups blanched almonds, halved	will do, if soft and juicy]
8 tablespoons (1 stick) butter	

Boil the rice until not quite tender, following the recipe for *chilau* (page 340). Drain and keep warm.

Fry the almonds in 4 tablespoons butter until just golden. Add raisins and dates, and stir gently over moderate heat for a few minutes longer. Add about ½ cup water and simmer gently for a further 15 minutes until the dates are soft and the water has been absorbed.

Melt a tablespoon of butter in a large, heavy saucepan. Add half of the rice and spread evenly with the date and almond mixture. Cover with the remaining rice and dot the top with butter shavings. Cover with a clean cloth and a tight-fitting lid, and steam over very low heat for about 30 minutes.

Roz ou Hamud / Rice with Hamud Sauce

An Egyptian specialty and a great favorite. This is rice served with a rich, lemony chicken soup or sauce called hamud. *For the soup version, see the recipe on page 110.*

Prepare 2 cups long-grain rice according to one of the recipes for plain rice at the beginning of this chapter, but do not start until the hamud *is ready.*

Use chicken giblets or leftover chicken bones and a carcass to make a rich stock. The stock left over from boiling a chicken would be ideal; it is also possible to use stock cubes, but, although acceptable, they are not as good.

Chicken giblets, bones, etc., or 2 chicken stock cubes	2–3 zucchini, thinly sliced
1 turnip, cut into pieces	2 tablespoons finely chopped parsley
1 large potato, cut into pieces	2–4 cloves garlic
2 stalks celery with leaves, chopped	Juice of 1–2 lemons, or to taste
2 leeks, thinly sliced	Salt and black pepper

Put all the ingredients in a large saucepan and cover with about 5 cups water. Bring to the boil and boil vigorously at first, removing the scum as it rises to the surface. Then lower the heat and simmer gently for 1 hour or more, until the meat comes away from the bones, the potato has practically disintegrated, the other vegetables are extremely soft, and the stock is rich and full of flavor. Add water if necessary to bring the volume of sauce up to about 2 cups. Remove all the bones but leave the pieces of chicken and vegetables in the sauce. It will be gently flavored with the leeks, celery, and garlic, with a sharp, lemony tang at the same time.

Serve the sauce and rice in separate bowls, and pour the sauce over each portion of rice with a soup ladle, as an accompaniment to chicken dishes.

Almond Sauce for Rice

This is an exquisite alternative to hamud *(above), a specialty of Damascus.*

⅓ cup ground almonds, or more for a thicker sauce
2½ cups chicken stock
Salt and white pepper
1 clove garlic, crushed

2 tablespoons finely chopped parsley
½ teaspoon sugar
Juice of 1 lemon, or more
Pinch of turmeric [optional]
Finely chopped parsley, to garnish

Mix the almonds and cold stock together in a saucepan. Bring to the boil, season to taste, and add all the other ingredients. A pinch of turmeric may be used to give the sauce an attractive pale yellow color. Simmer gently, stirring occasionally, for 20 to 30 minutes, until the mixture thickens and the ingredients have blended to give a rich, flavorsome sauce.

Serve garnished with chopped parsley as an accompaniment to plain rice (pages 339–41), with chicken dishes.

If you have some leftover chicken available, cut it into small pieces and add to the sauce with the other ingredients. One or two tablespoons of pine nuts can also be added 10 minutes before the end of cooking time.

Rice with Beid bi Lamoun

Beid bi lamoun is the Greek *avgolemono* sauce, made with eggs and lemon juice, and popular all over the Middle East.

The quantities and ingredients are the same as for *avgolemono* sauce for fish (see page 158), except that a rich chicken stock is used instead of the fish stock.

Serve hot as an accompaniment to plain rice, cooked according to one of the methods described at the beginning of this chapter.

İç Pilav / Goose Liver Pilav

A rich and delightful Turkish specialty. Chicken livers can be used instead of goose livers if necessary.

2 cups long-grain rice
8 tablespoons (1 stick) butter
¾ lb. goose livers, cleaned and
    sliced
Salt and black pepper
1 teaspoon ground allspice [op-
    tional]
8 scallions, finely chopped
1 medium-sized onion, finely
    chopped

1 tablespoon pine nuts
1 tablespoon raisins
1 teaspoon sugar
2 tablespoons tomato paste or 1
    large ripe tomato, skinned and
    chopped
4 tablespoons finely chopped fresh
    dill or parsley

Wash the rice as described on page 339 only if necessary. Heat 2 tablespoons of the butter in a frying pan. Fry the livers until just colored and remove. Season them to taste with salt, pepper, and a little ground allspice if liked. Toss well and reserve. In the same fat, fry the scallions lightly for a few minutes to soften them.

Put the rest of the butter in a large, heavy saucepan. Heat until melted and fry the onion until golden. Add pine nuts and prepared rice, and stir well over moderate heat. When the grains are well coated with fat, add 4 cups of water. Stir in raisins, sugar, and tomato paste (or the skinned and chopped fresh tomato), and season to taste with salt and pepper. Use a wooden spoon for stirring to avoid breaking the grains. Bring to the boil, cover, and simmer for 15 minutes until the rice is just cooked and has absorbed all the water.

Now return the fried goose livers to the pan with the scallions. Add freshly chopped dill or parsley, mix well, and stir lightly into the cooked rice. Cover the top of the pan with a clean cloth, put on the lid, and leave over very low heat for 20 minutes.

Rice with Quail

This delicious dish can also be made successfully with pigeons and other small birds.

6 small quail
8 tablespoons (1 stick) butter
Salt and black pepper
1 onion, finely chopped

2 cups long-grain rice, washed and
  drained
Pinch of grated nutmeg

Clean, wash, and wipe the quail. Sauté in hot butter in a large pan until colored all over. Remove to another pan. Cover with water and season to taste with salt and pepper. Bring to a boil, remove the scum, and simmer gently, covered, until tender (about 6 to 10 minutes). Drain and keep warm. Reserve the stock.

Now fry the onion in the same butter until soft and golden. Add the washed and well-drained rice, and sauté in the hot butter until all the grains are coated and transparent. Pour over it 4 cups of the stock left over from cooking the quail, adding water if necessary. Add a pinch of nutmeg. Bring to a vigorous boil, then reduce the heat and simmer very gently, covered and undisturbed, until tender, about 20 minutes.

Serve on a large tray, the quail imbedded in the rice.

PERSIAN KHORESHTHA,

OR SAUCES

Of all the dishes of Persian cooking, the most common are the sauces, or *khoreshtha*, or, since they are always intended to be served over rice, *chilau khoreshtha*. They are common only insofar as they are eaten daily and sometimes twice a day. Otherwise they deserve all the culinary superlatives. It is in these dishes, most of all, that the refined knowledge and experience of centuries have crystallized to give the exquisite Persian combinations of meat and poultry with vegetables, fruits, nuts, herbs, and spices; combinations which are never overpowering, but in which all the ingredients retain their dignity, enhanced and complemented by each other.

Khoreshtha are, by English standards, stews rather than sauces. An infinite variety of ingredients is used to make them. Meat and poultry are usually cubed or cut into smallish pieces. Vegetables are diced, sliced, or left in larger pieces. Fruits are sliced and cut, nuts chopped, and beans soaked beforehand. Fresh herbs are used if possible.

Delicate spices are used in small quantities—the sauces are never hot, peppery, or strong. Occasionally, a drop of rose water is added; sweet-and-sour pomegranate juice or sauce is also a favorite flavoring. Sometimes the sauces are colored brick-red with tomatoes, sometimes rich brown with the pomegranate sauce, green with spinach and herbs, or golden with saffron.

The ingredients are usually sautéed in butter or oil. Then water is added, never very much, and they are left to cook slowly and gently for a long time until the juices and flavors blend and fuse. The sauces are also good prepared a day in advance.

These *khoreshtha* vary slightly from family to family and according to which ingredients are in season. Generally, people are faithful to what they know and what has been passed to them by tradition. In the summer, all the local vegetables find their way into the *khoreshtha*. As they become more scarce, apples and quinces appear, and when they, too, disappear in the winter, their place is taken by nuts and dried fruits.

We are lucky in the West, inasmuch as we can always have recourse to canned and frozen vegetables which are, in many cases, quite acceptable. Cooked, leftover meat and chicken can also be used.

Since *khoreshtha* contain both meat and vegetables, they can be served at our Western tables as a meal in themselves, accompanied only by plain rice, preferably steamed in the Persian manner (page 340). In modern Persia they are often preceded by an egg dish or *kuku* (the Arab *eggah*)—see pages 150–1.

Spinach and Prune Khoresh

Meat and fruit dishes have recently become popular in the West, particularly in America. In the Middle East, they are a very ancient tradition. Moroccans and Persians excel in the art of those splendid combinations, each family daily repeating the dishes of the past with its own particular and individual variations.

1 onion, finely chopped
Butter or oil
1 lb. lean stewing beef or lamb,
    cubed
½–1 teaspoon ground cinnamon
¼ teaspoon grated nutmeg

Salt and black pepper
Juice of 1 lemon, or more
½ lb. prunes, soaked overnight
½ lb. fresh spinach, washed and
    chopped

In a large saucepan, sauté the onion gently in 3 tablespoons hot butter or oil until soft and golden. Add the meat and brown all over. Sprinkle with cinnamon and nutmeg, and season to taste with salt and pepper. Add about 2½ cups of water to cover, and the lemon juice. Bring to the boil, remove any scum, and simmer over a low heat for about 1½ hours, or until the meat is nearly tender. Throw in the drained prunes and spinach, and cook for a further 15 to 20 minutes. Add more water if necessary. This should be rather more liquid than a stew. Adjust seasoning and serve with plain cooked rice.

An apple and prune *khoresh* substitutes yellow split peas and apples for the spinach. Add about ¼ cup split peas to the meat together with the water, and simmer until the peas are soft and the meat is tender. Peel 1 or 2 tart apples. Slice and sauté in butter, then add them to the stew at the same time as the prunes. (You will need fewer prunes for this version, only 3 or 4 oz.) The flavorings are, again, lemon, cinnamon, and nutmeg, in about the same quantities.

Apple Khoresh

1 onion, finely chopped
5–6 tablespoons butter or oil
1 lb. lean stewing lamb, cubed
Salt and black pepper

1 teaspoon ground cinnamon
3 tart apples [cooking or eating
    ones]
Juice of 1 lemon, or more

Sauté the onion in 3 tablespoons butter or oil in a large saucepan until soft and golden. Add the meat and brown all over. Season to taste with salt and pepper, and sprinkle with cinnamon. Cover with about 2½ cups of water. Bring to the boil, remove any scum, and simmer gently for 1½ to 2 hours, or until the meat is tender. Add more water during the cooking time if necessary.

Peel, core, and slice or chop the apples into largish pieces. Sauté gently in 2 to 3 tablespoons hot butter until lightly colored all over. Add to the meat stew with the lemon juice. Cook for a further 5 minutes, or until soft. Do not allow the apples to disintegrate unless you prefer to mash them to a purée with a fork.

Serve with plain rice.

Yellow split peas can be added to the meat stew at the start of cooking for a richer texture, and chicken can be used instead of meat. Bone it before adding the fruit. Although not used in the Middle East, pork is also rather good in this sauce.

Peach Khoresh

Prepare the sauce as in the preceding recipe, using either meat or chicken, and substituting 4 peaches, preferably not quite ripe ones, for the apples. Peel them, remove the pits, and slice them or cut them into largish pieces. Fry in butter and add them to the sauce. Simmer for a further 15 to 20 minutes. Here again, lemon juice and cinnamon are a pleasant flavoring. Some people also like to add about 1 tablespoon sugar.

Rhubarb Khoresh

Butter
1 onion, finely chopped
1 lb. lean stewing beef, cubed
Salt and black pepper

¾ teaspoon ground cinnamon or
  allspice
1 lb. fresh rhubarb stalks
Juice of ½ lemon

Heat 2 tablespoons butter in a large saucepan, and fry the onion until soft and golden. Add the meat and sauté until well browned. Cover with water, season to taste with salt and pepper, and add cinnamon or allspice. Bring to the boil and simmer for 1½ to 2 hours, until the meat is very tender.

Trim the rhubarb stalks and cut them into 2-inch lengths. Sauté in 2 tablespoons butter for a few minutes, then sprinkle with lemon juice and cook for a few minutes longer. Add to the meat sauce and simmer for 10 minutes. Serve with plain white rice.

Eggplant Khoresh

Chicken may be used for this sauce instead of lamb or beef. A zucchini sauce is prepared in the same way, using 1 lb. whole zucchini.

2 eggplants, sliced	Black pepper
Salt	½–1 teaspoon turmeric [optional]
1 large onion	½ teaspoon ground cinnamon
Butter or oil	[optional]
1 lb. lean stewing beef or lamb, cubed	¼ teaspoon grated nutmeg [optional]
¼ cup brown lentils or yellow split peas, soaked for a few hours	2 tablespoons dried crushed mint
	1–2 cloves garlic, crushed

Sprinkle eggplant slices with salt and leave them to drain in a colander for at least 30 minutes to rid them of their bitter juices.

Chop the onion finely and set aside 1 tablespoon to use as a garnish. Fry the remainder in 2 tablespoons butter or oil until soft and golden. Add the meat and brown the cubes on all sides. Add the drained lentils, and cover with water (about 2½ cups). Season to taste with salt and pepper, and simmer gently for 1½ to 2 hours, until the meat is tender and the lentils are soft. A teaspoon of turmeric may be added if you like for color, and a little cinnamon and nutmeg may be included for a mild aroma.

Wash the salt off the eggplant slices, pat them dry, and sauté in about 2 tablespoons butter or oil until soft and golden. Add them to the stew and cook for 15 minutes longer.

A traditional and very tasty garnish is made by frying the reserved chopped onion in a little butter or oil until soft and golden, then adding dried mint and garlic, and frying for only 1 minute longer.

Serve the sauce in a bowl, garnished with this mixture, as an accompaniment to a large dish of plain, fluffy white rice.

A variation is to add the juice of 1 lemon (in Iran *oman*, or dried lemons, are used) and ½ lb. skinned and chopped tomatoes or 4 tablespoons tomato paste.

BREADS

Khubz

In the Middle East, as in much of the world, bread is the staff of life. Middle Eastern bread is round, flat, and only slightly leavened, with a hollow like an empty pocket running right through it. It is made with various qualities of wheat flour: a coarse flour makes an earthy, dark bread, a refined white one results in a delicate white bread. It is soft. Even the outer crust is not crisp but soft, while the inside is chewy, and good for absorbing sauces.

A religious and superstitious feeling is attached to bread, stronger in some Middle Eastern countries than others. To some it is, more than any other food, a direct gift from God; a hungry man will kiss a piece of bread given to him as alms. An invocation to God is murmured before kneading the dough, another before placing it in the oven. A piece of bread found lying on the floor is immediately picked up and respectfully placed on the table.

Although bread is available everywhere in towns, many people still prefer to make their own and send it to be baked in the oven of the local bakery, as is done in the villages. Children rushing through the streets balancing a large wooden tray or a flat wicker basket on their heads are a common daily sight. The trays hold rounds of flattened dough laid on a cloth, and covered by another cloth. At the bakery, the children stand close to the big oven, watching where their bread is put down so as not to lose it among the other loaves. People often mark their loaves with a pinch or brand it with a sign drawn with a stick in order to be able to recognize and claim their own when it comes out of the oven.

Bread is eaten with every meal. Sometimes people break off a piece and double it over to enclose and pick up a morsel of meat or vegetable, or dip it in a sauce or cream salad, holding it delicately between the thumb and the first two fingers. Sometimes it is cut in half and the pocket is filled with hot shish kebab and salads or *ful medames* (page 268). It can also be toasted, or broken into pieces and used as a base for various dishes such as *fata* soup (page 130), *fattoush* salad (page 75), and a few stews. Some people, my father among them, claim that they cannot truly savor sauces or juices, or anything in fact, without a piece of bread.

Arab proverb: "Take your bread to the baker even if he eats half of it."

Khubz (*Eish Shami*)—or Pitta Bread,

as it is more commonly known in the West

½ oz. (1 cake) fresh yeast or ¼ oz. (1 package) dried yeast	3½ cups all-purpose flour
About 1¼ cups tepid water	½ teaspoon salt
Sugar	Oil

Dissolve the yeast in about ¼ cup of the total amount of tepid water. Add a pinch of sugar and leave in a warm place for about 10 minutes, or until it becomes frothy and bubbly.

Sift flour and salt into a warmed mixing bowl. Make a well in the center and pour in the yeast mixture. Knead well by hand, adding enough of the remaining water to make a firm but not hard dough. Knead the dough vigorously in the bowl, or on a floured board or pastry cloth, for about 15 minutes, until it is smooth and elastic, and no longer sticks to your fingers. Knead in 1 or 2 tablespoons oil for a softer bread. Sprinkle the bottom of the bowl with a little oil and roll the ball of dough around and around to grease it all over. This will prevent the surface from becoming dry and crusty. Cover with a dampened cloth and leave in a warm place free of drafts for at least 2 hours, until nearly doubled in size.

Punch the dough down and knead again for a few minutes. Take lumps of dough the size of a large potato or smaller (according to the size of bread you wish to have). Flatten them on a lightly floured board with a dry rolling pin sprinkled with flour, or with the palm of your hand, until about ¼ inch thick and about 6 to 7 inches in diameter; however, the size can vary; it is the thickness that is important. Dust with flour and lay the rounds on a cloth sprinkled with flour. Cover with another lightly floured cloth, and allow to rise again in a warm place.

Preheat the oven set at the maximum temperature for at least 10 minutes. Oil two large baking sheets (one for each rack) and put them in the oven for an additional 10 minutes to make them as hot as possible. Take care that the oil does not burn.

When the bread has risen again, slip the rounds onto the hot baking sheets, sprinkle them lightly with cold water to prevent them from browning, and bake for 6 to 10 minutes, by which time the strong yeasty aroma escaping from the oven will be replaced by the rich, earthy aroma characteristic of baking bread—a sign that it is nearly ready.

Do not open the oven during this time.

Remove the baking sheets as soon as the bread comes out of the oven and cool on wire racks. The bread should be soft and white with a pouch inside.

Khubz Mbassis / Tunisian Semolina Bread

7 cups fine semolina
3 oz. (1 cake) fresh yeast or 1½ oz. (1 package) dried yeast
About 2 cups tepid water
Sugar
1½ teaspoons salt
5 tablespoons olive oil

1–2 tablespoons melted lard [traditionally, rendered lamb's tail fat]
4 tablespoons roasted sesame seed
1 teaspoon aniseed
1 egg, beaten

Put the semolina in a large mixing bowl. Dissolve the yeast in a little of the water with a small pinch of sugar, and leave in a warm place for about 10 minutes until it begins to froth and bubble.

Add salt to the semolina and mix well. Work in the oil and melted lard, followed by the yeast mixture. Knead vigorously, adding the remaining water gradually to achieve a soft dough. Then knead for at least 15 minutes longer. Cover with a clean, dampened cloth and leave to rise in a warm, draft-free place for 1½ to 2 hours.

When the dough has doubled in bulk, punch it down and work in the seeds, kneading well for a few minutes. Divide the dough into small loaves and arrange them on oiled baking sheets. Allow them to rise again in a warm place until doubled in bulk.

Brush the loaves with beaten egg and bake in a preheated hot oven (450°) for the first 15 minutes. Then lower the heat to 350° and bake for a further 20 minutes or longer, depending on the size of the loaves. Test the loaves by tapping one lightly on the bottom. If it sounds hollow, it is ready. If not, return the trays to the oven for a few minutes longer. Cool the loaves on wire racks.

Kahk / Savory Bracelets

Three recipes for "ka'ak" are given in the medieval Kitab al Wusla il al Habib. *Here is a modern recipe. It makes rather a large quantity.*

7 cups all-purpose flour
2 oz. (1 cake) fresh yeast or 1 oz.
   (1 package) dried yeast
About ½ cup tepid water
Pinch of sugar
16 tablespoons (2 sticks) margarine

1–2 tablespoons salt
½–1 tablespoon ground cumin
½–1 tablespoon ground coriander
1 egg, lightly beaten
Sesame seeds

Sift the flour into a large mixing bowl. Dissolve the yeast in a little of the tepid water, add a small pinch of sugar, and let it stand in a warm place for about 10 minutes until it begins to bubble. Melt the margarine (used instead of butter because it does not become rancid) and let it cool.

Season the flour with salt, cumin, and coriander to taste—I prefer the larger quantity given—mixing them in well. Work in the melted margarine and the yeast mixture. Add enough water, gradually, to make a stiff dough, kneading vigorously. Continue to knead for about 10 minutes.

Take walnut-sized lumps of dough and roll them into thin cigarette shapes about 4 inches long. Bring the ends together and press them firmly against each other to make little bracelets. Paint their tops with lightly beaten egg mixed with 2 tablespoons water, using a pastry brush or a piece of cotton. Dip the egg-coated surface in a plate containing sesame seeds. Some will stick.

Place the bracelets on an oiled baking sheet and allow them to rest and rise in a warm place for about 2 hours. Some people allow the dough to rise once in a large bowl covered with a damp cloth before shaping the little bracelets, and then again. Both ways work equally well.

I am told that a good way of knowing when the bracelets are ready for the oven is to put a small lump of dough in a glass of water when it is first made. It will sink to the bottom, but then it will slowly rise again. When this happens, the rest of the dough is ready for baking. (I hasten to add that for some mysterious reason this method does not always work for me, although others swear by it.)

Bake the bracelets in a preheated moderate oven (375°) for 20 minutes; then lower the heat to slow (325°) and bake for 1 hour. The bracelets should be firm and crisp right through and a pale golden color. If they are still a little soft, return them to a very slow oven (250°) to dry out.

Iflagun

A medieval recipe, described as the bread of the Franks and Armenians, in the Wusla il al Habib. *From the French translation by M. Rodinson.*

"Take flour and knead with *samna* [clarified butter] in the same way as described for *ka'ak*. Allow to rise. Shape into a round bread with a slightly ridged edge. Take an egg. Break it into a bowl and add a little salt, ground pepper, ginger, sesame seed, *chènevis*, aniseed, roasted *carvi*, cumin seed and poppy seed, and mix well with the egg. The pepper must be abundant for its warmth to be felt. Add *atraf at-tib*, wild rue and grated cheese. Add saffron, chopped pistachio nuts, and spread thickly over the bread. Put in the oven. This is an excellent recipe."

I found this recipe very intriguing and have adapted it to modern breadmaking methods and my own taste. Make an ordinary bread dough:

1¼ cups milk	1 tablespoon salt
1¼ cups tepid water	1½ oz. (3 cakes) fresh yeast or ¾
2 tablespoons lard	oz. (3 packages) dried yeast
2 tablespoons butter	2 lbs. (7 cups) all-purpose flour
2½ tablespoon sugar	Oil

Scald the milk. Add half the water, and the lard, butter, sugar, and salt, and allow to cool to tepid. Dissolve the yeast in the remaining water with a pinch of sugar, and leave in a warm place for 10 minutes, or until frothy. Then mix with the water-and-milk mixture, and pour into a large, warmed bowl.

Sift the flour and add it gradually to the yeast mixture, beating at first with a wooden spoon, then mixing by hand until a soft dough is achieved which does not stick to the sides of the bowl. Use more or less flour if necessary. Allow the dough to rest for 10 minutes. Then knead it on a pastry cloth or a lightly floured board. It will be slightly sticky at first. Knead vigorously for 10 to 15 minutes until smooth and elastic.

Grease a bowl with a little oil and roll the ball of dough about in it to coat the whole surface with oil. This will stop the surface from drying out and forming a crust. Cover the bowl with a damp cloth and allow the dough to rise in a warm place, free of drafts, until it has doubled in bulk. This will take about 2 hours.

Punch the risen dough down again and knead for a few minutes longer. Then pat it into a round, flat shape and place it on an oiled baking sheet.

Prepare the spice and seed mixture. Although a whole egg is suggested in the medieval recipe, I suggest using 2 eggs yolks instead. Beat them in a bowl and add the following:

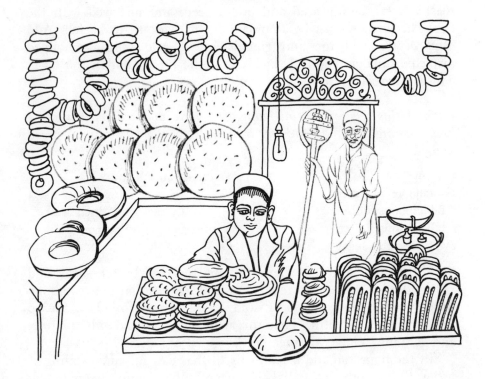

¼ teaspoon ground ginger
4 tablespoons roasted sesame seed
2 teaspoons aniseed
2 teaspoons roasted cumin seed
2 teaspoons poppy seed

4 tablespoons grated cheese [a dry crumbly one such as Parmesan, dry Cheddar, Lancashire, or Leicester]
2½ tablespoons chopped pistachio nuts
Salt
A generous amount of black pepper

Mix well into a rich paste and spread it over the top of the loaf. Allow the bread to rise again in a warm place until it has risen considerably though not quite doubled in bulk.

Bake in a preheated hot oven (450°) for the first 10 minutes, then reduce the heat to 350° and bake for a further 30 minutes. Test by tapping the bottom of the loaf. If it sounds hollow, it is ready. If not, return it to the oven and bake for a few minutes longer. Then remove it, and cool it on a wire rack.

Try this bread with all the seeds listed above or select those you prefer.

Semit / Bread Rings Covered with Sesame Seeds

Cairo vendors sell these bread rings covered with sesame seeds from large baskets, or sometimes threaded onto long wooden poles. In summer, they cry their wares at the entrances of open-air cinemas, or carry them around the tables and across the rows of chairs, chanting "Semit! Semit!" The audience eagerly collect provisions to last them through the performance: rings of semit, cheese, salted, grilled melon seeds or leb, peanuts and Coca-Colas. They while away the time as they wait for darkness to fall and the film to start by eating and chatting; or they watch the children running up and down the aisles, and dancing on the cinema stage to popular Arab and Greek tunes.

One can make excellent semit at home. Make an ordinary bread dough as described in the previous recipe. After its first rising, knead and shape it into large rings about 7 inches in diameter and ¾ inch thick. Brush them with an egg beaten with 2 tablespoons water, and dip them in a bowl of sesame seeds. Arrange on oiled baking sheets.

Leave to rise in a warm place until nearly doubled in bulk again. Bake in a preheated hot oven (450°) for the first 10 minutes, then reduce the heat to 350°, and bake for a further 15 to 20 minutes, or until the rings are golden and sound hollow when tapped.

Other more unusual and more refined types of *semit* are made with a rich dough containing butter, oil, and eggs.

Chorek

A sweet bun and an old Oriental favorite. Usually prepared in large quantities for tea, leftover chorek *can be sliced and lightly toasted in the oven, to be eaten the following morning at breakfast with butter and jam. The preparation is much less complicated than it may seem at first sight.*

2 oz. (4 cakes) fresh yeast or 1 oz. (4 packages) dried yeast	4 tablespoons melted butter
	A few drops of vanilla extract
½ cup tepid water	4 eggs
Granulated sugar	¾ cup superfine sugar
2 lbs. (7 cups) all-purpose flour, sifted	4–7 tablespoons milk
	½ cup raisins
Oil	

In a medium-sized mixing bowl, dissolve the yeast in ¼ cup tepid water with a pinch of sugar. Leave in a warm place for about 10 minutes. When the mixture begins to bubble, stir in about 2 cups of flour, taken from the total quantity, and the remaining ¼ cup tepid water, or enough to make a soft dough. Work the dough with your hands, then knead vigorously for about 10 minutes. Roll the dough into a ball and grease it all over with a teaspoon of oil. Cover the bowl with a damp cloth and leave in a warm place to rise for about ½ hour.

In another bowl, mix the rest of the flour with 2 tablespoons oil, the melted butter, and vanilla extract. Mix well.

In a third, rather larger bowl, beat 3 eggs with the superfine sugar until light and fluffy. Add the flour, yeast, and water dough, and mix well. Gradually add the contents of the second bowl, stirring vigorously with a wooden spoon. Add enough milk to make a soft dough. Knead vigorously for 10 minutes. Then add the raisins, and work them well into the dough.

Cover the bowl with a damp cloth and allow the dough to rise again for another ½ hour. Then take egg-sized lumps of dough and roll them gently into little balls. Grease your palms lightly with oil to prevent the dough from sticking. Transfer the balls to oiled baking sheets, spacing them quite widely apart, and leave them to rise yet again in a warm place. The balls should double their bulk and be like large apples after about 2 hours.

Brush their tops with the remaining egg, beaten, and sprinkle with granulated sugar. Bake in a preheated hot oven (450°) for 8 minutes, then reduce the heat to 350° and bake for a further 20 minutes, or until the buns are a warm brown color. Cool them on wire racks.

Arab saying: "Add raisins to your bread on the baker's birthday."

PUDDINGS, CAKES, AND SWEETS

Halawiyat

The sweet tooth of the Middle Eastern peoples is well known. Throughout the region, large quantities of pastries, desserts, jams, and preserves are enjoyed on every possible occasion.* To many, they are also symbols of generosity and friendship, happiness, rejoicing, and success.

As in the West, sweets are eaten at the end of a meal. Quantities are also made regularly and stored away, ready for the casual caller and the unexpected friend, who by Middle Eastern convention expects and enjoys a warm, enthusiastic welcome at any time of the day. He will invariably be received, even at an awkward time, with the famous Oriental hospitality, the ingrained courtesy and decorum which have been rooted deeply by centuries of custom. Pastries, jams, and preserves will be pressed upon him with a Turkish coffee.

Besides spontaneous calls, there are special occasions when visiting is obligatory. A new arrival in town, a return home from a trip, a sickness, a death, a birth, a circumcision, a wedding, and the innumerable Muslim festivals, the *mûlids*, all set the cake- and pastry-making and eating rituals in motion. Certain occasions call for a particular sweet. Pastries, jams, and preserves, sweet-scented creams, and delicately fragrant fruit salads are made days in advance and served to commemorate or celebrate an event, as symbols of joy or sadness. They are often beautifully colored and decorated.

Muslim festivals always seem to be in progress. They sometimes last for as long as ten days—ten days of continuous merrymaking. Nearly every week brings some excitement and has some saint to be honored, some memory to be cherished, or some rite to be performed. The first ten days of the sacred Moharram, the opening month of the year, are holy. The passion play of Hasan and Hoseyn follows, performed in reverence to the memory of the martyr Hoseyn. In the second month, caravans of pilgrims returning from Mecca are welcomed with a picnic celebration. In the third month comes the Rabi el Awal or Mûlid el Nabi, the festival of the Prophet's birth. Then come the Mûlid el Bulak, the feast of the Lady Zeinab

---

* Rose and orange blossom water, which are used quite often in these recipes, are not difficult to obtain. See List of Sources.

and the feast of the "miraculous ascent," the visit to Paradise. After the great fast of Ramadan follow the Id es-Saghir and the visiting of cemeteries. Then there is the procession of Kisweh, of the Holy Carpet, and that of the Mahmal, the Ark of the Covenant.

In Egypt, many of the festivals are not based on either the Muhammadan or the Coptic religions, but derive from ancient Egyptian pagan rites and customs. People want to enjoy themselves, and any occasion is a pretext for fun, for laughter and merrymaking, for dancing and singing in the streets, for glass- and fire-eating, for *Kara Guz* (the Egyptian Punch and Judy), and for tying colored papers to bicycle spokes. It is a time for putting on dresses in fabulous *baladi* colors—sugar pinks and oranges, mauves, purples, lilacs, limes, acid greens, and scarlets—and for wearing Western pajamas in the streets. It is also a time for buying, from the street vendors, brilliantly colored violet, pink, and pale green syrups, and sweet pastries made with nuts, honey, and sugar and painted yellow, pink, and green, the colors of joy and happiness.

At one particular festival, the day of the sacrifice of the bride of the Nile (the Bent el Nil), we used to buy a large sugar doll painted in many different colors, with red lips and pink cheeks, and dressed in frilled and pleated multicolored tissue and silver papers. To my mother's horror, I once ate the whole doll, licking and chewing it for a month, undressing it and dressing it again after every repast.

For me, sweets are particularly associated with feelings of well-being, warmth, and welcome, of giving and receiving, of crowds of people smiling, kissing, hugging, and showering hospitality. I remember how hard it was to refuse, when visiting our many relatives and friends, the delicacies and pastries that were literally forced upon us, after our mother had impressed on us that we should not take more than three stuffed vine leaves, two *kahk*, and two *ma'amoul* because it was discourteous to be too eager and it would appear that we were not properly fed at home. We learned to say "No" a few times before we accepted, and even today, after many years in Europe, I find it hard to say "Yes" the first time when offered a drink or something to eat, and then sadly regret the loss of a longed-for tea or pastry.

Many of the pastries are sold in shops which are famous for their specialties. They are also made at home. Every housewife prides herself on making a perfect *konafa* or the lightest *fila*, and will rarely divulge her secrets of success to anyone but her daughter. Or she *may* give the recipe under pressure, but with one deliberate mistake, so as to ensure failure when a competitor attempts it.

It is customary during periods of general festivity for every housewife to prepare mountains of assorted pastries on large trays, to be sent to all her sisters and relatives. She duly receives as many in return. On family occasions, relatives and friends come to help the hostess prepare a great variety of dishes days before the party. Sometimes a specialist is called in, a cook who comes to make one or two dishes for which she is famous, and then moves on to another house to make the same dish again. We always knew beforehand if we were to be served Rachèle's *ataïf* or Nabiha's *karabij* or *konafa à la crème*, and we could rejoice for a few days in advance at the thought.

Ever since my parents joined us in Europe, we have been making these specialties ourselves, and we have found them extremely easy to prepare. I am sure that every housewife who tries will be able to make them easily and successfully, so I have included them in this chapter with all the old, traditional family sweets.

FRUIT

Fruit is plentiful and varied. The market stalls glow with the brilliant colors of bananas, peaches, sweet lemons, mangoes, melons, figs, watermelons, pomegranates, grapes, and apricots. When fruits are in season they are served at both lunch and dinner, piled high on plates or, when it is hot, in large bowls surrounded by ice. Each person dips his fruit in an individual finger bowl of ice-cold water.

Fruits are sometimes served in the Persian manner, grated and mixed with crushed ice and scented water. They are also stewed and sometimes stuffed.

When fresh fruits are not available, jams and compotes, prepared while they were plentiful, are served, as well as stewed or macerated dried fruits. As with all dishes, people have their favorite combinations. Some families put extra apricots or nuts in their dried fruit compote; others prefer scented water to syrup. I have given below the quantities and varieties which are best known. Adapt them to your own taste.

Stuffed Melon

1 large melon
2 ripe peaches, pears, or mangoes, fresh or canned
A few grapes or pitted cherries, if available

3–4 tablespoons superfine sugar
1–2 tablespoons lemon juice
1 tablespoon rose or orange blossom water

Cut a slice off the top of the melon and set aside to use as a lid. Remove the seeds and scoop out as much of the flesh as you can, being careful not to bruise the outer skin. Scoop melon balls out with a rounded scooper, or use a spoon and then cut the chunks into small pieces.

Put the scooped-out melon in a bowl with the peaches, pears, or mangoes, peeled and sliced, and the grapes or stoned cherries. Add sugar and lemon juice to taste, sprinkle with rose water or orange blossom water, and mix well.

Return the fruits and juice to the melon shell. Cover with the top slice and chill for about 2 hours before serving. Serve from the melon shell, which can be decorated with flowers stuck into little holes made with a knitting needle, or tied with a bow like an Easter egg.

Arab saying: "He who fills his stomach with melons is like he who fills it with light—there is baraka [*a blessing*] *in them."*

Grated Apples

In an Egyptian Dream Book *translated into English by "a Lady" in 1231, it is said that "to dream of looking at apples betokens a wedding. To dream of eating apples is a sign of mourning, unless they are very sweet; then it is a sign of a great deal of prosperity in the marriage state."*

*Here is a typically Persian way of serving apples or other fruit. It is
ideal for a hot summer's day.*

6 eating apples	2 tablespoons rose or orange
Juice of 1 lemon	blossom water ‡
4–8 heaping tablespoons confec-	3–4 ice cubes, crushed
tioner's sugar	6 thin slices lemon

Peel and grate the apples into a glass bowl. Squeeze the lemon juice
over them to prevent them from discoloring. Add sugar to taste, sprinkle with rose or orange blossom water, and mix lightly. Chill for a
few hours.

Just before serving, add the crushed ice. The ice can be crushed
either in an electric blender or in a mortar. Decorate with thin
slices of lemon and serve.

Turkish Fruit Komposto

A dish of one kind of stewed fruit is always certain to be on the menu
of even the humblest café, usually spelled *kompot* in a Frenchified
manner. It is the "bread and butter" dessert, made with fresh fruits
when they are in season, dried fruit in the winter.

Although I call them "stewed," in actual fact fresh fruits, especially, should only be poached, dropped in a very little boiling water
or syrup, then simmered gently until they are just tender. They should
not be overcooked.

Apples should be simmered in water, with a little sugar added to
taste when they are nearly tender. Apricots, plums, cherries, and
grapes are best simmered in a boiling syrup made of one part sugar to
two parts water. Soft fruits such as strawberries, figs, peaches, and
pears are simmered in a thicker syrup made of equal volumes of
sugar and water.

When making a dried fruit *kompot*, wash the fruits only if necessary. Soak overnight if required. Bring to a boil in the same water
and simmer until tender. Add sugar to taste. Dried apricots, prunes,
apples, cherries, raisins, and figs can all be used. The *kompot* can be
flavored with a stick of cinnamon, a little lemon juice, rose water, or
orange blossom water. Serve hot or cold, on its own, or accompanied
by fresh cream or yogurt.

Fresh Fruit Compote

This compote can be made with any fresh fruits that are in season, and in various combinations to suit individual taste. I have listed more fruits than are needed for 6 portions. They will not all be in season at the same time, so use those that are available.

SYRUP
Water
Sugar
Lemon juice

2 cooking apples
2 pears
2 peaches
4 plums
4 apricots
A handful of strawberries or cherries

Make a syrup by boiling water with half its volume of sugar and lemon juice to taste, allowing it to simmer for about 10 minutes.

Wash, peel, core, and slice all the fruit, and remove pits where necessary. Put the sliced fruit in a large pan with the syrup, bring to the boil gently, and simmer for about 15 minutes, or until they are all soft. Chill and serve cold, with thick cream if you wish.

Quince Compote

2 lbs. quinces
½ lb. (1¼ cups) sugar

2 cups water
Juice of ½ lemon

Peel and core the quinces, and cut them into thick slices. Put the peels and cores into a thin syrup made by simmering the sugar and water with lemon juice. Cook for 30 minutes, by which time the syrup will have acquired a jelly-like quality. Strain the syrup and return it to the pan. Bring it to the boil again and poach the slices of quince until soft.

Serve hot or cold with thick heavy cream, whipped cream, or yogurt. This compote is excellent mixed with an apple compote, cooked separately.

Mixed Dried Fruit in Syrup

This dessert is particularly favored during Ramadan, the month-long fast during which Muslims fast all day and eat only after sunset. All through the hot day the people, hungry and listless, are hardly able to work, and dream of what they would like to eat. At nightfall, when the sky is a cherry red, the cannons boom through the cities to signal the end of the fast and the muezzins sing it from all the minarets. The silent city suddenly trembles and comes alive with the clatter of spoons and plates, glasses and jugs, and with the sound of relieved hunger and laughter, of music and merrymaking.

The longed-for dishes wait on tables and trays and on the floor, piled high with ful medames, falafel *and* bamia, *meatballs, kebabs, and stewed fruit.*

¼ lb. each of: dried apricots, figs, peaches, prunes, and cherries
½ cup seedless raisins
⅓ cup each of: blanched almonds, pistachio nuts, and pine nuts
Sugar

Wash and soak the dried fruits overnight if necessary. Use a larger proportion of the fruits which you like best. (I use ½ lb. apricots and no figs.) Put them in a large pan with blanched almonds and, if they are available, pistachios and pine nuts. If using only one kind of nuts, raise the amount to ⅔ cup. Cover with water, sweeten to taste, and bring to the boil slowly. Simmer gently until all the fruits are well cooked, at least ½ hour or longer depending on their quality.

Khoshaf / Dried Fruit Salad

A great Middle Eastern favorite in which the fruit is not stewed but macerated. A superb dessert. Various dried fruits may be used, but purists feel that only apricots and raisins should go into this classic dish, together with the nuts and almonds.

1 lb. dried apricots
½ lb. prunes
¼ lb. raisins
¼ lb. blanched almonds, halved
⅓ cup pistachio nuts or pine nuts
Sugar
1 tablespoon rose water
1 tablespoon orange blossom water

Wash the fruits if necessary and put them all in a large bowl. Mix with the nuts and cover with water. Add sugar to taste (from ½–1 cup is usual), and sprinkle with rose water and orange blossom water. Let the fruits soak for at least 48 hours. The syrup becomes rich with the juices of the fruit and acquires a beautiful golden color.

A less common variation is to add ¼ lb. each of dried figs and peaches, and a few fresh pomegranate seeds when these are available. Their luminosity brings out the rich orange, mauve, and brown of the fruit, and the white and green of the nuts. Some people dissolve *amardine* (sheets of dried compressed apricot) ‡ in the water to thicken and enrich it.

Apricot Pudding

The use of gelatin is a recent innovation in the Middle East, but this pudding, which was an aunt's specialty, is a favorite of mine and so I feel compelled to include it.

3 lbs. fresh apricots or 2 large cans [1 lb. 13 oz. each] apricots, drained
Juice of 2 oranges [½ cup juice]
Juice of ½ lemon
Superfine sugar
¾ oz. (3 envelopes) gelatin

½ cup hot water or juice from the canned apricots
Whipped cream [optional]
A few halved apricots and chopped almonds or pistachio nuts, to decorate

Choose sweet ripe apricots. Remove the pits and turn the apricots into a purée either by rubbing them through a strainer or by putting them in an electric blender with the orange and lemon juice. Add sugar if required, depending on the sweetness of the fruit, and the gelatin, which has been stirred in ½ cup hot water or fruit juice until completely dissolved. Strain the mixture and whisk it, or put it in the electric blender again and blend until smooth and creamy. Pour into a wetted mold and chill for 3 to 4 hours. It should be set very firmly.

To unmold, dip the mold for a few seconds in very hot water and turn out immediately onto a cold serving dish.

Decorate with whipped cream if you like, and with a few halved apricots and a sprinkling of chopped almonds or pistachios.

Orange Jelly

This is another modern, European-inspired dessert which is nevertheless Oriental.

¾ oz. (3 envelopes) gelatin	Superfine sugar
½ cup water	2 eating apples, thinly sliced
6 large juicy oranges	[optional]
1 lemon	A few pistachio nuts, chopped
2 tablespoons orange blossom water	

Stir the gelatin in the water over low heat until it dissolves. Then add the juice of 4 oranges and the lemon, and the orange blossom water. Sweeten to taste.

Peel the remaining 2 oranges, removing as much pith as possible. Slice thinly and halve. Place the half-slices decoratively along the sides of a moistened mold, with a few in the center to hold them in place. Slices of apple can also be arranged in the center of the mold at the same time as the orange slices.

Pour the liquid into the mold and chill until firmly set. Turn out onto a serving dish and decorate with little mounds of chopped pistachio nuts.

Riddle: She is the beautiful daughter of a handsome man. Her beauty is that of the moon. Her children are in her bosom, and her dwelling is high. Who is she?
Answer: An orange.

Prunes with Cream

This is a popular recipe in which alcohol is sometimes included, contrary to Muslim dietary law.

1 lb. prunes	4 tablespoons superfine sugar
Boiling tea	[optional]
¼ cup Cointreau or Kirsch	A few drops of vanilla extract
1½ cups heavy cream	

Wash the prunes if necessary and put them in a bowl. Pour boiling hot tea through a strainer over them to cover and let them soak overnight. They will swell and become very tender. Drain and place them in a serving bowl. Sprinkle with liqueur. (No sugar is required.)

Whip the cream until stiff, and stir in sugar to taste and vanilla. Smother the prunes with cream and chill for a few hours before serving.

Prunes Stuffed with Walnuts

1 lb. prunes	1 tablespoon lemon juice
Boiling tea	1¼ cups water
The same number of shelled walnut	1 cup heavy cream
halves as there are prunes	2 tablespoons superfine sugar
2 tablespoons sugar or more	[optional]

Wash the prunes if necessary. Pour strained boiling hot tea over them and let them soak overnight. Drain. Remove the pits, replacing them with half a shelled walnut. If you find this difficult, boil the prunes in the tea until nearly tender, then cool, remove their pits and stuff them.

Bring the water, sugar, and lemon juice to a boil and simmer for a few minutes. Drop in the stuffed prunes and simmer gently, covered, for ½ hour, adding more water if necessary. The walnuts will become impregnated with the rich syrup. Allow to cool and serve chilled with cream, whipped and sweetened with superfine sugar if you wish; or allow to cool, smother with the whipped cream, and chill together for a few hours. This last method is particularly delicious.

Modern variations which add to the aroma of the prunes include cooking them in sweet red wine (in this case using less sugar or none at all) or in the tea in which they have been soaked, flavored with a few drops of vanilla extract.

Amardine Cream

This exquisite pudding is traditionally made in Egypt during the period of Ramadan. The sheets of dried and compressed apricots called *amardine* can be found in most Greek and Oriental groceries.‡

Put about 1 lb. sheets of *amardine* in a bowl and cover with about 3½ cups water. Let the sheets soak for a few hours, then bring to the boil in the same water and simmer until they are very soft and have practically dissolved. Add sugar to taste if you wish, and cook gently until the mixture thickens into a rich cream. Stir occasionally with a wooden spoon and take care not to let the cream burn. Add a few halved blanched almonds, mix well, and pour into a serving bowl. Serve chilled, with whipped cream if you like.

I have found that a delicious cream, similar to the one above, can be made with ordinary dried apricots, which are more readily available and much cheaper. Use about 1 lb. good-quality apricots. Soak them overnight in about 3½ cups water. The following day, simmer them in the same water until soft. Turn them into a purée either by rubbing them through a strainer or blending them with their cooking water in an electric blender. Return to the pan, add sugar to taste and simmer gently, stirring occasionally with a wooden spoon, until thick. Stir in a few slivered almonds, pour into a bowl, and serve chilled.

Stuffed Apricots

18 fresh apricots
Juice of ½ lemon, or more
½ lb. (1¼ cups) sugar, or less if
   apricots are sweet

¾ cup ground almonds
½ cup superfine sugar
2 tablespoons rose water

Make a slit in each apricot and remove the pit, taking care not to break the fruit in half. Put the apricots in a large pan with the lemon juice and sugar. Warm the pan slowly, covered, and let the apricots simmer gently in their own juice, turning them and stirring from time to time, and moistening with a few tablespoons of water if necessary. Cook until the apricots are soft and have released their juice to form a syrup with the sugar. Allow to cool.

Make a paste with the ground almonds, superfine sugar, and rose water, and knead well. Fill the apricots with this paste and serve them cold in individual bowls, with the syrup poured over them. The apricots can also be served warm, in which case they should be returned to the pan and heated gently in the syrup.

A variation is to stuff each apricot with a whole blanched almond instead of the ground almond paste.

Belila

A sweet served in the Sephardic community on the occasion of a baby's first tooth.

½ lb. barley, soaked overnight
Sugar
2–3 tablespoons orange blossom or
   rose water

⅓ cup pistachios, chopped
¾ cup flaked almonds
¼ cup pine nuts

Simmer the barley in about 5 cups of water until only just tender, about ½ to ¾ hour.

Add sugar to taste and cook a few minutes, stirring, until well dissolved. Add orange blossom or rose water and the nuts. Add more water if necessary, so that the barley and nuts remain suspended in a light, scented syrup.

A FEW CREAM PUDDINGS

The Middle East possesses a wide range of desserts made with ground rice, cornstarch, or semolina, each with a subtle difference in texture and flavoring. The addition of such delicate flavorings as orange blossom, rose water, mastic,‡ or cinnamon, the incorporation of ground almonds, raisins, and nuts, and traditional decorations transform these humble ingredients into exquisitely fragrant Oriental desserts.

Balouza

½ cup cornstarch
6 cups water
½–1 cup sugar, or to taste

¼ cup orange blossom or rose water
¼ cup or more chopped blanched
   almonds or pistachio nuts

Mix the cornstarch to a smooth paste with a little of the water in a large pan. Add the rest of the water and the sugar, and stir vigorously with a wooden spoon until dissolved. Bring to a boil slowly, stirring. Lower the heat and simmer gently, stirring constantly, until the mixture thickens. A flame-tamer will help prevent the pudding from burning. To test if it is ready, dip a spoon in the hot mixture and see if it clings and coats the spoon. Another test is to drop a quarter-teaspoonful onto a cold plate—if it remains a solid little ball and does not flatten out, it is ready.

Stir in orange blossom or rose water and continue to cook for 2 or 3 minutes longer. Add the chopped nuts, stir well, and pour into a glass bowl. Chill.

This pudding is like white opaline encrusted with little stones. When it is served it trembles like a jelly. It is customary for an admiring audience to compliment a belly dancer by comparing her tummy to a *balouza*.

Balouza Muhallabia

This is a creamier, less firm version of the plain *balouza* above, made with milk instead of water and without the nuts, which are used as a garnish instead.

Chill the pudding in a large glass bowl or in individual dishes and decorate with chopped blanched almonds or pistachios, or both, making decorative patterns all over the top of the pudding.

"When I go to my house after a day of labor, the food tastes good to me though it be cheap. Does, then, the richest merchant in the city enjoy his quail and duck and partridges more than I enjoy my bread and dates? And can man be happier than I with my wife, for if there be not love, what pleasure has a man in a woman?"—Arab wisdom.

Balta or Hetalia

A beautiful and delicate dessert, like white blossoms and brown leaves floating in a pure scented stream.

1 recipe *Balouza* (p. 384)

SYRUP
About 3½–5 cups cold water
¾ cup sugar

3–4 tablespoons orange blossom or rose water
¾ cup raisins
¾ cup blanched halved almonds
⅓ cup chopped pistachio nuts, if available

Prepare the *balouza* and pour it into a large, moistened, square tray or mold. This will give you a wide thin sheet of *balouza*. Cool and chill in the refrigerator. When it has set firmly cut it into 1-inch squares with a knife.

Prepare the syrup in a very large mixing bowl or two smaller bowls. Pour in water and add ¾ cup sugar, or more if you like it sweet, and a little orange blossom or rose water. Stir until the sugar has dissolved. (This syrup is not cooked.) Taste again and add sugar if it is not sweet enough, or water if it is too sweet. Stir in raisins, almonds, and chopped pistachio nuts if available.

Unmold the squares of *balouza* and drop them into the syrup. Stir gently and serve. Serves 10 to 12 people.

Meghlie / Ceremonial Rice Pudding with Aniseed

This pudding is traditionally served to visitors and well-wishers on the birth of a son. It is said that a family will serve it on the birth of a daughter only if they are truly pleased to have one after a succession of four sons. Large amounts are made in expectation of many visitors.

This is a highly aromatic pudding. I recommend it to those who like the flavor of aniseed. Because it is strong, serve small portions only.

¼ lb. ground rice ‡
5½ cups water
11 tablespoons sugar
1 teaspoon caraway seed
1 teaspoon fennel seed
1 teaspoon aniseed

Pinch of ground ginger
To decorate: chopped blanched
almonds, pistachios, toasted
pine nuts, hazelnuts, whichever
are available

Mix the ground rice to a smooth paste with some of the cold water. Add sugar, caraway seed, fennel seed, and aniseed, and mix well. (The spices can be used in powdered form if more convenient.) Bring the remaining water to the boil in a large saucepan with a pinch of ginger. Add the ground rice paste gradually, stirring vigorously with a wooden spoon. Bring to the boil again, then allow to simmer, stirring occasionally. Cook until it thickens, about 1 hour. Pour into individual serving bowls or a large glass bowl, allow to cool, and chill until ready to serve.

Serve decorated generously with patterns of chopped blanched almonds, toasted pine nuts, chopped pistachio nuts, and hazelnuts. Use all or any that are available.

LULLABY FOR A SON*

*After the heat and after the bitterness, and after the sixth of the
    month,
After our enemies had rejoiced at her pain and said, "There is a stone
    in her tummy!"
The stone is in their heads! And this overwhelms them.
Go! O bearer of the news! Kiss them and tell them, "She has borne
    a son!"*

LULLABY FOR A NEWBORN GIRL*

*When they said, "It's a girl!"—that was a horrible moment.
The honey pudding turned to ashes and the dates became scorpions.*

* Maspéro, *Chansons populaires.*

When they said, "It's a girl!" the cornerstone of the house crumbled,
And they brought me eggs in their shells and instead of butter, water.

The midwife who receives a son deserves a gold coin to make earrings.
The midwife who receives a son deserves a gold coin to make a ring
    for her nose.
But you! O midwife! Deserve thirty strokes of the stick!
Oh! You who announce a little girl when the censorious are here!

Rice Pudding Flavored with Mastic

For those who like the flavor of mastic.

5–6 tablespoons [about 4 oz.]
    pudding rice
½ cup cold water
3¾ cups milk
5–6 tablespoons sugar

1 tablespoon orange blossom or rose
    water
¼ teaspoon pulverized mastic
Chopped blanched almonds and
    pistachio nuts, to decorate

Mix the rice with cold water. Bring the milk and sugar to the boil, and add the rice and water. Bring to the boil again and simmer gently over low heat for 45 minutes. The mixture will become beautifully creamy. If all the liquid is absorbed too soon, add a little more milk. Add the orange blossom or rose water and mastic pounded with a little sugar (a much loved flavoring in the Middle East). Continue to cook and stir for a few minutes more.

    Pour into a bowl and sprinkle with chopped almonds and pistachio nuts. Serve hot or cold.

Sholezard / Persian Yellow Rice Pudding

This excellent dish is traditionally served on the anniversary of the death of a member of the Prophet Muhammad's family. Saffron gives it its elegant color and distinctive taste.

5–6 tablespoons pudding rice
¼ teaspoon powdered saffron
2½ cups sugar
1 teaspoon lemon juice

⅓ cup blanched almonds, chopped
[optional]
1 teaspoon ground cinnamon
[optional]

Bring the rice to the boil in 5 cups water in which you have dissolved the saffron. Simmer gently for about ¾ hour until the rice is soft and swollen. Add a hot syrup made by simmering together the sugar, lemon juice, and ½ cup water. Cook all together for about ½ hour, until much of the liquid has been absorbed.

If you like, stir in some chopped blanched almonds. Allow to cool a little and pour into a glass serving bowl. Chill and serve dusted with a little cinnamon if you wish.

Muhallabia

This is the most regal and delicious of puddings.

1–2 tablespoons cornstarch
4 tablespoons ground rice ‡
5 cups milk
10 tablespoons sugar, or to taste

4 tablespoons orange blossom or
rose water,‡ or 2 tablespoons of
each
¾ cup ground almonds
Chopped almonds and pistachio
nuts, to decorate

Mix the cornstarch and ground rice to a smooth paste with a little of the cold milk. Bring the rest of the milk to a boil with sugar and add the paste gradually, stirring constantly with a wooden spoon. Simmer the mixture gently, stirring constantly but being careful not to scrape the bottom of the pan (the milk may burn slightly at the bottom, and if it is scraped it will give a burned taste to the whole pudding). When you feel a slight resistance to the spoon while stirring, and the mixture coats the back of the spoon, it has thickened sufficiently.

Add orange blossom or rose water, stir, and cook for a further 2 minutes. Stir in the ground almonds and remove the pan from the heat. Allow to cool slightly, then pour the pudding into a large glass bowl or individual dishes. Chill and serve, decorated with a pattern of chopped almonds and pistachios.

Some people pour a syrup made of honey boiled with water and scented with a little orange blossom water over the cold *muhallabia*. It can also be decorated with crystallized rose petals or violets.‡

Riddle: A sparkling saber, so sweet to pull out. The kings of the East and the kings of the West cannot put it back into its sheath. What is it?
Answer: Milk.

Ma'mounia

This is a medieval sweet which was probably invented for the Caliph Ma'moun in the tenth century. Rice seems to have been used at that time, but now it is made with semolina.

There are many well-known variations and these are generally called basbousa, halawa, *or* helva. *I have asked several people how they make* basbousa: *invariably, each has given me a different recipe.*

The basic ma'mounia *is now a Syrian, and even a particularly Aleppan, specialty. There, it is eaten almost daily for breakfast, but it also makes a delicious dessert. It is often served to a woman after she has given birth to help her regain her strength.*

2½ cups water	8 tablespoons (1 stick) unsalted
2¼ cups sugar	butter
1 teaspoon lemon juice	1 teaspoon ground cinnamon
¾ cup semolina	*Eishta* [page 392], clotted cream, or whipped cream

Make a syrup by boiling the water and sugar with the lemon juice, and allowing it to simmer for about 10 minutes, until slightly thickened.

Fry the semolina gently for 5 minutes in butter. Add the syrup and stir well. Leave the pan on the heat for a further 2 minutes, then remove and leave it to rest for 20 minutes. It is now ready to eat. Serve warm, sprinkled with cinnamon. Spread a tablespoon or so of *eishta*, clotted cream, or whipped cream over each portion. Serves 4.

Basbousa bil Laban Zabadi / Basbousa with Yogurt

Unsalted butter
⅓ cup blanched almonds
½ cup yogurt
¾ cup sugar
1 cup semolina
1 teaspoon baking powder
A few drops of vanilla extract

Eishta [page 392], clotted cream, or
   whipped cream [optional]

SYRUP
1 cup sugar
⅓ cup water
Juice of ½ lemon

Make a thick syrup by boiling the sugar, water, and lemon juice together and simmering until it thickens. Allow to cool, and chill.

Melt 8 tablespoons (1 stick) butter. Toast the blanched almonds and chop them finely. Beat the yogurt with the sugar in a large mixing bowl. Add the butter and all remaining ingredients except the cream, and beat well until thoroughly mixed. Pour into a large, rectangular, buttered baking tray and bake in a fairly hot oven (400°) for ½ hour.

Pour the cold syrup over the hot *basbousa* as soon as it comes out of the oven. Cut into lozenge shapes and return to the oven for a further 3 minutes.

Serve soused with 8 tablespoons hot melted butter and spread with *eishta*, thick clotted cream, or whipped cream if you like.

Basbousa bil Goz el Hind / Basbousa with Coconut

8 tablespoons (1 stick) unsalted
   butter
1½ cups semolina
¾ cup superfine sugar
½ cup flaked coconut
⅓ cup all-purpose flour
½ cup milk

1 teaspoon baking powder
A few drops of vanilla extract

SYRUP
1 cup sugar
⅓ cup water
1 tablespoon lemon juice

Prepare the syrup first by dissolving the sugar in the water and lemon juice and simmering until it is thick enough to coat a spoon (about 7 minutes). Allow to cool, and chill.

Melt the butter in a large saucepan. Add the remaining ingredients and beat well with a wooden spoon until thoroughly mixed.

Pour the mixture into a large buttered oven dish or baking tray, making a thin layer. Flatten out as much as possible. Bake in a moderate oven (375°) for about ½ hour. Look at it after 20 minutes to see if it has cooked enough. It should be crisp and a rich golden ochre.

Cut into squares or lozenge shapes as soon as it comes out of the oven, and pour the cold syrup over the hot *basbousa*.

Serve hot or cold.

Basbousa bil Loz / Basbousa with Almonds

2¼ cups water	¾ cup semolina
1½ cups sugar	Whole blanced almonds, *eishta*
1 teaspoon lemon juice	[below] or clotted or
¾ cup blanched almonds	whipped cream
½ cup butter	

Bring water, sugar, and lemon juice to a boil in a pan. Simmer for a few minutes. Chop the almonds finely and fry them in hot butter together with the semolina until they are a beautiful golden color. Add the hot syrup slowly, stirring constantly over low heat until the mixture thickens. Remove from the heat and cover the pan. Let it cool a little.

Pour into individual greased molds and flatten out on top. Unmold and serve warm. Decorate each portion with an almond or a dollop of cream.

Date and Banana Dessert

4–5 bananas	1¼ cups light cream
½ lb. pitted dates, fresh or dried	

Arrange alternate layers of thinly sliced bananas and halved dates in a serving bowl. Pour cream all over and chill for a few hours before serving. The cream will soak into the fruit and give it a soft, slightly sticky texture. A delightful way of eating dates.

Eishta / Thick Cream or Middle Eastern Clotted Cream

The rich *gamoussa* (buffalo) milk in the Middle East yields, when it is boiled, a thick cream which can be cut with a knife. Every family collects layers of this cream whenever the milk is boiled, to eat with honey or jam or with various pastries. A substitute, though not as splendid, can be made with heavy cream and milk.

Stir 5 cups milk with 1¼ cups heavy cream. Pour into a wide, shallow tray. Use the widest available to give the cream the greatest possible surface. Bring to the boil slowly. Simmer gently over very low heat so that it barely trembles for about 1½ hours. Turn off the heat and let stand for 7 hours before putting in the refrigerator. Chill overnight before using. A thick layer of cream will have formed on the surface of the milk. Using a sharp-pointed knife, detach the edges of the cream from the pan and transfer to a flat surface or a large plate. Cut into squares.

Lay the cream flat on pastries or curl it into little rolls.

Ordinary thick clotted cream or whipped cream is a good substitute for *eishta*.

Atr / Sugar Syrup

A traditional and constant feature of Middle Eastern sweets and pastries is the sugar syrup which is used to make, bathe, soak, or sprinkle most of them.

It appears almost everywhere, either thin and liquid, or thick and treacly, scented with rose water or orange blossom water, or both. These distilled essences can be obtained from every Greek store and from many pharmacists.‡

The syrup is extremely easy to make by boiling water and sugar together with a little lemon juice to prevent it from crystallizing.

The usual proportions for a syrup are:

2½ cups sugar	1–2 tablespoons or more rose water
1¼ cups water	or orange blossom water, or
1 tablespoon or more lemon juice	both

Bring sugar, water, and lemon juice to the boil, remove any scum, lower the heat, and simmer gently for 5 to 10 minutes until it has thickened.

Quantities of sugar and water can be varied according to the degree of thickness required for a particular recipe. However, one can also determine the thickness by the length of the cooking time. The longer it is simmered, the more it is reduced, and the thicker it will be. If a syrup is not thick enough, it may be thickened by further cooking and reduction. If it is too thick, it may be thinned by adding a little water, stirring, and simmering a little while longer.

The usual test to determine if a syrup has thickened is to see if it coats a spoon (a metal one). For a greater degree of thickness, one usually feels a slight (but only slight) resistance to the spoon as the syrup is stirred.

It is only when the syrup has cooled that one can know its true degree of thickness (since it always appears thin when hot). If this is not correct, it can be remedied as described above.

The flavorings of rose water or orange blossom water are stirred in at the end of the cooking and simmered for only a minute or two, as prolonged cooking impairs their aroma.

If used heavy-handedly, this syrup will give pastries the rather sweet sickly stickiness which characterizes badly made pastries in pastry shops outside the Middle East.

When syrup is used for making pastries, it must be added only when they are already baked, fried, or cooked. It is added *very cold* to the *hot* pastries. It is either poured over them as they come out of the oven; or the pastries themselves (such as *luqmat el qadi*) are dropped in for a few minutes, then lifted out, richly saturated. If this condition is not fulfilled, the result will be a failure.

Syrup can be made in advance and stored for many weeks in a glass jar, ready to be used.

ICE CREAM

Italian and French ice creams such as *sfogliatella, cassata,* and the *café liégeois* are made in masterly fashion in Egypt, but specialists excel in particularly Middle Eastern ice creams—*dondurma kaymakli,* a milk ice cream, and various granitas and fruit ices.

Ice creams are served in every café in Cairo and Alexandria. Groppi's, the Café Paradis, the Sans Souci, Cecil's, and the Beau Rivage were famous all over the world for their ices. These were made in large, barrel-shaped cylinders with hollow centers filled with a mixture of ice and salt. A rotating pole turned continually, stirring the ice cream so that it froze with a creamy soft texture. Water ices did not need stirring and were only made to freeze.

I have many happy childhood memories of long, hot afternoons spent eating ice creams. In the evenings, for a special family treat, we were taken before or after, or instead of, the cinema to "degustate" ice creams in an open-air café. There, we almost invariably met numerous relatives, friends, and acquaintances. Tables were joined together and grew to swallow up the whole café. The fragrance of the ice creams, made with ripe fruit, fresh eggs, butter, and thick cream, mingled with the scent of necklaces of threaded fresh jasmine which the fathers and husbands were compelled to buy for their women when the vendors came around the tables, their arms heavy with rows and rows of the little white flowers.

Dondurma Kaymakli / Ice Cream

A brilliantly white milk ice cream made with the starch of a root called sahlab *(sold under the name of* saleb *in England)‡ and flavored with mastic and orange blossom water. Its creamy, slightly elastic texture comes from the mastic, a hard resin which, when softened with ordinary candle wax, becomes the Middle Eastern chewing gum.*

1 teaspoon powdered *sahlab* or 1 tablespoon cornstarch	1¼ cups sugar
	¼ teaspoon mastic
3¾ cups milk	1 tablespoon orange blossom water
1¼ cups light cream	Chopped pistachio nuts, to decorate

Dissolve the powdered *sahlab* or cornstarch in a little of the cold milk. Put the rest of the milk in a saucepan together with the cream and sugar, and bring to a boil. Add the cold milk and starch mixture gradually, stirring all the time with a wooden spoon. Crush and pulverize the mastic by pounding with a little granulated sugar, and stir into the milk mixture. Simmer very gently over low heat for about 15 minutes, stirring occasionally.

Add orange blossom water, remove from the heat, and beat well with a wooden spoon. If the mixture is lumpy, use a blender to make it smooth. Pour into refrigerator trays, cover with foil, and freeze in the freezing compartment of the refrigerator, set at the lowest setting.

Beat the mixture well by hand three or four times at intervals to break up the ice crystals. Transfer to the nonfreezing part of the refrigerator for about 20 minutes before serving. The ice cream should be perfectly smooth and free of crystals. Serve in little bowls, sprinkled with chopped pistachios.

Lemon Granita— / A Sorbet

3¾ cups water
1¼ cups sugar

1 tablespoon orange blossom water
1¼ cups lemon juice

Boil water and sugar together for a few minutes, stirring until the sugar has dissolved. Cool and add orange blossom water and lemon juice. Stir well and pour into a mold or refrigerator trays. Cover with foil and place in the freezing compartment of the refrigerator, set at the lowest setting. As the ice freezes a little, beat lightly with a fork without removing it from the trays to reduce the size of the crystals. Repeat a few times at ½-hour intervals. Transfer from the freezer to another part of the refrigerator about 20 minutes before serving. Serve, if you like, in scooped-out lemon halves.

Orange Granita— / A Sorbet

2½ cups orange juice or 2 cups
    orange juice and ½ cup lemon
    juice

3¾ cups water
1¾ cups sugar
1 tablespoon orange blossom water

Strain the orange juice if you wish—I prefer not to. Add lemon juice if you prefer a slightly acid tang.
    Boil water and sugar together for 5 minutes. Remove from the heat and when cool stir in juice and orange blossom water.
    Freeze in the same way as the lemon granita above.
    A decorative way of serving the ice is to pack it into the scooped-out shells of small oranges.

PASTRIES

Baklava and Konafa (Kadaif)

Baklava and *konafa*, the grandest of Middle Eastern pastries, are the best known abroad. Unfortunately, they are known at their worst because, as with all food prepared commercially in a foreign country, they are invariably degraded. The cooking fats used are the cheapest, peanuts are sometimes used instead of pistachios and walnuts, and of course few people are in a position to judge if the pastries are well made.

Baklava and *konafa* prepared at home can be entirely different from those found in shops and restaurants. They should be light, crisp, and delicate. They may look elaborate, but they are easy and cheap to prepare, and they make an excellent dessert as well as pastries for tea.

Both can be prepared days ahead, stored in the refrigerator and baked on the day they are to be served. They also keep for several days after they have been baked.

Fila pastry, used to make *baklava*, and *konafa*, a shredded dough, can be bought at a few Greek bakeries and shops. I have described *fila* in greater detail on pages 96–8. In the old days in the Middle East, people used to make the pastry doughs at home, but today they are generally bought ready-made.

All over the Middle East, these pastries are present at every party and served at every occasion. No bakery or café could be without them. They even go in donkey carts on those national day-long picnics to the cemeteries, filling the huge baskets alongside the pickles, bread, lettuce, and *falafel* (page 47). They are part of the celebrations, the rejoicing with the dead, tokens of love for the departed, who are believed to come out from the tombs to play on the seesaws and swings, and to enjoy the merry dancers, musicians, jugglers, and *gala-gala* men with their relatives. *Baklava* and *konafa* are always brought to be shared in these happy reunions.

The pastries are not mentioned in medieval Persian or Arab works, and seem to have made their appearance in the region during the time of the Ottoman Empire. Can they be Turkish in origin, or Greek? I suspect Greek.

Baklava

1 lb. *fila* [about 24 sheets]
½ lb. (2 sticks) unsalted butter, melted
1–1½ cups pistachio nuts, walnuts, or almonds, coarsely chopped
2½ tablespoons sugar

SYRUP
1¼ cups sugar
½ cup water
1 tablespoon lemon juice
1 tablespoon orange blossom water

Buy *fila* ready-made in paper-thin sheets (see pages 96–8). You will need a large deep baking dish, round or square, and a pastry brush. Paint the dish (the sides as well) with melted butter. Fit half the number of pastry sheets in the dish one at a time, brushing each sheet with melted butter and overlapping or folding the sides over where necessary.

Mix the chopped nuts with sugar (little sugar is needed, as a syrup will be poured over the whole). Spread the nuts evenly over the sheets of pastry in the dish. Cover the remaining sheets of pastry, fitting layer after layer, folding the sides where necessary and brushing each sheet, including the top one, with melted butter. Cut diagonally into lozenge shapes with a sharp knife.

Prepare the syrup, unless you have made it earlier. Dissolve the sugar in water and lemon juice and simmer until it thickens enough to coat a spoon. Add orange blossom water and simmer for another 2 minutes. Allow to cool, and chill lightly in the refrigerator.

Bake the *baklava* for ½ hour in a preheated slow to moderate oven (350° to 375°), then raise the heat to 450° or 475° and bake for 15 minutes longer. The *baklava* should be puffed and a very light golden color. Remove from the oven and quickly pour the *very cold* syrup over the *hot baklava*. Leave to cool.

When cold and ready to serve, cut the pieces of pastry out again and place them separately on a serving dish; or turn the whole dish out (by turning it upside down onto a large plate and then turning it over again on the serving dish) and cut out again along the original lines.

A variation called *kul-wa-shkur* ("eat and thank") is filled with ground almonds mixed with half their weight in sugar. The syrup provides extra sweetness.

Konafa—called Kadaif by Greeks and Turks

The dough for this pastry can also be bought ready-made in Greek shops. It is made of flour and water mixed into a liquid batter and thrown through a strainer onto a hot metal sheet over a small fire. The dough sets in strands which are swept off the sheet very quickly and remain soft. They look like vermicelli or shredded wheat, only soft, white, and uncooked.

You can make konafa *with two different fillings, a cream filling or one of walnuts or pistachios.*

1 lb. *konafa* pastry
½ lb. (2 sticks) unsalted butter, melted

SYRUP
1¼ cups sugar
½ cup water
1 tablespoon lemon juice
1 tablespoon orange blossom water

CREAM FILLING
4 tablespoons ground rice ‡
2 tablespoons sugar
2½ cups milk
½ cup heavy cream
or
WALNUT OR PISTACHIO FILLING
2 cups pistachios or walnuts, coarsely chopped
2½ tablespoons sugar

Prepare the syrup by stirring the sugar, water, and lemon juice over moderate heat, then simmering until it thickens and coats a spoon. Stir in orange blossom water and cook for 2 minutes longer. Cool and chill lightly in the refrigerator. Prepare either of the following fillings.

Cream filling: mix ground rice and sugar to a smooth paste with ½ cup milk. Boil the rest of the milk and add the ground rice paste slowly, stirring vigorously. Simmer, stirring, until very thick. Then allow to cool, add cream, and mix well.

Walnut or pistachio filling: mix the chopped nuts with the sugar.

Put the *konafa* pastry in a large bowl. Pull out and separate the strands as much as possible with your fingers so that they do not stick together too much. Pour melted butter over them and work it in very thoroughly with your fingers, pulling the shreds and mixing so that each one is entirely coated with butter. Put half the pastry in a large, deep oven dish. Spread the filling over it evenly and cover with the rest of the pastry, evening it out and flattening it with the palm of your hand.

Bake in a preheated slow to moderate oven (350° to 375°) for 45 minutes, then in a hot oven (450° to 475°) for only 10 to 15 minutes longer, until it is a light golden color. Remove from the oven and immediately pour the *cold* syrup over the *hot konafa*.

Serve hot or cold.

Konafa can also be made into small, individual rolled pastries. This is the form in which they are most commonly sold in pastry shops. The threads of dough are wrapped around a filling of chopped or ground walnuts, chopped pistachios, or ground almonds to which a little sugar and some rose water have been added. One way of making them is to lay a flat bundle of threads of dough moistened with melted butter on a clean surface. Lay a flat stick or a wide skewer along it diagonally. Arrange the filling over the stick or skewer, then roll or flap the threads of dough tightly around the stick. Slip the stick out carefully, leaving the filling inside the roll. Arrange the rolls on baking trays and bake as described above. Then pour cold syrup over them as they come out of the oven. Cut into individual portions and serve, preferably cold. One traditional way of baking the rolls is to arrange them in a spiral in a round baking tin. A more uncommon but particularly delicious *konafa* similar to the cream-filled one is filled instead with a slightly salty, soft cheese such as Italian ricotta. The cold sugar syrup is poured over the hot *konafa* and combines with the cheese to give an unusually fine taste.

Luqmat el Qadi or *Zalabia* / Little Round Fritters in Syrup

Popularly known as *zalabia* in Egypt, these are tiny, light crisp, golden fritters soaked in an orange blossom and rose-scented syrup. A medieval recipe is given in al-Baghdadi's cooking manual for these doughnuts, bearing the same name, which means "judge's mouthfuls." In the Lebanon they are called *aweimat*. The Greeks have a similar sweet called *loukoumades*, and I suspect that the name is derived from the Arabic one. They are also very popular in Spain, where they were probably introduced by the Arabs.

Zalabia are often sold in the streets during festivals. They are deep-fried and thrown into a rich syrup, sometimes colored bright yellow or red for joy and happiness, then sprinkled with sugar, and sometimes cinnamon. They make a glorious party dish, served piled in a pyramid on a large platter, held together by the thick syrup.

Various recipes exist for the leavened dough, which is basically made of flour, water, and yeast mixed to a very soft, elastic paste. Here is one.

3½ cups all-purpose flour
½ oz. (1 cake) fresh yeast or ¼ oz.
   (1 package) dried yeast

1 teaspoon sugar
2½ cups lukewarm water [or 1¼
   cups water and 1¼ cups milk]

Sift the flour into a large, warmed mixing bowl. Dissolve the yeast with the sugar and a little of the water, and leave in a warm place until frothy. Add the remaining water to the yeast mixture, beating constantly. Add this to the flour gradually, beating vigorously. The very soft dough will be rather like a pancake batter, but not quite as liquid.

Cover with a clean cloth and leave in a warm place to rise for 1 hour. Beat vigorously and allow to rest and rise again; then beat again. The secret of making good, perfectly round *zalabia* is to beat the dough at regular intervals (at least three times, more often if possible) and allow it to rest again. This should result in a very elastic texture.

While the dough is resting, prepare a sugar syrup:

5 cups sugar
2–2½ cups water
2½ tablespoons lemon juice

2½ tablespoons rose water
2½ tablespoons orange blossom
   water

Dissolve the sugar in water and lemon juice, and simmer until the syrup thickens and coats the back of a spoon. Add the rose and orange blossom water, and continue to simmer for 2 minutes longer. Allow to cool, then chill in the refrigerator until required. The syrup must be very cold when used.

Gently heat 2 inches of corn or nut oil in a saucepan. Beat the dough. Take a small teaspoonful of dough with a wet spoon and drop it into the not too hot oil, or for a rounder shape, press dollops out of a pastry tube. Fry gently, only a few at a time. They will rise to the surface quickly in the shape of little round balls. Turn them over. When they are crisp and a beautiful golden brown, remove them with a slotted spoon and drain them on absorbent paper. Dip them in the cold syrup while they are still very hot and lift them out again. They will absorb the syrup immediately and become deliciously soaked. They can be eaten hot or cold, sprinkled with sugar and, if you like, dusted with cinnamon.

Ma'Amoul / Stuffed Tartlets

Ma'amoul *are glorious little stuffed pastries that can have many different shapes and fillings. It is always a thrill to bite them and to find walnuts, pistachios, almonds, or dates. They are an Easter specialty.*

An uncle told us of a baking competition organized by a dignitary in Aleppo many years ago. The maker of the best ma'amoul *would get a prize, the equivalent of about five dollars, to be paid by the dignitary. Hundreds of* ma'amoul *poured into his house, certainly more than five dollars' worth, and enough to keep him eating happily for months.*

This recipe makes about 40 ma'amoul.

2½ cups all-purpose flour
½ lb. (2 sticks) unsalted butter
1 tablespoon orange blossom or rose water

3–4 tablespoons milk or water
Date or Nut Filling [below]
Sifted confectioner's sugar

Sift the flour into a large mixing bowl. Work butter into the flour, and mix thoroughly by hand. Add orange blossom or rose water, followed by milk or water, and work the dough until it is soft, malleable, and easy to shape.

Take a walnut-sized lump of dough. Roll it into a ball and hollow it out with your thumb. Pinch the sides up to make a pot shape. Fill with either of the two fillings below, then press and pinch the dough back over the filling, making a little ball shape. Place the pastries on a large oven tray. Decorate the tops of the pastries with tweezers or make little dents with a fork. (This will help the confectioner's sugar to cling when they are baked.) Bake in a preheated slow oven (350°) for 20 to 25 minutes. Do not let the pastries become brown. They will become hard and their taste will be spoiled. While they are still warm, they will appear soft and uncooked, but on cooling they will become firm.

When cold, roll them in confectioner's sugar. They will keep for a long time in a tightly closed container.

A simpler version of this is the *ma'amoul* date roll. For this use only the date filling below. Divide the dough into four parts. Roll out and flatten each part into a rectangle 2 inches wide. Spread the filling over each rectangle thinly and roll up lengthwise into thick sausage shapes. Cut diagonally into 1¼-inch sections. Pinch tops or decorate with a fork so that they will hold the sugar better. Bake as above and, when cold, roll in confectioner's sugar.

Fillings for Ma'Amoul

1. DATE FILLING

Chop 1 lb. pitted dates. Put them in a saucepan with about ¼ cup water. Cook over low heat, stirring, until the dates have softened into a practically homogenous mass. Allow to cool.

2. NUT FILLING

1½–2 cups walnuts, almonds, or
    pistachio nuts, finely chopped
1–1¼ cups sugar

1 tablespoon rose water or ground
    cinnamon

Mix the chopped nuts with sugar. Add rose water if you are using almonds or pistachios, cinnamon if you are using walnuts. Mix well.

Karabij

This sweet consists of small round ma'amoul *pastries bathed in a brilliant white cream with a very distinctive flavor, called* naatiffe.

1 recipe *Ma'amoul* (p. 402)
1 recipe Nut Filling (above)

NAATIFFE CREAM
2–3 oz. Bois de Panama [erh halawa
    or "soul of the sweet"]*
1¼ cups sugar
1 tablespoon lemon juice
1 tablespoon orange blossom water
Whites of 3 large eggs

Prepare the *ma'amoul* dough exactly as described in the basic recipe, but leave out rose or orange blossom water, and use water rather than milk to bind. Shape the *ma'amoul* and fill them with nut filling. Do not decorate their tops. Bake as directed and cool.

Prepare the cream. Pulverize or grind the dried white branch of Bois de Panama. Soak it for several hours in ½ cup water. Transfer to a *large* saucepan together with the soaking water, and boil until the mixture has thickened and is reduced to about a quarter of the original volume. Take care while doing this, as the mixture foams and rises considerably. Strain through cheesecloth.

Heat the sugar with ½ cup water until dissolved. Bring to the boil and add lemon juice. Simmer until thickened. Add the orange blossom water, and remove from the heat. Add the hot solution of Bois de Panama (off the heat, as otherwise it will foam up and overflow), stirring vigorously with a fork. Leave to cool.

Beat the egg whites until very stiff. Add the heavy cold syrup mix-

* Available in Greek shops under the name of halawa wood.

ture gradually as you would add oil to a mayonnaise, beating vigorously all the time. It will froth and expand. You can use an electric mixer.

Dip each *ma'amoul* in this thick, brilliantly white cream, making sure it is well coated. Arrange them in a pyramid in a serving dish and pour the rest of the cream over them.

Sanbusak bil Loz / Almond Rissoles

These are prepared with the dough given under savory *sanbusak* on page 89, using a little sugar instead of salt, and a filling of 1 cup ground almonds mixed with 1 cup sugar and 2 tablespoons orange blossom water.‡

Roll the dough out thinly and cut into rounds with a tumbler. Put a teaspoon of filling in the center of each round. Fold in half, making a half-moon shape, and pinch and fold the edges firmly in a sort of festoon.

Deep-fry the pastries in hot oil until golden brown, and drain on absorbent paper. Alternatively, paint their tops with lightly beaten egg yolk and bake in a preheated moderate oven (375°) for ½ hour until a pale golden color.

Ghorayebah

These are charming, plain pastries that appear to melt in the mouth and are very simple to make.

1 lb. unsalted butter
1 cup superfine sugar
2 cups all-purpose flour, sifted

Blanched almonds or pistachio
nuts, to decorate

Cream the butter and beat it until it becomes white. Add the sugar gradually, beating constantly for about 5 minutes, or until it is a smooth cream. Stir in flour slowly and knead by hand. Although no liquid is added, this makes a very soft dough. If the dough is too soft, add a little more flour.

There are two traditional shapes for *ghorayebah*. Make walnut-sized balls, flatten one side of them on a baking tray, and stick a blanched almond on top of each one. Alternatively, roll the dough into 4-inch-long sausage shapes about ½ inch thick, and bring the ends together to make bracelets. Decorate the tops with chopped almonds or pistachio nuts. Place the bracelets on baking trays, a little apart, as they will spread slightly.

Bake in a slow oven (350°) for 20 to 30 minutes. Do not let the *ghorayebah* overcook or get even slightly brown. They must remain very white, and they taste quite different if they are even slightly browned.

Serve these delicate, light cakes with tea or coffee.

An exquisite variation is to replace 1 cup of the flour with 1 cup ground hazelnuts.

Assabih bi Loz / Almond Fingers

These pastries are extremely easy to make and delightfully light. They feature in medieval manuscripts as lauzinaj, *which were fried and sprinkled with syrup, rose water, and chopped pistachios.*

½ lb. fila pastry sheets [see page 96]	1 cup granulated sugar, or to taste
About 8 tablespoons (1 stick) unsalted butter, melted	1 tablespoon orange blossom water or ground cinnamon
1 cup ground almonds, pistachios, or walnuts	Superfine sugar, to decorate

Cut the sheets of *fila* into three rectangles approximately 5 inches by 10 inches. Brush the center of each rectangle with melted butter.

Prepare a filling of ground almonds or pistachios mixed with sugar and orange blossom water, or of walnuts mixed with sugar and cinnamon.

Put 1 heaping teaspoon filling at one end of each rectangle. Fold the longer sides slightly over the filling and roll up into a cigar shape. Place on a buttered baking tray and bake in a preheated slow to moderate oven (350° to 375°) for about 20 minutes, or until slightly colored.

Serve cold, sprinkled with superfine sugar.

You may deep-fry the pastries instead of baking them, in not very hot oil and for only a very short time, until lightly colored. Drain on absorbent paper and dust with sugar. Serve hot or cold.

Trovados

A Sephardic variation of the Arab sanbusak bil loz on page 405. The dough is made with sweet red wine, which gives the pastries an unusual color and flavor. Like the Arab version, these pastries are stuffed with a mixture of ground almonds and sugar, perfumed with rose and orange blossom water.

DOUGH
2 cups all-purpose flour
1 tablespoon sugar
½ lb. unsalted butter or margarine
1¼ cups sweet red wine

FILLING
1½ cups ground almonds
1 cup superfine sugar
2 tablespoons rose water

Sift the flour into a bowl. Add sugar and work in butter or margarine. Add wine gradually, working it in quickly, until the dough has the consistency of wet sand. Allow to rest for 15 minutes.

Roll the dough out thinly and prepare the pastries as in the recipe for *sanbusak*, but only 2 inches wide, putting a teaspoon of filling in each one. Bake in a preheated slow to moderate oven (350° to 375°) for about ½ hour, or until the *trovados* are done and lightly colored. They will be a soft pink color and have a faint taste of wine. This recipe makes about 40 *trovados*.

Serve on a wide, shallow dish, sprinkled with syrup (½ cup water and a little lemon juice to 1 cup sugar).

Ataïf / Arab Pancakes

Ataïf is a sweet dearly loved all over the Middle East, a medieval dish which has remained unchanged to this day. It was particularly favored by the Caliph Mustakfi of Baghdad in the tenth century, to whom a poem, written by a certain Mahmud ibn al Husain Kushajim about the merits of the sweet, was recited at a lavish banquet in honor of the Caliph.

Ataïf are basically pancakes dipped in syrup. Sometimes they are sprinkled with pistachios and eaten with thick cream, sometimes piled high on a platter in a pyramid of alternate layers of ataïf *and cream. Or they may also be stuffed with chopped walnuts, sugar, and cinnamon.*

They are eaten as often as possible during festivals and on happy occasions. Ataïf is the special sweet of the Id es-Saghir after the fast of Ramadan. It is also a wedding sweet. In Egypt, on the day of betrothal, a string of camels or donkeys brings the bride's furniture and belongings to the house of the bridegroom, while he gives a farewell "stag" banquet complete with dancers and singers. The young bride has a ritual bath and is then conducted to her new home by a colorful procession headed by buffoons and musicians, dancers, jugglers, sword swallowers, and fire eaters, and followed by numerous, lavishly decorated donkey carts. The first cart carries a coffee maker with pots and cups and a fire, making coffee for well-wishers. The second carries makers of ma'amoul and trays covered with these pastries to distribute. The third carries pancake makers, handing out ataïf *to passersby.*

When the bride arrives at the house, she sits down with her guests to a feast where hundreds of ataïf *are gleefully consumed.*

This was common in the past and is still done in some parts today.

Families nowadays usually buy their ataïf *ready-made from bakeries, and then stuff them and dip them in syrup. But the batter is easy enough to make at home. Several people I know always make it themselves. None have weights, nor do they measure quantities. They just look at the batter and add more water or more flour if they* think it requires it. *An aunt who lives in California and who has never ceased to cook in the Oriental manner uses the well-known pancake mix, Aunt Jemima, which is very acceptable.*

The recipe below will make about 36 ataïf.

BATTER
½ oz. (1 cake) fresh yeast or ¼ oz. (1 package) dried yeast
1 teaspoon sugar
1¼ cups lukewarm water
1½ cups all-purpose flour

SYRUP
2½ cups sugar
1¼ cups water
1 tablespoon lemon juice
1–2 tablespoons orange blossom water

Oil
Whipped cream or clotted cream
Chopped pistachio nuts or almonds

Dissolve the yeast with 1 teaspoon sugar in ¼ cup lukewarm water. Allow it to stand in a warm place for 10 minutes, or until it begins to bubble. Sift the flour into a large bowl. Add the yeast mixture and work it into the flour. Add the remaining water gradually, stirring constantly, until the batter is smooth. Leave the bowl in a warm place, covered with a cloth, for about 1 hour. The soft, almost liquid batter will rise and become bubbly and a little elastic.

Make a syrup by dissolving the sugar in water with lemon juice and simmering it until it is thick enough to coat the back of a spoon. Stir in orange blossom water and simmer for 2 minutes longer. Allow it to cool, then chill in the refrigerator.

When the batter is ready, dip a piece of cotton or paper towel in oil and rub a heavy frying pan with it so as to grease it with a very thin film of oil. Heat the pan until it is very hot, then reduce the heat and keep it at medium.

Pour 1 tablespoon of batter into the pan, tilting the pan a little to allow it to spread. It will not spread out too much and will remain in a small, round, fattish shape. (Do not try to spread it out too much.) When the pancake loses its whiteness, becomes bubbly, and comes away from the pan easily, lift it out with a palette knife. *Fry one side of the pancake only if you are making stuffed pancakes.* Otherwise, flip it over and cook the other side.

Put the pancakes aside in a pile on a plate. They should be somewhat thick and spongy.

The *ataïf* can be eaten flat, as they are. Dip each one in the cold syrup and spread with thick cream. In the Middle East a cream made from buffalo's milk called *eishta* is used (see page 392). You may, instead, use whipped cream or clotted cream. Sprinkle chopped pistachios or almonds over the cream. Serve 3 or 4 per person.

A beautiful way of serving *ataïf* at a party is to make the plain *ataïf*, fry them on both sides, and dip them in syrup as above. Put a layer of *ataïf* on a round serving dish, spread it with *eishta* (no other cream will do), and sprinkle with chopped pistachios or almonds. Repeat several times, making a pyramid, and ending with a layer of cream and nuts.

Stuffed Ataïf

To my taste, the stuffed ataïf *are the most exquisite ones. When making these, remember to fry one side of the pancakes only (the other side must remain moist so that its edges can be stuck together). Pile them up on a plate as you make them.*

1. ATAÏF STUFFED WITH EISHTA

Put a tablespoon of *eishta* (page 392) on the unfried side of each pancake. Clotted cream and whipped cream are not suitable in this case, as they would melt and ooze out when fried. (An unsalted cheese such as Italian ricotta may, however, be used.) Fold it in half and pinch the edges together firmly to seal them, making a half-moon shape and trapping the filling.

Drop each pancake in very hot oil and deep-fry for 2 to 3 minutes until a pale golden color. Remove with a perforated spoon. Drain well on absorbent paper. Dip the hot pancakes in syrup and serve hot or cold. If you have a very sweet tooth, serve them with the syrup poured over them.

2. ATAÏF STUFFED WITH NUTS

Make a filling of ½ lb. (2 cups) shelled walnuts, chopped, 4 tablespoons sugar, and 2 teaspoons ground cinnamon. Stuff and deep-fry the pancakes as above.

Arab saying condemning an ostentatious wedding: "The bride is a frog, but the wedding is a cyclone."

Eish es Seray or Ekmek Kadaif / Palace Bread

A popular sweet, not usually made at home. Some bakeries and cafés always have a tray full of the rich, translucent, golden-ochre bread soaked in honey and syrup. Numerous recipes exist, and of course the quality and taste of the dish depend on the bread and honey used.

Make a thick syrup by dissolving 3½ cups sugar in 1 cup water and 1 tablespoon lemon juice, and simmering until it thickens. Add ½ to 1¼ cups honey, preferably a delicate one (Hymettus or acacia), and 1 or 2 tablespoons of rose water. Stir well and simmer for 2 minutes longer.

Use a large round loaf, such as those found in Greek and Italian shops. Cut a round of bread horizontally through the widest part so that after all the crusts are removed it is ½ to ¾ inch thick. Dry out in a very low oven. Pour the syrup into a wide, shallow pan which will hold the whole bread. You can darken the syrup to a deep rich brown (the traditional color for this sweet) by melting 2 tablespoons sugar in another pan until it is a dark brown caramel and stirring it into the syrup. Bring the syrup to a boil. Place the bread slice in it and simmer very gently, squashing and pressing it down with a wooden spoon to help it to absorb the syrup better. Cook until the bread is entirely soaked through and is soft, rich, and heavy.

Turn out onto a round serving platter and allow to cool.

Serve spread with a very thick layer of clotted cream or whipped cream and sprinkled with chopped pistachios. In the Middle East they use the cream called *eishta* (page 392), which is thick enough to be cut with a knife.

Individual square slices of bread can be used in the same way as the large round and simmered until soaked through.

Another successful way of making this sweet, although not as authentic, is to use Holland rusks instead of bread. They need only be dipped in the syrup for a moment or two to become thoroughly soaked.

Sweet Turkish Börek

Ancient recipes call these little pastries taratir-at-turkman *or "bonnets of the Turks." The quantities below make a large number of pastries.*

5 egg yolks
½ teaspoon salt
4 tablespoons superfine sugar
2 tablespoons brandy

7 tablespoons yogurt
3½ cups self-rising flour
Oil for deep-frying
Confectioner's sugar

Place the egg yolks in a large mixing bowl, add salt, and beat until thick and lemon-colored. Add the sugar and brandy, and continue beating. Add the yogurt and mix well. Sift in the flour, stirring with a wooden spoon to begin with, and then working the dough by hand.

Knead on a floured board until the dough blisters, then roll out as thinly as possible with a floured rolling pin. Cut into ribbons about 1 inch wide, then divide into 3-inch strips. Make an inch-long slit down the center of each strip and pull one end through—or tie the strips in knots, which is rather easier.

Fry in deep oil which is not too hot until the pastries are puffed and just golden, turning once. Lift out with a perforated spoon. Drain on absorbent paper and sprinkle with confectioner's sugar.

SEPHARDIC CAKES

Among the minority dishes of the Middle East, there are some which are particularly Sephardic Jewish in origin. Besides peculiarities due to their religious dietary laws, such as the use of oil and vegetable cooking fats instead of butter or *samna* (clarified butter), the Jews brought with them their favorite dishes from previous homelands. The main feature of Sephardic cooking as distinct from Middle Eastern cooking, which the Jews also practice, is the evidence of Spanish and Portuguese influence.

During the fourteenth and fifteenth centuries, the time of the Inquisition, thousands of Jews left Spain and Portugal after a thousand years of life in the Peninsula. Many headed toward the countries of the Middle East. The local Arab Jews, overwhelmed by their superior intellect, high rank, and refined social manners, copied and adopted their language, manners, and customs, as well as their dishes. These dishes, similar to those prepared in Spain today—some still bearing Spanish names—are still faithfully prepared by Middle Eastern Jews. Among them are cakes baked specially for the Jewish Passover, made with ground almonds instead of flour. During Passover dried bread crumbs are not used either, nor is the baking pan floured. Instead, fine matzo meal is substituted for both.

These cakes, which are half pudding, half cakes, can never fail. If they are undercooked they make a fine dessert with cream. They are too moist ever to be overcooked or to dry up.

Orange and Almond Cake

2 large oranges
6 eggs
1½ cups ground almonds
1 cup sugar

1 teaspoon baking powder

Butter and flour, for cake pan

Wash and boil the oranges (unpeeled) in a little water for nearly 2 hours (or ½ hour in a pressure cooker). Let them cool, then cut them open and remove the pips. Turn the oranges into a pulp by rubbing them through a strainer or by putting them in an electric blender.

Beat the eggs in a large bowl. Add the other ingredients, mix thoroughly, and pour into a buttered and floured cake pan with a removable base if possible. Bake in a preheated moderately hot oven (400°) for about 60 minutes. Have a look at it after 1 hour—this type of cake will not go any flatter if the oven door is opened. If it is still very wet, leave it in the oven for a little longer. Cool in the pan before turning out. This is a very moist cake.

Another Orange and Almond Cake

5 eggs	1 tablespoon grated orange rind
½ cup sugar	1 tablespoon orange blossom water
⅓ cup ground almonds	
3 tablespoons matzo meal or fine dry white bread crumbs	Butter and flour, for cake pan

Beat the eggs well in a large bowl. Add the remaining ingredients and mix thoroughly. Pour the mixture into a buttered and floured cake tin and bake in a preheated moderate oven (375°) for about ¾ to 1 hour. Cool in the pan, then turn out.

Chocolate Cake

½ lb. bitter or plain chocolate	6 eggs, separated
2½ tablespoons milk	Butter
¾ cup ground almonds	Flour
8 tablespoons sugar	Superfine sugar, to decorate

Melt the chocolate with the milk in the top of a double boiler over boiling water. Mix the melted chocolate with the ground almonds, sugar, and egg yolks, and beat well. Fold in the stiffly beaten egg whites and pour into a buttered and floured cake pan, preferably one with a removable base. Bake in a preheated moderate oven (375°) for about ¾ to 1 hour.

When the cake is cool, turn out and sprinkle the top with sugar.

Similar cakes are made with matzo meal or farina potato flour instead of ground almonds, used in the same proportions. They are very good, but not as rich or full of flavor.

Hazelnut Cake

6 egg whites
8 tablespoons sugar
2 cups hazelnuts, coarsely ground
2½ tablespoons matzo meal or fine dry white bread crumbs
Butter
Flour

FILLING
6 egg yolks
8 tablespoons sugar
6 oz. cooking chocolate
1 tablespoon butter

DECORATION
4–5 tablespoons sugar
Handful of shelled hazelnuts

Beat the egg whites until stiff and fold in sugar thoroughly. Fold in coarsely ground hazelnuts. (Do not grind them too finely or they will be oily. They should be felt in the cake.) Fold in the matzo meal or bread crumbs. Pour the mixture gently into a buttered and floured cake tin, preferably one with a removable base. Bake in a preheated moderate oven (350° to 375°) for ¾ to 1 hour. Cool. Turn out and split into two layers.

Make the filling. Beat the yolks until lemon-colored. Add the chocolate, melted in a double boiler. Soften the butter and blend it into the mixture. Return to the double boiler and cook over boiling water, stirring, until the filling thickens. Allow to cool.

Spread the filling between the layers, put them together, and spread remaining filling over the top.

If you like, heat a little sugar in a small pan until it becomes liquid and brown. Stir in a handful of shelled hazelnuts and pour out onto an oiled slab or plate. When it is hard, break it into small pieces with a knife, or pound in a mortar. Arrange in a pattern or sprinkle over the top and sides of the cake.

Walnut Cake with Coffee Filling

6 eggs, separated
8 tablespoons sugar
1 cup walnuts, coarsely ground
1 cup matzo meal or fine dry white
    bread crumbs
A few drops vanilla extract
Butter
Flour
Chopped walnuts, to decorate

FILLING
8 tablespoons (1 stick) butter
½ cup superfine sugar
1 small coffee cup strong black
    coffee or 2 tablespoons instant
    coffee dissolved in a little boil-
    ing water

Beat the egg yolks with the sugar until lemon-colored. Add the walnuts. These are better only coarsely ground; if too fine, they might be a little oily, and the merit of the cake lies in distinguishing their texture. Add the meal or bread crumbs and vanilla sugar. Mix well. Fold in the stiffly beaten egg whites and pour into a buttered and floured cake pan, preferably one with a removable base. Bake in a preheated oven (375°) for ¾ to 1 hour. Allow to cool, then turn out of the pan.

When cold, cut the cake into two layers and spread the bottom layer with part of the coffee filling. Make this by creaming the butter, adding sugar, and beating well; then add the coffee, beat again to blend, and allow to cool until firm. Put the two layers together again and spread the top of the cake with filling as well. Sprinkle with chopped walnuts.

Coconut Cake

6 eggs, separated
8 tablespoons sugar
4 oz. flaked coconut
1 tablespoon orange blossom or rose
    water ‡ or a few drops of va-
    nilla extract
Butter
Flour
½ cup each heavy and light cream

FILLING
4 oz. flaked coconut
½ cup sugar
A drop of lemon juice
1 tablespoon orange blossom water

Beat the egg yolks with sugar until thick and lemon-colored. Add coconut and flavoring, and mix well. Fold in the stiffly beaten egg whites and pour into a buttered and floured cake pan. Bake in a pre-heated moderate oven (375°) for about 45 minutes. Allow to cool and cut in two layers.

Prepare the filling. Sprinkle the coconut with cold water to moisten it thoroughly. Make a syrup by dissolving sugar in about ⅓ cup water and a drop of lemon juice. Simmer for about 5 minutes. Add coconut and simmer for a few minutes longer. The coconut will swell and become creamy. Stir in orange blossom water. This is really a coconut jam.

Whip the cream. Spread half the coconut between the cake layers and pour what is left of the syrup over them. It will enrich the cake. Put the layers together again and spread the thick whipped cream over the top of the cake. Finish with the rest of the partially drained coconut jam spread over the top.

Hojuelos de Haman

A Sephardic Jewish specialty commemorating the defeat of Haman by Esther and Mordechai. The pastries symbolize Haman's ears and are usually prepared for the feast of Purim. The pastry itself, though authentic, is not particularly exciting, but its shape is. For a tastier pastry I suggest that you try the one given for Turkish sweet börek *(page 412) instead.*

3 eggs	Oil for deep frying
½ teaspoon salt	Cinnamon sugar or clear honey or
2 tablespoons superfine sugar	sugar syrup
2¼ cups all-purpose flour	

Beat the eggs until light and thick. Add salt, sugar, and 4 tablespoons water, and beat well. Sift in enough flour to make a rather soft dough which does not stick to the fingers. Knead until smooth.

Roll the dough out thinly on a lightly floured board. Cut it in half-moon shapes with a pastry cutter. Pinch the centers of the shapes like bow ties and fold the two leaflike ends up to make "ears."

Deep-fry in hot oil until golden, turning the pastries over once.

Serve hot or cold, dusted with cinnamon sugar or sprinkled with clear honey or sugar syrup.

A variation is to replace 1 or 2 tablespoons water with the same quantity of rose water or orange blossom water,‡ or to replace all three with sweet white or red wine. Two tablespoons of melted butter may be added to the dough. In this case, use only one egg.

PETITS FOURS

Among Middle Eastern pastries there are some very small delicacies which are easy to prepare in large quantities, and which make excellent *petits fours* to serve at large parties or after dinner with coffee. Several are made with ground almonds and sugar. There are also apricot drops, dates, and walnuts stuffed with ground almonds, caramelized hazelnuts, pistachios, and walnuts.

Various recipes exist for almond paste. Some date back to medieval times. All are still very popular today. Many are traditionally cut into lozenge shapes: in fact, it is believed that the etymology of the word "lozenge" is derived from these Arab sweets made with almonds, the word for which is *loz* in Arabic.

I was surprised to find these same little sweets in every bakery and pastry shop in Portugal, where they are said to be a national specialty. Their Spanish names, such as *mogados* and *maronchinos*, are still used in Middle Eastern Sephardic circles today. The Spanish Sephardic saying "A los añnos maronchinos?" (Does one give *maronchinos* to donkeys?) denotes the high esteem in which these delicacies are held.

Almond Drops

These are the simplest to make, and my favorites.

¾ cup ground almonds
¾ cup sifted confectioner's sugar
4–5 tablespoons orange blossom
    water ‡

Additional confectioner's sugar and
    halved almonds or pistachio
    nuts, to decorate

Mix the ground almonds, confectioner's sugar, and enough orange blossom water to make a stiff paste; knead by hand until smooth. Let the paste rest for a few minutes. Wash and dry your hands, and shape the paste into little balls the size of large marbles. Roll them in confectioner's sugar. Decorate if you like with halved almonds or pistachio nuts imbedded in the top of the balls. Serve in individual little paper cases.

A variation is to stuff the almond balls with chopped pistachios. This is really superb. Make a little hole in each almond ball with your finger and fill it with chopped pistachios mixed with granulated sugar. Close the hole over the pistachios and shape into a ball again. Roll the balls in confectioner's sugar and place them in small paper cases. Decorate the top of each ball with a whole or half pistachio which has been stripped of its thin skin to make its greenness apparent.

Arab proverb: "A year in which there are plenty of almonds and dates increases prosperity and life."

Kahk bi Loz / Almond Bracelets

Use a paste similar to that given for almond drops above. To 3 cups ground almonds mixed with 5 cups confectioner's sugar and enough orange blossom water to make a firm, dryish paste, add the white of 1 small egg, stiffly beaten. (For a paste made with 1½ cups ground almonds, only half the amount of egg white is necessary. Do not be tempted to add more.)

Mix the paste and egg white well, and roll into thin cigarette shapes. Bring the ends together and flatten them, making bracelets the size of small napkin rings. Decorate, if you like, with a few blanched almonds. Alternatively, make little round, flattened ball shapes and stick a blanched almond in the middle. Arrange on well-buttered baking trays.

Bake in a preheated slow oven (350°) for about 10 minutes. The bracelets must not be allowed to color. They will be soft while hot, but become firm on cooling.

These almond bracelets are favorites at engagement and wedding parties. They are also traditionally served at the ritual bath of a young bride. My mother went through this ceremony on her wedding day, but today, although it is still common in rural districts, the custom is fast disappearing from modern town weddings.

The bride goes to the public bath accompanied by her female relatives and friends. She walks with a woman at each side, under a canopy of silk borne by four men. Married ladies head the procession, followed by young, unmarried girls. The bride walks behind.

At the bath, she washes in scented water, watched by all the women and girls. A feast follows. While the guests are entertained by female singers, large trays piled high with pastries are passed around. No feast of this type could be without the traditional *kakh bi loz.*

Among the songs sung at the bath, one goes as follows:

Shimmering, shimmering, little lettuce heart, shimmering!
O my little brother, she is white, and her whiteness is tinted with
*   pomegranate!*
O my little brother, she is white, and her whiteness is seductive!

On such occasions the relatives try to assess if the girl will make a good wife and if she will be able to bear children easily. Remarks abound on the width of her hips and the size of her breasts.

A PERSIAN TALE*

A peasant went into town. As he walked through the bazaar, he came across a confectionery shop with all sorts of brightly colored confectionery displayed on the street. The owner of the shop sat on the doorstep.

The peasant went up to him, pointed two fingers at his eyes and said: "Hou!"

The confectioner asked him why he had done that.

"I thought you were blind and could not see me!" came the reply.

* Christensen, *Contes persans.*

"But I am not blind!" said the confectioner.
"Then how," asked the peasant, "if you can see, can you resist eating your sweets?"

Stuffed Walnuts

¾ cup ground almonds
½ cup superfine sugar
4 tablespoons or more orange
 blossom water ‡

20 shelled walnuts
½ cup granulated sugar

Make a firm paste by mixing the ground almonds, superfine sugar, and orange blossom water together thoroughly. Add more orange blossom water if necessary, to bind the paste. Squeeze about 1 teaspoon of the paste between two walnut halves. Place these on a cold oiled surface.

Make a little caramel by heating and stirring the granulated sugar until it melts and turns a light brown color. Pour a little over each walnut. When it is cold and hard, it will hold the walnut halves together.

Place in little paper cases to serve.

Glazed Nut Clusters

Caramelized almonds, hazelnuts, and pistachio nuts were among the range of confectionery sold on the beaches of Alexandria when I was a child. Young vendors paced the sands carrying confections and sweetmeats in large, flat wicker baskets, chanting *"Fresca!"*—a name probably originating from the Italian, meaning "fresh." They balanced the baskets on their heads, resting them on a coiled piece of soft cloth, and sometimes carried a second basket perched on one hip and held at the other side by an outstretched hand. Their chant was echoed by that of other vendors singing: *"Casquette, baranet, pantofla, pastillia, chocolat!"* (caps, hats, slippers, pastilles, chocolate), or *"Gazouza, gazouza!"* (lemonade). Some sold salted roasted peanuts and pistachios as well as confectionery, and they gambled for these in games of odds-and-evens with their customers.

To make nut clusters, put about 1 lb. hazelnuts, almonds, or pistachio nuts together in little heaps on an oiled marble slab or on a large oiled plate. Melt 2 cups or more granulated sugar over very low heat, stirring constantly. Allow the caramel to become light brown, then pour it over the nut clusters. As it cools, the caramel will harden and hold the nuts together.

Alternatively, and perhaps more simply though less attractively, the nuts or almonds can be thrown into the hot, light brown caramel and stirred until they are all well coated. Pour the whole onto an oiled slab or plate. When it has hardened, crack it into pieces.

A less common variation is to simmer the nuts in honey instead of caramel for ¾ hour until it thickens.

Sesame seeds are also sometimes used in this manner.

Apricotina / Apricot Drops

½ lb. dried apricots   A few pistachio nuts [optional]
Icing sugar

Wipe the apricots with a damp cloth. Do not soak or wash them, as this would make them too moist. Mince or chop them very finely. Add a few tablespoons confectioner's sugar to taste, and knead thoroughly by hand, wetting your hands from time to time to make a smooth, soft, slightly moist paste. Shape into marble-sized balls. Roll them in confectioner's sugar and let them dry overnight. You can insert half a bright green pistachio nut on top to offset the rich orange of the apricots.

A splendid variation is stuffed *apricotina*. Use 1 tablespoon ground almonds or finely chopped pistachios mixed with 1 heaping teaspoon sugar. Make a small hole in the center of each *apricotina*. Put in a little of the filling, close the hole again, and roll in confectioner's sugar.

Rahat Lokum / Turkish Delight

This little sweet epitomizes luxury, pleasure, and leisure. No harem film scene could be without it. Most Middle Eastern homes have platefuls lying on little tables in the living room, and in the past these were largely responsible for the extra weight put on by the ladies of the leisured classes.

Luscious lokum, some stuffed with fresh cream, others with nuts of various kinds, are made by specialized confectioners famous throughout the Middle East. Unfortunately, their recipes are closely guarded family secrets.

Here is a basic recipe which gives a rather large quantity. Although easy, it does require a certain expertise.

1 lb. glucose

5½ lbs. granulated sugar

¾ lb. cornflour

Juice of 1 lemon

1 teaspoon pulverized mastic

A few drops of cochineal or other food coloring if desired

3 tablespoons orange blossom water or rose water

3–4 oz. almonds or pistachios, chopped

Cornflour to dust the tray

Icing sugar

Put the glucose and the granulated sugar into a large pan with 2 cups of water. Stir well and bring to a boil, stirring occasionally.

Put the cornflour into another large pan. Add 6 cups water gradually stirring until well mixed. Bring to the boil slowly, stirring all the time, until you have a smooth, creamy white paste. Add this slowly to the hot sugar and water syrup, stirring vigorously so that no lumps form.

Bring to a boil again and cook, uncovered, over a constant low flame for 3 hours, stirring as often as possible with a wooden spoon. (In the commercial preparation, a mechanical stirrer operates continuously.) If the flame is too high, the bottom of the mixture will tend to carmelize.

The mixture must be cooked until it reaches the right consistency. This takes about 3 hours, and on this depends the success of the recipe. To test if the consistency is right, squeeze a small blob of the mixture between two fingers. *Only when it clings to both fingers as they are drawn apart, making gummed threads, is it ready.* It may then have acquired a warm golden glow.

Add the lemon juice and the flavorings. The mastic should be ground with a little granulated sugar to be successfully pulverized. Add coloring if you wish. Stir vigorously and cook a few minutes longer. Add the chopped nuts and mix well.

Pour the hot mixture out about 1 inch deep into trays that have been dusted with cornflour to prevent sticking. Flatten it with a knife and leave it to set for at least 24 hours. Then cut into squares with a sharp knife, and roll in sifted icing sugar.

The *lokum* will keep for a long time packed in a box.

For a richer flavor, a few tablespoons of grape juice are substituted for some of the water added to the cornstarch. An excellent *lokum* is made by P.S.P. Confectioners Ltd. in England: 1 lb. walnut halves are threaded onto 4-foot lengths of strong button thread, the first and last walnuts tied securely at each end to hold them all firmly. This is dipped into the same *lokum* mixture and coated thoroughly. It is then removed, and allowed to cool and set. The process is repeated at least three times until the walnuts are well covered. They are then hung up to dry for a few days, and finally rolled in confectioner's sugar.

JAMS AND PRESERVES

Murabbiyat

Like the pastries, jams remind me vividly of my childhood, of visiting relatives, of sitting on low sofas surrounded with bright silk cushions, of being enveloped by perfumes, faint and delicate or rich and overpowering.

My father's sisters, whom we visited regularly, were always fragrant with their favorite homemade soaps perfumed with violets, rose water, orange blossom, and jasmine. Their homes were intoxicating with the frankincense which they used in every room—*bakhoor el barr*, benzoin or aloes wood—with musk and ambergris, and the jasmine, orange blossom, and rose petals which were left soaking in water in little china or crystal bowls.

Candied orange peel, quince paste, coconut, fig, date, rose, tangerine, and strawberry jams would be brought in as soon as we arrived, together with pyramids of little pastries, and accompanied by the tinkling of tiny silver spoons, trembling on their stands like drops on a chandelier. Delicately engraved and inlaid silver trays carried small crystal or silver bowls filled with the shiny jams: orange, brilliantly white, mauve, rich brown, deep rose, or sienna red. They were arranged around the spoon stand, next to which was placed a glass of water, ornate with white or gold arabesques.

The trays were brought around to each of us in turn as the coffee was served, for us to savor a spoonful of each jam, or more of our favorite one, with one of the little spoons, which was then dropped directly into the glass of water.

At our beautiful Aunt Régine's we would be served the best date jam in existence, our favorite rose jam was made by our gentle Aunt Rahèle, and Camille made an inimitable *wishna*. *Harosset* and coconut jam were traditionally made for our Passover celebrations by my mother. We ate them all the more rapturously because they appeared so rarely.

Although they can be eaten with bread, these jams and preserves are at their best savored on their own with black coffee or a glass of ice-cold water, or as a dessert with thick cream.

Tangerine Jam

This magnificent jam makes a delicious dessert if served with thick cream.

2 lbs. tangerines   4 cups sugar

Cut the tangerines in half and squeeze out the juice. Pour into a bowl and set aside. Remove the thin skins which separate the segments inside the peel. Then simmer the peel in water until soft, say 7 to 10 minutes. Drain well, cover with a fresh portion of cold water, and soak for 12 hours or overnight, changing the water once or twice if possible to get rid of all the bitterness.

Drain the peel and put it through the coarse blade of a mincer, or chop it roughly, using a *mezzaluna* chopper if you have one.

Pour the reserved tangerine juice into a large saucepan. Add the sugar and minced or chopped peel; simmer until the syrup is slightly thickened and the juice forms a firm jelly when a drop is left on a cold plate. It takes 15 to 30 minutes. Let the jam cool slightly, then pour it into clean warmed jars and seal tightly.

Strawberry Jam

2 lbs. strawberries, preferably wild   Juice of ½ lemon [optional]
  ones
4 cups sugar

Hull the strawberries. Wash them only if necessary. Layer strawberries and sugar in a large glass or earthenware bowl, or in a deep china dish. Leave them to macerate for 12 hours or overnight.

Transfer the strawberries and their juice to a large pan and add a little lemon juice if you like. Bring to a boil very slowly, stirring gently with a wooden spoon or shaking the pan lightly, and skimming off the white froth as it rises to the surface. Simmer for 10 to 15 minutes, depending on the ripeness of the fruit. Wild strawberries will require only 5 minutes, sometimes even less.

When the strawberries are soft, lift them out gently with a flat, perforated spoon and pack them into cleaned, heated glass jars. Let the syrup simmer for a little while longer until it has thickened enough to coat the back of a spoon or sets when tested on a cold plate. Pour over the strawberries, and when cool, close the jars tightly as usual.

Naring / Bitter Orange Peel in Syrup

An exquisite preserve which is particularly good made with bitter orange peel. Since orange peel keeps well in any tightly closed container in the refrigerator, you can collect it gradually. Choose thin-skinned oranges. Rub lightly with a grater to remove some of their bitterness, then peel in six strips.

2 lbs. orange peel	3¾ cups water
4 cups sugar	Juice of ½ lemon

Boil the peel in water for about ½ hour, until soft. Drain well and soak in a fresh portion of cold water for a day if using the peel of ordinary oranges, changing the water once or twice if possible. If using bitter orange peel, it should be left to soak for 4 days and the water should be changed twice a day.

If the peel is very pithy, scrape some of the white pith away with a spoon, to make it less pasty. Roll the strips of peel up one by one, and thread them onto a thick thread like a necklace to prevent them from unrolling. Drop the necklace into a syrup, made by boiling the sugar with water and lemon juice, and simmer for about 1 hour, until the peel has absorbed the syrup thoroughly. Lift out, remove the thread, and drop the peel rolls into a clean glass jar.

If the syrup is not thick enough, boil vigorously to reduce it until it coats the back of a spoon. Cool slightly and pour over the orange peel to cover it completely. Close the jar tightly.

Serve the rolls of peel either with some of their syrup, or rolled in sugar syrup like crystallized fruits.

Dates in Syrup

This preserve must be made with fresh dates. The red or yellow varieties which occasionally appear in Greek shops will do. Treated in the following manner, they are totally different from the dried dates with which people in the West are so familiar.

2 lbs. fresh dates	Juice of ½ lemon
3 cups sugar [or the weight of pitted dates]	3–4 cloves

Peel the dates carefully. Boil them in enough water to cover for about 1 hour, or until they are very soft. Drain them, reserving the water, and remove the pits.

Measure the date liquor and make up to 3¾ cups with cold water. Add sugar and lemon juice, and bring to a boil. Simmer for a few minutes, then drop in the dates and cook for a further 20 minutes. Lift the dates out carefully with a flat perforated spoon and put them in a clean glass jar, burying the cloves among them.

Thicken the syrup by allowing it to boil until it coats the back of a spoon or sets when tested on a cold plate. Pour over the dates and close as usual. These dates are also delicious stuffed with chopped, candied orange peel (about 3 oz.) or ¾ cup halved blanched almonds. They should be filled as they are pitted, before cooking in the syrup.

Apricot Jam

2 lbs. fresh apricots
3 cups sugar, or the weight in sugar of pitted apricots

Wash and pit the apricots. Layer them with sugar in a large glass or earthenware bowl and leave overnight to macerate. The following day, pour the contents of the bowl into a large saucepan. Bring to a boil very slowly and simmer gently for about 40 minutes, until the apricots are soft and translucent, and the juice has thickened enough to set when tested on a cold plate. Stir occasionally to prevent the fruit from sticking to the bottom of the pan and burning.

Let the jam cool in the pan, then pour into clean glass jars and close as usual.

Apricots in Syrup

Use the same proportions of apricots to sugar as above. Wash and pit the apricots. Bring sugar to the boil with 2½ cups water and the juice of ½ lemon, and simmer for a few minutes. Drop in the apricots and cook gently until soft, about 40 minutes. Lift them out carefully with a flat perforated spoon and put them in clean, heated glass jars.

Thicken the syrup considerably by boiling it down until it falls in heavy drops from a spoon. Cool slightly and pour over the fruit, covering it entirely. Close as usual.

Green Walnut Preserve

A delicacy which should be attempted whenever green walnuts are available.

1 lb. fresh green walnuts, shelled
2 cups sugar
2 cups water
1 tablespoon lemon juice
2–3 cloves

Skin the walnuts carefully, trying not to break them. Soak them in cold water for 5 to 6 days, changing the water twice a day to remove any bitterness.

Make a syrup by boiling the sugar and water with lemon juice until thickened enough to fall in heavy drops from a spoon. Let the syrup cool, then add the well-drained walnuts. Bring to a boil gently and simmer for ½ hour. Remove the pan from the heat and leave the walnuts submerged in the syrup overnight.

The following day, bring to a boil again and simmer for a further ½ hour. Add cloves, and pour the walnuts and syrup into a large, clean, warmed glass jar. Allow to cool, and close as usual.

Green Figs in Syrup

2 lbs. young green figs
3½ cups sugar
2½ cups water

Juice of ½ lemon
1 tablespoon orange blossom water
or a few drops of vanilla extract [optional]

Choose small, unblemished, slightly underripe figs. Wash them carefully. You can leave them unpeeled if they have perfect skins. Trim their stems, leaving only a little part.

Boil the sugar and water together with the lemon juice for a few minutes until slightly thickened. Soak the figs in this syrup overnight. The following day, bring to a boil and simmer until the figs are soft. Lift them out with a flat perforated spoon and put them in a clean glass jar. If the syrup is a little thin, reduce it by simmering for a few minutes longer until it is thick enough to coat the back of a spoon. When it is ready it can, if you like, be flavored with a little orange blossom water or vanilla. Pour the syrup over the figs and close as usual.

Dried Fig Jam

2 lbs. dried figs
3 cups sugar, or to taste
3 cups water
Juice of ½ lemon
1 teaspoon ground aniseed

4 tablespoons pine nuts
1 cup walnuts, coarsely chopped
¼ teaspoon pulverized mastic

Chop the figs roughly. Boil the sugar and water with the lemon juice for a few minutes, then add the figs and simmer gently until they are soft and impregnated with the syrup, which should have thickened enough to coat the back of a spoon. Stir constantly to avoid burning. Add the aniseed, pine nuts, and walnuts, and simmer gently, stirring, for a few minutes longer. Remove from the heat and stir the mastic in very thoroughly. (To be properly pulverized, it must have been pounded with sugar.) Pour into clean, warmed glass jars and close as usual.

Wishna / Sour Black Cherry Jam

A magnificent jam and a great Middle Eastern favorite. Serve as a dessert with thick cream, or plunge a tablespoonful into a glass of iced water, then drink the syrupy water and eat the fruit left at the bottom.

2 lbs. pitted sour or morello cherries [pitted weight]

4–5 cups sugar, or to taste
Juice of ½ lemon [optional]

Layer the pitted cherries and sugar in a large glass or earthenware bowl, and leave them to macerate overnight. The following day, pour the cherries and juice into a large pan and bring to the boil very slowly, stirring frequently to prevent them from burning. Let the cherries simmer in their own juice for about ½ hour, or until very soft, adding a little water only if necessary. If the syrup is still too thin at the end of the cooking time, remove the cherries carefully to glass jars with a flat perforated spoon and simmer the syrup for a few minutes longer until it coats the back of a spoon. The juice of ½ lemon is sometimes added during the cooking.

Pour into clean, heated glass jars and close as usual.

If sour cherries are not available, you can make a very good, though not, to my taste, as wonderful, jam with ordinary sweet cherries. Prepare them as directed above, using more lemon and less sugar. Dried sour cherries, available in some Greek groceries, also make an excellent jam. Soak them in enough cold water to cover for at least 24 hours. Drain and pit them. Then drop them into a boiling syrup made by simmering 4 cups sugar with 3¾ cups water and a little lemon juice for a few minutes. Simmer gently until the cherries are soft, stirring frequently with a wooden spoon to prevent them from burning. Lift the cherries out of the syrup with a flat perforated spoon and pack them into clean, heated glass jars. Cover with the syrup, which has been simmered for a few minutes longer to thicken and reduce it. Close up as usual.

Harosset

This is my mother's recipe for a traditional Jewish Passover date and raisin paste which, according to tradition, symbolizes the cement used for building and the hope that Jews will continue to build. To the Jews of Egypt, the color and texture of harosset *are reminiscent of the rich, red Nile silt.*

½ lb. pitted dates
½ lb. large raisins

½ cup sweet red Passover wine
½ cup walnuts, chopped, to garnish

Finely chop the dates and raisins. Put them in a bowl with enough water to cover, and leave them to soak overnight. The following day bring them to the boil in the same water and simmer over very low heat, stirring constantly with a wooden spoon to prevent the fruit from burning, and squashing it to a smooth, thick paste against the sides of the pan. No sugar is required, as the fruit is already sweet enough. You can make the paste even smoother by puréeing it in an electric blender. Allow the paste to cool.

Just before serving, add the wine and stir well. Serve in a glass bowl, garnished with chopped walnuts.

If you wish to keep this preserve longer than a few weeks, it is preferable to cook it with about 1 cup of sugar. This will help it to keep better. Otherwise, store it in a cool place. Add the red wine only just before serving, using just enough for the quantity being served. You can also vary the amount of walnuts, and mix some of them into the paste. An excellent variation is made by adding 2 sweet apples, peeled and grated, about ¼ cup ground almonds, 1 teaspoon ground cinnamon and ½ teaspoon ground mixed spice to the soaked fruits before cooking them. Another is to add about ½ lb. chopped dried and pitted cherries and prunes, which should be soaked together with the dates and raisins. If you do so, reduce the quantity of raisins by about half. *Harosset* can be made into a thicker and drier paste by using less water. Allow it to cool and roll it into marble- or walnut-sized balls. Serve sprinkled with ground almonds or walnuts.

Coconut Jam

This fragrant, brilliantly white coconut jam is another of my mother's traditional Passover recipes. Make it at least a day before serving.

1 lb. flaked coconut
2 tablespoons orange blossom or rose water
2 cups sugar
1 tablespoon lemon juice
⅓ cup pistachio nuts or blanched almonds, chopped

Put the coconut in a bowl and sprinkle with orange blossom or rose water and a little fresh cold water, fluffing it with your fingers as you do so. Leave the coconut overnight to absorb the moisture. It will swell and become soft.

Make a thick syrup by simmering the sugar with the lemon juice and ½ cup water for a few minutes. Add the softened coconut to the hot syrup and bring to the boil again slowly, stirring constantly with a wooden spoon. Remove from the heat as soon as it boils. Over-cooking will make the coconut harden and become slightly yellow. It should be a pure, translucent white. Allow to cool. Mix in the nuts, pour into a glass bowl, and serve.

If it is not to be used within a day or two, store in a tightly sealed glass jar. Serve as a dessert or to accompany coffee.

Pumpkin Jam

1 large pumpkin
Sugar
1 tablespoon lemon juice
¼ teaspoon mastic
⅓ cup blanched almonds, slivered

Peel the pumpkin and discard the seeds. Grate the flesh in thick shreds. Measure the grated flesh.

Make a syrup with the same amount of sugar as grated pumpkin, half this amount of water, and the lemon juice. Bring to the boil, stirring, and simmer gently until the syrup is thick enough to coat a spoon thickly. Stir in the grated pumpkin, and continue to simmer until it is soft and transparent.

Pound the mastic to a powder with a little sugar and mix well with the jam. Cook for a few minutes longer, then stir in the slivered almonds.

Pour into clean, warmed glass jars and close up as usual.

Quince Jam

2 lbs. quinces   2 cups sugar

Peel, quarter, and core the quinces, and then slice them. Simmer them in a little water until just tender; then remove them carefully with a flat perforated spoon and set aside.

Measure the water left in the pan and make it up to 1¼ cups with more water. Add the sugar and heat gently, stirring, until the sugar is dissolved. Simmer the syrup gently until it is thick enough to coat the back of a spoon. Return the quince slices to the pan and continue to simmer until they are very soft. Mash them with a wooden spoon and cook for a little while longer, stirring, until the jam thickens.

A more jelly-like jam can be made by tying the peel and cores up in a cheesecloth bag, and simmering them in the syrup with the quince slices. In this case, the water should be made up to 2½ cups instead of 1¼ cups. Remove the cheesecloth bag before mashing the fruit.

Pour into clean, warmed glass jars and close up as usual.

Quince Paste

2 lbs. quinces   A few blanched almonds, to
2 cups sugar   decorate
Juice of 1 lemon

Wash the quinces and quarter them, but do not peel or core them. Boil them with very little water, or steam them for 20 to 30 minutes, until very soft. Rub through a fine strainer.

Heat the sugar and lemon juice with about ½ cup water, stirring constantly, until the sugar has dissolved. Bring to a boil and simmer for a few minutes to thicken the syrup. Add the quince purée and cook over very low heat, stirring constantly with a wooden spoon, until the paste thickens and comes away from the bottom of the pan.

Turn the paste into a wide, shallow mold or tray and spread it out evenly. Leave it to dry for several days. The drying period can be shortened by placing the tray in a warm oven several times or in an airing cupboard.

Store the jelly-like sheets of paste wrapped in waxed paper or foil.

Serve with coffee, cutting them into small squares or triangles, and putting a blanched almond in the center of each one.

An interesting variation is to spread a layer of ground or halved blanched almonds between two layers of paste before it is cooled and dried.

Rose Petal Jam

An exquisitely delicate jam which I have not been able to prepare successfully with the roses from my own garden. The petals remained tough under the tooth, whereas they should offer only a slight resistance.

I have, however, recently been told that certain varieties of rose exist such as the "wild eglantine" which would be suitable for jam making. I am therefore giving the recipe for those who are fortunate enough to have a rose which will make a good jam.

1 lb. fresh rose petals, preferably red   2–3 tablespoons rose water
Juice of 2 or more lemons   [optional]
2 cups sugar

Pick fresh, mature, red petals. Make sure they have not been sprayed with insecticide. Cut off their white ends. Wash and drain them. Leave them whole if you like, or mince them finely with some of the lemon juice.

Simmer the petals in 2½ cups water until tender. It may take only a few minutes or much longer, according to the variety of rose used. Add the sugar and lemon juice, and cook until the syrup thickens—usually about 10 minutes. Add a little rose water if the petals do not have a strong perfume of their own.

SHERBETS
AND DRINKS

Sharbat

"The Egyptians have various kinds of sherbets or sweet drinks. The most common kind is merely sugar and water, but very sweet; lemonade is another; a third kind, the most esteemed, is prepared from a hard conserve of violets, made by pounding violet-flowers and then boiling them with sugar. This violet-sherbet is of a green color. A fourth kind is prepared from mulberries; a fifth from sorrel. There is also a kind of sherbet sold in the streets which is made with raisins, as its name implies; another kind, which is a strong infusion of liquorice-root, and called by the name of that root; a third kind, which is prepared from the fruit of the locust tree, and called in like manner by the name of the fruit." *

I have long been haunted by the cries and songs of the street vendors in Cairo in my childhood. Most often, it was drinks that they were selling, to quench the thirst of passersby or, as they sometimes chanted, to give them strength and health. As the vendor went by, people would rush down from their flats to drink several glasses as though the thirst for wine of which Omar Khayyam sang could be quenched by the heavenly sherbets. The vendors carried a selection of sherbets in gigantic glass flasks, two at a time, held together by wide straps and balanced on their shoulders. The flasks glowed with brilliantly seductive colors: soft, pale, sugary pink for rose water, pale green for violet juice, warm, rich, dark tamarind, and the purple-black of mulberry juice. As they went through the street, the vendors chanted their traditional, irresistible calls of "*Arasous!*" and "*Tamar-hindi!*," accompanied by the tinkling of little bells and the clanging of the metal cups which they carried with them.

Water vendors, too, had a large clientele. They carried their water in large earthenware jars, whose porous surface helped to keep the water cool by its constant evaporation. The water vendor has a powerful position in Middle Eastern folklore. A story is told of the vendor who, greedy of power, established himself by a desert road, displaying cool and curvy earthenware jars. As a thirsty traveler approached and asked for a drink, the vendor would take a very long

* Lane, *Manners and Customs of the Modern Egyptians.*

time to reply, then he would point to a jar. When the traveler approached the jar, the vendor would snap: "Not that one! The one next to it!" Then, as the unfortunate man took this one up to his lips, he would be sworn at again: "Not that one, you fool! That one, I said!" This would go on until the poor traveler was on his knees, begging to be allowed to buy a drink. As a protection from this sort of experience, an Arab proverb advises: "The water of the well is better than the favor of the water vendor." However, beggars are never refused water, which is considered the most blessed of alms.

Sherbets are also served at home at all times of the day, and when guests have already had Turkish coffee and it is time to have something else. A fragrant almond drink and a rose syrup were favorites in my home. They were bought ready-made.

In *Manners and Customs of the Modern Egyptians*, E. W. Lane goes on to describe how the sherbet is served.

"The sherbet is served in coloured glass cups, generally called 'kullehs', containing about three-quarters of a pint; some of which (the more common kind) are ornamented with gilt flowers, etc. The sherbet-cups are placed on a round tray, and covered with a round piece of embroidered silk, or cloth of gold. On the right arm of the person who presents the sherbet is hung a large oblong napkin with a wide embroidered border of gold and coloured silks at each end. This is ostensibly offered for the purpose of wiping the lips after drinking the sherbet, but it is really not so much for use as for display. The lips are seldom or scarcely touched with it."

Although this description was written a hundred years ago, the same customs still go on, as I remember from my own childhood.

Always use a wooden spoon when stirring syrups and sherbets. A metal one may give a metal tang to the drink.

Orange Syrup

This is rather sweet, as syrups are apt to be, particularly if compared to fresh orange juice, but to my taste, delightful. Use the smallish, slightly acid oranges with thin skins.

Wash the oranges and squeeze them in the usual manner, removing the pips. Strain the juice if you like—I prefer not to. Ten oranges will yield about 2½ cups juice. Add sugar, between one and one and a half times the amount of juice, according to taste, and stir briskly until the sugar is completely dissolved. Use an electric blender to achieve this if you have one.

Pour the sweetened juice into a saucepan, add the juice of ½ lemon, and bring slowly to the boil. Remove from the heat as soon as it reaches boiling point. Cool and pour into thoroughly washed and dried bottles.

If you wish to store the syrup for a long time, here is a traditional method for preserving it. Grate the rind of 1 or 2 oranges, then squeeze it through a piece of cheesecloth. Float a teaspoon of this oily "zest" at the top of each bottle. It will act as a perfect protection. Before starting the bottle, remove the oily crust with a point of a knife.

Serve diluted with ice-cold water.

Milk of Almonds

The proportions for this excellent syrup vary according to taste. Here is one recipe.

1½ cups ground almonds	1 tablespoon cornstarch [optional]
3¾ cups water	2 tablespoons orange blossom water
4 cups sugar, or more	

Put the ground almonds in a bag made of several layers of cheese-cloth. Tie it at the top, leaving a lot of free space inside for the ground almonds to move freely.

Soak the ground almonds in the water in a large bowl for about 1 hour, rubbing, squeezing, and shaking the cheesecloth with both your hands at intervals. Allow the water to penetrate the almonds and soak them, then squeeze it out again, taking with it the milk of almonds, beautifully white and fragrant.

When you feel that the almonds have given out as much "milk" as possible, squeeze them dry. Pour the almond milk into a saucepan, add sugar, and bring to the boil slowly, stirring until the sugar has dissolved. *Use 4 cups sugar at least if the syrup is being made to last.*

Simmer gently until the syrup thickens enough to coat the back of a spoon.

Some people like to add a tablespoon of cornstarch diluted in a little water, stirring it in gradually, then allow the syrup to simmer and thicken even further. But I do not feel that this is necessary.

Two minutes before removing the pan from the heat, perfume the syrup with orange blossom water. Allow to cool, pour into clean, dry bottles, and close tightly.

Serve diluted with ice-cold water.

Rose Water Syrup

2 cups sugar
1¼ cups water
1 tablespoon lemon juice

2 teaspoons red food coloring
¼ cup rose water‡

Make a thick sugar syrup by simmering the sugar, water, and lemon juice together slowly, stirring, until it coats the back of a spoon. Add the coloring and stir well. Then stir in the rose water and simmer for 1 or 2 minutes longer. Allow to cool and pour into a clean, dry bottle. Close tightly.

To serve, dilute with ice-cold water.

Mulberry Syrup

Pick very ripe, black mulberries. Extract their juice by putting them in a cheesecloth bag and squeezing them tightly. Alternatively, squash them with a wooden spoon through a very fine strainer. Measure the amount of juice in a measuring cup and pour it into an enameled pan. Add double the amount of sugar and a tablespoon of lemon juice per 1 cup juice, and bring to the boil slowly, stirring constantly. Simmer gently, stirring occasionally, until the syrup thickens and coats the back of a spoon. Skim off any froth as it rises to the surface. Let the syrup cool and pour it into thoroughly washed and dried bottles. To serve, dilute about 1 tablespoon of syrup in a glass of iced water.

Tamarind

In Egypt, this dark, thick, rich, sweet-and-sour syrup was usually bought ready-made. It was diluted with ice-cold water to make a superb and refreshing drink, and also used in small quantities as a flavoring for stews and other dishes like stuffed leeks (page 328).

The syrup is also very common and extremely popular in Italy, where it is sold by pharmacists. Dried, cinnamon-colored tamarind pods are sold in many Indian shops under the name of imli or sometimes tamarindo,‡ usually cracked open and with their seeds removed. They require preliminary cleaning and careful washing (as they are often gritty) before lengthy soaking. The syrup made from these is not as dark as that made from the pods in the Middle East.

1 lb. tamarind pods   2–4 cups sugar, or more

Clean and wash the pods thoroughly. Soak overnight in 3½ cups cold water. They will become very soft. Rub the pods through a fine strainer, squashing them with a wooden spoon. Hard seeds and fibers will be left behind. Strain the pulp back into the soaking water. Now strain the diluted pulp through cheesecloth into a saucepan, squeezing the pulp as much as possible with your hands. Add 2 cups sugar if you like a sour tamarind; increase the amount if you prefer a sweeter one. (Add the larger quantity if the syrup is to last.) Bring to the boil slowly, stirring constantly until the sugar has dissolved, and simmer gently until the syrup thickens. Cool and pour into clean, dry bottles. Close tightly.

Sekanjabin

A Persian vinegar and sugar syrup. The proportions for this refreshing drink, in which one can detect a similarity to the English mint sauce for lamb, vary from one family to another.

2½ cups water

4 cups sugar

1 cup wine vinegar

6 sprigs fresh mint

Bring water to the boil with sugar, stirring constantly until the sugar has dissolved. Add the vinegar and simmer for 20 minutes longer. Remove from the heat and submerge the sprigs of mint in the syrup. The flavor of the mint will penetrate the syrup as it cools. Serve diluted in ice-cold water.

Sometimes a little peeled, grated cucumber is added to the drink.

Riddle: What is sweeter than honey?
Answer: Free vinegar.

Yogurt Drink

An excellent and deliciously refreshing drink, called abdug *by Persians,* ayran *by the Lebanese, and* laban *by others. It is consumed extensively all over the Middle East and particularly in Turkey and Persia, prepared in homes and cafés, and sold by street vendors.*

2½ cups yogurt

2–2½ cups cold water

Salt

1–4 tablespoons dried crushed mint, or to taste [optional]

Beat the yogurt well in a large bowl. Add water and continue to beat vigorously until thoroughly blended together. Use an electric blender if you have one. Season to taste with salt and dried crushed mint if you like.

Serve chilled, preferably with a lump of ice.

Sahlab

An excellent winter drink made with milk and a powdered resin called sahlab (saleb *in Greek*).*

2½ cups milk	2 teaspoons finely chopped
1 teaspoon *sahlab*	pistachios
	Ground cinnamon

Heat the milk. Add the powdered *sahlab*, beating vigorously, and cook over very low heat, stirring all the time, until it thickens (about 5 to 10 minutes). Serve in cups, sprinkled with finely chopped pistachios and cinnamon.

Zhourat / Infusions

Infusions are extremely popular throughout the Middle East and are recommended as a winter drink, particularly for those suffering from colds. Boiling water is thrown over dried crushed leaves of mint (*Mentha viridis*), verbena, sage, sweet basil, sweet marjoram, amber, jasmine, black elder, and rose petals. They are drunk very hot, sometimes lightly sweetened.

Turkish Coffee

Coffee first became popular in the Middle East in the Yemen and Saudi Arabia. It was probably transplanted there from Abyssinia, where it grows wild. According to legend, it was particularly favored by the Yemeni Sufis, who believed that its effects facilitated the performance of their religious ceremonies, hastening mystical raptures. Accordingly, it came to receive a ceremonial character.

Today, the serving and drinking of coffee is still surrounded by tradition and ceremony. Walking past cafés, one cannot help but remark on the almost mystical ecstasy with which coffee drinking still affects people.

---

* This is sometimes available in a hard resin form, in which case it must be pulverized, preferably in an electric grinder.

Coffee drinking is a very important activity in the Middle East. Men spend hours during the long summer nights, and whenever they can during the day, sitting in cafés, sipping coffees one after the other, sometimes accompanied by a lokum or pastry, while they sharpen their wits entertaining each other, telling jokes or tales of Goha, setting riddles, and playing charades and tric-trac (backgammon).

Business and bargaining are never done without coffee. At home, it is served as soon as visitors arrive, always freshly brewed, usually with freshly roasted and pulverized coffee beans. It is always prepared in small quantities as each visitor arrives, in small, long-handled copper or brass pots called tanaka, holding from one to five cups.

Coffee cups are very small, usually cylindrical. In some countries they have no handles; in others, china cups fit into small metal holders which match the serving tray made of copper, brass, or silver. The tray is usually beautifully ornamented. Traditional patterns and Arabic writing (often blessings and words in praise of God) are chiseled into the metal. Sometimes the carvings are inlaid with a thin silver thread.

People have their favorite blends of coffee beans. Mocha beans from the Yemen are popular; so are Brazilian and Kenya beans.

Rules of etiquette are observed in the serving of coffee. A person of high rank is served first, then a person of advanced age. Until a few years ago, men were always served before women, but today in the more Europeanized towns women take precedence.

Since sugar is boiled at the same time as the coffee, guests are *always asked their preference—whether they would like sweet* (helou or sukkar ziada), *medium* (mazbout), *or unsweetened* (murra)—*and they are served accordingly. In cafés, it is customary for waiters to take thirty orders for coffee at a time, all varying in sweetness, and supposedly never to make a mistake. There is a well-known joke about the waiter who takes an order for a large gathering of inevitably differing tastes, makes them all exactly the same, medium-sweet, brings them all together on a huge tray and hands them round with a show of concentration, saying:* "Helou, mazbout, helou, murra, murra, helou . . ."

The occasion may determine the amount of sugar added to the coffee. At happy ones, such as weddings and birthdays, the coffee should always be sweet, while at a funeral it should be bitter, without any sugar at all, regardless of the tastes of the people. At deaths it was customary for some families in Cairo to erect huge tents, which stretched right across the narrow streets. The ground was carpeted and filled with gilt chairs and the tents were decorated with sumptuously colored appliqués. Relatives, friends, and passersby came to pay their respects. They sat on the gilt chairs, solemnly drinking black, unsweetened coffee to the wailing of the professional mourners.

An excellent account of how coffee was made in Egypt in the last century is given by E. W. Lane in Manners and Customs of the Modern Egyptians:

"In preparing the coffee, the water is first made to boil; the coffee (freshly roasted and powdered) is then put in and stirred; after which the pot is again placed on the fire, once or twice, until the coffee begins to simmer, when it is taken off, and its contents are poured out into the cups while the surface is yet creamy. The Egyptians are excessively fond of pure and strong coffee thus prepared, and very seldom add sugar to it (though some do so when they are unwell) and never milk or cream; but a little cardamom seed is often added to it. It is a common custom, also, to fumigate the cup with the smoke of mastic; and the wealthy sometimes impregnate the coffee with the delicious fragrance of ambergris. The most general mode of doing this is to put about a carat weight of ambergris in a coffee-pot and melt it over a fire; then make the coffee in another pot, in the manner before described, and when it has settled a little, pour it into the pot which contains the ambergris. Some persons make use of the ambergris, for the same purpose in a different way—sticking a piece of it, of the weight of about two carats, in the bottom of the cup, and then pouring in the coffee: a piece of the weight above mentioned will serve for two or three weeks. This mode is often adopted by persons who always like to have the coffee which they themselves drink flavoured with this perfume, and do not give all their visitors the same luxury."

Here is my method.

PER PERSON
1 very heaping teaspoon pulverized coffee (very finely ground, *not* powdered)

1 heaping teaspoon sugar, or less to taste
1 small coffee cup water (Turkish size)

Although it is more common to boil the water and sugar alone first and then add the coffee, it is customary in my family to put the coffee, sugar, and water in the *tanaka* or pot (a small saucepan could be used, though it is not as successful), and to bring them to the boil together. By a "very heaping teaspoon" of coffee I mean, in this case, so heaping that it is more than 2 teaspoons. A level teaspoon of sugar will make a "medium" coffee.

Bring to the boil. When the froth begins to rise, remove from the heat, stir, and return to the heat until the froth rises again. Then remove, give the pot a little tap against the side of the stove, and repeat once again. Pour immediately into little cups, allowing a little froth (*wesh*) for each cup. (Froth is forced out by making your hand tremble as you serve.) Serve very hot. The grounds will settle at the bottom of the cup. Do not stir them up or drink them.

Try flavoring the coffee with a few drops of orange blossom water or cardamom seeds, adding the flavoring while the coffee is still on the stove.

It is common practice for people in some circles to turn their coffee cups upside down on their saucers when they have finished drinking. As the coffee grounds dribble down the sides of the cup they form a pattern or image from which at least one member of the company can usually read the fortune of the drinker. A friend has a coffee cup which she brought from Egypt and has kept in a cupboard in England for many years now, carefully wrapped in fine tissue paper and rarely disturbed. She is convinced that it bears the protective image of Rab Moshe (Moses) traced out in coffee grounds at the bottom of the cup.

Moroccan Mint Tea

A refreshing infusion of green tea and mint, the preparation of which is considered an art. It is traditionally served in a richly engraved silver pot, and poured from a great height into ornamented glasses. The mint must be of the Mentha viridis (spearmint) variety. The infusion is sweetened in the teapot.

2 tablespoons green tea
Handful of fresh or dried whole
    mint leaves

Lump sugar, to taste

Heat the teapot. Add the tea leaves and pour a little boiling water over them. Swirl around and quickly pour the water out again, taking care not to lose the leaves. Add mint and sugar to taste, and pour in 4–5 cups boiling water. Allow to infuse for about 5 to 8 minutes, then skim off any mint that has risen to the surface. Taste a little of the tea in a small glass, and add more sugar if necessary.

    Serve in glasses.

BIBLIOGRAPHY
<hr>

LIST OF SOURCES
<hr>

INDEX
<hr>

Bibliography

Malja-at-tabbahin by Muhammad Sidqi Effendi. Translated from Turkish into Arabic. Cairo, 1886.

A Cookery Book by Ekrem Muhittin Yegen. Inkilàp-Kitabeir, Turkey. Third impression, 1951.

Middle Eastern Cooking by Patricia Smouha. André Deutsch, London, 1955.

In a Persian Kitchen by Maideh Mazda. Charles E. Tuttle Company, Rutland, Vermont, and Tokyo, Japan, 1960.

Art of Lebanese Cooking by George N. Rayess. Librairie du Liban, Beirut, 1966.

Treasured Armenian Recipes by The Detroit Women's Chapter of the Armenian General Benevolent Union Inc. New York, 1963.

Food from the Arab World by Khayat and Keatinge. Khayats, Beirut, 1965.

Contributions to the Culinary Art: A Collection of Family Recipes and Cookery Clues by Monah Oppenheim for the Young Peoples Group of Congregation Shearith Israel. New York, 1961.

Fès vu par sa cuisine by Madame S. Guineaudeau. Morocco, 1958.

"A Baghdad Cookery-book" by Professor A. J. Arberry in *Islamic Culture*, No. 13, 1939.

"Récherches sur les documents Arabes relatifs à la cuisine" by Maxime Rodinson in *Revue des études islamiques*, Nos. 17–18, 1949–50.

"Ghidha" by Maxime Rodinson in the *Encyclopédie de l'Islam*. Second edition, Livraison 39, 1965.

Manners and Customs of the Modern Egyptians by E. W. Lane. John Murray, London, Fifth edition, 1860.

Modern Lebanese Proverbs by Anis Frayha. American University of Beirut, 1953.

Contes Persans en Langue Populaire by Arthur Christensen. Andr. Fred. Høst & Søn, Copenhagen, 1918.

Chansons Populaires Recueillies dans la Haute-Egypte: De 1900 à 1914 by Gaston Maspéro. Imprimerie de l'Institut Français d'Archéologie Orientale, Cairo.

Recueil d'Enigmes Arabes Populaires by le R.P.A. Giacobetti des Pères Blancs. Adolphe Jourdan, Algiers, 1916.

The Wit and Wisdom of Morocco: A Study of Native Proverbs by Westermarck. London, 1930.

The Wild Rue by Bess Allen Donaldson. Luzac and Co., London, 1938.

Folk Medicine in Modern Egypt by "A Doctor." Translated by John Walker, 1934.

List of Sources

CALIFORNIA
Greek Import Co., 2801 W. Pico Blvd., Los Angeles
Nassraway's Pastry Shop, 4864 Melrose, Los Angeles
New Santa Clara Market, 799 Haight St., San Francisco
Mediterranean and Middle East Import Co., 223 Valencia St., San Francisco
G. B. Ratto & Co., International Grocers-Importers, 821 Washington St., Oakland

CONNECTICUT
Dimyan's Market, 116 Elm St., Danbury

FLORIDA
Joseph's Imported Food Co., 621 Fields Ave., Jacksonville
Greek-American Grocery, 2691 Coral Way, Miami

HAWAII
Gourmet Bazaar, International Market Place, Honolulu

ILLINOIS
Columbus Food Market, 5534 W. Harrison St., Chicago

INDIANA
Athens Imported Food, 103 N. Alabama St., Indianapolis

KENTUCKY
A. Thomas Meat Market, 315 E. Jefferson St., Louisville

LOUISIANA
Central Grocery Co., 923 Decatur S., New Orleans

MAINE
Model Food Importers, 115 Middle St., Portland

MASSACHUSETTS
California Fruit and Produce Center, 637 Mt. Auburn St., Watertown
Cardullo's Gourmet Shop, 6 Brattle St., Cambridge
Syrian Grocery Impt. Co., 270 Shawmut Ave., Boston

MICHIGAN
Mourad Company, Grocers, 13847 Hamilton St., Highlaw Park

MINNESOTA
The Pavo Co., Inc., 119 N. Fourth St., Minneapolis

MISSOURI
Demmas Shish-Ke-Bab, 5806 Hampton Ave., St. Louis
Italo American Impt. Co., 512 Franklin Ave., St. Louis

NEW JERSEY
N. Nafash & Sons, 2717 Bergenline Ave., Union City

NEW YORK
Malko Importing Corp., 185 Atlantic Ave., Brooklyn
Sahadi Importing Co., Inc., 187 Atlantic Ave., Brooklyn
Kalustyan Orient Expt. Trading Corp., 123 Lexington Ave., New York City
Kassos Brothers, 570 Ninth Ave., New York City
Oriental Wholesale Foods & Gifts, 6530 Seneca, Elmo

OHIO
Shiekh Grocery Co., 652 Bolivar Rd., Cleveland
Metropolitan Coffee Co., 451 Cuyahoga Falls, Akron

PENNSYLVANIA
Stamoolis Brothers Grocery, 2020 Penn Ave., Pittsburgh
Sherwood Grocery, 790 Garrett Road, Upper Darby

RHODE ISLAND
Near East Market, 253 Cranston St., Providence

TENNESSEE
Barzizza Brothers, 351–353 S. Front St., Memphis

TEXAS
European Importing Co., 910 Preston Ave., Houston

VIRGINIA
Green American Importing Co., 518 E. Marshall St., Richmond

WASHINGTON
Angelo Merlino & Sons, 816 Sixth Ave. So., Seattle

WEST VIRGINIA
Haddy's Food Market, 1503 Washington St., Charleston

WISCONSIN
Topping & Co., 736 N. Second St., Milwaukee

CANADA
Sayfy's Groceteria, 265 Jean Talon East, Montreal, Quebec

INDEX

almond(s)
basbousa with (*bil loz*), 392
bracelets (*kahk bi loz*), 419–21
cakes, orange and, I, II, 413–14
drops, 418–19
fingers (*assabih bil loz*), 406–7
meatballs with dates and (*rutabiya*),
250–1
milk of, 441–2
pudding (*muhallabia*), 385
rice
with dates and, 353–4
sauce for, 355
rissoles (*sanbusak bil loz*), 405
salad (*nougada*), 77
sauce for fish (*khall wa-kardal*), 159
tahina cream salad with, 43
Amardine cream, 382–3
anchovy sauce, with garlic, for fried
fish (*zemino*), 160
apple(s)
grated, 376–7
khoresh, 359–60
lamb with sour cherries and, 249
stuffed, Persian (*dolmeh sib*), 322–3
apricot(s)
drops (*apricotina*), 423
jam, 431
lamb stew with (*mishmishiya*), 247–8
polo, lamb and, 348–9
pudding, 380
stuffed, 383
in syrup, 431
zucchini, stuffed with, 310–11
artichokes and artichoke hearts, 285
and fava beans in oil, 293–4
pickled, 332–3
stewed in oil, 50
stuffed, 319
artichokes, Jerusalem (*tartoufa*), 294–5
in tomato sauce, 295
assabih bi loz, 406–7
assafeer, 198
ataïf (pancakes), 407–11
atr, 393–4
avgolemono, see *beid bi lamoun*

avocado
purée, carmel, 57
with cream cheese, 57
with tuna, 57
salad, orange and, 67

baba ghanoush, 46–7
baklava, 397–9
banana and date dessert, 392
barley pudding (*belila*), 384
basbousa
with almonds (*bil loz*), 392
with coconut (*bil goz el hind*), 391–2
with yogurt (*bil laban zabadi*), 391
beans, see brown beans; fava beans; string
beans; white beans, dried
beef, 201–2
brochettes, Moroccan, 206–8
ground
fillings for vegetables, 300–2, 320
fingers with ground rice (*kofta bil
roz*), 218–19
grilled on skewers (*kofta meshweya*),
206
kibbeh hamda, 232–3
kibbeh in tray (*bil sanieh*), 229
kibbeh with matzo meal (*massa*), 231
koukla, 219
loaf in tray (*kofta bil sania*), 221
meatballs (*terbiyeli köfte*), 220
meatballs, leek, 225–6
meatballs, Turkish (*kadin budu*),
219–20
meatballs, Turkish, with eggplant
purée, 236–7
meatballs with pine nuts and tomato
sauce (*daoud pasha*), 223
meatballs with spinach and chickpeas,
242
meatballs, zucchini or eggplant, 224–5
mefarka, 237–8
moussaka, 289–92
rolls, stuffed with hard-boiled eggs,
222–3
rolls, with pine nuts, 224

date(s) (*continued*)
  paste, Passover raisin and (*harosset*),
    434
  rice with almonds and, 353–4
  shad stuffed with, 172–3
  in syrup, 430
dfeena, 251–2
dietary laws, 23–5
dolma, 33–6
döner kebab, 203
duck
  browned, 196–7
  faisinjan, 193
  with orange juice, 197–8

eggah (*see also* eggs and egg dishes,
    eggah), 135, 143–4
eggplant(s) (*betingan*), 284
  baked *rishta* with, I, II, 292–4
  cream (*hünkâr beĝendi*), 292–3
  deep-fried, 295–6
  eggah, 146
  fried with yogurt, 37
  filling for savories (*khandrajo*), 88
  khoresh, 361
  marinated, 331–2
  meatballs, 224–5
  meat stew with, 236
  medias, 308
  moussaka, 289–92
  in oil, with tomatoes and green peppers,
    288
  pickled, 330–1
  pilav, Turkish cold, 346
  purée, 36
    Turkish meatballs with, 236–7
    with yogurt, 37
  slices stuffed with cream cheese, 52–3
  stuffed, 303–4
    imam bayildi, 305
    with meat and pine nuts (*Sheikh el
      Mahshi*), 305–6
    mock, 311
    with rice, cold, 307–8
    with rice and meat, 306–7
  Turkish filling, 302
  with *tahini* (*baba ghanoush*), 46–7
  with tomatoes, 386–7
egg(s) and egg dishes, 135
  chakchouka, 141–2
  deep-fried eggs, 139

egg(s) and egg dishes (*continued*)
  eggah
    with brains (*bi mokh*), 149–50
    bread and zucchini (*bi eish wa
      kousa*), 144–5
    chicken and noodle (*bi ferakh wa
      rishta*), 148
    eggplant (*bi betingan*), 146
    fava bean, fresh (*bi ful akhdar*), 145
    leek (*bi korrat*), 146–7
    meat (*bi lahma*), 147–8
    with sausages, Tunisian (*ojja bil
      Mergaz*), 149
    spinach (*bi sabaneh*), 147
    zucchini (*bi kousa*), 145
  fried eggs
    with cheese (*beid bi gebna maqlia*),
      140–1
    with chicken livers, 141
    with garlic and lemon (*beid bi tom*),
      140
    with vinegar (*beid masus*), 139
  hamine eggs (*beid humine*), 135, 136–8
  hard-boiled eggs, 138–9
    with chicken and whole wheat (*feri-
      que*), 186–7
    with cumin (*beid maduq*), 136
    fried (*beid mutajjan*), 136
    meat rolls stuffed with, 222–3
  and lemon soup, 111
  omelets, 135
    herb, 152–3
    kukuye sabsi, 150
    potato, Persian (*kuku sibzamini*), 151
  poached eggs with yogurt, Turkish, 142
  scrambled eggs with vinegar, 139
  tagine of *kofta* and, 245
  with tomatoes (*beid bi tamatem*), 140
eishta, 392–3
etiquette and social customs, 14–23

falafel (*ta'amia*), 47–50
fasulyeli paça, 258–9
fattoush, 75–6
fava beans
  dried, 262
    beef stew with, 244
    salad (*ful nabed*), 75
    soup (*ful nabed*), 115
    ta'amia (*falafel*), 47–50

A Note About the Author

Claudia Roden was born and brought up in Cairo, where she participated in the customs and cultures of the Arab world, and of the many small communities that go to make up Middle Eastern society —Armenian, Coptic, Jewish, and European. She left Egypt to finish her education in Paris and England, and traveled widely in Europe and South America. She then studied art in London, and has since exhibited some of her work, in which she tries to express the flamboyance and color of the Middle East.

Mrs. Roden lives in London with her husband and three children.

A Note on the Type

The text of this book was set in Electra, a typeface designed by W(illiam) A(ddison) Dwiggins for the Mergenthaler Linotype Company and first made available in 1935. Electra cannot be classified as either "modern" or "old style." It is not based on any historical model, and hence does not echo any particular period or style of type design. It avoids the extreme contrast between thick and thin elements that marks most modern faces, and is without eccentricities which catch the eye and interfere with reading. In general, Electra is a simple, readable typeface that attempts to give a feeling of fluidity, power, and speed.

Typography and binding design by Cynthia Krupat.